MW00887471

BRING ME WILD ROSES
AN ALASKAN ODESSY
by
Celestia Oborn Whitehead

DEDICATION

This book is dedicated to the numerous descendants of Clermont and Gwynne Oborn. I hope that this little peek into their unique lives will stay in your hearts and increase your understanding of your family roots. You came from some hearty and colorful progenitors.

Author's Note

This book is history, memoir and story-telling combined. It is a product of unpublished journals and family memorabilia, as well as the author's memories, and those shared with the author. The photographs are from the old family albums, and in some cases may be grainy, but they help to evoke the time and place. Some minor characters' names are fictional because no one recorded them, and when names of more major characters are changed it is noted with an asterisk (*). Intimate thoughts and feelings of characters, other than the author's, have been imagined, with the object of staying as true as possible to the real events portrayed.

FORWARD

This is more than an account of an Army Air Corps veteran and his sweetheart, who proved up on the first homestead in Kenny Lake, Alaska. It's the story of a time and place that are nearly forgotten, and some of the real characters who made things happen in post World War II Alaska.

Writing this book necessitated researching not only my own family records, but also historical events that took place in Alaska during the first half of the twentieth century. Alaska, as my parents encountered it in 1947, when they first arrived, had already been shaped by the Yukon Gold Rush, commercial mining, government policies, and the military. World War II had a lasting impact on the territory. As part of the war effort, the government attempted to build infrastructure, establish shipping ports, and excavate tunnels through mountains to connect the coast of Alaska to the interior. After WWII, the military abandoned projects such as roads, ports, railroads, and airfields, turning them over to civilian contractors. With the opening of the Alaska Highway to civilian traffic, in May of 1947, veterans and others streamed north, seeking employment and opportunities in a new Territory.

They came to homestead, build roads, teach school, work for the government. Others built up communities in the wilderness, became bush pilots, or rejoined the military. Incredibly, our father did all of these things in Alaska during the years from 1947 to 1955.

In 2009, my mother, Gwynne Paxton Oborn, died at age 85. During her life, Gwynne wrote memories of her early years in Alaska. After her death, my sister and I combed through files pertaining to our family's Alaskan history. We found letters, receipts, official papers relating to the Homestead at Kenny Lake. There were newspaper clippings, and a joint journal, written by Cler and Gwynne, as well as her drawings and some photographs. Taken together with our own memories, we knew this was a story that needed to be told and preserved for posterity.

Gwynne and Clermont Oborn arrived in Alaska on July 4, 1947, and filed on their homestead in September. They received their certificate at the Land Office in Anchorage, on July 16, 1952, Patent Number 1135891.

The Copper River Basin is vast in area, but in 1947 there was only a small community of individuals and families who lived there, and they depended on each other. There were the old timers, like Ben Pinks, Ma Barnes, and the Ahtna native family of "Mama George," who helped our parents during the first critical years. There were new families who came to Kenny Lake, some recruited by our father. They became our friends and neighbors, who worked together with our parents, to build a community in the wilderness. Nature has erased much of their struggle: land they worked so hard to clear is overgrown with brush; most of their cabins are gone. Today Kenny Lake is a small, but thriving community, and our homestead is a place where, over the intervening years, we Oborns have returned, again and again, with our children and grandchildren.

We, the children of Gwynne and Clermont Oborn, are getting old, but we were there; our very characters were molded by the duality of delight and hardship that pervaded our childhood in Alaska. We witnessed many of our parents' triumphs, as well as their defeats. With the input of my siblings, I have been privileged to tell some of our parents' story, and stories from our own lives that are part of the larger account of post war Alaska.

Gwynne M. Paxton and Clermont Arave Oborn's children are: Corrie Lynne Player, Clermont Paxton Oborn, Celestia Oborn Whitehead, Charles Benjamin Barnes Oborn, Howard Mahle Oborn (Butchy)

PROLOGUE

Clermont and Gwynne 1942

When the Second Great War ended, optimism spread across America, like Hope escaping from Pandora's box. In the tree-lined streets of Ogden, Utah, the promise of post-war prosperity shimmered over Ogden Valley, just as it did everywhere in America. Hope was plentiful, but job opportunities for all those returning veterans were few.

Clermont Oborn, and his young wife, Gwynne, lived frugally in a little white house near the Ogden Army Depot. Cler was an officer and a pilot. The government didn't need so many pilots now, so Cler worked at the Base as an aircraft electrician.

He and his bevy of army buddies at the Depot were all in the same boat: no one had much money, but there were a lot of possibilities on the horizon. They just had to be alert and open the door when opportunity came knocking.

Cler was one of those men that other men want to follow. Although sure of himself, he was never full of himself. He didn't get ruffled easily. There was a centered calm about him, but also a certain fearlessness. He seemed to have inherited some of the qualities of his great grandfather, Nelson Arave, a prominent pioneer of Utah. At seventeen, Nelson had driven a wagon across the plains, over twelve hundred miles from Nauvoo, Illinois. In Utah, he'd founded several towns, and was known as a great friend of the Indians. Cler's mother was the granddaughter of Nelson Arave. According to family lore, Nelson was half French and half Canadian Indian.

Gwynne fell in love with Cler in high school. She thought he was the most handsome boy at Ogden High. He was six-foot-two, lean-muscled, with thick, curly brown hair, dark brown, almost black eyes, and tawny skin. He had a way of smiling so his dimples showed, and an easy manner. His nose was straight, cheekbones high. He had full, beautifully-shaped lips, and a strong, cleft chin.

Gwynne was five-foot-six, with an hourglass figure other girls envied. Her Scottish blood showed in her ivory skin, and clear, hazel eyes with dark lashes. Her nut-brown hair flowed in waves down her back. Cler was crazy about her.

On December 7, 1941, when the Japanese bombed Pearl Harbor, Cler was a senior in High School and Gwynne a Junior. Cler could hardly wait to graduate, so he could join the Army Air Corps. Like hundreds of other young men, he wanted to be a pilot, and help defeat the Axis Powers.

In April, a month before graduation, Gwynne and Cler were married. He was 18 and she was 17. That summer, he enlisted in the Army Air Corps, and left for seven weeks of basic training in Texas.

Gwynne stayed with his parents, in Ogden. While her husband was still away, Gwynne suddenly went into labor, two and a half months early. With the life of his wife and child at stake, Cler was allowed emergency leave, and he rushed back to Utah.

The baby was born on October 6, 1942. Her tiny body was nearly fleshless, her skin transparent, over tiny bones. The doctors placed the premature baby in an incubator, telling her parents that her chances of survival did not look good.

Cler's father, Ernest, helped him give the infant her name and a blessing. He reached into the incubator to touch her head, which was no bigger than an orange, and the baby grasped her grandfather's finger with her miniature hand.

"Whoa! This one's a fighter!" Ernest exclaimed. "This baby will live!" And she did. As her parents had agreed, she would be called Corrie Lynne, a name Gwynne had once read in a Scottish novel. It was a tribute to her Scottish heritage.

By the time Cler made it back to see his wife and daughter, they were both doing well. Gwynne was almost afraid to touch her, but Cler gently lifted his daughter, as if he were an old hand at fatherhood. He held her in the palm of one hand, and touched her tiny cheek, "Hello, there, little Corrie Lynne!"

He was only able to stay a day or two, just long enough to see that all was well, and then he had to return to basic training. After Basic, he was selected to go on to Officers Candidate School.

When Cler was located on a training base called Kelly Field, some distance outside of San Antonio, Texas, Gwynne and the baby were allowed to join him.

Gwynne and Cler purchased a small trailer, which they towed behind their roadster. The little car had a good engine, and was able to pull the trailer as they moved from base to base, wherever Cler was sent. They lived in the trailer over the next three years, as they were transferred from Texas, to Tucson, Arizona, to Barstow, California, and back to Tucson.

Gwynne returned to Ogden for her second baby's birth. Corrie Lynne was a spunky, but undersized thirteen-month-old, when her brother, Clermont Paxton, was born November 18, 1943. He was a sturdy boy, and by the time he was a year old, he was as big as his older sister. To avoid confusion with his dad's name, they called him Paxton.

At each level of training, Cler's ability to learn, and his quick mind got him rapidly promoted. He received his pilot wings, and commissioned a second lieutenant in 1943. Then he was sent to Tucson, Arizona, to teach other pilots. By this time, pilots were returning from combat, and needed retraining for peacetime purposes. Cler was frustrated at being kept out of combat so long, having to retrain men who had hundreds more hours flying than he had.

As the war wound down in Europe, the Army Air Corps focused its military might on the War in the Pacific. Tens of thousands of new pilots strengthened the Pacific fleet on aircraft carriers, and island bases.

In the spring of 1945, Cler and Gwynne were living outside of Tucson, and he was stationed on Marana Army Base. In August, Cler received orders to go to a staging base in North Dakota, where he was supposed to pick up his squadron, prior to going to the Pacific. He had permission to take the children and Gwynne to Utah, before he had to report to the base in North Dakota.

They hooked up the trailer and drove over to Marana Army Base, to pick up paperwork pertaining to his orders. Gwynne stayed in the car with the two small children, while Cler went into the main building, where he found a party going on, with much cheering and laughter. When he managed to talk to an officer about picking up his orders, the man looked puzzled. "What orders?" he asked, "Haven't you heard? The war is over!" The Japanese had surrendered. It was August 15, 1945.

Not having a radio, Cler and Gwynne had not heard the news. Cler told the officer he was on his way to take his wife and

10

children to Ogden, and was told to go ahead and do that. He could be mustered out at Hill Field, which is what the Ogden Army Depot was by then called.

The trip home started out fine, and the weather was good. They found a place to park the little trailer and camp each night. When they traveled over a steep, winding mountain pass, they encountered a snow storm, and the little car began to slip backwards down the hill and into the oncoming lane.

With Gwynne pushing with all her might on the brakes, Cler got out and tried to put rocks behind the tires. He finally managed to pull the car and trailer out of the wrong lane, just as a Greyhound bus came rushing down the hill, unable to stop. In the driving snow, Cler edged the trailer and car just off the road and helped his wife and children slip and slide into the trailer, where Cler led his family in fervent prayer, and they settled down for the night. They were not parked on level ground, so the heater didn't work, but they piled on the blankets and managed to sleep fitfully until morning.

In the morning, Cler opened the trailer door. "Gwynne! Come here! Look at this!"

She rolled out of bed and stood peering into the bright morning. The trailer was parked with its wheels less than eighteen inches from the edge of the steep cliff. In stunned silence, Cler and Gwynne knelt beside their bed. They gave thanks to a loving Heavenly Father for watching over them, imploring His continuing, watchful care as they made their way home to Utah. This miracle was only one of the many that this young family would experience over the next decade.

Though Cler was severely disappointed that he wouldn't be taking off with his squadron, he was practical. There would be other work for him to do; other challenges, and other hills to climb. Gwynne, for her part, was relieved. She knew how badly Cler had wanted to go to the Pacific, but she thanked the Lord daily for keeping him safe with her and the children.

In Ogden, they sold the little trailer, and traded their vintage roadster for an Army surplus jeep with good tires and a reliable engine. With peace in the world, Cler and Gwynne, like so many other couples at that time, decided to have another baby.

As time for their third baby's birth drew near, Gwynne fell sick with a fever, and the doctors at Dee Hospital worried they'd lose both the mother and the child. Thankfully, Gwynne rallied; her fever and blood pressure stabilized. Since the baby was not yet full term, Gwynne was allowed to go home. The next day, on his lunch hour, it must have been inspiration that led Cler to fix the windshield wipers on the jeep.

That night it was pouring rain when they sped to the hospital. They arrived just in time for the doctor to deliver a healthy baby girl. They named her Celestia Alice, after her two great grandmothers.

It was May 24, 1946. Life was good; their baby was perfect, the world was safe for Democracy, and anything was possible.

Clermont and Gwynne Oborn 1947

1

FALL, 1946

CALL OF THE YUKON

It was August 15, 1946, exactly one year after Japan's unconditional surrender to the Allied Powers. The little house near the Ogden Army Depot was sweltering; there was no lawn to speak of, and no trees to cool the air.

Gwynne had left the door open, and pushed up the kitchen and front room windows, in a futile attempt to create a little draft. She had stripped the baby, Celestia, to her diaper, and laid her in a bassinet, where she kicked her feet and cooed softly. The toddlers, Corrie Lynne and Paxton, sprawled on the kitchen linoleum, playing with a set of wooden blocks.

Gwynne stood at the small, painted table, rounding off a generous ball of bread dough; she tucked it into a ceramic bowl and laid a clean, white dishtowel over it. Just as she left it on the counter to rise, she heard the jeep rumble up to the house.

Cler strode through the door with a sparkle in his eyes, and a cheerful grin lighting up his face. He slipped his arms around Gwynne and lifted her off the floor, swinging her around.

"Cler! What on earth..." She giggled as he set her down, "I'm going to get flour all over you!" She rubbed her hands together over the breadboard; little pills of dough fell onto the flowered surface.

Corrie Lynne and Paxton grabbed one of their father's long legs. He took a few steps as they clung to him, giggling, then he ruffled their hair, and sent them off to play.

"I've been thinking it was about time we went to Alaska," he said, pulling out a chair from the table, and dropping onto it.

"Alaska! Alaska?" she asked, padding in her slippers, to the sink. She twisted the knobby handles to get the water running just right, and stuck her hands underneath. As she soaped her hands, she said, "Alaska. You still want to go?"

This wasn't the first time they'd talked about heading North. Alaska had been in the news often during the war. The government feared an invasion by the Japanese, and wanted to be ready by fortifying the territory. President Roosevelt authorized the building of a road into Alaska's interior. Seven regiments, about 10,000 men, of The Army Corps of Engineers were enlisted to build fifteen hundred miles of road from Canada's Yukon, to bases in Fairbanks, Alaska.

14

When the Japanese bombed Dutch Harbor, on the Aleutian Chain, the men building the road were reminded that what they were doing was essential to the war effort, and they sped up their efforts. Meanwhile, bases, airfields, and outposts were established in a number of remote places around the territory.

While constructing the Alaska Highway, the Army Corps didn't just start at one end of the road and go to the other end. They set teams of men and equipment at different points, and worked in two directions. Engineers marked out a path about ten miles ahead of the teams of bull dozers that followed, knocking down trees and clearing a fifty to ninety-foot wide path. In spite of muskeg, bogs that swallowed heavy equipment, and permafrost, which was mud frozen solid, the engineers developed ways of coping with the conditions. There were mosquitoes to torment them in summer, and before October, the men were getting frostbite. The last pieces of the highway came together by October, 1942. They had accomplished this enormous feat in less than eight months. The Alaska Highway was considered to be the greatest accomplishment since the Panama Canal.

Gwynne's grandfather, George Anthony Paxton, left Utah for Nome, Alaska, in the gold rush of 1899. He was twenty-five years old. George took out a mining claim, and brought out enough gold each year, to make a comfortable living. He spent six months in Alaska, and six months at home in Ogden, Utah. When he came home for the winter of 1902, he married a twenty-nine-year-old Scottish woman named Alice Crosby. They had a son, Charles, who, when he was a teenager, went with his father to help work the claim. George was one of the fortunate few who managed to find gold, let alone make a living from his efforts. Of the estimated 100,000 who went to the Yukon and Alaska during the Gold Rush, only 30,000 actually arrived in the gold fields along the Klondike River, and of those only 4,000 actually found gold. There is no family source that tells exactly where George found his.

At that time, the writings of Canadian poet, Robert Service, were wildly popular, feeding the Public's interest in Alaska. Thousands loved and quoted The Spell of the Yukon, while the literary bards called it doggerel.

George Paxton, perhaps identified with some Service's sentiments.

"I wanted the gold, and I sought it,
 I scrabbled and mucked like a slave.
Was it famine or scurvy -- I fought it;
 I hurled my youth into a grave.

I wanted the gold, and I got it --
 Came out with a fortune last fall, --
Yet somehow life's not what I thought it,
 And somehow the gold isn't all." (Robert Service)

Gwynne first remembered her grandfather, George, when she was six-years-old. By this time her grandfather was fifty-seven, and was no longer going to the gold fields, though he had become somewhat of a wealthy man. He was getting old, and his wife, Alice, was not well. George always considered his adventures in Alaska to be the highlight of his life. Alice, on the other hand, had good reason to believe those same adventures corrupted both her husband and her son, Charles.

Gwynne loved her father, Charles Paxton, but not her grandfather, George. The old man drank and swore, and was not kind to her grandmother. It was understandable that Gwynne would have mixed feelings about gold mining, and Alaska in general.

When Cler fell in love with Gwynne, he also fell in love with current romantic notions about Alaska; he wanted to go there, not to look for gold, but to build a home in a pristine land. At some point, he, like Gwynne's grandfather, discovered the spell of the Yukon.

"...There's the land. (Have you seen it?)

16

It's the cussedest land that I know,
From the big, dizzy mountains that screen it
To the deep, deathlike valleys below.
...I've stood in some mighty-mouthed hollow
That's plum-full of hush to the brim:
I've watched the big, husky sun wallow
In crimson and gold, and grow dim...
The strong life that never knows harness:
The wilds where the caribou call;
The freshness, the freedom, the fairness—
O God! How I'm stuck on it all." (Robert Service)

The Second World War, of course, had intervened, but Cler's dream of going to Alaska persisted. He started thinking about it again after the war, while he was working at the Ogden Army Depot. He had a lot of Army buddies working there, too, and the men began to talk about their plans for the future.

Cler liked his hometown, but he didn't plan to stay there for the rest of his life. There was a whole world out there. His older brother, Bill, had gone to California, made money in radio and silent pictures, and started working for the movie industry. His other brother, Frank, worked for a national canned food outfit, and traveled all over the West. Only his sister, Ella, stayed in Ogden, living across town from her parents.

THE PLAN

Cler was twenty-two, and Gwynne twenty-one, that day when Cler came home and announced he wanted to go to Alaska. "We've been thinking about this for a long time," he said, even though Gwynne had not really been thinking about it. She'd been concentrating on nursing her baby, tending her toddlers, baking bread when the little house was already sweltering, washing and hanging a dozen diapers on the line every day. It was Cler who was thinking about Alaska.

He did notice that Gwynne didn't seem all that enthusiastic, but he attributed her silence to her mulling over the practical considerations. Cler picked up the wooden spoon that lay on the table. He bounced it like a drum stick on the bread board, tat-a-tat-tat.

"There's no hurry, Sweetheart; we can take the whole winter to get ready," he told her. "With the new highway opening, getting there will be easy."

Gwynne dried her hands on her apron and joined him at the table, sitting across from him. She took the wooden spoon away from him so his drumming wouldn't wake the baby.

"So tell me. You're not thinking of going up there to pan for gold, are you?"

Cler laughed. "It's not about gold, although if we run across any, we'll certainly grab it! No, it's about homesteading. I have some buddies at work who want to go, too. We've been looking into what it takes."

"What do you actually know about Alaska, Cler? I mean, my grandpa used to only go up there in the summer. You're talking year-round, right?"

"Yes, but it's not all ice and Eskimos. I have a friend who actually worked for the Army Corps of Engineers, building the Alaska Highway. He says it's wonderful country. Of course, he lost a couple of fingers to frost bite, but..."

"He still wants to go up and homestead, even though he lost his fingers," Gwynne said, dryly.

"No, he doesn't, but some of us do. We want to take advantage of what the government is offering us." The Homestead Act of 1862 had been renewed and revised to help veterans returning home after World War II. There were articles in all the papers, and even in the Reader's Digest. The news was out: Alaska was open for homesteading; free land just for living on it. Of course, if you read the fine print, it was all pursuant to certain Acts in 1946, in which the government reserved its "right to build roads, railroads, power lines, etc." across any homestead.

18

The new acts also reserved, to the government, "any gold or thorium that might be on the property."

After the war, the Territorial Government had to frequently remind Washington of Alaska's strategic importance. To support the military, the civilian population also needed to increase; previously maintained by the military, bridges, roads, tunnels, ports, and even the railroad were turned over to civilian contractors, so they needed men and material. As of May, 1947, the Alaska highway would be open to civilian traffic, which the government hoped would increase the workforce and build up the Territory.

The baby began to cry, and Cler stepped over to the bassinet and picked her up, "How's my little angel?" he cooed, holding her close to his face, and kissing her damp little forehead. She continued to fuss, turning her head, looking for something to suck.

"I'll take her," Gwynne said, reaching for the baby. "I'll feed her if you'll punch down the bread dough. It's so warm in here, it's already risen above the bowl."

Cler handed the baby over, and it only took two steps across the small kitchen to reach the sink, to wash his hands. He dried them on a clean dishtowel, and returned to the table, where he removed the towel that covered the mound of dough. He cleaned and floured the breadboard, and emptied the glutinous mass of dough onto it. As he worked it under his hands, he continued to talk about Alaska. Gwynne nursed the baby, without covering herself, because of the heat.

Cler said, "One thing that excites me is that we veterans get a special deal now. We don't have to farm, or even clear a certain amount of land. Of course, we'd have to build a place to live, and that means we'd still have to clear some land. Alaska is covered over with trees and brush so thick, even the moose hate to go through the woods! At least, that's what my buddy at work told me."

"The guy with eight fingers?"

"Yup, that guy. Anyway, one other good thing is that we'll get a four hundred dollar a month stipend."

"Really? That would be nice," she said.

With a practiced hand, he sliced the dough into quarters, and formed four loaves, tucking them into greased bread pans. He set them next to each other in a row, and spread the dishtowel neatly over them.

Then he sat down at the kitchen table, leaning back on his chair, balancing on two chair legs. He often did this balancing act because he was too tall to sit comfortably on most kitchen chairs.

"Watch out or you'll fall over on your head," Gwynne teased.

The baby pulled away, and Gwynne covered herself, and put Celestia on her shoulder, patting her little back until a loud burp erupted.

Cler laughed, "Now, that's a healthy baby!"

Corrie and Paxton climbed up on their father's lap, one on each knee, forcing him to set his chair on all four legs. He wrapped his arms around them, and clasped his hands. They giggled, as he wiggled his thumbs and they each tried to grab and hold onto a thumb.

Gwynne said, "You know, my father went up to Alaska when he was fourteen, to stay with Grandpa Paxton. Grandpa had a placer mine somewhere up there, but I don't know where."

"Your dad told me a little about that one night when he'd been drinking a bit. Placer mining was mining gold from rivers or streams, so they moved around. I guess the gold fields were a pretty wild place in those days."

"They were, although Daddy never told me much about it."

"Not a story for a little girl?"

"That's my take on it. You knew my grandmother, but by that time she was bedridden. When she was well, my grandmother was a gentle and refined woman. She was appalled by the things Dad learned when he was with his father in Alaska, but there was nothing Grandma could do about it. "

20

Cler said, "Well, that was then. I'm sure things are a lot more civilized up there now."

"I wouldn't bet on it," Gwynne said, darkly.

Tired of playing with Dad's thumbs, Corrie and Paxton slid off his lap and ran out the open door, into the front yard, to play in the dirt.

Cler leaned back, balancing on two chair legs again. "Gwynne, I know Alaska's still the wilderness, but when your dad was there, well, you're talking about camps full of ruffians and fortune seekers; men, drinking and gambling. Now, I believe Alaska offers a different kind of life for a man and his family."

Gwynne shrugged, "All I know is my grandpa had to stop going up to the goldmines because Grandma got sick. She just took to her bed. I used to help take care of her after school, and feed her. She'd stopped talking by then, but I could tell she liked me to come."

Cler asked, "So what was wrong with her, or do you know?"

"No one knew. She just took to her bed, and never got up again. The doctor said that if there was a fire, she'd be the first one out the door. I don't know. Maybe, she just couldn't handle life anymore."

Gwynne stood up and laid the baby back in her bassinet. For a few moments, she just stood there watching the rosy infant sleep.

"We don't have to go," Cler said, bringing the chair legs to the floor with a thump.

She came up behind him and put her arms around his neck, laying her head on top of his, nuzzling his curly hair.

"No," she said, "If you want to go, I want to go. With you, I'd go to Timbuktu!"

PREPARATION

21

During the following winter, four other veterans from the Depot, and their wives, met with Cler and Gwynne around the Oborn's kitchen table. They poured over pamphlets and articles about Alaska, studying everything they could about the climate, and the opportunities for homesteading. In the spring, they planned to drive the Highway, making the journey together. They would caravan, like a modern wagon train.

After much discussion and research, the group decided they'd all go to south-central Alaska, and homestead on the Kenai Peninsula. There, the weather was supposed to be milder and there was plenty of available land.

They came to the conclusion that the climate on the Kenai was similar to Northern Utah. Temperatures in the interior of Alaska, and further North, could reach 60 degrees below zero, but they were set on going to the Kenai, so they weren't worried.

While Gwynne and Cler stockpiled supplies, their friends began to have second thoughts. One by one, each of the other couples dropped out.

By spring, Gwynne and Cler had gathered all the things they thought they'd need in Alaska. They bought a two-wheeled trailer to haul their supplies, to be pulled behind the jeep.

The list was long: kerosene lanterns and kerosene, down sleeping bags, wool army blankets, canned food, flour and sugar, warm clothing. They needed tools: an ax, a hatchet, a sledge hammer and cross-cut saw. Gwynne needed a wash board and galvanized tub, for scrubbing clothes by hand, bars of brown, lye soap which would serve for every cleaning need, from laundry soap to shampoo. They bought a Dutch oven for cooking over campfires, and a cast iron frying pan. They needed extra Jerry cans of gasoline for the jeep; there would be many miles between places where they could buy gas.

By May, Cler and Gwynne felt they were ready to leave the comfort and civilization of Ogden. Their baby, Celestia, was almost a year old. She would sleep curled on a folded blanket, on top of a tin bread box, which was squeezed between the two front seats of the jeep. The other two children would ride comfortably among sleeping bags, blankets and pillows in the back seat. The two-wheeled trailer was packed high and tied with a tarp covering the bulging top.

They didn't know what lay ahead, but they were setting off on the adventure of their lives. Cler and Gwynne bid his sobbing parents goodbye and headed north.

SPRING, 1947

THE JOURNEY

The trip was going fine until four-year-old Corrie Lynne came down with mumps in Missoula, Montana. This forced them to stay in a motel, which cost precious time and money. Cler tended the children, while Gwynne worked temporarily as a waitress in a coffee shop. When Corrie was better, they continued on their journey.

Traveling through Montana and what is now Glacier National Park, they were thrilled by the towering peaks and clear rivers, but they were not going to stop in Montana. Homesteading there was not an option. It was Alaska, their own promised land, that beckoned to them.

Paxton and Celestia came down with the mumps together. They stopped at a motel near the border. Gwynne and Cler were able to work at the motel restaurant where they stayed. Gwynne also sold her sterling silver in order to get enough money to cross into Canada. The Canadian Government required travelers to have enough money when they entered Canada, to leave again. The Canadians were not heartless, but they remembered the Gold Rush. Now, with so many people streaming north, they had no desire to be stuck caring for indigents.

When Cler and Gwynne arrived at the Canadian Border, officials took their only gun, a single shot .22 rifle, and broke it down, attaching a seal that had to stay in place, until the family crossed out of Canada again, far up in Yukon Territory.

On they traveled, over grassland and prairies, until they reached the Canadian Rockies. They passed through canyons of jagged rocks and tumbling waterfalls . There were small cities and little towns, but as they traveled north, signs of civilization dwindled. At night they pitched a tent near a river or stream, where they could build a fire to cook on, and refill their water can.

They reached Dawson Creek, the beginning of the Alaskan Highway, in the latter part of June. The highway seemed to be little more than a wide cow path. When the weather was dry, they choked on dust; it seeped into every pore, coated the jeep's plastic windows, the canvas top, and the tarp-covered trailer. After rain, or when the road wound through muskeg, mud sucked at the tires.

Cler gunned the jeep up switch-backs carved into the sides of granite mountains, the heavy trailer dragging like a stubborn beast, threatening to pull them backwards, off a cliff. At the top of each mountain, they'd reach a summit, cheering, and then head down again. Now it was a fight to stay ahead of the trailer. Cler would gun the engine, in order to pull ahead, and then shift down to slow, to make the curves, fighting the weight of the loaded trailer all the way to the bottom. And so it went, up and down again, over a mountain, through another tree-covered valley , over still another roaring river, on a swaying pontoon bridge.

Once, after rain, the trailer slid off the side of a muddy embankment. Gwynne grabbed the baby, terrified they were going to roll. Cler stomped on the gas and tore down the embankment, fighting to stay in front of the trailer. The jeep careened along the side of the hill, dragging the trailer behind, until Cler was able to steer it up and onto the road again.

They finally came to the border on July 4, 1947, and crossed into Alaska Territory. At Dawson Creek, they met another young couple, Larry and Laura Straley, who were also going to the Kenai to homestead. The Straleys had started north on horses, but had sold the horses and bought a car. The country was just too vast to travel on horses and still get to Alaska before winter.

24

The two couples hit it off immediately. Laura was a dark-eyed beauty, with a competent air about her. She had a way of making Gwynne, who was naturally shy, feel at ease. Larry and Cler seemed like old buddies who had just rediscovered each other. The couples traveled together, and when they stopped for the night, they pitched their tents near each other and shared their fire.

Cler was always a careful camper. Near the camp, but far enough for privacy, he always dug a little pit for a toilet. He set up a hand washing station with soap and water, and waste was burned and tin cans taken away with them after the camp was dismantled.

Larry and Laura stayed with Gwynne and Cler until they were almost to Tok Junction, 93 miles inside Alaska.

The families camped in the woods near the road, and in the morning Larry and Laura said goodbye and headed to Anchorage, where they promised to meet up again.

Gwynne and Cler had only driven a few miles down the road, when the jeep started making a terrible, grinding noise. He jumped out, walked around the jeep and then looked back on the road. He could see something a few yards away, sitting on the gravel. When he came back, he was holding several pieces of metal. "We're not going anywhere," he said.

Gwynne sat listening to the silence, and even the children didn't make a sound. They were all watching Cler. He leaned against the fender, holding what were obviously essential parts of the jeep. There was nothing around but the cloudy sky above and the dusty road winding ahead into the trees.

They heard an engine noise, and it grew louder. The sound of scraping, and crushing gravel. A road grader, looking like a giant, yellow insect, rumbled up behind them. The driver stopped when he saw the jeep, and turned off the shuddering racket of his engine. He jumped off the grader with a big smile.

"Howdy folks! Need some help?"

He was a stocky fellow with a full, bushy brown beard. He was wearing a dusty tan coat and equally dusty denim pants, with heavy leather work boots.

"Well, I guess I do," Cler said, showing him the broken pieces of metal.

"Looks like it. I'm Forest Triber, by the way," the amiable driver said. "I can tow you into the camp at Tok Junction; it's only about ten miles down the road. I'm headed that way."

Forest hitched a chain onto the disabled jeep, and attached it to his road grader. Cler steered the jeep, as the grader towed them into the Road Commission camp.

At this junction, the Alaska Highway met the Richardson Highway. A traveler could take the Richardson west, to Valdez and the coast, or the Glenn Highway south to Anchorage and the Kenai Peninsula. Also from Tok Junction, the Alaska Highway headed north to Fairbanks.

BEN PINKS

At Tok, the Road Commission camp sprawled onto the tundra. This was where the government kept workers, trucks, road graders and bull dozers. There were several long buildings in the camp, and numerous out-buildings. Men who worked on the road lived in the camp's dorm during the summer and fall, until road-construction was halted. The grader, with jeep in tow, bounced into camp and parked near other heavy equipment in the broad clearing.

Three-year-old Paxton's eyes grew wide as he spied the fascinating machinery. "That's a big tractor," he said in awe.

"It's called a bull dozer," Cler told him. "That tan one over there, that's an Allis Chalmers. That big blade can tear up trees and move huge boulders."

"Wow," Paxton said, staring at the bull dozer that was only a few feet away.

"Come on, gang, let's get out and look around. I'll ask if we can camp over in those trees."

26

There was a crystal clear, gurgling stream along the edge of the clearing. Across the stream from the camp, Forest helped Cler pitch a tent. He invited the family to share supper with the men in the dining hall.

It was there that they met the camp cook, Ben Pinks. He was a bandy-legged little man with sparkling blue eyes in a face like wrinkled leather, and he wore a brown beard. Gwynne looked around the dining hall, full of bearded men, chatting and laughing as they ate at a dozen tables. In the interior, it seemed, men didn't bother shaving, and maybe they grew beards, she thought, to keep their faces warm.

Dinner was social hour at the camp, a time to sit around and talk. Ben finished dishing up dinner, and came to join Forest and Cler's family, at their table. He asked, "Where are you folks headed?"

"We intend to go south to the Kenai Peninsula," Cler told him.

Ben chewed on his lower lip, tasting a bit of his fuzzy beard, while he listened to Cler extol the virtues of the Kenai.

Ben said, "Cler, you say you want elbow room. Maybe the Kenai's not for you. For one thing, I heard there's fires down there. There's too many folks headed down to Anchorage, anyways. You need to see my Kenny Lake. I know you'll like it there."

In the green Army tent, Cler tucked the children into their sleeping bags, "I think we should keep on going south, don't you?"

"Yes," Gwynne said, as she knelt on their sleeping bag, unpinning her coiled braids. With her fingers, she began to loosen her hair, in order to brush it out. "We don't want to be too far from civilization."

"But not too close, either," he said, crawling over to their bag. He pulled off his boots. "Let's have prayer," he said, kneeling beside his wife.

"We thank Thee, Heavenly Father for the angels who rescued us today. We thank Thee for helping us thus far on our journey to travel in peace and safety."

After the prayer, as he undressed down to his long johns, he began to softly sing a popular song once recorded by Gene Autry. Cler sang it partly as a lullaby for the children, whose three little pairs of eyes looked up at him, wide awake, and partly as a love song to his wife. The gurgling creek accompanied his clear, baritone voice.

"With someone like you,
A pal good and true,
I'd like to leave it all behind,
And go and find
A place that's known to God alone;
Just a spot to call our own.
We'll find a perfect peace
Where joys will never cease,
Somewhere beneath a kindly sky.
We'll build a sweet little nest,
Somewhere in the West,
And let the rest of the world go by..." (J. Keim Brennan and Ernest Ball)

He crawled into their double sleeping bag, and Gwynne wriggled in beside him.

"I love you," she said, rising up on one elbow to kiss him.

They could hear someone talking over in the camp, and a man laughed. Nearby, there was only the murmur of the stream.

The next day, Ben Pinks introduced Cler to a forest ranger friend of his. During their conversation, the ranger said, "You might want to rethink going down to the Kenai. The whole place is on fire right now. The animals are gone."

Ben added that they really should try the Copper River area. His eyes shone as he said, "There's plenty of salmon in the rivers, and all the moose you can stand. It's the most beautiful place on earth, Cler; God's own country."

The entire Copper River Basin was barely inhabited. In fact, at this time, across the thousands of square miles making up Alaska, (over 586,000) there were only about a hundred thousand people, including all the native peoples scattered along the rivers, and in villages from Southeast Alaska, on the panhandle, to the Aleutian Chain, from Canada to Alaska's western seacoast, and all the way to the Arctic Circle. Cler and Gwynne were among the 12,000 hopeful individuals who arrived from the States that year, after the opening of the highway. The Oborns would be among the fewer than three thousand souls who stayed.

One problem was the extreme weather, and the other was access to the land. There were only three highways, and they connected at Tok Junction. Most of the state was inaccessible, even by plane, and there were few airfields, hundreds of miles apart. Air travel in Alaska was always dangerous, even in summer. The weather was unpredictable, and planes were forced to fly over immense stretches of uninhabited country to get from point A to point B. There were vast glaciers, that created their own bad weather, and mountain ranges too high to fly over.

While Cler was working on the jeep, Ben Pinks let Paxton and Corrie tag around with him and his curly, black lab, Buddy. The dog loved the attention the children gave him, wagging his bushy tail and trying to lick their hands.

Ben Pinks was an irresistible character, outspoken and good-natured at the same time. He said he came to Alaska seeking gold over forty years before. He'd done many things; he'd cooked on fishing boats, and had trapped beaver and muskrat, hunted moose and bear.

Ben hated bears with a vengeance. He'd had a hunting partner who was killed by one. During the week that Gwynne and Cler were at the camp, Ben shot several bears. It was a pattern they recognized: some time during the night, they'd be awakened by Ben's dog barking, deep and low. In a few moments, they would hear a shot or two ring through the trees.

The next morning they would find out Ben had shot a bear that was coming around camp. To the old trapper, they were a danger and a nuisance, and it was his job to keep the camp safe.

The old man took to Cler's family as if he'd known them all his life. He doted on the children, loved conversing with Cler about Alaska, about the war, about Cler's military training. He seemed drawn Gwynne, with her fresh beauty, but he was always a gentleman. He often expressed fatherly concern for her welfare.

Ben insisted on feeding the family dinner in the dining hall, and continued to bring food that was supposedly left over. Gwynne thought he was cooking and baking too much, on purpose.

Cler borrowed a tripod and pulled the engine on the jeep, with Forest Triber's help. He discovered what part needed to be replaced. He hoped the part wouldn't cost more than he had, which was a total of fifty dollars. On the third morning at the camp, he hitch-hiked into Anchorage to buy what he needed. He was only gone a day, having been fortunate to get rides, and the people who picked him up even bought meals for him. When he got back, he told Gwynne of his good fortune.

"Everyone who gave me a lift treated me like a buddy. And when I went to buy the part, I couldn't believe it, but it was only ten dollars! It's like a miracle, Gwynne. I still have forty dollars left!"

Cler had seen Anchorage, with its raw, dirty streets, its fledgling down town, and its row of bars on Third and Fourth Avenue. The air was tainted by smoke from the forest fire that was burning up the Kenai. While he was in Anchorage, Cler began to reconsider homesteading on the Kenai, and to think seriously about settling down in Copper River country.

Ben said there was land available, and easily accessible, near his hunting tent at Kenny Lake. He called the tent a "baraba."

"You can stay at my camp until you get a cabin built. There's cleared land there, ready to build on, because Kenny Lake used to be a rest stop for men and horses, back in mining days.

30

It's on the road to the mine at Chitna. Why don't you go see it? I'll draw you a map. I just know you'll fall in love with it."

Ben Pinks had a friend who'd filed on a homestead, a hundred-and-sixty acres, at Kenny Lake, but the friend had left Alaska. In September, that land would become available for someone else to file on. Cler could be that fortunate man. On the map of Kenny Lake, he sketched in the area of his friend's abandoned tract of land. "You can stay in my baraba," the old trapper said. "Might as well get some use out of it. I'll come out to Kenny Lake in a few days, to see how you're getting along."

Cler was surprised, but he grinned, "Well, sure, Ben. I guess you're pretty certain we'll like the place."

"One look; you'll like it." Ben said.

When the jeep was fixed, Cler and Gwynne thanked their friends, Forest and Ben, who'd helped them so much. They took down the tent, packed up, and drove off to see Kenny Lake.

It was about a hundred and seventy-five miles from Tok Junction to Kenny Lake. On the way, they stopped at Copper Center, a small settlement of mostly native people. There was a large road house there, built out of squared logs. Besides rooms and a restaurant, the Copper Center Road House had a bar, grocery store and gas pump. Gwynne and the children gratefully climbed out of the jeep to use the restroom facilities, while Cler filled the jerry cans and the tank of the jeep with gas.

When Gwynne returned, the children scrambled back into the jeep again. "How much further is it?" Gwynne asked, settling the baby onto her lap.

Cler said, "They tell me it's only about twenty-two miles from here to Kenny Lake."

2
COPPER RIVER COUNTRY

SUMMER, 1947

When it came to natural grandeur, Ben had not exaggerated when he spoke so highly of Copper River country. It was indeed breath-taking: the area was surrounded by immense, snow covered mountains that spawned sprawling glaciers, which in turn fed rivers. Rivers from a dozen different glaciers flowed into the mighty Copper, which, over eons of time had carved a canyon through a vast plateau. Granite bluffs along the river rose up through the lush landscape. Willows, alders, quaking aspen and birch trees covered the land like a fuzzy blanket of pale green. Stands of dark spruce broke up the vista of leafy trees. Receding glaciers had left a thousand lakes in their wake.

Cler drove along a gravel highway that wound its way over the low hills and around the meadows of tall grass and glittering ponds. Gwynne felt her heart stir with awe and gratitude; it was all just so beautiful!

They followed the rough map's directions as they left the gravel highway and turned onto a narrow dirt road, called the

Edgerton Cut-off. Ten miles from the turn-off, would be Kenny Lake, and Ben's hunting tent, or "baraba," as he called it. Seventeen miles past Kenny Lake was Chitna, a town built for a huge copper mine in 1918. The mine had been closed in 1938, and the town was now a ghost town, they were told, although there was a little store there, run by a family who was paid to guard the mine.

They identified Kenny Lake by its size. It was larger than most of the lakes in the area, but still small enough that a man could walk around it in a few hours. The nearly round lake was like a mirror; its still water reflected the sky in a perfect image of snowy mountains, dark spruce, and fluffy clouds.

On the shore of Kenny Lake, nearest the road, lay remains of a log barn, its roof caved in. Across from the lake, Cler followed a track up a modest rise, through a grassy area. On their right, lay a stand of spruce trees. They passed a pit filled with blackened boards noted on Ben Pinks map as "road house, burned down in '36."

They followed the trail north and slightly uphill, and found the small structure that was Ben Pink's hunting tent. It was white canvas, with a wood frame, sidewalls, a peaked roof, and a wooden floor.

Cler parked the jeep, and then he and Gwynne climbed out and stretched, looking around. Paxton and Corrie scrambled out, too, glad to be able to run across the grass. Gwynne carried the baby on her hip while they checked out the baraba.

Opening the canvas door and ducking under the frame, they entered the cozy space. Light filtered through the white canvas, eliminating need for a window. A cot and a small iron stove, as well as a little table, a chair and a cupboard furnished the inside.

Stepping out into the clean, moist air, Gwynne took a deep breath. She lowered her wiggly baby down to stand, as she took in the panoramic view of mountains and forest.

"Oh, Cler! It's so beautiful here! I love it!"

Baby Celestia, now called Lestie for short, wobbled as she took hold of her mother's skirt, clinging to it, rubbing the soft cotton against her little face.

Cler moved to join them. He surveyed the open space with its willows on the west and forests of spruce on the north and east.

"Part of that grass field could be planted into a garden, couldn't it?" Gwynne asked, indicating a weed-filled patch.

Cler said, "I think it could. You know, Honey, we need to appreciate how much open land there is here. And how high and dry it is. No marsh close by. We wouldn't even have to clear brush in order to build a cabin. Look, we could build it over there, by those spruce trees. I could even make a landing strip. See? A plane could come in over the lake, and land down there, on that open field, with plenty of room. Maybe I'd have to clear a little brush over there, but…"

Gwynne picked up Lestie, and brushed her off.

"Really? A landing strip? Well, first, I guess, we'd better build a cabin, right?"

"Absolutely!" Cler bent to kiss her on the lips.

Thus it was decided. The Oborns would take out their homestead at Kenny Lake.

For now, they had to get busy on the cabin. July was half over, and snow would fly before October. They figured they had to be in a snug, warm cabin before the end of September.

They pitched their army-green tent beside Ben's tent. Cler, Corrie, and Paxton slept in the army tent, while Gwynne and the baby slept on the cot in the baraba, where Gwynne also was able to cook and the family could eat at the small table.

Celestia's earliest memory is of waking in the white tent, with sunlight filtering through the canvas. She's sitting on the cot, which is neatly tucked with an army blanket. She stares at the metal stove, and then at the table. She's hungry, but doesn't cry; alone, but unafraid. She can hear her parents talking just outside the tent.

34

BUILDING THE CABIN

In Copper Center, Cler obtained a survey map of the area, and located the quarter section of land he intended to file on in September. The land extended from the road and ran north of their camp.

On a grassy, open space, Cler began his cabin by digging a trench around a twenty-foot by twenty-foot square he'd laid out with stakes and strings. When he finished the trench, he filled it with gravel, ready for the first logs.

Gwynne thrived in the glistening light of high summer. She felt herself blossom, like the wild roses that suddenly appeared on bushes along the roadsides, wherever the sun could touch them. They showed fresh and pink among dark, green leaves, giving off a sweet fragrance.

There were countless other wild flowers: blue bells, and purple lupine, fireweed, like flames of fuchsia, white daisies, Indian paint brush and tiny, blue forget-me-knots, which she discovered among the tall reeds, beside the lake.

Often, when the children were napping, and Cler didn't need her, she took a little knife and went walking, returning to the tent with a miniature bouquet to arrange in a small glass bottle, an offering to beauty, glowing on the faded wooden table in the baraba.

Ben stopped by to see how the family was doing, and when he saw that Cler had not cut any logs yet, he asked, "Did you notice that abandoned barn down across the way?"

"Yes," Cler answered, "Who owns it?"

"Nobody, now. It used to be a way-station for horses and wagons hauling freight to and from the mine at Chitna. The old roadhouse also stabled horses there. The mine and everything else was abandoned back in '38. Nobody owns it now. You could drag those big old logs up here. Be perfect for your cabin."

Ben ruffled Celestia's curls and patted Corrie on the shoulder. "You kiddies stay close to your folks, you hear?" he said,

35

stooping a little to look Corrie in the eyes. In a scary voice he intoned, "They's bears in this country."

Corrie and Paxton solemnly promised to stay close by.

Before he left, Ben handed Cler a powerful, 10 gauge shot gun. "You can give it back after you buy yourself a gun," he told Cler. "You can't stay here without a gun."

Cler handled the gun, checking it over. "Guess you think my .22 won't kill a rabbit."

Ben laughed. "A rabbit, you bet. But not a bear." He reached into his pocket and pulled out a box of shells. "This single barrel ain't that powerful, but it's better'n nothin'. I got a bear gun, but I need it out at the camp."

Cler agreed to accept the loan of the shotgun, but promised he'd buy his own gun, the first chance he got.

"Think about tearing down that barn," Ben said, walking with his characteristic uneven gait, back to his very old Ford. Cler had heard him joke that if his car was one model older, he'd be starting it with a crank. The engine sputtered to life and Ben left in a cloud of exhaust.

After he left, Gwynne and Cler looked at each other. "What do you think about tearing down that old barn, as Ben suggested?" Cler asked.

"I don't want old, rotten, logs for our new home," she said, and Cler agreed.

With his chain saw, he energetically went to work clearing brush so he could get the jeep back to a stand of large spruce trees on their own land.

Using ax and chain saw, Cler felled some big spruce trees, watching them crash down, slamming into the ground below with branches and limbs set quivering. He trimmed the branches off and then dragged the logs out one at a time, on a heavy chain behind the jeep. Back at the building site, Gwynne used a small hatchet to trim bark off the logs. Cler wielded an ax to cut log-sized notches near the ends, and used a double-handed draw-knife to flatten one side, so the bumpy, round logs would lie flat against each other. Gwynne also helped by working the winch attached to the jeep.

The winch, a sort of motorized pulley, raised the heavy logs, while Cler maneuvered them into place and fit them together. He secured the logs at the corners with iron spikes.

THE OLD BARN

Building the cabin walls with newly cut, green logs, turned out to be incredibly difficult. The logs were heavy as iron and the thick, gooey sap dulled the ax. It was almost as bad as chopping rubber, Cler said.

Progress was agonizingly slow. Cler and Gwynne had managed with great effort to build the cabin walls two logs high all around. July was going fast.

That day the family made a trip to the little store in Chitna for groceries. When they returned to Kenny Lake, Gwynne glanced at the ruins of the old barn. Those logs were looking better to her now. She didn't say anything, because she thought it was Cler who wanted to build their cabin out of new logs, thinking the barn logs were rotten.

They drove up the trail, and reached the clearing where the cabin stood, with walls only two logs high. Gwynne felt her chest compress with anxiety; she was afraid she'd have an asthma attack. They'd never finish the cabin before winter, at the rate they were going.

As Cler stopped the jeep and they all piled out at the camp site, Gwynne took a deep breath of the crystal air to calm her nerves. She led the children to the big tent and began to make a little lunch, while Cler started again on the cabin. She packed two loaves of bread into the tin bread box and kept one out to slice for sandwiches.

While Gwynne sliced bread, the hollow "thunk" of Cler's ax echoed through the clearing. A magpie scolded from a nearby Birch tree.

The three small children sat on the floor, waiting patiently for their food. Their mother began spreading a thin layer of jam on each slice of bread. She would take two slices to Cler when she went out to help him winch the log into place.

Corrie and Paxton began to fret. "I get the first piece!" Corrie shoved her brother, who, though younger, was as big as she was.

"Mama!" Paxton wailed.

Gwynne sighed, handing each of them a slice at the same time. The baby noticed and opened her little mouth to object, but Gwynne quickly handed her a half-slice.

"Give Lestie the other half," she told Corrie. "If she doesn't want it, you and Paxton can share it."

Corrie said, gravely, "Yes, Mama," but Gwynne saw the glance she gave her brother.

"If the baby's still hungry, she'll cry," Gwynne said. She left the children sitting on the wood floor, eating their bread and jam, and walked the short distance along tire tracks made by the jeep. The tracks had pressed down the grass until there was only dust, soft under her shoes. She reached the building site and a thrill of fear passed through her again. Winter was coming.

Cler was leaning on his ax, taking a breather.

"Cler," she said, shading her eyes with one hand, "Can we go down and look at the old barn again?" She handed him the bread and jam, pressed together into a sandwich.

He took a bite and chewed thoughtfully, searching her face. After he swallowed, he asked, "You think we should?"

"It might make things easier..." she said, swatting at a mosquito that whined near her ear. "If the logs aren't rotten, anyway."

"Let's go look at the barn," he said, energized by the thought. He slammed his ax blade into the stump he used as a chopping block.

They checked on the children, who had finished eating. Celestia had crawled up onto the cot and was sound asleep. Gwynne sent Corrie and Paxton to the Army tent to take their naps. They were tired, and immediately sprawled on the sleeping bags. While he waited for the kids to fall asleep, Cler fixed himself another sandwich and made one for Gwynne, who hadn't eaten. Once the kids were all asleep, Gwynne and Cler walked hand in hand down the track to the lake, and surveyed the ruins of the barn. The roof had caved in and the roof boards were rotten. Green moss and orange lichen covered the weathered, upended boards. The logs making up the walls, however, looked solid.

Cler smoothed his hands over the dry, weathered logs. He thumped one and it sounded hollow, like a drum. With his pocket knife, he sliced a thin peel off the surface, revealing healthy wood underneath.

"I don't think these logs are rotten at all," he said, carving off another peel. He walked around the perimeter of the structure while Gwynne followed, thumping each log as they passed along the walls. This could save them so much work.

When they reached the front of the barn, Cler gazed at the dry logs of Sitka Spruce. "These babies must have been harvested along the coast and hauled in from Valdez. They're so much bigger than what grows around here."

He thumped the nearest log. "All I have to do is… " He let out a long breath, "all I have to do is take these apart. It'll be some work, but worth it."

Gwynne leaned her head on his shoulder, emitting a little sigh.

"I know," he said, "we should have listened to Ben."

She lifted her head, "I didn't say that…"

"You thought it, though."

"No," she said, honestly, "I always believe you can do anything."

He laughed then, turned her to him and kissed her, holding her close. They fit together so perfectly. He kissed her again in spite of weariness, with the passion of a young husband.

That same day, Cler drove the jeep to the old barn, and using a crowbar, began to pull it apart. As he loosened each log, he wrapped a chain around it, climbed into the jeep, and pulled the log away from the wall. Little by little, he began to dismantle the old barn. He needed to keep at it. By now they were losing daylight by five or six minutes every day.

Fortunately, the dismantling went fairly quickly, as the barn logs were dry and came apart more easily than Cler had figured they would. He and Gwynne noticed layers of a gray, felt-like substance pressed between the old logs, and decided it was dried moss.

"Do we need to put something between the logs as we place them?" Gwynne asked when they found the dried moss.

Cler considered; gathering and drying moss would take time. They didn't have much time.

"The logs already fit together pretty tight. Let's just get the walls up first," he said.

Gwynne agreed. "Chinking is something I can do while you're putting the roof on."

The walls rose steadily. Gwynne worked the winch, while Cler set them into place and, using a sledge hammer, drove a spike into each corner. At night, the exhausted couple could barely crawl into their sleeping bags, they were so tired.

Corrie helped by tending the other children during the day, while her parents worked on the cabin. It wasn't easy for the four-and-a-half year old, especially when three-year-old Paxton escaped and she frantically ran after him. Once, she thought she'd lost him for good and was afraid to tell Mama, but the little boy was only hiding behind a big tree. She heard him laughing and sneaked up on him. She angrily grabbed his hand, dragging him back to the tent.

"Don't you know bears will eat you?" she scolded.

Another time, Corrie herself wandered into the nearby trees and was quickly lost. She had no idea which direction to go back to the tent. Panicking, and fearing she'd run into a bear, she began to run, and came out of the woods into the clearing, where her father and mother were working on the cabin. She ran back to the tent, where Paxton and Celestia were playing in the dirt nearby. Her parents didn't even know she'd been missing.

Kenny Lake trees 1947

NIGHT VISITOR

After Ben left the shotgun, Gwynne began thinking about bears. With only canvas for shelter, what would keep a bear from tearing through the tent and making off with one of the children? She began to obsess about it. One night, when the children had been put to bed, her stomach churned with anxiety.

"I don't want to sleep in the baraba tonight. I want to sleep with you in the Army tent."

Cler glanced at her as he ducked into the tent, "That's fine with me. We'll just squeeze in together. But I have a gun, now. I think we'll be OK." He didn't say it, but the truth was, only a cabin could keep them safe from a bear. Each night they knelt together and prayed for a safe night's rest, then went to bed and left their little family in the Good Lord's keeping.

Being high summer, it was light all night, even though the sun dropped below the horizon. In the dim light of one early morning, Cler was awakened by rustling in the brush, and the heavy breathing and grunting that could only be a bear.

He leaped out of bed, and grabbed the shotgun. Three-year-old Paxton watched his father dive out the tent door. The boy peered out to see what was happening, just as Cler aimed the gun at a nearby stand of birches.

When the bear spotted Cler, it rose up on its hind legs like a very tall, hairy man, behind a birch tree. Cler could tell it was a brown bear, even though a tangle of branches and leaves hid its face. Cler took a bead on the spot that he figured was the bear's head and pulled the trigger.

The shotgun exploded with a deafening blast that ripped a hole through the tree trunk. Cler glimpsed the bear's face framed by the hole in the tree, like a picture. Thrown backwards by the recoil, Cler hit the ground on his butt, and rebounded like he was on springs, in time to see the bear, blinded by lead shot and wood shrapnel, running around in circles.

The baby screamed, and Gwynne was propelled out of bed by the sound of the blast. She nearly collided with Cler, as he ducked into the tent and jumped into his boots. Snagging a handful of shells, he ducked out, hot after the wounded bear, which, by this time, had recovered enough to take off in a lumbering gallop, its huge rump disappearing into the brush.

Cler reloaded the shotgun as he tore after the bear.

Gwynne watched Cler in his long underwear, gun in hand, dashing into the thick brush. She waited in agonized suspense for him to return.

More than an hour later, he came back.

By this time, Gwynne had managed to settle her children down, and get them into bed again. She sat guarding the door of the tent, terrified, but determined to protect her children with the cast iron skillet she held on her lap. She spied her husband's pale, gray underwear before she saw his face reappearing through the trees. Setting the frying pan on the ground, she ducked out of the tent to meet him.

"You get him?" she whispered, when he came close enough to hear her. She didn't want to wake the children; or, if the bear was close, alert the bear. As for the bear, he was long gone. As for waking the children, they were all wide awake. Paxton slipped past his mother to get a glimpse of his dad.

Cler shook his head. "I tracked that so-and-so for more than a mile, but no dice. All we can hope is that face full of splinters and lead will put the fear of God into him so he won't come back!"

"So you did shoot him, but not enough to kill him?"

"That tree over there took most of the impact, but I think I blinded him. I kind of feel bad that I couldn't put him out of his misery. Truth is, killing a brown bear with a shot gun isn't such a good idea, anyway. I've got to get a better gun."

Gwynne stared at the big birch tree. One side of the trunk was blasted away, as if some giant had taken a bite out of it.

It was too late now to crawl back into bed, so she got up and carried the frying pan back to the little stove in the baraba, where she began to build a fire for breakfast.

Cler took his gun and headed up the track. "I guess I might as well start working on the cabin. Let me know when breakfast is ready," he said.

Gwynne gave him a wry look over her shoulder. "Maybe you should put some clothes on, first!"

HEALTH NURSE ARRIVES

One day, a young woman, driving a dusty Oldsmobile, stopped at the building site. She climbed out of the car and stretched, smoothing her tan denim jacket. She took in the tents and the three grubby children playing in the sawdust near the partial cabin walls.

"I'm Clarissa Mann," she announced, smiling, as Cler approached her car. "I'm the public health nurse."

"Cler and Gwynne Oborn," he said, reaching out to shake her hand.

"I'm checking families in the area, homesteaders and natives alike, for health issues. How are you folks?"

"I'm sure we're all in good health," Cler assured her. By now the children were shyly standing by their parents.

"May I?" Clarissa asked as she leaned down to inspect Paxton, checking behind his ears and parting his tousled brown locks, apparently looking for lice. She felt his neck for swollen glands, and put one hand on each little scrawny shoulder, as if measuring whether or not they were even.

Corrie watched with interest as Paxton was given the once over, but when the woman moved to assess her, she shrank from the stranger's touch. Clarissa ignored Corrie's reticence, and continued her examination. Corrie was very thin and her hair was stringy, dusty from playing in the dirt.

Gwynne felt ashamed; she could suddenly see her children through the nurse's eyes and they looked uncared for. She'd been so busy helping Cler, that she hadn't done much except feed them.

The nurse finished checking Corrie, and then she spotted Lestie, hiding behind her mother's skirts. Clarissa bent to examine the baby, who was wearing a soiled blue dress. Her little bare feet and legs were dusty. The child had lumps on her face, forehead, and underneath her hair; all over her head, in fact.

"What on earth is wrong with her?" The nurse asked, feeling the lumps on Lestie's head.

Cler swept his baby up into his arms, and brushed the wispy curls back from her forehead.

"Oh," he said, "this is a case of mosquito bites. They really love her." He kissed the baby's sweaty, dirt-smudged forehead, setting her down again. "We love her, too."

The health nurse tried to smile. "She must be very allergic. Do you have any mosquito repellent? You need to keep it away from her eyes, but..."

"We'll get some," Cler promised.

"I need to vaccinate the children for tuberculosis," Clarissa said, stepping to her car and reaching for a black bag.

"Tuberculosis?" Gwynne repeated, worried.

"It's epidemic among the natives," the nurse said. "We're trying to vaccinate all the homesteader's children, too."

The vaccinations completed, with all three children crying, Clarissa bid the little family "good-bye" and returned to her car. As she drove away, Gwynne took the baby from Cler.

"I think I'll wash the children, and put them all down for naps," she said. "What should we do for Lestie's allergy to mosquito bites?"

Cler said, "If we had some vinegar and soda, we could make paste for the itching. It's what my mother would do." He carried Lestie back to the baraba and Gwynne followed leading the other two children. Cler poured water from a jerry can into the basin, and wet a washrag , touching it to the bar of soap. He gently washed the baby's swollen forehead, and continued over her sparse hair until he'd washed and rinsed her face and head. Gwynne watched him for a moment. "Here," she said, reaching out, "I'll finish washing the children, and you go back to work."

Cler swatted a mosquito on his neck. He ducked out of the baraba. "Well, it'll soon get too cold for mosquitoes, anyway."

To Gwynne, this was not a comforting thought.

3

PROGRESS

From the ruins of the burned-out road house, Cler and Gwynne scavenged a window for the kitchen, and a long frame with four small windows for the opposite side of the cabin. The kitchen window had four small panes of glass in it that weren't even cracked. The other window frames needed new glass.

The barn logs were so big around that the cabin walls rose quickly. On the front of the cabin, Cler built a long porch, shaped like the prow of a ship. He built the walls five logs high, connected to upright poles that supported the roof. It spanned the width of the cabin. This porch would shelter his winter's firewood.

The fat logs from the old barn also made fine rafters, and a ridge pole over the center of the cabin and porch, forming a low, slightly peaked roof. Using small, straight poles, laid close together over the rafters, Cler and Gwynne created a roof. Cler scaled the corner logs like a ladder to access the roof.

Once he had poles covering the entire roof, he intended to put a layer of dirt on top of them, to act as insulation and water-proofing, but there were small cracks between the poles, where dirt would sift through. He salvaged some twisted sheets of corrugated tin from the roadhouse ruins. Using a sledge hammer, he beat the tin flat, and then soldered the nail holes in it. The result was not pretty, but it would do. He tacked the tin over the poles on the roof.

Once the tin covered the roof, Cler needed Gwynne's help to put a layer of dirt on top. He hoped the dirt would act as insulation, as well as help keep the roof from leaking. He rigged a rope and pulley onto the winch attached to the jeep, and then he shoveled dirt into 2 buckets. He tied a filled bucket to the rope, and climbed up onto the roof to dump and spread it out.

It was Gwynne's job to work the winch, and bring the buckets up to the roof. After every two buckets, Cler climbed down to fill the empty buckets and scrambled up to the roof again. When she could, Gwynne climbed up with him, and helped spread the dirt around.

When they had a few inches of dirt all over the roof, they decided to quit.

"I'm done for," Cler panted. "Let's pray it's enough."

They turned their attention to finishing the cabin, so they could move in before the cold weather hit.

Fish wheel on the Copper River 1947

THE GEORGES

Down the road, about a half mile, was a small settlement of Alaskan natives. Their cabins had been empty all summer. Cler found out that the people were down on the Copper River at their

47

fish camp, where they spent the summer catching and drying fish. The dried fish was a staple in their diet, and also fed their sled dogs over the winter.

The Copper River flowed only about a half mile away, accessed by a narrow dirt road leading from the native settlement, down to the river.

One day in late July, Cler and Gwynne loaded the kids into the jeep to go meet their neighbors, and maybe buy some fresh salmon, if they could. They arrived at the clearing on the river bank, where a dozen natives were working at the fish wheel. This was made from tied and bent willows, with paddle boards that turned with the river's current. When a salmon was scooped up by the boards, it slid into a trough on the river bank.

Cler parked the jeep and jumped out to talk to some of the men. A native man snagged a huge King Salmon from the catch box, using a hooked spear. He carried it to a long board table, where the women were gutting the fish, and filleting it into narrow strips.

A very old native woman, in a long sleeved, flowered dress was laying strips of salmon on a willow rack over a low, smoky fire.

Gwynne and the children climbed out of the jeep to look around. In the air there was a rich, salty smell of drying fish and wood smoke. Gwynne lifted Lestie, settling her on one hip. Corrie and Paxton followed their mother to where the women were working. A young woman about Gwynne's age looked up from filleting a hunk of the dark, red salmon, and watched her approach.

"Hello," Gwynne said. "I'm Gwynne Oborn, and these are my children. That's my husband, Cler, over there. We're from down the road at Kenny Lake. We're building a cabin there."

The young woman pointed to herself, "Emma Bell." She indicated another woman who bent over, adding a few sticks of wood to the smoky fire under the fish racks. "That Ina Lincoln, my sister. We live those cabins. We know you live Kenny Lake. Think we come visit you maybe."

48

"I'd love that!" Gwynne said.

The old woman in the flowered dress joined Gwynne and Emma. She was holding a couple of foot-long sticks of smoked salmon. It was dark red, and stiff, like a stick with bark on it.

"Hello," Gwynne said. The old woman nodded and grinned, showing her tiny yellow teeth. Her face was wrinkled, like a walnut shell, and her black eyes sparkled with good humor. She offered the stick of smoked salmon to Gwynne, then tore the second one in half for Paxton and Corrie.

"Mm, good!" she said.

Gwynne's mouth watered; she was hungry. She tore off a piece of the fish and gave it to Lestie to chew on, and then she chewed on the end of her own piece. "Delicious!"

Emma said, "This Mama George. She our mother."

"Nice to meet you, and thank you for the fish," Gwynne said. The dried salmon tasted like it smelled: smoky, a bit oily, and salty.

While Cler talked with the men, he found out that the natives who lived in the little cluster of cabins were of one family. Though the daughters had different married names, everyone referred to them as the Georges.

The Oborns left the fish camp with the gift of a large salmon, and promises on both sides to visit each other when fish camp was over.

At Kenny Lake, there were nights when a bear came around the tents, but the sleeping occupants didn't hear it. Cler saw the scat in the morning, and tracks in the soft dust, so he knew. Even though he didn't tell her, Gwynne soon realized they were having night visitors.

"I wish we had a dog," she said.

"We'll move into the cabin soon, I promise," Cler told her.

When the Georges returned from fish camp, they were interested in what was happening at Kenny Lake. They began visiting Cler and Gwynne, bringing gifts of fish, both fresh and dried. The children loved the old woman, and called her Grandma George.

The Georges were some of the last of a large group of Athabasca, who had lived along the Copper River for generations. The local natives called themselves the Ahtna people. Many of these people had died from various diseases brought by explorers and gold miners. In the little settlement near Kenny Lake, there lived only "Mama" George and her two daughters, with several small children, and an eleven-year-old grandson named Franklin, who was the only "man" in the group, other than Ina's husband, Nick. The other men had all died from measles a few years before. Emma spoke better English than her mother, and often translated for her.

Gwynne was glad to have neighbors close by, and the fish supplemented their diet, that consisted mostly of canned vegetables, bread and oatmeal. Cler had been too busy finishing the cabin, to go hunting.

One day, during breakfast, there was a gentle knock on the door frame of the tent. Cler rose from the cot, where he and Gwynne sat, eating their oat meal, and the children sat on the floor nearby. He lifted back the canvas to find Emma and her mother. The old lady had a 30-30 Winchester rifle over her shoulder. She was dressed in the traditional summer parka made of colorful flowered cotton that came down almost to the tops of her mukluks, or hand-made leather boots. Emma had on a gray cotton dress and sweater.

Cler invited the women in and Gwynne got up from the cot and shook hands with her friends. They offered Grandma George the wooden chair, and the other women sat on the cot. Cler perched on a short, fat log that was used as a stool.

Emma said, "Mama George worried about you have no gun."

The old woman spied the shotgun on the willow rack over the doorframe, and pointed. "No good," she said. She handed Cler the 30-30 rifle. "The bear she walk."

Emma said, "She want you keep until you get bear gun."

After many thanks, their visitors left, and Cler placed the 30-30 on the willow brackets, with Ben's shotgun. The .22 was wedged above the center pole.

As he sat back down on the cot, Cler shook his head. "The Georges are probably thinking these Chechakos know very little about bears."

Gwynne glanced up at the guns and then reached down and spooned the last of Celestia's oatmeal into her little mouth.

Cler leaned his elbows on his knees and ran his hands through his matted, brown curls. "I know. You don't have to say it."

Ben Pinks, the old trapper, was also thinking of the little family living in tents at Kenny Lake. He sent a letter that Cler should come to Tok and get his dog, Buddy. He explained that when the road commission camp closed for the winter, he was going to take the job as jailer in Copper Center. The beaver and muskrats were getting pretty scarce, he said, and he didn't feel well enough to come out to Kenny Lake and trap as he had done for so many years. Cler might as well dismantle the baraba, he added, and use what he could for his cabin.

The day after they received Ben's letter, Gwynne, Cler and the three children made a trip to Tok Junction. Cler brought the shot gun to give back. If Ben was giving him Buddy, the least he could do was give back his shotgun. Grandma George's 30-30 was better for bears, anyway.

When they finally pulled into the parking area, they climbed out of the jeep weary and dusty, as there had been no rain for a week or two and the gravel highway was bone dry. Every mile, the tires kicked up dust and the canvas top did little to keep it out.

They waved to Ben, who emerged from the cook tent followed by Buddy, the big, black dog. Buddy spotted the children and leaped ahead of his master to greet them. Within seconds, the kids were giggling and petting the dog, while Buddy's tail was wagging like a flag in a strong breeze.

With Lestie on her hip, Gwynne watched Ben as he approached across the parking area. He was bowlegged, and his characteristic limp was even more pronounced than the last time she'd seen him. It looked like the arthritis in his back was getting worse. He waved, calling out, "Howdy folks! Nice to see you!"

A bit out of breath, Ben reached the family, and glanced at his dog with the kids. He said, "You got more use for this good bear dog than I'll have in town."

"I don't know what to say." Cler reached out and shook his hand. "Thank you. While I'm here, Ben, let me give you back your shotgun."

Looking a bit surprised, the old man took the gun. "Thanks. You bought yourself a gun? What'd you get?"

"Actually, Grandma George loaned me a 30-30. I'm still planning on buying something."

The old man ran his fingers over his fuzzy beard. "You should do that. I was hopin' you wouldn't have occasion to shoot a Grizzly with this here shotgun," he said.

"Well, actually, I did shoot a brown bear..."

Ben's head jerked up and he stared at Cler. "Did he go down?"

"No, but he ran away!" Cler told him the story of shooting the tree, and the bear with its face full of splinters.

Ben laughed until tears came. When he recovered, he said, "Hey, I gotta get back to the cook tent. It's dinner time, so come on over."

The road crew had already filled most of the tables. They were eating, talking and laughing as the Oborns filed in. The Oborns filled their plates and sat down at the one empty table. While they were visiting in the dining hall, Ben took his shotgun, and left for a few minutes. He came back carrying a hefty rifle, and handed it to Cler.

"It's a thirty-ought-six and you can bet it'll take down a Grizzly. And here's a box o' shells I got left over, Cler. You can pay me when you get the money. Watch the little feller with this gun around," he grinned at three-year-old Paxton, whose brown eyes were wide and interested in that big gun.

Cler was stunned. "Ben, I can't…"

Ben put a hand on Cler's arm, "As I said, you can pay me when you got the money. I don't aim to be huntin' bears in Copper Center. I'm getting' too old. I'm feeling it in my bones."

Ben had given Cler the two essential items he needed to protect his family and survive at Kenny Lake: a gun that would stop a grizzly, and a good dog. But Ben was still concerned. When the family had finished eating, he walked with Cler back to the jeep. The children ran ahead and urged Buddy into the back seat, where Corrie and Paxton wrapped their arms around him, snuggling his furry body.

Ben laughed to see how the children loved Buddy, but then he sobered. "How's your cabin fixed for winter, Cler?"

Cler stood straighter, feeling like he was being interrogated by a short, but tough, drill sergeant.

"It's almost finished, Ben. We'll be fine."

Ben's eyes were like battered blue marbles held in place with wrinkles. The old man had seen all that this country could deliver. He smiled like he believed Cler, but he wasn't through, "If push comes to shove, and you want to move into Copper for the winter, there's cabins you could rent. I got one, furnished, you could have for cheap."

"I'll see how it goes out at the lake," Cler said, not wanting to be any more indebted to his friend than he already was.

"Take care my dog, now, you hear?" Ben called to the children.

4
FILING ON THE HOMESTEAD

Lestie and Buddy

Fall, 1947

At Kenny Lake, the Aspen leaves had turned bright yellow and the woods were a golden mass at the edge of the field. It was September, time to file on the homestead at Kenny Lake. Gwynne and Cler had already committed themselves by building a cabin, but it felt wonderful to go into the land office in Anchorage and officially claim the homestead.

The family made a trip to Anchorage, to file their papers. When they signed the papers, Gwynne kissed her husband. Cler grinned, "All we have to do now is live on it!"

While they were in town, they bought a few groceries. They also stopped at the pound and got a little, black kitten.

"That's a peachy cat!" Paxton exclaimed as his dad handed him the kitten. The cat's name became Peachy, an improbable name for a black kitten who would grow into a large, black tomcat, but it stuck. Peachy would keep the cabin free of shrews, the tiny, mice-like creatures that came around to eat whatever their sharp teeth could get into.

When they brought Peachy into the jeep, Buddy sniffed at him curiously. "Nice kitty," Paxton said, petting the kitten. Buddy accepted him, and thereafter, Peachy and Buddy became friends. The children adored them both.

ONE TINY PROBLEM

It was sometime in September that Gwynne suspected, to her utter dismay, that she was pregnant. She didn't say anything to Cler about it, because it shocked her; she must have been pregnant before they even left Ogden! She was sure that if she had known, she would never have agreed to leave Utah. For the last month or so, she had often felt sick to her stomach, but at the time she thought it was exhaustion. With all the work and hurry of trying to get the cabin finished, she had put any thought of a possible pregnancy out of her mind.

Now, as her true condition dawned on her, she was afraid; the baby would most likely come in February, one of the coldest months of winter.

In a panic to be alone and process her predicament, Gwynne hurried out of the baraba without saying anything to Cler, and headed to the woods. She followed a leaf-strewn animal path that led her further into the brush. If a bear came along, she wished it would eat her. No, she told herself, as she dodged willow branches that caught at her sweater. She really didn't want to be devoured by a bear, but she was more terrified of her situation than of a bear at this point. She felt betrayed by her own body; how could she carry a baby, or give birth here? Would a newborn even survive? It was all too horrible to contemplate.

She felt breathless, light-headed, and thought she would faint. She found a silvered, partially burned tree that had fallen, half hidden in the tall, dead grass, and she dropped onto it, resting her elbows on her knees, clutching her head in her hands.

"Dear Father in Heaven. I don't know what to do!" A sob escaped her lips, and she bit it back, sucking in a deep breath. She held her breath until she thought she'd pass out, and then expelled another sob, letting go. She cried with her whole body, like a child. After a few minutes, she stopped crying and wiped her face with the tail of her flannel shirt, that fell below her sweater.

She lifted her head and listened to the silence all around. The breeze rustled a few dead leaves above her head, but there wasn't even a magpie to be heard. The silence forced her to be still, and listen to her own thoughts. It dawned on her that over the summer she'd been pregnant, lifting heavy logs, shoveling dirt around, on the roof. Somewhere inside, had she known? It occurred to her that maybe she'd purposely ignored it; had worked herself to exhaustion, risking a miscarriage. Wouldn't that be better than having a baby without a doctor, and watching it get sick, or freeze to death in the cabin?

"Forgive me, Lord," she whispered.

She knew it wouldn't be long before she'd have to tell Cler. Well, OK, then, but she'd wait until she showed. Just wait and see. That was the answer. She rose from her seat on the log and made her way back to the camp.

HOME

The nights were getting too cold to sleep in the tent. The children were cold, and the baby cried with an earache. Gwynne treated Lestie's ear with warm oil, but told Cler that if they didn't get into the cabin soon, all the children would catch colds. It was time to start moving into the cabin, whether it was finished or not.

The thing they needed most now, was to get a stove built and installed. They'd brought with them, from Ogden, a kit to make a wood-burning stove out of a fifty-gallon steel drum, set on cast iron legs, but they needed to find a barrel. Cler remembered seeing a bunch of steel drums stockpiled behind the store in Chitna, probably left over from the mines.

When Cler went to Chitna to get a few groceries, he decided to ask about buying one of the barrels, even though he didn't have much money. Before he bought the groceries with the almost all he had in his wallet, he asked, "What do you want for one of those steel drums out back?'

"I'll throw it in with the groceries," the storekeeper said.

"That's great!" Cler told him. "Know anyone who could cut the steel for me? I'm making a drum stove. Got to get moved into the cabin, today, if possible."

There was a man in the store, sitting on a chair by the stove, drinking a bottle of beer. "I'll do it for nothing," he said, standing up. He introduced himself as Sam Blaylock, and he lived only a mile or so down the road.

Sam and Cler went out back, selected a good barrel, with minimum rust on it, and threw it into the back of the jeep. Cler followed him to his house, and Sam cut a circle out of one end with a torch, and another hole on the side, for the chimney. As he worked, he and Cler talked amiably, and when they parted, Cler told him to be sure and stop by Kenny Lake for a cup of coffee, anytime.

At the cabin, Cler put together the "drum stove," as it was called. He placed it in the center of the cabin, on its cast iron legs. On top of the drum, he used screws to attach the flat piece of steel, meant to hold cooking pots. The chimney was made from short lengths of black tin fitted together, and the first length contained a damper, which was a round piece of steel inside the chimney, that could be adjusted with a wire-wrapped handle on the outside. The chimney rose straight up through the tin circle that protected the roof.

As soon as the stove was installed, Cler began to build the first fire in it, to try it out. Paxton wanted to help. He carried a piece of log that was nearly as big as he was, and dropped it by the stove with a loud thump.

"Thanks, pal," Cler smiled, patting him on the head. He shoved the log into the stove and added another short log, then he added kindling.

Finally, he opened the damper and lit the fire. As the kindling took hold, flames began to crackle, and he clanged the heavy iron door shut, and adjusted the grate. In a few moments, the chimney began to smoke. With a piece of kindling, he tapped a joint straighter, and it stopped smoking. In only a few moments, the fire was going strong.

Gwynne dragged in a bench Cler had made earlier in the summer from split logs. She placed it near the stove, so they could all sit down. The fire cracked and popped gaily, and the cabin grew warmer. Paxton and Corrie reached out their hands to the welcoming heat, while Gwynne held Lestie in her lap, to keep her away from the stove until she got used to the fact it was hot. A feeling of peace filled Gwynne's heart as she leaned against Cler's shoulder.

"We're home," she said.

"Home!" the children echoed.

After a few minutes of savoring the fire, Cler stood up, "Well, let's get the rest of our things in here, and I'll take down the army tent."

They left the warmth of the new stove, and hurried to move their few belongings into the rough shelter of the cabin. There was no floor. Floor joists made of logs, placed every five feet, were already in place, but there was no money to buy boards. There was no door, either, so Cler nailed a flap of canvas over the opening, as a temporary door.

He took down the baraba, and used the portable floor, which was about six' by eight', to make a flat place for their bed, in the northwest corner of the cabin. Earlier, they'd found an old bedspring in the ruins of the roadhouse, and Gwynne had filled a mattress cover with dry reeds from the lake. When the bed was finished, and made up with sleeping bags and blankets, Cler lay down on it, while Gwynne stood over him.

"What do you think?" she asked.

"It's a little better than the ground," he said.

She slapped him on the shoulder, "After all my hard work, that's all you have to say?"

He looked up at her with a sparkle in his eyes, "It's great!" he laughed, "Just great!"

In the northeast corner of the cabin, the three children would share the cot; two little girls at one end, Paxton at the other.

At first, the dirt floor was damp, and not bad to live on. The baby got filthy, though, and since they had no floor, walking was a struggle for her. She would just get toddling along, and run into a log as high as her waist. Then she'd lie on top of the log and roll over it, get to her little feet, and toddle off again.

When the dirt floor dried to fine dust, Gwynne cut soft, green spruce boughs and laid them between the floor joists to keep the dust down. Corrie and Paxton complained of the "prickles," but the branches gave the cabin a sweet, piney smell. Gwynne told the kids that if they didn't like the prickles, they needed to put their shoes on. Lestie had outgrown her baby shoes, so Gwynne dug in her cedar chest for the pair of high-button shoes she, herself, had worn as a baby, and put them on Lestie to protect her feet. The pine boughs, however, were the last straw for Lestie. She gave up trying to walk, and sat in the dirt, waiting patiently for someone to pick her up and carry her.

After they'd settled into the cabin, Cler wrote that they'd be staying in Kenny Lake for the winter. Ben wrote back right away. He said that he'd contacted the store keeper at Chitna and told him to charge any groceries Cler might need for his family.

"I told him to send the bill to me," Ben wrote.

Gwynne's eyes filled with tears as she and Cler read the letter together.

Cler wrote back. "We received your letter and kind offer. We don't know how to thank such a good friend as you have been to us. I hope to be getting my veteran's allotment in a few months and will be able to pay back anything we may have to charge."

Emma George's cabin

4

Fall, 1947

FRIENDS

Emma George knew where to go to pick berries in the fall, and how to dry wild rosehips. Rosehips were plentiful, rich in vitamin C, and if they were seeded, they could be eaten like raisins. They also contained a lot of pectin, which could be added to any other berries to thicken jam.

When Gwynne, Emma, and Ina, her sister, went out to pick berries, one of them was armed with a rifle, in case they encountered bears, which competed for the berries. Fortunately, when they did see a bear, it was too busy eating berries to notice them, and remained on the other side of the berry patch. The women picked blueberries, high bush cranberries, and wild raspberries, too. These gifts from nature added greatly to their homestead diet.

While the autumn days were still nice, Gwynne and the kids put on their coats and walked the half mile down the road to visit Emma, Ina, and their mother.

One day the women were all sitting in Grandma George's little cabin. It was the largest and nicest of the three homes, with a piece of worn linoleum on the floor that Grandma George kept scrupulously clean. She had brightly flowered cotton curtains on the two windows in the front room, a couch covered with a bearskin, plus several chairs. The iron stove hummed as it burned, making the room seem friendly and inviting.

The four women sat companionably sipping raspberry leaf tea from heavy china cups, which were chipped and striated from years of use. Celestia played on the floor with Emma's toddler, Vivian, while the older children played outside.

Sometimes, Gwynne asked Grandma George to tell about her life, and she was happy to do it, though Emma had to translate, as best she could. Grandma George was born in a village down on the Klutina River and had three brothers. She didn't know exactly how old she was but said in the old days, nothing was written down. She was maybe thirteen when she married a man and moved to a village further down the river. Those were good days, she maintained. "Plenty fish, plenty beaver." When the great fire burned all the trees, the beaver left. Gwynne assumed she was talking about the fire that had swept the area in 1926.

As Grandma George rattled on in her Copper River dialect, a form of the Ahtna language, she sometimes sprinkled her conversation with English. Emma didn't always know how to translate. Sometimes Emma, Ina and their mother would all burst into giggles, as if something risqué had been said. Gwynne wished she'd been able to understand the jokes. Over many visits, she learned many words in their dialect.

The old woman remembered seeing white men for the first time when she was a little girl. A large group, many hundred men, came over the mountain from Valdez and floated the Copper River on rafts, headed for the Yukon River. Gwynne knew that the Copper flowed into the Yukon, and surmised that the men were trying to reach the gold fields. There were no giggles as the old woman told about seeing only a few boats come back in the fall. Those white men stopped at her village for a time.

Grandma George heard the elders say that many men had died in the river, their boats overturning in swift water. They left supplies scattered in their empty camps along the river. The Ahtna people encountered their camps, and benefited from the supplies left behind.

Emma said, "Two, three years ago, we still see some those camps on the river. Not much left there. People take. You know how it is."

Gwynne nodded. Just months ago she would have been shocked at the idea of scavenging anything left behind by others. Now, she, herself, had become something of a scavenger. Her mother would be horrified, but here in the wilderness, it was a necessity.

As time passed, the Oborns and the Georges became good friends. When Cler shot a black bear, he gave the skin to Grandma George. She tanned it and made big, black, furry mittens for him and a furry hat. He shared the meat, and both families were able to enjoy it. The black bear meat was tender, and tasted much like pork.

The local dialect that the Georges spoke was dying out. The few old people, who had survived the measles, still spoke this form of Ahtna, but their children and grandchildren spoke more English. This worried Gwynne.

She inquired and found out the local dialect had never, to anyone's knowledge, been written down, so she began to compile a dictionary, writing the words phonetically, and putting together sentences. As she learned the language, she began to understand Grandma George better, and Grandma George loved Gwynne all the more for her efforts.

NOT READY

Autumn was marked by the migrations of thousands of water fowl. Snow-white trumpeter swans arrived at Kenny Lake, shouting their presence and staying only to feed for a few days on the abundant algae and lake weed that floated in the water. Flocks of Canadian geese, with their black heads and speckled wings, skidded silver trails behind them, landing on the water to rest and feed among the huge swans. During the height of the invasion, the local ducks and loons gave way to their bigger cousins, hiding out in the reeds, while the muskrats ducked into their holes, along the lake's edge.

Over several weeks, Kenny Lake hosted legions of water fowl, that landed and took off again as regularly as war planes from a busy aircraft carrier. All day the honking and quacking carried across the crisp air. At night the big birds were quiet, hiding their heads under their wings, but the sorrowful call of loons drifted up to the cabin. Soon, the swans left, signaling their departure with trumpeting calls, causing the people on the ground to look up, "Listen! There! The swans are flying south!"

Later, the black-headed geese, too, abandoned the lake, taking off in a rush of wings, forming up and leading their great bird squadrons south, to warmer climates.

The weather had turned and the canvas flap that served as a door would not do to keep out the cold. Cler had been working on making a door, but wasn't finished, what with all the other things he had to do, including duck hunting and cutting a winter's supply of firewood.

Chinking the logs, after building the walls, proved to be much more difficult than he and Gwynne had anticipated. The slimmest cracks were almost impossible to stuff with moss, or anything else. The drum stove put out a lot of heat, but the cabin remained chilly near the walls.

GIFTS AGAINST THE COLD

While the canvas flap was still the door, Grandma George and her grandson, Franklin, who was about twelve years old, came carrying some bundles. They hallooed at the opening and were immediately welcomed inside, where Gwynne was cooking some rutabagas in a frying pan on the drum stove.

The vegetables steamed the cabin with a sweet, caramelized fragrance. They were a gift from the pastor of a church in Copper Center. He had brought out a bag of clothes for the children, and also included the root vegetables. Gwynne had felt uneasy being considered a "charity case", but the family could use the clothing, and they did enjoy the fresh vegetables.

Now Grandma George had brought more gifts.

Gwynne opened the bundles to reveal soft, tanned moose-skin mukluks. "These are wonderful," she exclaimed.

The little woman just grinned.

Franklin said, "She make them."

Cler and Gwynne chorused, "Thank you so much. Thank you!"

Gwynne gave her a little hug, and then sat down on the bench to try her mukluks on. They fit her perfectly. Corrie and Paxton sat on the dirt floor to put on their own mukluks.

"See how they fit me?" Paxton grinned, strutting around in his new footwear.

Cler's mukluks came up to his knees. The tanned moose hide was flexible from being chewed, and they were sewn together with tiny, moose-gut stitches.

"They're wonderful! How did you know our sizes?" He asked.

The old woman pointed to her eyes, and then at Cler's feet. Somehow, she had fitted them by simply looking at their feet. She took a last gift from her bundle: a pair of little moccasins, with the fur on the inside. They were decorated with a geometric design worked in tiny, colorful beads.

"For baby girl," Mama George grinned.

She said something in Ahtna and Franklin translated, "She say you make mukluks warm with grass. Here." He pointed to the sole of his own mukluks. He meant that mukluks were insulated with dried grass, but Cler was able to find some felt boot liners for his and Gwynne's, and lined Corrie and Paxton's mukluks with old wool socks.

The air turned bitterly cold; even with the new door installed, keeping the cabin warm was almost a fulltime job, when bitter winds blew against the log walls and the snow sifted in through the tiniest cracks. The cabin would have been warmer, they realized, if they had stopped to put the moss between the logs as they set them in place. Now, some of the chinking actually blew out of the cracks with the wind. Gwynne wadded scraps of paper and rags to chink where she could, but tiny spaces still let in the cold. On the walls next to the beds, they tacked cardboard over the logs, to cut down on the draft.

One day, eighteen-month-old Lestie was sitting on her parents' bed with a pencil she had found on the nearby box they used for a night stand. She discovered that the pencil could make marks on the cardboard wall. She sat there and drew a primitive figure.

Gwynne saw her with the pencil and hurried to take it away before the baby hurt herself. As she snatched the pencil, she took a closer look at the marks Lestie had made on the cardboard. She'd drawn a person: an irregular circle with dots for eyes, a curved line for a mouth, and lines flowing from the circle for arms and legs. Gwynne, who was herself artistic and had taken art classes in High School, was amazed. "Cler! Come here and look at this. The baby just drew a recognizable figure on the wall."

Cler had been adding a log to the drum stove. He shut the iron door and stepped over to the bed.

"Look," Gwynne pointed, "right there!"

He peered at the figure. "Aren't kids usually about three or four before they draw something like this?" he asked.

"Yes, at least. They call it a spider person. It's the way kindergarteners draw people."

Cler picked up his baby, who still hadn't started walking again, and didn't talk. He lifted her to look into her round, blue eyes. "You think you have us fooled, but you are really a smart little cookie, aren't you? Gwynne, we may have another Rembrandt right here in Kenny Lake!"

One frigid night, Cler and Gwynne tucked the children into their down bags. Corrie and Lestie shared one, while Paxton was bundled into another one, at the end of the cot. Cler and Gwynne huddled in bed together, listening to the wind howl. It whistled around the cabin, sifting snow in under the door, through slim cracks between logs, and along the roofline.

"You never know where you have to put more chinking until the wind blows," Gwynne said, trying to joke about it.

"Yeah," Cler said, pulling her closer to him under the covers. "Like you never know how much the roof leaks until it rains."

Gwynne groaned, "If it weren't already frozen solid, I'm sure the roof would leak, too!"

Cler patted her tummy, paused, and felt it again. She heard his breath catch.

"Sweetheart, are you…"

"Yes," she said, tears filling her eyes. "I'm so sorry."

Cler was silent for a few moments. "But we've been careful…how could you be…?"

"I'm sure I was pregnant before we ever left Ogden," she said. "I wish I had known, then."

"It's OK, Sweetheart. Don't worry about it." He leaned over and kissed her on the lips, then he rolled onto his back and stared up into the darkness, listening to the wind howl. After a moment, he said, "Don't be sorry. Everything will be all right."

She was glad he knew now. He would take care of her. She knew there was no money for a doctor or hospital, even if she was able to get to one at the right time. It would be OK, though, she told herself. If Cler had to, *he* could deliver their baby. She trusted him completely.

In November, a letter came from Ben. Cler tore it open and they read it together, standing by the small row of windows for light. The drum stove was roaring, cherry red in places, but it was cold beside the window.

Ben wrote that he was worried about them. "I'm the one who told you to homestead at Kenny Lake, but you haven't had time to really get ready for winter, and I feel responsible. Won't you come into Copper and stay in a little house I have? It's furnished. The tenant has moved out and I'm going to sell it in the spring."

Gwynne's eyes traveled to the children who were huddled together in a single Army blanket, trying to stay warm by the crackling drum stove. The dirt floor was frosty, frozen solid near the walls. Outside, the snow was already two feet deep around the cabin and on the roof.

"The only good thing is that if the snow gets much deeper, it might bury the cabin and It will actually get warmer in here," she told Cler, trying to laugh. It was no laughing matter, though, and they both knew it.

Cler put his hand on her shoulder as they stood there together with Ben's letter.

"What do you think?" he asked softly.

"Oh, let's go into town!" Gwynne exclaimed. "Can we?"

"We can always go look at the house," Cler said.

They bundled the children into their coats, hats and mukluks, and settled them into the back seat of the jeep, with wool Army blankets tucked around them. Cler left the jeep door open, and called to Buddy, who leaped in beside the children, bringing snow with him. Then they drove to see the house Ben was offering them.

COPPER CENTER

Winter, 1947

Copper Center was a small settlement on the confluence of the Klutina and the Copper Rivers. The settlement was mostly a native village, with a few hardy souls who made their living hunting, gold-panning and fishing on the rivers.

The Oborns found Ben at the little log jail, and he gave them directions to the house and a key. The house was situated near the Klutina River, which was nearly frozen over, but they could see black water rushing by in the middle of the river, and hear the water rumbling under the ice.

The house was frame, rather than log, and it was sturdy and insulated with saw dust. It had a raised main floor, with the front door and porch opening onto the river side. The enclosed porch was situated at ground level, while the main floor was a few steps higher. When the Oborn family entered the little house, the children stared wide-eyed at the finished walls and floors.

"It looks like Heaven," Gwynne whispered. It had a kitchen stove, table and chairs, a heating stove, smooth painted floors, cupboards and several rooms. The main portion of the house was built on top of a cellar that provided cold storage and had a small window.

Ben said they could have any of the furniture that they wanted to take with them when they moved back to Kenny Lake, because he meant to sell the house unfurnished.

Cler sat down in a large rocking chair with black leather seat; a crack in the leather showed it was padded with horse hair. The chair fit Cler's tall frame and he rocked back with an appreciative moan.

"Ah, now this is comfort!"

Since Cler had just received his stipend money from the government, he could pay Ben the rent. He and Gwynne decided to move in right away.

They returned to Kenny Lake for the few things they'd need. By Thanksgiving, Cler and Gwynne were snuggly ensconced in the little house on the bank of the Klutina river. They celebrated Thanksgiving around the new table with a supper of canned salmon and Gwynne's homemade bread, baked in the oven of the wonderful wood range.

A few miles away, the Copper Center Road House stood on a small rise. When Gwynne and Cler went there to buy groceries, they encountered the crusty, but sociable woman who owned the road house. They had already met her several times, when they had come in for supplies during the summer. She was gray-haired, about medium height, and stocky. She had a tough competence that drew people to her. Under her tough exterior, she had a kind heart.

Mrs. Barnes greeted Cler and Gwynne, "I guess you agreed to come into town for the winter," she said, "Ben's glad you did, that's for sure. So am I." Her eyes dropped to the bulge that protruded from Gwynne's coat. Gwynne couldn't even button her coat over the baby now. He was due in three months, she thought, but still wasn't sure.

Ma Barnes smiled at Gwynne, but didn't say anything about the baby. She didn't have to. Staying out at Kenny Lake would have been more than fool-hardy in Gwynne's condition.

At first, Cler was a bit surprised that Ma knew so much about them. Of course, she knew everything that went on in Copper Center and the whole Copper River Basin.

"We're glad to be here," he told her. "Ben was right, we weren't quite ready for winter."

Ma Barnes leaned over the counter and greeted the children, "Well just look at these kiddies, will you? They've really grown, now, haven't they?"

Corrie and Paxton stood up a little taller, grinning back at her. She always gave them a piece of candy, and this time they left sucking happily on large gumdrops.

Her name was Florence, but everyone called her Ma Barnes. She was a well-known and influential character in the Interior at that time. Mr. Barnes had died many years before, and Ma had carried on with the Road House and prospered. Since 1922, her road house had been a vital necessity in the vast, barely populated region. All sought her good will. She especially loved the native people and looked out for them. She and her husband had adopted an Alaskan native girl, who was now grown up. Other than the adopted girl, Florence Barnes had never had a child.

FLOODWATERS

In January, the Klutina River froze over and giant ice blocks built up, blocking the water, which was backing up over the ice. When the river rose above its banks, it would be forced into its old bed, where a number of houses had been built, including the one Cler and Gwynne were renting.

One bitterly cold morning there was a knock on the door. It was a man Cler had met at the roadhouse, who had a cabin near the river. The man was bundled in coat, wool hat and scarf. He stepped inside, but he was clearly agitated.

"Cler, we're getting some men together to go try and blast the ice before we're all flooded out. I heard you've been in the Army. What do you know about dynamite?"

"Some," Cler said, going for his down parka, bearskin hat and gloves. "My military training included explosives. What do you plan to do?"

"We figure if we dynamite the ice jam, the river will stop backing up."

Cler left with the man. While he was gone, Gwynne listened at the window, but didn't hear anything for a couple of hours. Then she heard a dull boom not far away. There were more

70

explosions and her heart jumped every time she heard another boom. Cler returned just after dark.

"We can only work during daylight," he told her as he hung up his wet, frozen coat and laid his gloves on the back of the kitchen range to thaw. "It's too dangerous to dynamite in the dark. I just hope the daylight lasts long enough to do what we have to." Gwynne slipped into his arms and clung to him, wordlessly telling how relieved she was to see him safely back.

For a day or two the dynamiting seemed to work, but then the weather grew even colder, the ice blocks froze together to form a dam, and the water kept rising. There was nothing to do then, but keep blasting the ice jam as it formed.

"Isn't it someone else's turn to go?" Gwynne asked, as Cler got ready to leave for the fourth day in a row.

"There's only two of us who know how to handle the dynamite," he said, "and the other guy is an old timer, who used to work in the mines."

After Cler left, Gwynne stood by the small window that looked over the river; she wrapped her arms around herself. It was warm in the little house with the kitchen range crackling, but Gwynne shivered. She could see the water had backed up over the ice, and was rising to the top of the riverbed.

She felt a chill from the window and pulled her sweater around her belly. The baby was due soon. A month maybe. Fear sat like a hot coal behind her breastbone and angry tears filled her eyes. Why did it have to be *her* husband out there, risking his life with dynamite? She needed him!

She prayed, "Please, Lord, let this be the last time they have to blast."

The relentless sub-zero cold continued and every day now they dynamited during the short hours of daylight. For a while, the water seemed to flow away, but then the ice froze over again, and off Cler had to go.

"I might have to be gone all night," Cler told her, as he dressed to go out again. "The water is still rising."

"How will you work in the dark?" she asked, thinking of huge bonfires.

"We'll have to use flashlights," he said.

Of course, Gwynne thought. Bon fires would just burn through the ice and go out. Long after dark, she could hear the booming of dynamite. She put the children to bed, taking Lestie with her into her own bed.

The toddler cuddled against her mother, both of them shivering under the covers. Lying there, Gwynne heard a crash and glass breaking. She lifted her head from the pillow and could hear water running.

She sprang out of bed and lit a candle, holding it out in front of her, as she tried to follow the sound. It was coming from the cellar. She rushed to the stairs and saw black water glittering in the candle light. It was up to the third step from the bottom. She eased down the cellar stairs and saw a waterfall pouring through the broken window. She fled back to the main level and dressed her feet in a hurry, pulling on a pair of battered rubber boots. She shrugged into a long coat over her nightgown and bundled Lestie into her coat, then she woke the other children, wondering how she would get them all out of the house.

Corrie and Paxton protested sleepily, as she struggled to get them into their coats, but in moments they quieted, sensing their mother's terror. Gwynne was determined to carry all three of the children somehow, wading through the rising water to safety. Corrie Lynne might be able to hold onto her neck, piggy-back style, and somehow she'd manage Paxton and Lestie, one in each arm.

The candle flickered as she tried to carry it in one hand with Lestie on her hip. She set it on a small table, as she reached the front door with Corrie and Paxton clinging to the hem of her coat. The living room was dry, so she left Corrie and Paxton there, while she pulled the door open, only to find the enclosed porch flooded, the wicker laundry basket and clothes floating on top of the water, which was only inches from the top of the steps.

72

Carrying Lestie, who was clinging to her neck, Gwynne stepped down into the freezing water, where she sloshed through the porch and dragged open the porch door. Her heart sank. The house was surrounded by black water. How deep was it? Could she wade it with three children clinging to her? Then she heard voices and saw a lantern; light reflected on the black ripples. A rowboat was coming!

Gwynne waited in the flooded doorway, her stomach protruding from her coat and her toddler on her hip. She watched a man in hip boots climb out of the boat and splash towards her.

"How many are there, ma'am?" he called out.

"Three children and myself!" Gwynne hollered back. When he was closer, she gestured behind her, "The other two are in there."

Corrie and Paxton stood shivering in the living room doorway as the man waded past Gwynne, and picked up both small children, lugging one in each arm. They clung to his neck as he made his way out to the rowboat and handed them over to another man, who placed them on a board seat, and wrapped a blanket around them. The first man slogged back to Gwynne; she let him take Lestie from her.

Lestie was wide-eyed, but didn't cry. She stared at the lights reflecting on the water and wrapped her arms around the man's neck, feeling the rough wool of his scarf against her cheek, smelling the oil of his hair. When they reached the rowboat, she reluctantly let go of the stranger, as he handed her to another man. Then she was cuddling under a blanket with her big sister, fearful of the rocking motions of the boat, but warmed by the familiar comfort of her sister's arms around her.

It was Gwynne's turn to be carried to the rowboat. As the stranger lifted her into his arms, she felt awkward and heavy, embarrassed by her condition. She clung to him, terrified and angry. Cler should be there; she needed him! The man struggled through the deep water; she wanted to cry and beat her fist against the stranger's back.

Winded, the man nearly dropped her into the rowboat on the seat across from her children. She watched her little ones huddled, holding on to each other, against the frigid night and the rocking boat. There was not room enough for her on the other seat, so she had to stay where she was, clinging to the board seat, as terrified as her children looked. The hems of Gwynne's nightgown and coat were soaked, and quickly freezing into ice. Lantern light danced crazily on black ripples, as the men rowed toward shore. In minutes, the little family was deposited onto a snow bank, where other refugees milled around in the darkness. Everyone was waiting for cars to take them to shelter.

Gwynne's feet were freezing inside the flimsy rubber boots, and she felt like she and the children would be frost-bitten before they got to safety. In a few minutes, they piled into an old car. The Copper Center Roadhouse became a gathering place, since it was built on high ground. The car's driver let them out there, and went back for more passengers.

Stumbling with her toddler in her arms, and Corrie and Paxton clinging to her coat, Gwynne made her way toward lights and shelter. Inside, gas lanterns brightened the lobby and a fire burned in the big rock fireplace, welcoming the wet and frozen victims and, as the night wore on, many of the rescuers who had, themselves, been flooded out of their homes.

When Cler returned from dynamiting the river, he found his family safe in the Roadhouse. There was coffee being served, but the kitchen had been closed to the public since November, when the cook had left.

Ma Barnes handed Cler a cup of coffee. He looked half frozen. "You look like you could use this," she said. "I wish I could offer these folks something to eat, but I don't have a cook."

"I can cook," Cler said, sipping the hot mug. "I'm a pretty good cook, actually. Took a course in High School."

"Is that right? What would you say to my offering you a job? You folks will need a place to stay, for a while. Stay here, and cook for me. I'll trade you board and room for your whole family."

74

Cler reached out to shake her hand, "You've got yourself a deal!" Ma Barnes announced to all that the restaurant would be open in the morning for breakfast.

The fact that Ma Barnes offered board and room in return for a cook was nothing new. In fact, barter was common in the Interior. If a person needed something but had no money, there was often a way to trade for it, even if the trades took three or four individuals into the deal, before everyone had what they needed. The lobby of the Road House, for instance, was cozy with fur rugs made from creamy mountain goat skins and black bear furs, that Ma Barnes had taken in trade for supplies. There was a spectacular, hand carved banister and rails of diamond willow on the stairway to the upper rooms. This, she said, she had taken in trade. A man had lived all one winter in the roadhouse, carving it for her.

Cler was a good cook. He'd once wanted to be a chef. Of course, the War and the Army Air Corps had taken his life in another direction, but he still enjoyed cooking. Now the kitchen in the Copper Center Road House was his domain.

The day after the flood, a friend of Cler's picked up Buddy and Peachy from the flooded house and took them home with him. Later, friends took Peachy, and Ma allowed Buddy to join the Oborns at the Roadhouse.

Copper Center Road House
(Drawing by Celestia Whitehead)

FEBRUARY, 1948

IN THE COPPER CENTER ROADHOUSE

It was a time of plenty for the family. Corrie and Paxton could not remember such bounty. They filled their little tummies with all sorts of good food they had not had the luxury of eating on a regular basis, particularly cold storage vegetables like cabbage, carrots, turnips, parsnips, and pumpkin. They ate their father's sourdough pancakes, biscuits, and bread. Cler also baked cakes and pies for the restaurant, but the children actually preferred vegetables, even if they were occasionally offered a treat. They were not used to eating sweets, and their little bodies must have craved the vitamins the vegetables gave.

Ma Barnes took a special interest in the children, and indulged their childish antics. Corrie and Paxton seemed to have their run of the place. They played hide and seek in the halls and main rooms. One day, Paxton discovered a heating vent upstairs, and wondered where it led. He took the grate off, climbed into it, and got stuck. Corrie tried to pull him out, but couldn't do it. She ran downstairs and saw his little legs dangling from the ceiling. She found her daddy in the kitchen and Paxton was extricated, but both children received a firm scolding from their father.

Meanwhile, Gwynne took care of Lestie in the room, or sat in the lobby with her feet up, reading, while her toddler played on a fur rug, with a spoon and a cup.

Gwynne felt as big as a house, but she didn't know when her baby was actually due. Immobilized by her fears, she had been trying to ignore the whole issue, but now it was February, and if she went by when she first felt life, the baby could be due any day.

She was worried. First, the closest hospital was nearly two hundred miles away, in Palmer. If somehow she managed to get there, how could Cler possibly pay for it? No, she decided. *Going to the hospital is out of the question. I'll have the baby right here in Copper Center. Here, in this room.*

Gwynne was sitting on a small chair beside the bed in their room. Her belly was so distended that she barely fit in the chair. Lestie was playing on the floor with a newspaper, shredding it into little pieces. She was making a mess, and her face and hands were black, but she was occupied.

Cler came into the room. "Thought I'd come check on you. Everything OK?"

Gwynne rubbed the lower side of her belly, where it ached. "Fine, I'm doing fine. I guess I'll just have the baby here in Copper Center," she told him.

He turned pale, and sat down on the edge of the bed. "What are you thinking, Sweetheart? There's no doctor here!"

"Well, for one thing, there's a nurse here part of the time , who could help me. And...and you with your first aid training..."

"My first aid training? That didn't cover delivering babies! Well, maybe there's something in the book about it, but honestly, Gwynne..." He saw the stubborn look in her eyes, so he tried another tack. "Honey, what did Doc Graham* (not his real name) say when you saw him last Fall?"

She hung her head. "I know. He said, 'Come to Palmer when you feel the baby drop.' "

"And he told us that with your medical history, you shouldn't take chances."

Gwynne did not want to hear it. "I'm hoping things will be different this time."

Cler leaned forward, and took her hands in his, "I'm hoping so, too. Maybe we won't be able to get you to Palmer in time, anyway. Criminy! I don't know, Gwynne."

"Well, how do you think I feel? It's like I'm carrying a ticking bomb..."

Cler leaned over and put his ear to her tummy, "Not a bomb..." he said, straight faced.

She pushed him, "It's not funny, and you know it!"

He sat back on the bed, "I'm sorry. It isn't funny at all, but I really believe everything will be alright." He stood up, "Hey, I have to go start making dinner for the troops. I'll see you downstairs in an hour or so, OK?"

After he closed the door, she pushed herself up from the chair and rolled onto the bed, where she buried her face in the pillow and sobbed. The truth was, the day after the flood, Gwynne had felt her baby drop, but hadn't said anything to Cler, or anyone else. Dropping usually meant the baby would come within two weeks. That was nearly two weeks ago.

Ma Barnes was at least as worried about Gwynne and the baby, as Cler was. Gwynne was so young; about to have her fourth child at age twenty-three. Ma couldn't help feeling protective, as if the baby were her own grandchild.

The day after Gwynne's decision to have her baby in Copper Center, Ma got wind of it, and decided Gwynne needed a talking to. She found Gwynne settled onto the sofa in the lobby that evening after supper, and sat down beside her.

"I don't want to interfere, Honey, but I have to say..."

"I know," Gwynne said, "You think I should go to the hospital."

Ma looked surprised, "Well, that's what I wanted to talk to you about, dear. Staying here to have your baby—it just won't do! You mustn't take chances. If you had complications before, it could happen again. I'm just saying..."

Gwynne felt her heart soften, touched by the old woman's concern, "I.. I guess maybe I'll go, if I can decide when it's time."

Ma patted Gwynne's hand, "Ah, that's the thing, dear. I just wouldn't want anything to happen to you or that precious baby."

The next morning, in the lamplight, Gwynne lay in bed, watching Cler dress for work. He put on a blue cotton shirt over his long underwear and a pair of dark, wool pants. Then he sat down on a chair near the bed and pulled on his socks.

Gwynne lay with her hand on her belly, feeling the baby kick. She'd been awake during the night with intermittent pains, that she considered "false labor." It had happened to her before; the uterus practicing for real labor. The pains had scared her, though. Maybe it really was getting close to her time.

"I've changed my mind," she said, "I guess I'll go in to Palmer for the baby."

Cler stopped lacing his boots and looked at her sideways. "What made you change your mind?" he asked, hoping she meant it. When she didn't answer, he sat up, and turned to look at her. She was so beautiful. Her glossy hair lay loose, dark against the white pillow. The lamplight glittered in her eyes, making them luminous.

"I'm scared," she said. "I think I need a doctor to deliver this baby."

"It'll be good to go to the hospital, Sweetheart," he told her.

"I know, but the hospital will cost money. Doctor Graham knows a couple I can stay with, but we'll have to pay for that, too," she said.

"I'll get the money; don't worry. In a month or two, I can take a job working for the Road Commission, building the Tok Cutoff."

Cler was relieved that she would agree to have the baby in a hospital, but he felt sick about the cost. They only had a few dollars they'd need for gas and groceries when they left the roadhouse. The road commission job wasn't for sure, and the stipend he was supposed to get from the government had not come for two months.

Later, the same morning, Cler was at the stove, cracking eggs onto the huge griddle. The eggs sizzled, turned white with the sudden heat, and the yokes lay on top like quivering mounds of yellow gold. He chopped at the hash browns with the edge of his broad spatula and turned them over. As he began to slide the spatula under the eggs, he heard the half-door squeak on its hinges.

"How's it going, pal?"

Cler expertly turned the eggs "over easy" and then glanced behind him.

Forest Triber, the energetic man they'd first met driving a road grader, was standing there, wearing a red and black wool coat and his usual ear-to-ear grin. He was working for Ma Barnes now, helping manage her affairs. Forest had told Cler that Ma hadn't been feeling up to snuff lately.

Cler flipped over the last egg, "Hi, Forest. Things are going fine."

Forest came to the point, "Ma is sending me to Anchorage for supplies today. She insists that I offer Gwynne a ride to the hospital in Palmer."

Cler slid the spatula under the three eggs and slipped them onto a warm plate. He added some hash browns and slid it onto the shelf that opened into the restaurant. The waitress, a young native girl, retrieved it.

Forest asked, "So what about my taking Gwynne?"

Deftly pouring rounds of batter onto the sizzling griddle, Cler said, "Ma Barnes must have read my mind. I was wondering how I was going to get Gwynne to Palmer. I can't take the chance of her having the baby here. She had complications last time..."

80

Forest patted Cler on the shoulder, "I think Ma knows about that. So... I'll be leaving around noon. That work for you and Gwynne?"

Cler couldn't help but smile, "I'll finish up here and let her know."

Gwynne quickly packed her bag and a small one for Lestie. At noon, she climbed into Ma Barnes' car, while Forest happily held the door open for her and then lifted the toddler onto her knees. Gwynne moved Lestie over to the center of the bench seat and tucked a baby blanket around her.

Forest closed the door with a slam and hurried around the car. Once behind the wheel, he grinned at his passengers.

"I'm just tickled to have you, Gwynne," he said. "And you, little lady." He patted Lestie's curly head and she gave him a dimpled smile. He started the engine with a roar, shifted gears, and they were on their way.

"This will be fun!" he exclaimed. As they drove down the highway, he continued his cheerful banter, cracking jokes and even flirting with Gwynne.

She was taken aback. Forest had always been a friendly man, but today he was a bit more than friendly. She didn't understand it. He was twice her age, and she was about ready to have a baby. She didn't realize it at the time, but the man was simply thrilled to have a beautiful woman in his car to make the journey with him.

The day was sunny and cold. The roads were fair, but there were many icy patches, and Forest drove faster than Gwynne was used to. Going over Sheep Mountain Pass, the old car started sliding toward the cliff. There were no guard rails, and the mountain dropped away hundreds of feet into the tundra below. Forest cranked the steering wheel, bringing the car out of the slide, but then it started sliding the opposite direction, into the mountain. He cranked the wheel and they headed back toward the cliff.

Gwynne didn't know when she'd stopped breathing, and thought her heart had quit on her, but finally, Forest was able to slow down and regain control. It was a relief when they stopped at Sheep Mountain Lodge for a hot drink and a sandwich, and to use the facilities.

Forest was a good driver, or so it seemed, because he managed not to go careening off any cliffs, but Gwynne hugged Lestie to her side and prayed silently much of the way into Palmer.

The hospital was a collection of three Quonset huts left from the war. Still, it was a hospital with a real doctor and nurses. Gwynne kept telling herself that she was doing the right thing to be there, in spite of what it was going to cost.

Forest left his passengers at a small home a few blocks from the hospital. The home belonged to Irene and Leo, people recommended by Doctor Graham.

A few days later, Forest stopped by Irene's house and handed Gwynne an envelope. "Ma Barnes knows your situation, Gwynne. You can't fool that old woman!" He turned uncharacteristically serious, "When she found out you needed money to pay the doctor and hospital, she insisted. She says Cler can work it off later."

Gwynne opened the envelope and her eyes grew wide. Four hundred dollars! She couldn't help throwing her arms around the surprised man, and managed to say through her tears, "Tell her thank you, thank you!"

Sadly, Ma Barnes died before the baby was born and Forest, who was managing her estate, told Cler that he was sure Ma would not have wanted that money paid back.

(The Copper Center Road House, largely under one other owner, remained a popular stopping place and tourist spot, for the next sixty-four years. It was on the National Historic Register, when it burned to the ground on May 20, 2012.)

NEW BABY

Irene and Leo had two bedrooms in their house. Gwynne learned that the extra room was intended to be a nursery, but their first baby had died and they had no other children. Irene was in her forties, a pretty, petite brunette with gray eyes and an aura of what people used to call "old money" about her. She had a slight southern accent, and told Gwynne that she was from Virginia, where her family had lived for generations in the same house.

Leo was an accountant, broad across the chest and sandy haired with freckles sprinkled over his face that made him look boyish. When Gwynne asked what brought Irene to Alaska, she smiled and replied, "Leo."

Gwynne and Irene, in spite of the difference in their ages, became fast friends. They chatted about books they'd read and songs they loved. They told each other about their families.

One day they were out in Irene's back yard hanging clothes on the line. The weather seemed mild for February and the sun was out, though there was still plenty of snow on the ground. Leo had shoveled a path from the back porch and under the clothes line. Both women were bundled in coats and scarves.

"My mother was an artist," Gwynne said as she bent down to pick up a towel from the basket on the ground.

Irene heard Gwynne's moan.

"Here, I'll do the bending over for both of us," Irene laughed, as Gwynne put a hand on the small of her back to help her straighten up.

Irene handed her a towel, "So did your mother's talent rub off on you?"

Gwynne reached up and pinned the corner of the towel to the line. "She taught me to draw, and even gave me paper and pastels to bring with me to Alaska."

"So you're an artist, too?" Irene asked around the clothes pin in her mouth.

"I've done a few pastels of Kenny Lake, and the cabin, but I haven't had much time for it, since we've been here. Busy just surviving, I guess. But I do love art. I grew up with the scent of oil paints. Mother took classes at the University and worked at home on her paintings."

83

"What did she paint?" Irene asked.

"Houses, landscapes, flowers, nudes..."

Irene laughed. "Nudes? I can just picture a little old lady--"

Gwynne smiled, "Mother is only 21 years older than I am. She's—"

"My age," Irene laughed.

Gwynne said, "I'm sure when she *is* a little old lady she won't be much different."

"You must miss her."

Gwynne rubbed the small of her back again, to ease the ache. "I guess I do. Mother was—is—quite a lady. She always sets a beautiful table."

Irene noted the wistful tone in Gwynne's voice. "My mother was like that, too. We're really far from home, aren't we?" Irene said.

Gwynne smiled, "Yes, but home is where the heart is, they say. I'll be glad when it's summer and we can go back to Kenny Lake. Right now," she patted her stomach, "I'm most interested in getting this baby born."

Finished hanging the wash, the two women returned to the house with red, chapped hands. It was too cold to stay outside very long.

Irene seemed glad to have Gwynne staying with her, and she doted on little Lestie. With her fair curls, dimples and big blue eyes, Irene called her a "winsome child." Lestie was always watching, seeming to analyze the world around her, but she was twenty-two months old and she didn't talk.

Irene said, "She's a bright little thing, you can just tell, even if she doesn't say much. You can almost see the cogs turning, can't you?"

"I know," Gwynne said. "I think she's had so much upset in her little life, that she's taking her own time. Before she stopped talking, she said a half-dozen words, even at a year old. Then, I don't know exactly when it started, but we noticed she'd stopped talking. When we moved into the cabin, she could walk, but then

84

she just gave up for a while. Now she's walking again, and I suppose she'll start talking, too."

One day Irene took Lestie's hand and led her to a large steamer trunk that sat on an enclosed porch. Irene knelt on the floor and lifted the lid. The child watched with interest as the woman took out a little white rattle and a colorful wooden top and offered them to her. Lestie received the objects hesitantly. She had never had a toy and didn't know what to do with them.

Still kneeling by the open trunk, Irene lifted out a small blue dress and touched it to her own cheek for a moment. She held it up to to the toddler.

"Too small, I guess," she said, laying the dress reverently back in the trunk, with tears in her eyes.

Lestie could feel Irene's sadness, and leaned into her arms for a hug. Irene hugged her for a long moment, before letting her go.

"You darling child," she said, taking Lestie by the shoulders, and looking into her eyes. "You know everything that's going on, don't you?"

It was nearly the end of February, but Gwynne had still not had her baby.

Meanwhile, Cler moved from the roadhouse, back into the house on the river. The flooding had stopped once the water was able to flow through its old channel for a while. As the weather warmed, the water cut a path through the ice, and the river went down.

The house was dry on the main level, even though the porch was a frozen block of river water and clothes. It took some work and a portable stove, but Cler managed to thaw the iceberg that was the porch and get the clothes washed.

He still cooked at the roadhouse, taking Corrie and Paxton with him. One day during dinner he broke a tooth. This meant he had to go to Palmer to see a dentist. By this time, Gwynne had been there over two weeks.

He left the children, along with the dog and cat, with the Georges and arrived in Palmer, fully thinking he would see the dentist and leave in a day or two with his wife, daughter and a new baby, but it didn't happen. First he had complications with his tooth, which bled and became infected. He was in a lot of pain and had to go back several times to the dentist over the next three days. Gwynne still didn't have the baby. On top of all that, Irene slipped on the ice, fell, and broke her leg.

Now, Irene needed Gwynne's help more than ever, and couldn't take care of Lestie. Cler left Palmer the next morning with his toddler, and drove to Kenny Lake to pick up Corrie, Paxton, Buddy and Peachy from the Georges. He took them all back to the little house in Copper Center. He went back to cooking at the roadhouse, taking the children with him during the day.

When Gwynne began having pains two days later, Leo drove her over to the hospital. There was an emergency surgery going on at the time, and Gwynne had to wait her turn, lying on a gurney in a small room, as there was only one operating table and one doctor. The nurse said she would deliver the baby, if she had to, but Gwynne intended to wait for Dr. Garret. She ignored the nurse and timed her contractions. The pains got worse and worse, until she thought she would die from the pain. The nurse said Gwynne's body wasn't cooperating, and that the baby was too big.

Finally, the emergency operation on the other patient was over, and Gwynne was rushed into the room and moved onto the operating table. Dr. Graham checked her and the next thing she knew, the anesthesiologist had an ether mask over her face. Still in excruciating pain, she sucked in the ether too fast. Before the room went black, she heard someone say, "We're losing her."

The baby was born by C-section on March 2, 1948. He was chubby as a little doll, with a lusty cry that told the world he was strong and healthy. When Gwynne was awake, the nurse brought her husky little boy to her. He clutched at her gown with a grip she'd never seen in her other three babies, but then, she'd never had a nine pounder before.

"You're a tough little monkey," she said, looking into his round, dark eyes. They looked like Paxton's had, as a baby, with kind of a blue tint, but Paxton had turned out to be brown-eyed, and she was sure this boy was going to be brown-eyed, too.

"I'm so glad you're here," she whispered.

Before Gwynne left Palmer, Dr. Graham examined her and the baby, to make sure all was well.

"You need to come back in a few weeks," he told her.

"I'm alright, aren't I?" she asked.

Dr. Graham was washing his hands at the little sink in the exam room. He reached for a towel, and turned to face her, as he dried his hands. He looked at her intently.

"Gwynne, you made it through this pregnancy, but just barely; you were lucky. With your history, you really should not have another baby. You need to come into Palmer to have an operation, to insure that you will not get pregnant again."

While the doctor talked, Gwynne cuddled her newborn. She felt the warmth of his little body, smelled the sweetness of him. She'd been through so much difficulty, that she couldn't imagine being pregnant again, ever.

"If you think I should, I'll come back for the operation," she promised.

Gwynne returned to the little house on the Klutina River with her new baby, Charles, named after Gwynne's father. Cler had built a little cradle for him, but the cradle was too small, so they improvised, using a large dresser drawer. The tiny pink cradle made a perfect bed for Corrie's baby doll.

The children were glad to have their mother again, and Lestie would hardly leave her side. Gwynne had to stay in bed a while longer because of the C-section, so she cuddled Lestie on one side, with the new baby on her other. From her bed, Gwynne was able to take care of her children, while Cler was working. Corrie or Paxton helped by bringing things to her and playing with Celestia.

The cabin at Kenny Lake and the Army Surplus Jeep 1948

6

BACK TO THE HOMESTEAD

Before the family moved back to Kenny Lake, Cler bought a load of boards and trekked out there to lay the floor. The boards were wide and dark, made of spruce. They were old, with knotholes, but the worn planks would be easier on bare feet than new, rough lumber, anyway.

It was April, and there was still a lot of snow on the ground, but temperatures were mild. Little by little, the snow pack evaporated from the top down. The top foot or so of the ground would remain frozen until well into June. After the top layer thawed, the permafrost never thawed at all.

Cler filled the two-wheeled trailer with much of the furniture from the house by the Klutina River, as Ben had encouraged him to do. He took the double bed's mattress, which was a great improvement on the dried reeds they'd slept on before. He took the big rocking chair, the couch, and a hospital cot that fit all three children with room to spare. With help from his friends, he was able to haul the wood-burning kitchen range, and the kitchen cupboard, with its mouse-proof bins for flour and sugar.

When they had settled into the cabin, Gwynne felt, again, that she was "home." To add to her happiness, spring was on its way. She always felt better when there was more daylight, and she could hardly wait for summer, when she could be outdoors enjoying trees, mountains, wild roses, and birdsong.

Until then, she'd have to take care of her usual tasks: nurse the baby, wash diapers, scrub clothes in the wash tub, and hang them up outdoors. Kneading the dough hurt her wrists, so Cler did that part, but Gwynne enjoyed baking big, fluffy loaves of bread, in a real oven, in her kitchen range. Before the oven, she'd only been able to bake biscuits in the cast iron kettle.

While Gwynne took care of things inside the cabin, Cler was tromping through the last of the crunchy snow in the woods, checking his snare line. Rabbits, like money, seemed scarce. Today, he only found one rabbit in a snare. He had to admit it had been a difficult year. Cler's stomach clenched at the memory of dynamiting ice on the Klutina River, day after day, trying to keep the river flowing in its channel.

That last night, before they finally gave up, was a nightmare. Setting explosives in the dark and brutal cold; and all for nothing! His mind recoiled at the futility of it. The river had defeated them; the ice had closed in. Nature had won, and it had to be a miracle that he was still alive.

After lighting that last fuse, while running away, he had stepped into a hole in the ice, and sprawled, bruising his ribs on a jagged chunk of ice. He would never tell Gwynne how close he came to getting blown up that night.

As he was walking through the woods, his mind on his mortality, Cler thought of his old friend, Ben Pinks, who was still working as sheriff in Copper Center, but the last time they'd talked together, Ben didn't look very well. That was a couple of weeks ago, and Cler hoped he was feeling better by now. What a kind-hearted, good old guy! He was one of those people the Bible calls "the salt of the earth."

Cler turned back toward the cabin. He was soon out of the brush, heading for the wood pile, which, right now, he'd better tackle. He needed kindling for the kitchen range, and logs for the drum stove, before the kids woke up.

As he entered with an armload of wood, and a rabbit on top, he noticed how small the cabin felt, with its few windows, and low ceiling. The corner by their bed was crowded with a bassinet and a dresser, but at least they had a floor now, and with a little more work, he'd have the place fixed up even better. He'd seen another cabin where a man had used a sawdust mixture to fill the spaces between the logs, like frosting. He planned to get to that as soon as he replaced the dirt roof with boards and tar paper.

Gwynne was still in bed, so Cler lifted baby Charles from his bassinet. He changed his diaper, and put a dry nightgown on him. Gwynne woke up and nursed the baby, and gave him back to his father, to burp him.

"I just don't feel very well this morning," she said, rolling to face the wall. "Please let me sleep a while longer."

Cler took the baby and put him over his shoulder, patting him, but he didn't burp, and began to cry. Charles cried louder, so Cler laid him over his forearm, face down, in a position that usually worked to calm him. With the baby on one arm, Cler walked the few steps into the kitchen area of the cabin, and, one handed, began to mix up the batter for sourdough pancakes. Later, he'd make a batch of bread.

Cler and baby Charles in front of Copper River Bluff

A SACRED GROVE

On Sunday, the first of May, the sun came out like a benediction, melting the rest of the snow, wherever the sun shone. All that was left was under the trees, or on the north side of the cabin. After a breakfast of powdered scrambled eggs and toast made from the last of the bread, the family was sitting around the cabin, enjoying the sunshine that came in the kitchen window, from the east.

Paxton and Corrie were making a little replica of the cabin, on the floor, using chips of wood. Lestie was on her father's lap, and Gwynne was settled on the couch, nursing the baby for the second time since dawn.

"He's a good eater, that's for sure," Cler commented, listening to the guzzling sounds coming from under the blanket Gwynne had thrown over her shoulder and the baby.

"Growing like a weed, too," Gwynne said, proud of their healthy, chubby son. She said, shyly, "My doctor in Ogden said I was a Jersey cow."

Cler laughed, "Lots of cream, I guess! Well, it sure shows."

For a few minutes, they sat there together, enjoying the quiet. They could hear a magpie scolding somewhere near the cabin; maybe he was even sitting on the roof.

"I've been thinking I need to give the baby his name and blessing, Gwynne."

"Do we need to go into Anchorage? Try to find a branch of the Church?" She asked, unlatching the baby, and putting him on her shoulder. She held him in place with her chin while she buttoned her blouse.

Cler looked thoughtful. "No, I was thinking of going to a place in our own woods that's just as sacred as a church building. I've found more than one Sacred Grove out there."

Gwynne laid the sleeping baby on her lap and looked down on his rosy little face. He had a skiff of brown hair, that curled up on the top of his head.

Cler stood up, and gathered the baby from his mother's lap. "I'll bring him back in a little while." He picked up the blanket and laid it flat on the couch, then wrapped the baby in it.

Corrie Lynne watched her father leave, with the baby cradled in his arms. A corner of the creamy, crocheted blanket trailed over his forearm, as he carried Charles out of the cabin. After the door closed, she ran to the kitchen window, over the sink, to try and see what her father was going to do with the baby. At five, she wasn't tall enough to see out, but she jumped up so her tummy rested on the edge of the sink, something she'd done many times before. She saw her father, with the baby in his arms, heading toward the woods.

It wasn't long before he returned. He handed Charles back to his mother, who was still seated on the couch. "Charles Benjamin Barnes Oborn," he said, smiling. Benjamin was for Ben Pinks; Barnes was in memory of Ma Barnes; two people without whom this baby might never have made it safely into the world.

The next morning, Gwynne stepped out of the cabin into the gray morning, before anyone was up; she was headed to the

92

outhouse, wrapped in her quilted robe. She was pleasantly surprised at how warm it felt outside. It was at least in the forties.

When she emerged from the little wood building, she took in her surroundings, in no hurry to return to the dark cabin; the air felt so nice out here. Last night, rain had eaten away the last mounds of dwindling snow. Her eyes took in the sodden fields of winter-dead grass that rolled downhill to the road. The fields spread to a stand of willows that had already turned red-tipped with spring growth, and cottonwoods had sprouted orange shoots, glowing in the damp gray of morning. All these fields had been cleared by others, now gone, before she and Cler ever came here. She thought about yesterday, and the name Cler had given to their baby, in memory of Ben, and Ma Barnes. They could have added the name George in memory of Grandma George, too, but that would have been too many names! The thought made her smile. There were so many good people who had helped them since they came to Alaska. Honestly, Gwynne wondered, without those others, how would we have survived this first year?

Before she pulled open the heavy cabin door, she whispered a prayer. "Thank you, Heavenly Father for sending angels to aid us."

Celestia and Buddy 1948

Spring, 1948

MAKING A GARDEN

The sunlight was cold. A layer of thin clouds left the sky white, and prevented any heat from getting to the ground. Gwynne and Cler, bundled in coats, strode hand in hand, down the track they called a driveway, to the piece of ground they thought would make a nice garden. Now, it was just a patch of dry, tangled grass and weeds.

"It won't be long," Cler said. "We can start the garden in a week or two, I think, but we'll need a plow."

"Seeds and a plow. That might cost a lot," Gwynne said.

"Not really. I can get seeds down at the Chitna store. And you know, I saw an old rusty plow in a meadow, when I was on my way down there the other day. When I stopped to look at it, I also spotted a wagon with iron rimmed, wooden wheels. It has remnants of orange paint on it, so I think maybe it belonged to the road crew that built the cut-off."

"But don't they belong to somebody?" Gwynne asked.

"I ran into the sheriff while I was at the store and asked him about the things. There's a rake, too. He said I could take them if I wanted them. Says they no longer belong to anyone. So, I think we can plant that garden, as soon as the ground thaws a little bit more." He hugged her around the shoulders.

Gwynne felt her heart lighten with a little flurry of excitement. "Oh, go get the plow and things!" she begged, "Go today, just in case someone else gets to them first!"

Cler laughed, "OK, I'll go get them, but you know they've been sitting there for ten or twenty years, don't you? Not likely someone is going to run and get them today..."

"Someone is!" Gwynne said, leaning up to kiss his cold cheek, "You!"

"Yes, I am!" he said. Gwynne made him a sandwich of bread and jam, and Cler left in the jeep, taking some tools and

94

rope with him to pick up the plow, rake and wagon from the old hay field down the road.

He found the wagon to be perfectly sound, with an iron and wood tongue he could refit to be pulled by the jeep, instead of horses. In order to get it back to the cabin, he merely used the rope to tie it to the trailer hitch on the jeep. He figured he could build a new wagon box on the frame and wheels. He also found a serviceable, howbeit very rusty, hay rake. He came home pulling the old wagon behind the jeep, with the worn and pitted plow on the wagon, and went back for the hay rake.

On a mild morning, when the mud finally dried out, Cler and Gwynne excitedly began their garden. Cler hooked up the plow to his jeep. He would handle the plow, while Gwynne drove the jeep. "Start slowly," Cler said. "I'll guide the plow."

"Got it," Gwynne said. She sat erect, hands on the wheel, ready to drive.

He ran back and grasped the handles.

"OK, let's go!" he hollered.

Gwynne shifted into gear and eased on the gas. The jeep didn't move, anchored to the ground by the plow, which dug into the half-frozen dirt and seemed to be stuck there.

"Give 'er more gas!" Cler yelled, so Gwynne stomped on it, without looking back. The engine roared and the jeep jumped ahead and kept on going.

The plow nearly jerked Cler off his feet, but he held on. The blade churned up dirt, roots and grass. Gwynne kept pouring on the gas.

Enveloped in a cloud of exhaust, Cler lost his footing, sprang back up, and leaped after the jeep, still gripping the plow.

"Whoa! Stop!" he yelled at the top of his lungs, but Gwynne didn't hear him over the roar of the engine.

Pleased with herself, she kept her foot steady on the gas pedal, while the jeep was apparently plowing up soil like crazy. Then she glanced back to see Cler, almost flying through the air.

She slowed to a stop.

"I'm sorry; I'm sorry!" she called out.

Waiting for him catch up, she expected him to be mad, but he was so out of breath he couldn't say a word. He leaned forward, panting, his hands resting on his knees. When he finally could speak, he gasped, "A little slower, OK? Let's go!"

After only a few rows, Cler was exhausted. He signaled to Gwynne to stop and she turned off the ignition. He slid into the passenger seat, his hands shaking from the effort of controlling the plow.

"I'm beat," he panted. After he'd rested for a moment, he said, "I have an idea. With three furrows around for a fire break, maybe we can burn the rest of the weeds. Thaw the ground and add nutrients to the soil, while we get rid of the weeds at the same time. What do you think?"

She considered, checking how much they'd done so far. "Sounds fine with me," she said.

It wasn't long before they had the three furrows plowed, and decided they were ready to burn the rest of the grass in the center.

The children were playing near the cabin. Corrie sprawled on a blanket in the sun, with Lestie and baby Charles, while Paxton followed his dad to the east side of the cabin. Cler opened the cellar door and climbed down to retrieve some burlap bags. He and Paxton carried them over to the garden, and wet them down with water from a jerry can.

Cler made a bundle of dried grass for a torch, and then lit the grass in the center of the fire break. The flames flickered for a few minutes, and then the fire took off with a whoosh! exploding across the patch, while Cler, Paxton and Gwynne stood by, ready with wet gunny sacks in their hands. The flames roared and in seconds they jumped the firebreak and blazed in several directions, leaping up in a dozen different places. Cler slashed at the flames with his sack, running around like a mad man. Gwynne and Paxton rushed into the smoke to help.

Cler yelled for Corrie to take Lestie and Charles to the cabin, but Gwynne saw the fire headed that way and screamed,

"No! run to the field; over there, over there!" waving toward the east.

The baby protested loudly, as five-year-old Corrie lugged him to the far field, half running, half walking. Lestie ran after, until finally, Corrie stopped, hoping they were far enough from the fire. All she could see was a curtain of white smoke beyond the cabin. She dropped onto the ground with her chubby baby brother, and little sister sat down beside her. Corrie watched dirty gray smoke turn white, as it curled into the sky.

She jiggled the baby on her lap, but he continued to bawl; he felt wet, and heavy, so she eased him onto the grass. He fell back and lay kicking his chubby legs and waving his fat little arms in the air. Finally, he stopped crying, and stared at his fist, bringing it to his mouth, sucking greedily.

Cler, Gwynne, and four-year-old Paxton flailed at the fire, slapping their bags into the flames, but it seemed hopeless: as soon as they beat down one burning patch, another erupted somewhere else. In minutes, the grass fire shot against the west wall of the cabin; for a few seconds flames licked at the logs. With scorched bags, Cler and Gwynne beat down fire along the logs, and the flames died. Exhausted, they glanced toward the east, ready to tackle that leg of the blaze, but the center of the fire had burned out and the rest faded. All they saw was a blackened expanse of burned field, tendrils of smoke rising everywhere.

Their pint-sized son was right behind them. With one little leather boot, he stomped on a flame still burning in the charred grass. His parents were bent over now, panting with exhaustion, coughing from inhaled smoke.

Gwynne and Cler dropped their scorched gunny sacks and glanced at each other. Soot coated their hands and faces; rivulets of sweat, like muddy water, streaked their cheeks. They burst into a fit of laughter from sheer relief. Laughter made them cough harder, and coughing got them laughing again.

A little puzzled, Paxton watched his parents hilarity. He didn't know it, but he looked as black as they did, although he wasn't coughing as much. Being closer to the ground, he hadn't inhaled as much smoke.

Cler and Gwynne sobered in time to see a forest service truck tearing up the driveway, dust billowing behind. The driver slammed to a stop and jumped out, his eyes scanning the blackened field.

"I saw the smoke," he panted, as the disheveled, sooty couple approached him. "I'm Judd. I work for the forest service."

"Hello," Cler managed to say, still trying to recover his breath. He held out a hand, "Cler Oborn and this is Gwynne."

The man shook hands, "Good to meet you. I'm glad to see the fire's out."

"We are too," Cler cleared his throat, which was sore from the smoke.

Judd smiled, "Can you let me know when you want to burn again, folks? I can bring a pumper truck to stand by."

"You'll do that?" Cler asked.

"Sure will. I live about six miles down the road with my wife, Mina." He jerked his head toward Chitna. "I thought I was seeing the first wild fire of the season when I saw your smoke," he laughed.

Cler thanked Judd and invited him and his wife to come visit their cabin, anytime.

The next day, Cler and Gwynne got the children settled in the cabin after breakfast and returned to finish plowing the garden. Warmed by the fire, the ground was easier to till. They still had no seed, but Cler wanted to turn the soil, ready for the crops they intended to plant.

They did get a little seed, and planted oats, cabbage and carrots. As the ground dried out, they took the jeep down to the lake and filled cans of water for their little garden. They soon realized that carrying water from the lake would become an enormous task during the hot, dry summer.

Cler said, "Next year, I'll buy a pump and pipe the water up to the garden!"

Gwynne let out a long sigh. Most of what was growing was weeds. Money was scarce, and food was not plentiful, either.

Corrie Lynne on the porch wall. Jeep on the right.

Summer, 1948

TIME TOGETHER, TIME APART

During the glorious days of early summer, Cler and Gwynne stole an occasional hour to be alone together. They slipped away while the little ones napped and Corrie kept track of Paxton in the cabin. They took a gun, and ordered Buddy to stay with the children.

One warm afternoon, they found a grassy haven not far from the cabin, and spread a blanket on the ground. The aspen leaves fluttered their green and silver leaves like little coins above them, and tiny wild flowers, blue, pink and white, sprinkled the grass around them. Mosquitoes had not yet hatched out, and it seemed like Heaven that day, lying together in the tender sun; they were healthy, young and very much in love.

Cler was on his back, with his head resting on folded arms, and his eyes closed. He was enjoying the warmth of the sun on his face, when something cold and wet nuzzled his cheek. He sat up abruptly, opening his eyes.

"Buddy! What are you doing here? You're supposed to be watching the kids!"

Gwynne giggled, "He must have escaped. I guess he's trying to tell us we'd better get back." She sighed.

As they walked back to the cabin, Cler said, "I can work on the Tok Cutoff, anytime I can get out there." He pulled back a branch of willows and let her pass in front of him. When they were both on the other side of the clump of brush, and walking along an animal trail, he said, "I know you hate to have me go, but with the phone line to Chitna running right by here, I'm going to put a phone in. Then, when I leave, you can get a message to me, if you need to."

"A phone! That would be wonderful!"

In single file, they walked along a narrow path used by animals, and listened for the sound of cracking twigs or brush. A moose thumping down the trail towards them meant they'd better get out of the way!

When the trail broadened out, Gwynne took Cler's hand, "If you have to go, I'm not going to complain. We need the money. How soon would you leave?" she asked.

"I could leave now, except for helping Dan* (not his real name) on his cabin."

"He'll never get that well dug at the rate he's going," Gwynne murmured. "He never listens to you."

"I know," Cler said, "but I promised. A lot of people helped us when we were in a bind..."

She didn't need to be reminded that Cler was always the first to help, whether or not anyone else did. It was just the way he was made. Some people were easier to help than others, Gwynne thought, and Dan was one of the hard ones. He was a

100

stubborn, know-it-all sort of man, but Gwynne and Cler rather liked the guy.

A few weeks earlier, in May, Dan and his wife Mary had showed up at Kenny Lake. They had filed on land next to Gwynne and Cler, and wanted to build a cabin in the woods on the east, near a small lake. Dan didn't know much about homesteading or building, he admitted, and asked Cler to help him. However, the man wanted to do things his own way. Instead of building his cabin first, and then digging a well where Cler suggested, the guy had insisted on digging the well on the bare ground, in the center of his partially built log walls.

It proved to be a bad location, as the permafrost was close to the surface there, and he had to light a fire to thaw the ground, then dig a bit and light another fire. It was also a bad location, because it meant he had to finish his well before he could finish his cabin.

Dan's struggle was enhanced by the fact that his wife, Mary, hated roughing it in a tent, waiting for her husband to build shelter for them. She just wanted to go back to Anchorage and live like real people again. She was miserable, but her husband made promises in order to appease her.

Cler was anxious to leave for his job on the Road Commission crew, but Dan begged him to stay in Kenny Lake long enough to help him with his cabin. When Dan had his well dug, Cler helped him finish the walls, and get a roof on. In return, Dan promised that after Cler left to work on the Tok Cutoff, he would look in on Gwynne and help with whatever she needed.

Even while helping Dan on his cabin, Cler managed to set telephone poles, and run a phone line from the road to his own cabin. He paid for his phone by helping two other homesteaders down the road connect phones, as well. The phone line to Chitna was strung on the top of a three-legged arrangement like a jack fence. This was necessary in order to set the poles over swampy places, where the permafrost and water made any other kind of pole line impossible.

The phones they used in those days were little more than a wooden box mounted on the wall, with a receiver on the box, and a speaker on a wire, to put up to your ear. The phones required the caller to crank a number, using some pattern of long or short rings, to call others. Cler and Gwynne's number was two longs and two shorts. The phone would ring for every phone on the line, so they had to listen for their own combination of longs and shorts, before they answered.

After Cler left, Gwynne struggled. She couldn't haul water for the garden, because Cler had the jeep. Without enough water, the garden failed, but she managed to harvest a few small cabbages and some carrots.

Even in the summer, she needed wood to heat the cabin and cook on the stove. Because Cler had spent so much time helping Dan, he hadn't been able to cut and haul all the wood Gwynne would need while he was gone, but Dan said he'd make up the difference. Besides keeping the fires going, Gwynne hauled a bucket of lake water each day, for washing, and half-filled a jerry can (she couldn't carry a full one) with water from a well down by the road, that the Georges also used to get water. Often, Lincoln or Franklin would fill her can for her, too.

Help from Dan never came, and by the end of September Gwynne had used up all the wood Cler had left her. Cler called her once a week to see how she was, but she didn't tell him she was having a hard time, because she knew how desperately they needed the money.

"I'm doing fine," she insisted, hoping Dan would step in and help like he promised.

Since she didn't have the strength to wield an ax, she had to use a buck saw to cut scavenged logs into stove lengths. Between nursing the baby and taking care of the kids, she spent the rest of the daylight hours trying to find wood. Paxton helped her gather dead wood, but Gwynne was working herself to exhaustion trying to drag it back to the cabin to saw. With a new baby, she felt a bit desperate and tried to get a message to Dan through the mailman, Don Goodman. Dan told Goodman to relay back to Gwynne that he'd come soon and cut wood for her, but he never showed up.

In October the weather turned ugly, but it didn't snow. The road crew wouldn't stop until the snow stopped them. Back in Kenny Lake, the bitter weather necessitated a constant fire. One night Gwynne put two pieces of rotten wood in the stove and went to bed with the baby tucked next to her. In the morning, she climbed out of bed and realized the cabin was frigid. All she had to build a fire with was one piece of rotten wood, and she needed kindling, but didn't have the strength to go hunting for it in the woods. She sat down on the bed, tucking the blanket around her baby, afraid to even change his diaper for the cold. It was the last straw.

She marched to the phone and cranked the number of the Road Commission camp. "Hello? This is Gwynne Oborn," she yelled over static on the line. "I'm trying to get a message to my husband, Cler."

The party on the line said they'd get a message to him. "What do you want to say?"

"Tell him Dan's not helping, we're out of wood and we're freezing!"

Cler came home that day. When he entered the frigid cabin and saw his wife and children huddled in bed, his face hardened.

Gwynne rolled out from under the covers and hurried to meet him. The look on his face frightened her; she was afraid he'd go after Dan, but he let the moment pass. He took her in his arms and held her as she wept.

"I promise I'll never leave you again, Gwynne. I promise," he whispered into her hair.

Cler could have worked into December plowing snow, but with the money he had already earned, he was able to buy cases of canned goods, lamp oil, and other provisions for the winter.

Before winter really hit, Dan and his wife, Mary, abandoned their homestead and moved into Anchorage, where they got a divorce and Dan hired on with the Highway Patrol.

Months later, he stopped by to visit and brought his new wife with him. Gwynne thought the new wife was a good change for him. Cler kept his thoughts to himself.

Fall, 1948

HUNTERS IN TROUBLE

It was only a few days after Cler had come home from working for the Road Commission. The afternoon sun shone cool and pale into the cabin, and Cler was cleaning his 30-06 in preparation for hunting. Gwynne was in the kitchen making stew with potatoes, cabbage, and moose meat.

The children were looking at some Highlights magazines for children, that Grandma Oborn had sent them. In the magazines there were hidden pictures and dot-to-dot, stories Corrie could read to the others, and pictures to color.

Buddy jumped up from his spot by the drum stove and started barking just before there was a sudden pounding and shouting at the cabin door. Cler left his shotgun on the table and ran to open the door, where a tall, bearded man was standing, looking frantic. Everyone else stopped what they were doing and waited to see what was happening.

"Please, help me! My friend's badly injured!" the man cried.

Out in the driveway, the man had left his car with the door open. Another man was curled in the back seat, rolling back and forth, groaning and crying. A coil of wire was wrapped around the man's left arm and shoulder. Cler left the coil of wire as it was, as he helped ease the man from the back seat. Under the wire, the man's flannel shirt was shredded, and his left arm was mangled, bleeding badly.

"Benny, it's OK!" the bearded man kept saying. Together, he and Cler half-carried Benny into the cabin, and laid him on the couch, but now he hardly seemed conscious.

104

"What's this?" Cler asked, as he eased the coil of wire off the man's arm. Instantly, Cler pulled out his pocket knife to cut away the bloody shirt, and almost simultaneously tore a piece of the shirt into a tourniquet he tied above the gash, to stop the bleeding.

"We found the wire in the woods," the bearded man said, rambling on, "Maybe it was left from back when they put in a telephone line. Anyway, we decided it might come in handy," he said, watching helplessly as Cler worked on his friend.

Gwynne brought hot water, soap and clean rags, and Cler washed around the torn flesh, then poured sulfa powder into the wounds, and bandaged it all tightly.

"So what happened?" Cler asked. He figured it had to be a bear.

The man said, "Just after we picked up the wire, and Benny coiled it around his arm, a bear came charging out of the woods and knocked him down. He warded it off with the wire as the bear tore into his arm."

"The bear was chewing on the wire?"

"Yeah, roaring like thunder while it tore at the wire," he said, shaking his head. "It was the darnedest thing. Benny was screaming, I was trying to get a bead on the bear, but I didn't want to shoot my friend. The bear got a mouthful of metal, which didn't seem to agree with it. It suddenly dropped Benny's arm and ran off. I don't have a clue why the bear attacked like it did."

Cler said, "Probably had cubs nearby."

"Makes sense," the man said. Once the mangled arm was tightly bandaged, Cler loosened the tourniquet, so the arm wouldn't die from lack of blood flow.

They put the injured man in the Jeep, and Cler took off as fast as he could drive to get to the hospital in Glenn Allen, forty miles away. The other man followed in his car.

In Glenn Allen the hospital was right off the highway. A large Army tent had been set up as a clinic and hospital only a few weeks earlier. The men carried Benny into the emergency tent calling out, "Bear attack!" as a man in khakis came running to help and got him onto a gurney.

The man in the Army shirt was apparently a doctor. He threw his stethoscope around his neck and checked the wounded man's vitals, then took scissors from a nearby metal tray. The patient was too much in shock to do more than moan.

"Looks like he's already had some help," the doctor said, carefully cutting away the blood-soaked bandages, while Cler and the bearded man stood around watching.

"You might need to know I poured sulfa into the wound after I cleaned around it." Cler said. "It's deep. I had to put a tourniquet on it."

"I've got it covered," the doctor said. He was a small, intense young man with a shock of black hair and an air of competence. He'd obviously seen bear attacks before.

The doctor's assistant was also a young man. The assistant, too, was wearing khaki. He was ready with clamps, and iodine. He set them on a small table and brought over the suturing tray. As the bandages were pulled away, the main wound began to gush blood. The doctor immediately gripped the two jagged sides of the gaping wound to hold it together while the assistant put clamps on it in several places as the doctor directed.

Benny didn't even cry out. He was gray with pain and loss of blood, but his arm was probably numb from trauma. When things had settled down, the doctor said to Cler, "Your quick action likely saved this man's arm. You an Army vet?"

"Pilot," Cler said.

"Good work," the doctor said. He nodded toward his assistant, "Casey and I were both medical corps."

The bearded man spoke up, "I'm pretty sure this man saved my friend's life." He glanced at Cler. "We both thank you. You, too, Doc."

With his patient out of the woods, so to speak, the doctor was more inclined to chat. "Bear attack, huh?"

106

"A brown bear. A really big sow. I couldn't get a bead on her with my gun, but the coil of wire kept her from chewing off Benny's arm."

The doctor frowned, looking up from his stitching. "Coil of wire?"

"Just something we found in the woods," Benny's friend said. And then he told the doctor the story.

When he'd finished, the doctor just shook his head, smiling. "I've seen a few bear attacks, and heard a lot of stories. But this is one for the books. Saved by a coil of telephone wire!"* (the real names of these men were not recorded.)

WINTER

Winter descended thick and fast: one storm followed another; snow buried the grass, the weeds, and then the willows. It piled up for weeks like cumulous clouds, and the wind blew it into drifts. Ground and sky blended together, creating a perfect whiteout. Finally, gray skies cleared to crystal blue and the temperature dropped to ten, then twenty, then forty below zero.

Even with the sun shining, a man or child's breath would freeze into ice crystals as it hit the air. When Cler went out to chop wood, he put on the black bear mitts Grandma George had made him, and the fur hat. He always came in bringing the cold with him; the wood covered in frost. Then he'd leave again, to check his trap lines and try to get back before daylight ran out.

When he brought home a rabbit, he skinned it and gave it to Gwynne to cook. She discovered that the rabbits tasted best when they were dredged in flour, salt and pepper, and fried crisp, then simmered in their own gravy until they were tender.

In sub-zero temperatures, simple tasks like doing laundry became more difficult, but still possible. Gwynne braved the cold to hang laundry on the lines, where sheets, towels, and clothing froze stiff as boards. When she brought them inside, they began to soften. In only a few moments, they were dry; the water had frozen right out of them.

With a new roof, and a floor, the cabin was a warm and cheerful refuge during these bitterly cold months. Daylight lasted only about five hours at most, but the family gathered in the safe, yellow circle of a glowing kerosene lamp.

The drum stove, standing in the center of the cabin, was the literal and figurative center of family life. As logs popped and crackled inside the steel drum, the chimney softly roared. The stove emanated reassuring heat, drawing the family from cooler corners of the cabin. There, the children drank warm drinks made of hot water, sugar and canned milk. Gwynne toasted slices of bread on the flat top of the stove and passed them to all, crisp and hot.

Since there was no school at Kenny Lake, and Corrie had turned six, Cler applied to the Territory of Alaska for a correspondence course. Territory officials sent a Calvert Course, that had everything, including lined paper, crayons and fat pencils, for teaching a child reading, writing, and arithmetic.

7

TROUBLE

February, 1949

A whole year had gone by, but Gwynne had put off even thinking about the operation she was supposed to have. It was February of their second winter at Kenny Lake, and Charles was nearly a year old.

By now, the baby had grown out of his bassinet and slept in a crib near his parents' bed. He could pull himself up on his crib bars and stand now, as well. This was a perfect stance, the baby had learned, to throw his glass baby bottles out of the crib, sometimes hitting the drum stove. He'd squeal with delight to hear them shatter!

When Charles broke the last baby bottle, Cler put a nipple on a Coke bottle. When the baby broke the last Coke bottle, Cler said, he'd have to learn to drink from a cup. By the time he was a year old, Charles was drinking his milk from a cup.

One night, when the children were asleep, Cler lay on the couch with his head in Gwynne's lap, talking about their plans for spring. "One thing, Gwynne, I'm a little worried about," Cler said.

"What's that?" she asked, coyly stroking his cheek. "You need a shave," she giggled.

Cler sat up and turned toward her, taking her hands in both of his, "I'm talking about that operation Dr. Graham wanted you to have. We've been taking chances with your health, Sweetheart."

Her smile vanished. "I just feel cold whenever I think about it," she said. "I always thought we'd have five children."

Cler said, "I know, but I don't want to lose you; I don't think I could bear it. We've just been putting off the inevitable," he said softly.

"OK," she sighed. "I suppose it's time I went in to Palmer and got the operation over with."

Arrangements were made, and a few days later, Gwynne took the baby, leaving the three youngest children with Cler, and rode with the mailman, Don Goodman, to see Dr. Graham. Don made the run from Anchorage to Chitna and back. He and his wife and three children lived on a homestead in between Kenny Lake and Chitna. It was February of 1949.

She saw Doctor Graham at the clinic. She liked the kindly doctor, who worked so hard as the only physician in the area. He was a large man, with big, meaty hands. His face was wrinkled and soft with compassion.

Now, as she met with him, his hair seemed whiter, and his complexion seemed gray. He didn't look well.

After examining Gwynne, Doctor Graham said, "I'd like to schedule this as soon as possible."

She was suddenly very nervous. "I don't have the money for the operation," she told him.

Dr. Graham was firm. His pale blue eyes held hers. "That's alright. You can make arrangements. Gwynne, with your history..."

"I know..." She was crying now.

The doctor was silent. He stripped off his gloves and dropped them into a waste basket. Then he approached his young patient and put a hand on her shoulder. His hand felt heavy, and her tears kept flowing.

"You know you shouldn't have any more children, Gwynne," he said. He stepped back and turned to wash his hands.

She felt panic. She couldn't do it. "I just have to talk to my husband, first."

Doc Graham sighed. "That's fine. I'll schedule the operation for Friday, but you can cancel if you're not ready."

Gwynne used the phone at the desk to call the mailman, who was still in Anchorage, ready to make another run to Chitna, via Kenny Lake, in the morning. She stayed the night at Irene's, and the next morning Don picked her up. She arrived back at the homestead in the early afternoon.

110

Cler heard the mail truck approach the cabin and stepped outside. His jaw dropped when he saw Gwynne climb out. "We have to talk," she said. After Cler thanked Don, he walked to the cabin with his arm around Gwynne.

"What's the matter?" he asked. She was shaking and seemed weak, so he took the baby from her, and led her into the cabin and over to the couch. The children, who were busy at the table eating their lunch, stopped chattering and watched their parents.

"Why are you back here? What's wrong?" Cler asked, sitting down beside her with Charles on his lap.

"I just wanted to be sure..." her voice trembled. "I didn't know if I should go through with this."

"Sweetheart, we've already decided," he said gently.

She agreed that they had, but now she was frightened.

"You like Dr. Graham," Cler said, "He'll take care of you." He glanced down at the baby, "Four is a good number..." He took her hand between both of his and warmed it. It was cold as ice. He wanted her to have the operation. Another child might take her from him.

She sat rigid, feeling stiff all over. Cold. Drained. "I guess you can catch Don in Chitna," she said, finally.

Cler stood up and ducked sideways to avoid the low-hanging gas lantern. He crossed to the phone, his boots thumping on the floor. His voice seemed too loud in the small cabin, but the line was full of static, "Hello, Mac, is Goodman still there? Thanks. Say, Don, do you think you could pick up Gwynne and the baby again on your way back today? She just had to come talk to me..."

Don said he'd stop and pick her up again. "You don't have to explain anything," he said.

While his wife was in Palmer being operated on, Cler stayed at the homestead with his eldest three children. Corrie was six, Paxton five, and Celestia would be three in May. Gwynne planned to stay with Irene after the operation, and Irene agreed to take care of the baby, Charles.

At Kenny Lake, the weather was cruel. It was still below zero outside. In order to stay warm, Cler had to keep a roaring fire in the drum stove, but the cold came in fast through the log walls, if the fire died down.

One day Cler was out chopping wood for the fire, while Corrie entertained her younger siblings on the single bed all three children shared. She played patty-cakes with Lestie, who repeated the rhyme, "Pat a cake, pat a cake, baker's man. Bake me a cake as fast as you can. Roll it and pull it and mark it with "C" and shove it in the oven for Lestie and me!"

"I want pancakes," Paxton whined. "Corrie, can we get off the bed now? When's Daddy going to make us pancakes?"

Before she could answer, Cler stumbled into the cabin with a load of wood, dropped it near the stove and collapsed on the couch.

"Corrie," he croaked, "come here."

The little girl went obediently to her father, who looked very pale and sick. He leaned over and began to cough, unable to stop for a few minutes. When he finally caught his breath, he lay down on the couch. "You kids stay on the bed until I wake up, OK?"

Corrie looked in the tin bread box on her way to the bed. There was a small hunk left of the last loaf. She tore off half of it, and climbed back on the bed to share the bread. Hours went by and the fire died down so the three children cuddled under the covers. As they lay there, six-year-old Corrie told the story of Little Red Riding Hood, complete with voice changes. After the story, the children lay in bed, listening to the fire pop and crackle. When the fire died down, Corrie climbed out of the bed and tried to wake up her father.

"Daddy, wake up! The fire is going out!"

He stirred enough to sit up and choke down some sulfa medicine the doctor in Palmer had given him earlier for strep throat. He struggled to his feet, stuck two logs in the stove and then fell back onto the couch. When the logs burned down, Corrie again tried to wake him, but couldn't. She called Paxton to help her. They used hot pads to lift and open the heavy door and together the two small children wrestled a log into the stove.

They climbed back onto the bed. There was a little potty chair by the bed and water in a bucket, but they were all hungry.

Corrie took the last chunk of bread into bed with them; the three shared it and went to sleep.

The next morning their daddy was still asleep and the stove was cold. Corrie dreaded climbing out of bed into the frigid air, but knew she had to. She had to take care of Paxton and Lestie. Her stomach hurt. What if Daddy died? The cold had already taken over the cabin.

Corrie braced herself and began to slip out from under the covers, trying not to wake Lestie, who had curled against her in sleep. Lestie was disturbed by the movement of her sister and the sudden chill. She began to cry without even opening her eyes.

As soon as Corrie was free of the blankets, in her stocking feet on the icy floor, she made her way to the water bucket, which had a thin layer of ice on top. She broke the ice with the tin dipper and used it to fill a cup of cold water. She drank some and took the cup to her father, but he didn't rouse, so she set the cup down and covered him with another blanket from the rocking chair. When she kissed his cheek, he felt very hot. Maybe he didn't need the blanket after all. She stood there watching him for a moment, and a terrible dread came over her.

With trembling hands, she carried the water to her small siblings. Lestie sipped the water. "No, Co-wee! I want milk!" She pushed the cup away and began to cry. Paxton drank the rest of the water without a word.

Shivering with cold, Corrie climbed back into bed and tried to comfort Lestie.

Paxton said, "Is Daddy going to die?"

"No!" Corrie scolded. "Don't you dare say that!" But she had already thought it.

The three children huddled under the blankets. Corrie lay there too cold, hungry and worried to sleep. With so little to eat for three days, her stomach had stopped growling.

More time went by, but Cler didn't wake up. The cabin was freezing and Lestie began to cry again, "Pease, Co-wee, pease some milk!"

Corrie knew her sister was cold and hungry, but there was nothing else a little girl could fix to eat. She patted Lestie and wrapped the blankets closer around her, and her cries became a soft whimper. In the quiet, Corrie heard a voice outside the cabin.

"Hullo! Anybody in there?"

Corrie went to the door just as it swung open and there was Franklin George, bundled in furs against the bitter cold.

"We no see smoke," he said, "you got trouble?" He peered into the dim cabin, his eyes resting on the drum stove. Franklin knew what to do; he slipped back outside for wood. Corrie could hear the ax chopping and Franklin soon returned with an armload of logs and kindling. In a few minutes he had a roaring fire going.

Paxton started to climb out of bed. "Too cold." Franklin gestured for him to get back under the covers. "I come back," he said when he left. The sound of the fire crackling in the drum stove cheered the children as they huddled beneath the quilts, waiting for Franklin to return. Corrie wanted to ask him to make them something to eat.

It seemed a long time, but was only a half hour before they heard the put-put of Emma's old car, and then voices at the door. Emma and Franklin entered the cabin with packages in their arms and dropped their bundles on the kitchen cupboard.

Franklin disappeared outside, while his mother, Emma, approached Cler on the couch. She gently touched his forehead. Then, in one swift motion, she shed her parka and scarf, hanging them on the coat pegs behind the door, and hurried to the water bucket, her mukluks shuffling across the floor. She filled the tea kettle, setting it on the drum stove to heat. She dipped more water from the open bucket, into a bowl. Corrie and Paxton had climbed out of bed by now and stood in their stocking feet by the drum stove, warming themselves, as Emma bustled around the cabin. With a wet towel, she bathed Cler's face.

114

He jumped at the touch of cold, and opened his eyes for a moment, but could barely whisper, "Emma? What..."

She smiled shyly and asked, "You sick, Cler?"

He pointed toward the sulfa bottle on the counter, "I have medicine, over there," he croaked.

She handed him warm water to drink, a teaspoon, and the bottle of sulfa medicine. Cler leaned up on one elbow and took a few sips, swallowing painfully. He gave himself a dose of sulfa and set the cup of water on the floor as he was wracked with a painful coughing spell. When he finally lay back down and closed his eyes, Emma busied herself with the children. She coaxed Lestie out of bed, and found that the child was wet. Corrie located some clothing, a little flannel dress and sweater, with a tiny undershirt and drawers. Emma washed and dressed the child.

Corrie and Paxton were already dressed, having slept in their clothes, in an effort to stay warm. All three children sat up to the table, where they were fed warm, canned milk and fresh bread. With the children settled, Emma again ministered to Cler. He was burning with fever, but she managed to wake him, and coaxed him to drink some raspberry tea.

Franklin went home to help his grandmother, but Emma stayed. She washed the sheet on the children's bed, and dried it on a chair by the stove. She aired the blankets, baked some biscuits, heated water, washed the dishes, and fed the children.

In the afternoon, Cler's fever broke. He sat up and coughed until he gagged, and when he could breathe again, he drank some water. By this time, it was getting dark, and he told Emma she should go tend to her family, but she just smiled. "Ina takes care of Vivian for me."

She gave Cler tea with milk and sugar, and fed the children a supper of canned salmon, bread and milk, and tucked them into bed.

"I can manage during the night," Cler whispered, "You need to go take care of your own family, but thank you so much."

"I come back in the morning," she said.

The next day, Emma again cared for the family. The following day, Cler was still coughing, but he was able to move around and take care of his own needs. Emma wouldn't let him go outside to get wood, so Franklin stockpiled a whole stack inside the cabin, and Emma made enough bread to last a week.

Cler convinced Emma that he could manage, and although he embarrassed her with his multiple expressions of gratitude, she left smiling.

For the next week, while Gwynne was gone, Cler continued to get stronger. He fed the children, kept the fire going and slept a lot. When he felt a little better, he gathered them around him and told them stories. He told them about his great grandfather, Nelson Arave, a pioneer of Utah. Once, a group of angry Indians rode up to his cabin, ready to attack Nelson's family. Nelson talked to the chief, trying to find out what he was so angry about. It had to do with some white men stealing Indian horses. Nelson pacified the chief by volunteering to take him to talk to the chief of the Mormons. He then walked 30 miles beside the chief's horse, to Salt Lake City, where he introduced the chief to Brigham Young, and the Indian was able to tell his story, and be paid for his horses.

Another subject was Cler's own childhood in Utah. He told about fishing in the Ogden river, and floating down it on an inner tube. The stories they liked best were the ones when he was a bit naughty, like when he and his friends put rotten tomatoes on the street car tracks so they'd pop, and splash on passers-by. It was hard to picture, though. They had never seen a garden, much less tomatoes going to waste. Cler ran out of strength, before he ran out of tales to tell, and his voice stayed too hoarse for singing, but Corrie remembered many of those stories.

When Gwynne returned home, she looked pale, and seemed more quiet than before she had gone for the operation. The night she came home, after she had Charles settled into bed, and the other children were asleep, she and Cler crawled into bed. He tried to snuggle up to her back, but she pulled away.

"What's the matter?" he whispered.

116

"Nothing," she whispered back. "I just don't feel very well yet."

"I was just going to cuddle, Sweetheart. I don't feel all that well myself. I had pneumonia while you were gone."

Gwynne rolled over and put her hand on his forehead. "Are you sure you're better? I noticed you were coughing when you brought wood in tonight, but I thought it was just the cold air."

"I'm still working on getting better." He stroked her arm, "We sure missed you. Don't go away again, OK?"

"OK," she said. Leaning up on one elbow, she kissed his forehead, and rolled onto her back with a sigh.

"I missed you, too."

There was silence as they lay side by side. Gwynne was staring up at the ceiling. Starlight came in the windows and bounced around, making the walls and ceiling visible, but just barely.

Gwynne whispered, "Cler? There's something I want to tell you. About the operation."

He didn't answer. She listened to the soft, rhythmic sound of his breathing. He was fast asleep.

Don Goodman's children and the Oborn children at the Bluff overlooking the Copper River.

Spring, 1949

GRAND-DADDY GROUNDHOG

In the spring, when Celestia was three, she stood watching her father cut up a large carcass with his machete. He had the animal all skinned out and lying on the split-log table. She asked, "What is that, Daddy?"

Her father looked down and winked at her. "Why, can't you tell? This is a grand-daddy groundhog!"

She had never before heard of a groundhog, but she accepted his answer.

For some minutes, her father continued to carve sizeable chunks of meat off the bones, making a neat pile of roasts. Buddy, the dog, lay under the table waiting for a tidbit to fall to the floor. He jumped up suddenly and ran to the door with a single "woof!"

There was rapping on the door.

"Someone's here," Gwynne said, as she glanced at Cler with his hands bloody from the meat. She hurried to answer the knocking, and swung open the door to a man in a khaki uniform. He was tall and heavy-set and like Cler, he had to duck to come through the doorway.

"Hello," he greeted Gwynne, and then called across to Cler, "How are you folks doing?"

"Hello, Branson. Come on in." Cler stepped away from the table and went to wash his hands in the basin. "What brings you this way?"

"I'm headed up to Chitna, but I've been stopping in to visit folks along the road. So how're the little ones?" He glanced at Corrie and Paxton sitting together on the couch with books; they had stopped reading when they heard the knock and were eyeing the stranger with interest. Lestie still stood by the table.

Branson started to cross the room, but stopped when he saw the meat. "What have you got there, Cler?"

118

What Cler had there was an out-of-season moose. And Branson was the game warden. Cler's heart sank. He'd been caught literally red-handed. The man needed to do his job; he would have to confiscate the meat and fine Cler for killing a moose.

At this awkward moment, the blue-eyed child at the game warden's feet piped up, "Well, mister, can't you tell? That's a grand-daddy groundhog!"

Branson 's eyes dropped to the angelic-looking child, surprised. Then he broke out laughing.

After a moment, Cler laughed, too. The conversation changed to the weather and, shaking hands with Cler, the game warden left.

When the door was firmly shut, Gwynne and Cler exchanged glances. She murmured, "Well that was..."

"Unnerving," He finished. "Out of the mouths of babes..." he quoted, patting his little daughter on top of her curls.

"Well," Gwynne sighed, "We certainly need the meat."

"He knew that," Cler said, and went back to cutting up the moose.

HAULING WATER

Cler carried water from the old well by the road for drinking, but the water level in the well was going down, so it was reserved only for culinary water. Lake water was usually used only for washing. It contained duckweed, small shrimp and other creatures, but it was potable if it was strained and boiled. Cler said, "The only good thing about lake water is that it's wet." It didn't taste all that great, but the children didn't seem to know the difference, and drank it without complaint.

Cler brought water home from the lake by siphoning it into fifty gallon barrels. He hauled the barrels on the wood wagon, pulled by the jeep. Filling and hauling the barrels was a major task.

In spite of the problem of hauling water, Gwynne insisted on bathing her kids at least once a week. Cler thought "sponge baths" were adequate, especially in the winter, when he had to cut a hole in the ice to get water. "Sponge bathing" meant being washed from a small basin. Cler maintained the children didn't get that dirty in the winter, but Gwynne was adamant. If it was humanly possible, she would bathe the kids.

"They might catch a chill," Cler teased, as he hauled the wash tub to the kitchen and gathered towels and soap.

"Better goose bumps than head lice," Gwynne retorted.

Into the wash tub she poured hot water from the kettles, adding cold to make it just right. The children stripped down under a blanket and their mother set them one at a time in the water, giving them a wash cloth to cover their eyes. Then, using a sauce pan, she poured bath water over their heads. She scrubbed each child from head to toe with coarse, brown soap and poured another saucepan of water over his or her head to rinse off.

Gwynne didn't waste the bath water. She knew how to use and then reuse every drop. The water would do for washing out socks and underwear. After that, it could still be used to mop the floor. If it were summer, the dirty water could be thrown out to keep the dust down in the dooryard. In winter, it had to be carted away from the cabin before it was dumped, because it froze immediately into a patch of ice. Dumped again and again in the same place, it created a rather interesting ice sculpture.

Gwynne

8

COPING

spring, 1949

Gwynne was used to having a blue day or two, especially during the winter, but after the operation in Palmer, the blue days became more frequent; she often felt overwhelmed by feelings of loss that she did not understand. One morning, she was brushing her long hair, with its soft, brown waves falling forward, as she bent over. She hadn't cut her hair since seventh grade, and it reached almost to her waist when she stood up.

Sitting on the chair by her bed, she parted her hair without looking in a mirror and began to braid it on one side. As her fingers manipulated the silky strands, she began to think about the operation in Palmer, three months earlier. Until now, she had put the events in Palmer out of her mind, but now, it all came back, and sadness filled her whole body, like black smoke in a bottle.

That February day, when she had arrived in Palmer for the operation, it was late, so she asked Don to leave her at Ilene's. The next morning, she walked to the Quonset hut hospital and told the nurse at the desk that she had come back to have the operation that Dr. Graham had scheduled. The nurse was tall, almost gaunt, a pale sort of woman who looked ill, but was probably just tired. She seemed surprised to see Gwynne, but she led her to an exam room and asked her to wait.

In the cool, bright room, Gwynne clasped her icy hands in her lap to keep them from shaking. Outside the window, she could hear the humming engine of a gas-powered generator that provided electric lights in the hospital. She felt nervous as a cat, and began to get a headache, believing she could smell the exhaust fumes from the generator.

After some time, a young man in a white coat, with smooth, dark hair and eyes, strode into the room. He was slightly officious, brusque in his manner, "Good morning, Gwynne. I guess Dr. Graham has you on the schedule for later this afternoon, but I'll be performing your surgery," he told her.

A sudden chill struck her. "What? Where's Dr. Graham?"

"Oh, no one told you? Doctor had a heart attack yesterday."

It was probably Gwynne's shocked expression that made him add, "He's alive, but he's going to have to retire. He's literally worked his heart out. There's too much damn—sorry. Too much work to do. At any rate, I have your records here and it looks like Dr. Graham planned to do a hysterectomy. Is that right?"

She nodded, but his words struck her like fists. She had expected the kindly Dr. Garret, and here was this stranger. She had no idea there was another doctor in Palmer, and was too stunned to say anything. There was nothing to do but go through with the operation Dr. Graham wanted her to have.

Later, she knew it was later, because it was dark outside, she woke in a room with intense pain in her abdomen. The same tall nurse was checking her pulse with a cool hand.

"I need something for pain," Gwynne whispered. "I can barely breathe."

"You're fine," the nurse told her and walked briskly out of the room.

"What a mean lady," Gwynne thought. She must have dozed a bit, because the next thing she remembered was the new doctor and nurse talking out in the hall. She didn't catch every word, but she heard phrases.

The nurse said, "... Doc Graham knew about the fetus?"

Gwynne felt her heart leap. *What?*

The new doctor said, "I'm sure he did...the mother's health, and all, but still..."

The nurse's voice was amplified in the empty hallway. Gwynne heard, "Well, I don't agree with it, but it's done now."

It's done now. Done.

Gwynne's thoughts returned to the cabin, where spring was shining outside. With a heavy heart, she finished braiding her hair.

"Honey," Cler called as he entered the cabin, the door thudding behind him. "Oh," he said, spying her sitting on their bed. "There you are."

He saw the expression on her face and crossed the room in a few steps, sitting down beside her. He put an arm around her shoulders, "Another bad day?"

She buried her face in his flannel shirt, letting her tears come. After a minute or two she raised her head, "I'm alright," she said, sniffling. "Really I am." She used a bit of old towel to wipe her face.

Cler watched her for a moment. She was OK, then. He left her making up the bed, while he headed to the kitchen to build a fire in the cook stove. Breakfast was late, but the children were playing some game with buttons on the floor by the drum stove and didn't seem to notice. He would stir up some corn meal mush.

MACHETE

The Oborn children thrived having both of their parents around. Paxton, especially, idolized his father and followed him everywhere he could, asking questions, offering help. Cler enjoyed teaching the precocious little boy.

In everyday use there were guns, knives, fire, kerosene; all sorts of dangers that might intrigue a small boy. Cler had been such a boy himself, curious about everything, with no real sense of danger. He felt all the more anxious to teach his son to use all these potential hazards safely.

Cler had a huge knife for cutting meat. Its blade was about twelve inches long and the wooden handle was wound with narrow cord. He kept it sharp on a whetstone. He was standing at the kitchen sink sharpening the knife and five-year-old Paxton was watching him carefully.

"That's a big knife, isn't it, Daddy," the boy said. "Why is it so big? What kind knife is it? You can cut up a moose with it, can't you?"

Cler smiled. "I can do that, yes. This is a machete. It's like the blades explorers used to whack their way through the jungle." He noticed that Corrie and Lestie were also listening to his explanation. He continued rubbing the knife in circular motions on the whet stone. "You kids must not touch this knife, do you understand?"

Three little heads nodded; little faces solemn.

Cler added a little water and continued sharpening the machete. "I earned this knife when I was in high school, when I worked for a butcher in Ogden. That's where I learned to cut up meat. In Ogden, people ate meat from chickens, pigs, sheep and cows. Here, we eat moose and rabbits, and ducks." Cler's brown eyes sparkled and his dimples appeared when he smiled.

"What's Ogden, Daddy?" Paxton asked.

"That's a place far away in the States. One of these days we'll take a trip down south and you can see your grandparents."

"I remember Grandma," Corrie said. "I kind of liked her."

Cler laughed. "Which Grandma do you remember?"

Corrie brushed a strand of hair out of her eyes, and tucked it behind her ear. She squinted, as if having to wrack her brain for the answer, but it had only been two years. "I remember the pie-baking grandma. With a smile and white hair."

"That would be my mother," Cler said. "Your other grandma has brown hair. She's your mama's mother. We can see them when we go on a trip. And your grandpas, too. One of these days."

"Is Ogden nice, Daddy?" Corrie asked. "I can't remember."

"Oh, it has big, spreading, leafy trees. And fruit trees." He felt a little wistful, thinking about it. "Sometimes my mouth just waters when I think about those big, black cherries that grew on a tree in our yard. And peaches. Oh, we'll have some fresh peaches when we go there again, that's for sure."

Gwynne was rocking Charles in the big rocking chair, listening to Cler talk about Ogden. Her heart felt empty with the loss of something she couldn't quite put her finger on. Certainly, life at home with her parents hadn't been wonderful all the time, which is one reason she married Cler when she was seventeen.

But it wasn't Utah she missed, so much as civilization. Bathtubs, and hot, running water. Floors you could mop. Fresh tomatoes. Department stores, and pretty clothes. Her mother was always so particular about how she dressed. She would never go to town without her hat and gloves ...Gwynne sighed.

"Oh, Mama," she murmured, glancing down at her stained cotton dress. "You would say I've let myself go. You'd be appalled..."

MAMA AND DADDY HAVE AN ARGUMENT

The children were sitting on their bed, waiting for breakfast. Charles still slept in his little crib. Cler was cooking sourdough pancakes on an iron griddle, and Gwynne was setting the table, but her face was like a dark cloud and she was upset about something.

The children sat wide-eyed and silent, watching the argument between their parents, carried on with brusque movements and scowling faces. After a few low words the kids didn't quite hear, their mother stormed out of the cabin and tried to slam the door, but it was so heavy it bounced and she had to come back to shut it.

Cler kept cooking breakfast, flipping over a griddle-sized pancake. He called the children to the table. They climbed off the bed and Celestia and Paxton took their places on the split-log bench. Charles was awake now, so Corrie stopped to lift him from the crib and set him in the middle of the bench.

Cler divided up the pancake into triangles and gave one to each child. The baby picked his up and ate it like a slice of bread. He said, "Num!" but he was the only child making any noise. The others ate silently and when they finished, they filed to the other side of the cabin to sit on the couch. Corrie cleaned up the baby, got a diaper and changed him on the floor. She held Charles on her lap, jiggling him to keep him quiet.

Daddy was in the kitchen doing dishes and cleaning up, but where had Mother gone?

An hour passed. Cler finished rinsing a plate and set it on the cupboard. He abruptly left the sink and crossed the room, snagging his rifle as he ducked out the cabin door. After the door thudded closed, the children sat together on the couch, watching dust motes float through a patch of sunlight on the floor in front of them. It was so still they could hear a magpie squawk in the spruce tree outside. Then they heard three gun shots echo through the woods, not far from the cabin.

Corrie whispered, "Daddy shot Mother!"

Paxton and Celestia began to cry. Charles joined in, and Corrie commanded them all to "Be quiet!"

Soon Cler returned to the cabin, acting unconcerned. He resumed wiping the counter and stepped outside to throw the dish water on the little birch tree that Gwynne had planted. When he came back inside, he noticed the children huddled silently together on the couch.

Corrie spoke up, "Did you shoot Mother?"

Cler stared at his children, who stared back at him more with curiosity than fear in their eyes. He was stunned by Corrie's question.

"Of course not! How on earth could you think--? I would never..."

"We heard shots," Corrie said.

Cler frowned, "Shots? I fired into the air! The shots were signals!"

The children didn't ask what signals meant, but at that moment, the door swung open and Gwynne slowly entered the cabin. She stood silently for a minute.

"All right. I admit it: I was lost. Thank you." She crossed to their bed and uncoiled her braids. Then she curled up on the bed like a small child, her face half- buried in the pillow.

Cler felt defeated. The anger that had been simmering in his chest slowly dissipated as it dawned on him that their little children thought he was capable of shooting their beautiful mother.

He turned back to the kitchen sink and stared out the window, so the children wouldn't see his tears. This wilderness living was hard on Gwynne. He would get some more money and add onto the cabin, as soon as he could.

A few days later, Cler received a letter from his brother, Willis, called Bill, who lived in Hollywood Hills, California. He said he and Nan wanted to come to Alaska in July. He didn't say so, but Cler suspected that his mother, Gwendolyn, had put Bill up to it. She was worried about Cler and his little family. Mother Oborn had never left Ogden, Utah, and Cler knew she felt bereft, as if her youngest son had moved to Timbuktu.

Cler smiled; whatever the reasons, it would be great to see his beloved big brother.

Forest and Cler putting new roof on the cabin 1949

9

ADDITION

Summer, 1949

Cler spent the month of June working on the house. He harvested timber from his own property, and set up a saw mill. To do this, he bought a used John Deere tractor he could pay for over time, and used it to haul logs, and as the engine for his saw mill. He built a platform for a saw table, then rigged the blade to a belt attached to the tractor engine. With his saw mill, he cut boards for an addition to the cabin, and a new roof.

Before he started on the addition, Cler climbed up and shoveled the dirt off the old roof. Forest Triber helped him put the new roof on the cabin and the front porch. They sheeted the whole with rough lumber and made it waterproof, using tar paper and tar.

Cler built the addition out of logs, making it twelve feet long and the same width as the cabin, which was twenty feet. Rough lumber was used for the interior walls, floor and roof. He also built a backdoor from rough lumber. Layers of translucent plastic covered the windows.

With his chain saw, he cut a door in the back wall of the cabin to access the addition, which consisted of two tiny rooms on one side of a hallway, each one big enough for a set of bunk beds with a little space to walk in. There was one room for the girls and one for the boys. Across the hall, was a slightly larger room for the parents, and a wash room with a wash stand, basin, and chemical toilet. A curtain over the door provided privacy. In the summer, everyone went outside to the outhouse, but for small children, nighttime and winter, they now had the luxury of "indoor facilities."

BILL AND NAN COME TO VISIT

In July, Willis, called Bill by everyone but his mother, took his wife and flew to Alaska. He and Nan were older than Cler and Gwynne and had no children. Cler picked Bill and Nan up at Elmendorf Field, where they arrived in a commercial plane, even though Elmendorf was a military installation built by the Army during the War. The new Anchorage International Airport wouldn't be finished until two years later.

Cler watched his brother's wife emerge from the airplane. Nan stopped for a moment to scan the tarmac, shading her eyes from the July sun with one hand, carrying a small, red leather suitcase in the other. Bill followed, guiding his wife down the portable stairway. They were a handsome pair, slim and dark-haired. Nan wore a blue, tailored skirt and jacket, while Bill sported khaki slacks and a leather jacket. Nan and Bill descended from the plane like a movie star couple.

When they reached the tarmac, Cler ran to meet them, and Bill dropped his suitcase and grabbed his brother in a hearty hug. They held each other, slapping each other's backs in a wordless embrace that brought tears to their eyes.

"Man! It's good to see you," Bill exclaimed when he finally let go of his little brother.

Bill was brown-eyed, wide shouldered, and handsome like Cler, with the same dark curly hair, but he was a head shorter than his "little" brother.

"Great to see you, too," Cler grinned, picking up his brother's suitcase in one hand and taking Nan's from her, in the other. "Nice to see you, Nan," he said.

The fact that Cler's hands were full, didn't stop Nan from wrapping her arms around him and leaning up to kiss him on the cheek.

"How are you, Cler? Oh, it's wonderful to finally get here! The winds aloft were fierce!"

Bill grinned, "They weren't as bad as all that, but it's good to be on solid ground again."

"Aren't you Hollywood people used to flying all over the world?" Cler teased. Bill worked in the movie industry, and was now involved in pioneering the new medium of television.

"Too busy working," Bill laughed. "But I'm on vacation, now, thankfully. We're anxious to see some of this country. Even from the air, it looks beautiful."

"And vast, and cold!" Nan added, "We flew over some massively large glaciers. Ice fields, the pilot called them. But now that we're on the ground, it's almost hot out here."

Cler said, "Wait 'til we get inland. It'll be even hotter at Kenny Lake. At Kenny Lake it can hit ninety this time of year."

Bill looked surprised, "No kidding?"

They were walking to the Quonset hut terminal, to wait for their bags to be unloaded off the plane. A row of military gray, metal chairs offered the only seating, once they arrived indoors.

Nan and Bill planned to stay for two weeks. While they waited for their baggage, they talked about how Gwynne and the

130

children were (doing fine), how the homestead farm was coming along (slow, but making progress), places they might want to see (the Matanuska Glacier, which was on the way to Kenny Lake, the Chain Lakes near Chitna, where they could fly fish for lake trout, and the scenic Copper River).

Even in the jeep, the long drive to Kenny Lake flew by, as Bill and his brother caught up on each other's lives, and Nan exclaimed over the breathtaking scenery. The air blew in through the spaces in the canvas top, and Nan exclaimed it was exhilarating.

When they arrived at the cabin, Gwynne and the children spilled out to greet them. Gwynne felt shy as she watched her glamorous in-laws climb out of the jeep. Nan was slim, well-dressed and self-assured; the picture of a city girl.

After hugging Gwynne, Nan said, "All the way here, I just stared at the vistas. Everywhere I look is stunning. I don't know how you bear it darlings. It's just too much beauty to take in!"

Gwynne laughed and felt a little less anxious. "We feel like we can live just on the view, sometimes. Come on inside, Honey, and we'll have some lunch. Are you hungry?"

"We had a snack at a place called Sheep Mountain, but I'm famished," Nan told her as the two women entered the cabin. It was cool, and seemed dark, until their eyes adjusted to being out of the sun. Gwynne had cleaned and dusted the cabin, mopped the piece of blue linoleum that covered the boards on the kitchen floor, and put a red cloth on the split-log table. On the table she'd placed a glass jar, filled with white and yellow wild flowers.

Now she thought she could see her home through Nan's eyes, and anxiety clutched at her heart. The cabin was small, dark, crowded, and rough. The board floor was uneven, and the low ceiling seemed to close in on them.

But Nan seemed not to notice.

"Oh!" Nan exclaimed, "Your cabin is so cunning. I love it!"

Bill and Cler put up the Army tent for Nan and Bill to sleep in while they were visiting. Energetic Nan was game to do just about anything, from shooting tin cans with Cler's .22, to hiking back to the Bluff. She was out-going and friendly, enjoying her visit to the wild. Sometimes she talked about their life in California, the palm trees and beaches, their Hollywood friends, their new house.

Gwynne, a natural introvert, often busied herself in the kitchen at the stove or sink, when she could have been sitting around with the other adults, laughing and talking together. Bill explained the latest technical breakthroughs in television, and Cler told about life in the wilderness, not above exaggerating the challenges, but all in good humor.

"You know it got so cold last winter, that if I stood still when I was outside getting wood, my feet would freeze to the ground! I had to holler for Gwynne to come rescue me by pouring hot water over my mukluks!"

Sometimes Nan grew wide-eyed at Cler's jokes, but Bill always broke out laughing.

On the last evening of their visit, the men were telling stories in the living room and the children were coloring pictures at the table. Gwynne was bathing Charles in the wash pan, on the kitchen cupboard, while Nan watched from a nearby chair.

When Gwynne lifted the baby from his bath, all pink and dimpled, Nan jumped up and grabbed the towel, "Here, may I dry him?"

Gwynne handed her baby to Nan, who wrapped the towel and took him to her chair near the drum stove. The baby laughed and cooed as she dried him.

"You precious, precious little thing!" She snuggled the chubby baby against her, and kissed his damp hair. When she gave him back to Gwynne to diaper, she said, somewhat wistfully, "Oh, darling, you're so lucky, you know. You and Cler make such beautiful babies together!"

It was then that Gwynne realized she need not envy her glamorous sister-in-law; Nan actually envied *her*.

Not long after Nan and Bill returned to their home in California, they wrote to Gwynne and Cler with good news. They had adopted a toddler, a little Samoan child they named Cathy.

NEW NEIGHBORS

That spring, other homesteaders had moved in. Scot and Maxine McDaniel filed on the claim abandoned by Dan and Mary, with its cabin on the tiny lake where Cler liked to hunt ducks.

Maxine was a pretty woman with abundant red hair. Scotty showed his ancestry in his sandy hair, fair skin and clear blue eyes. He was a beautician by trade, but an artist at heart, and he had a rare talent for painting scenes of Alaska's wilderness. He could skillfully capture qualities of winter dawn and summer sunsets, of snow and of tundra.

Cler helped Scotty finish the cabin left by Dan, and the two men became instant friends. When Scotty had to go into Anchorage, Cler would check on Maxine, and the baby, Donna.

FIRE!

One sunny morning, Lestie awoke in the tiny room she shared with her sister. Corrie was still asleep on the top bunk. Lestie lay listening to the whir of the chain saw as Cler cut fire wood out in the yard. She watched a fly buzzing against the translucent plastic window at the end of the bunk beds, where the sun filtered in. The sound of the saw quit. Someone outside was screaming and crying, and dogs were barking. Lestie wriggled out of her sleeping bag and ran to the back door, squinting into the morning sunshine. There was Maxine McDonald, running across the field, her red hair flying, with her baby under her arm. The McDaniel's two black cocker spaniels scrambled to keep up. Maxine was yelling, "Cler, Cler, our cabin's on fire!"

Buddy began to bark, alerted by all the confusion.

Dropping the saw, Cler looked up to see black smoke spreading over the tops of the spruce trees, into the blue sky. He yelled to Maxine, "Tell Gwynne to call the Forest Service!"

Maxine reached the front door just as Gwynne opened it. "My cabin's on fire!" Maxine exclaimed over her baby's screams. "Call the Forest Service!"

Cler sprinted to the tractor, which was parked at the side of the driveway, with the wagon still attached, and a load of six fifty- gallon drums of water, which he had just hauled from the lake. He jumped on, started the engine, and tore off down the drive. A barrel fell over and rolled off the back of the wagon, bursting off the cap when it hit the ground.

Paxton was standing in front of the cabin. He saw the barrel fall, water gurgle onto the dirt. He watched his father disappear down the road. There was black smoke billowing into the sky, drifting over the spruce trees.

If sparks caught the woods on fire, the Oborn's cabin would be next. Paxton shuddered. He was seven now, but he still remembered the fire when he was four: the searing heat, choking smoke. He remembered the terror, as he worked beside his parents, beating at the flames.

Cler braked just enough to keep from tipping over the barrels; he wrenched the steering wheel and turned onto Scotty's dirt road. The cabin was engulfed; the roof blazed, the windows had shattered, flames flared between the logs. There was no way to save it.

He backed around to dump the barrels, turning his efforts to stopping the blaze from spreading through the grass and catching the trees. He leaped from the jeep and up into the wagon, shoving and rolling each barrel off the back. Each barrel fell off and rolled on the ground, colliding with the others.

He wrangled the barrels so that they lined up in the scanty yard between the roaring fire and the trees. Sprinting from barrel to barrel, he tore off the caps. Heat from the blazing cabin scorched his face as he lifted the butt end of each barrel, emptying water into the dry grass.

Gwynne cranked the Forest Service number, but apparently the lines were down. She couldn't even call the store at Chitna.

"We'll have to run to Copper Center. Corrie Lynne, help me get the kids in the jeep; we have to get out of here!"

Gwynne glanced at Maxine, standing breathless, dazed, clutching her sobbing baby. Gwynne saw the angry red burn on Donna's forehead.

"I'll get something for her burn," Gwynne said, rushing to the sink. She snatched up a clean dishtowel, wet it in cool water, and laid it gently on the baby's forehead. Donna startled, and grasped at the towel, but Maxine kept it pressed over the burn, and in a moment, the baby stopped struggling and merely whimpered.

Corrie had awakened with all the uproar, and now she rousted Charles out of bed, and herded him past their mother, out the door.

"Come on, Maxine, we have to get to another phone!" Gwynne hustled her friend to the front seat of the jeep, which was already loaded with kids. There was nothing to do but leave the dogs to fend for themselves.

Copper Center was only twenty miles away, but it seemed further. As Gwynne sped down the highway, Maxine had calmed down, and could talk about what had just happened. She said Scotty had gone to Anchorage on business. She was sleeping, when the roof must have caught on fire, and a burning piece of ceiling fell on the baby's face. She woke to the baby's screams, and snatched her out of her crib, tearing out of the smoke-filled cabin.

"If Donna hadn't screamed..." Maxine shuddered.

"It's too awful to think about, but you're safe now," Gwynne said. She glanced at the baby, who was whimpering in her sleep, with the wet cloth still on her forehead.

At Copper Center, Gwynne called the Forest Service to report the fire. They said they'd alert the ranger down the road, who had a water truck. Besides a phone, the ranger had a two-wave radio, which was good, since the lines were down.

The children sat quietly on the white sheepskin rugs which were scattered around the main lobby of the road house. They were still wearing whatever they'd slept in, looking grubby and disheveled. Their feet were bare. Corrie held on to Charles, who was trying to escape, while Gwynne talked quietly with Maxine, who was still in shock. Guests of the roadhouse passed and stared at the tousled haired children, and the two distraught mothers. They didn't know the enormity of what had happened.

Back at Scotty's Lake, Cler had managed to contain the fire to only the cabin, until the forest service truck arrived. The ranger pumped water onto the blaze to cool it down and prevent sparks from spreading to the trees.

Scott and Maxine's cabin burned to the ground, and they lost everything they had in it. They moved back to Anchorage for a time, but later returned to Kenny Lake and began to build another cabin across the road from their original one. It seemed like the property on Scotty's Lake was doomed to be abandoned.

BLACK BEAR

The family made a trip into Copper Center for groceries. They bought flour and sugar, lard, canned milk and canned vegetables. While they were in town, they stopped at the jail to see how Ben Pinks was getting along.

Ben was sitting on a chair in the jailer's office, with his stocking feet propped up on a wooden box, beside the stove. He had his boots off, drying by the fire. There was an enamel coffee pot on the stove, and he was sipping coffee from a mug. He was gripping the mug with both hands, as if warming his hands on it. His stubby fingers hurt sometimes with what he called the "rumatiz." Ben looked up when he heard the heavy wooden door whine on its hinges, as Cler opened it.

136

"Well, howdy, folks! How's things going out to Kenny Lake?" he said jovially, putting his feet down on the floor. "Can I get you a cup of coffee?"

Cler shook his head, "Oh, we're fine, Ben. We just stopped by to see how you were getting along."

Gwynne sat on the only other chair, while Cler and the kids crowded into the small room and stood along the walls.

Ben spotted the kids, "How're you kiddies? Bein' good to your ma?"

"We're always good to her," Corrie told him.

"You got candy in your desk?" Lestie asked. The last time they'd stopped by, he had some jelly beans.

"Got some pieces of horehound, if you like that. It's good for what ails ya', if your folks say it's fine for you to have it."

"Sure. I'd like a piece of that myself." Cler said.

Ben opened the top drawer on his battered wooden desk and drew out a small paper sack of candy. He passed it to Cler, who gave each of the children one, as well as Gwynne, and popped one in his own mouth, handing the bag back to Ben. Horehound drops were made from an herb and considered a good remedy for coughs, similar to cough drops.

"So you're feeling pretty good, are you, Ben?" Gwynne asked.

"To tell you the truth, I've been pretty low lately. It's a good thing my job as sheriff don't amount to much more than locking up a drunk now and then. The trouble is, my bones ache. I guess it's the rumatiz, but I got no energy, if you know what I mean. I'd like to go huntin' for bear, like in the old days, but I'd be hard pressed to follow a trail. The bear'd have to come up and lay down by my feet, just to get his self shot!"

Cler laughed. "As bad as all that? I'll tell you what. I know you like bear meat, and if I get one, I'll drive all the way back here to Copper Center just to give you a piece of him."

"You'd do that for me?"

"I would. You've done more for me than I could ever do for you."

Ben took another drink of his coffee. "Now you're embarrassin' me, doggone it."

After the visit, the family stopped and bought a few groceries at the Roadhouse, and then headed back to Kenny Lake. Cler had his 30-06 in the jeep, and he was thinking that if he saw a bear on the way back, he'd shoot it and take some meat to Ben. The man deserved that much and more.

When they rounded the bend in the circle driveway, they saw a black bear sitting on the porch, leaning up against the front door. Cler stopped the jeep where it was, and said, "Keep the kids quiet, OK? And everyone stay put."

He took his gun from under the seat and loaded a shell into it, dropping a handful into his coat pocket. He climbed stealthily out of the jeep and sneaked closer to the cabin. The black bear just sat there. He'd found some canned goods stored on the porch and was biting into a can of peas, using his incisors like a can opener, sucking out the juice.

The black bear had a white patch of fur on the front of his neck. He was gnawing on the tin can, and he ignored Cler. This must be Ben's bear, Cler thought, the one that just sits there waiting to be shot. He raised his 30-06 and pulled the trigger.

The bullet killed the bear, but it also went through the cabin door and shattered some dishes on the cupboard. Gwynne cleaned up the broken dishes while Cler skinned the bear. He tacked the unusual hide on the back wall of the cabin to dry, and when the meat was cured, he made a trip into Copper Center to give a quarter of it to Ben.

It was only a few weeks later, that he found out from Forest Triber that Ben had died.

Corrie Lynne, age 7

10

NEW ARRIVALS

October, 1949

It was late fall in the Copper River Valley. The willows were bare, and the birches reached black, naked fingers into the pale, gray sky, where the clouds seemed to be holding back snow. Cler was out splitting wood for kindling, when he heard some dogs barking down at the lake. He thumped his ax into the chopping block and strode down the hill to investigate, with Buddy following. There was a car and trailer parked by the lake.

A man and woman were leaning against their car, taking in the scenery. As Cler approached, two dogs set up a racket, and

Cler told Buddy to heel. One of the dogs was smaller, black and white, while the larger dog was just a pup. He looked part wolf, scrawny, with yellow eyes and a ragged, grayish coat. The man spoke sharply to his dogs, "Dinah, quiet! Dan!" He kicked at the wolf dog, "Quiet!"

The dogs quieted and wagged their tails. The wolf pup hesitantly approached Buddy, who stood his ground. He took a reading on the man's dogs and decided they weren't a threat. He stayed close to Cler, although he deigned to wag his tail in greeting.

The man was about Cler's age, in his mid-twenties, of medium height and build, with the blue-eyes and coal black hair they used to call "Black Irish." He was dressed for the Bush, with boots, khaki pants littered with pockets, a matching vest, and a red flannel shirt. His sleeves were neatly turned back at the cuffs, exposing a sprinkling of black hair above his wrists. He stuck out his hand, "Hi, I'm Dennis Reilly.* My wife, Mildred."* (not their real names.)

"Hello, Dennis," Cler shook his hand. "Mildred. Nice to meet you."

The woman smiled shyly. She was lean-faced, with dark hair slicked back and knotted at the nape of her neck. She wore loose fitting jeans rolled at the ankle, high-topped boots, and a cable knit sweater that came down to her thighs.

"So where are you folks from?" Cler asked.

"North Dakota. We left Bismarck two months ago, with two riding horses and a pack horse. We just packed up and headed north."

"No kidding?" Cler grinned. "How'd that work out?"

Dennis struck a casual pose, leaning back against his car's hood, and spreading out his hands. "Listen, horses don't break down or run out of gas, but they are pretty slow!" He laughed.

Cler was interested, "I knew some other people who started out on horses to come north. How long did it take you to get here?"

140

Dennis looked at his wife. "Well, we got to Montana, but by then we figured we couldn't make it up the highway before winter, so we sold the horses in Missoula, and bought this outfit." He indicated the Ford car and aluminum trailer.

"Nice," Cler said. "My friends didn't end up making it to Alaska on horseback, either, so don't feel bad. So where are you headed now?"

"We're looking for a place to homestead."

Mildred started to say something, but Dennis interrupted, "To tell you the truth, we haven't found what we want, yet, though we intended to go further south. Fella said this was great country, so I thought we'd check it out."

This is just what Cler had been hoping for: more homesteaders in the area, to build up the community. But this couple had arrived way late in the season. "I have to be honest with you, Dennis," Cler said, "I think you'd be better off to head on south to the coast; maybe stay in Anchorage for the winter. It's too late to build a cabin this year, and the winter can be brutal here in the interior. But I'd love to see you come back next spring."

"I think we can tough it out in the trailer," Dennis said, "If I decide I want to stay, anyway. I didn't come all this way to give up without a fight."

Cler bit his lip. "Course, it's up to you. You're welcome to stick around Kenny Lake. Since you're here in moose country and it's hunting season, it's a good time to get a moose if you want one."

"Maybe I'll do that," Dennis said, standing a little taller, although he only came up to Cler's shoulder.

Cler said, "Well, how about coming on up to the cabin? I'll introduce you to my wife."

The Reillys agreed, and followed Cler up the hill, while the dogs ran happily ahead. Meanwhile, Gwynne had come out of the cabin. She met them walking into the yard.

"This is Dennis and Mildred Reilly, Honey. They might take out a homestead somewhere near here, if they can find what they want."

"It's so nice to meet you!" Gwynne said, "Come on inside where it's warm."

Dennis sized up Gwynne, who was looking pretty in a flowered house dress, with her shiny, brown hair braided in a coil around her head.

"Nice to meet you," he said, nodding toward her. Dennis and Cler followed the women into the cabin.

Gwynne noticed that Mildred looked tired, drawn around the mouth, with smudges of purple under her eyes. "You must be tired after your drive. Let me get you something hot to drink." She began getting cups out of the cupboard, and moved the coffee pot from the back of the kitchen range to sit over a burner.

By warm drink, she meant Postum, a popular cereal drink, and coffee substitute that many people had learned to like during the war, when coffee was rationed. Cler's mother even made it herself, and Gwynne had learned from her. On a cookie sheet, she toasted ground wheat or barley with molasses, until it turned almost black. The resulting mixture was then percolated in the coffee pot. It was good with canned cream and sugar. Everyone in the Interior drank coffee, but when they ran out, they sometimes made this ersatz coffee.

Gwynne turned to Mildred. "So how do you like Alaska?"

Mildred said, "It's beautiful. I just wish we'd get settled somewhere soon. Things just seem to go wrong, you know? Like yesterday we got the trailer stuck in the mud somewhere between here and no where..."

Dennis said, "That was not my fault," and went back talking to Cler.

Mildred lowered her voice, "I think we're going to like it once we get settled, but I hope it's soon, that's all I'm saying."

As the guests were seated on the sofa, their hands cupped around mugs of Postum laced with milk and sugar, Cler introduced the children, who were gathered around a

Montgomery Ward catalogue at the table. "Those are our children: the girl there in glasses is Corrie Lynne, our eldest. That's Paxton next to her. Curly Locks is called Lestie, and the little guy is Charles." He called over to the children, "You kids make up your minds about which shoes you want?"

"Yes, sir!" Paxton said, "We're just looking at toys, now, Daddy." Christmas was two months away, but reading the Catalogue was entertainment in itself. The children actually looked forward to new shoes, as much as toys. Toys they might only dream about, but new shoes were coming in a few weeks.

Gwynne had traced around each of their feet with pencil, on brown paper, so the people at Montgomery Ward could tell which size to send to them.

Corrie glanced down at her worn leather lace-ups. She'd had those shoes for a long time. They had belonged to her cousin, Francia before her, and Aunt Ella sent them in a box. At one time, the shoes were too big. But she had grown. A month ago they pinched her toes so much she told her father. He reached for one shoe and took out his pocket knife, flipping open the blade. He set the shoe on the table and neatly cut out the toe, making her shoe into a sandal. Corrie slipped the shoe over her little gray sock, and found it fit just right. She handed her father the other shoe. Until tonight, when she saw all the new shoes in the Catalogue, she had liked her "sandals" very much. Now they looked old and worn out to her.

For the next hour, Dennis and Cler talked about the cost of gas, the jobless situation since the War, and Dennis' flat feet that had kept him out of the Army.

Cler and Gwynne assured their guests that it was fine if they camped here at Kenny Lake for a while. Dennis was adamant that his little trailer would work just fine as a place to live, until he had a cabin built. He told them he was sure he'd find a good homestead in the nearby area.

Cler wanted the community of Kenny Lake to grow. Neighbors helped neighbors, and everyone benefitted from having more people around. He wanted the Reillys to stay, but he knew Dennis was being unrealistic about homesteading this year, though he didn't say so. He thought the man would figure it out without being told.

Dennis changed the subject, "I really want to spend a day or two hunting while the weather is good," he said.

"Ever been hunting, Dennis?" Cler asked.

Dennis shrugged. "How hard can it be? I guess everyone in Alaska hunts, so why not me?"

The two men continued talking, while Gwynne and Mildred prepared a lunch of creamed salmon and fresh-baked bread.

While they were all eating, Dennis said, "I'd like to take you up on your offer to go hunting with me. I've got a new gun that I can't wait to try out."

Cler was taken aback. He had said nothing about taking the man hunting, but decided it wasn't a bad idea. "Sure, if you want to share the meat."

"Of course. What would I do with a whole moose, anyway?" Both men laughed.

After lunch, Dennis and Mildred left, and the older kids followed them out the door. Their dogs greeted the children, with tail-wagging and attempted face-licking. The big pup jumped up and put his heavy paws on Corrie's chest, trying to lick her face, while she was giggling, pushing him away.

"Down!" Dennis ordered, without looking back. Mildred said, "I'm sorry," to Corrie, and dragged the big pup away by his collar.

Just after dark, there was a knock at the door, and Paxton answered it. Dennis and Mildred had come to visit, where the gas light had been lit, and the stove was popping cheerfully. In each hand, Dennis gripped a rifle by the stock. "What do you think of these, Cler? Isn't this thirty-ought-six a beauty?"

Cler was relaxing in his rocking chair. "Nice. The shot gun looks good, too. You could get some ducks with that. There are still some on the lake."

144

Dennis set his shotgun so it leaned against the log pillar by the drum stove.

"That gun loaded?" Cler asked, nodding toward the shotgun.

"I don't think so."

"Why don't you check to be sure," Cler said, mildly.

Dennis picked up his shotgun, and broke it open, glancing into the barrel. "Not loaded."

He set it down again, and took up his rifle. Laying it across his lap, he perched on the end of the couch nearest Cler's rocking chair. The others, including the children, were seated around the cabin, the women and Paxton on wooden chairs, and the rest of the children on the floor.

Dennis said, "This Winchester, I'm told, will take down a moose, easy." He lifted the rifle, brought it to his shoulder, and sighted it directly at Paxton's head.

Cler reached out with his index finger, and casually moved the barrel a couple of inches to the side. The gun went off with a deafening bang. The bullet zinged past Paxton and thunked into the cabin wall.

Dennis lowered the barrel, so it aimed at the floor. "Sorry," he said, "I didn't know it was loaded."

"It's always a good idea to check," Cler said, but he was thinking that Dennis was dangerously ignorant about guns.

Mildred gave her husband an icy stare, and Dennis dropped his eyes, pretending to study the floor. The Reillys excused themselves, and got to their feet. Mildred whispered, "Goodnight," to Gwynne, giving her a peck on the cheek. Dennis caught up with his wife at the door.

"Well, guess we'll head off to bed," he said lamely, taking his guns with him.

The next morning, he came into the cabin, apologetic. "I'm really sorry about last night."

Cler was at the griddle, turning over hotcakes. He was the one who had brought the Reillys home with him, and he figured he owed it to Dennis to help him.

"You folks had breakfast?" he asked.

"Yeah, we ate in the trailer."

Cler said, "So what's your plan for today? Are you going to go look for a homestead? Or do you want to help me go after wood?"

Dennis' face darkened for a moment, "No thanks. Actually, I was hoping you'd take me moose hunting. How about it? Looks like it'll be good weather."

"Let me get the family fed, and we'll talk," Cler said, pouring batter onto the griddle from a ladle.

Dennis left.

After last night, Cler wasn't keen on getting accidently shot by the fellow. Cler sighed. Well, he'd try to give him a few pointers along the way.

An hour later, dressed in his coat and a knit hat, Cler stepped outside into an overcast morning, with his rifle in his hand, carrying his pack with the other. His machete, in its leather case, was strapped to his pack. The weather was not too cold; a perfectly good day for hunting. Seeing Cler with his gun, Buddy ran over and heeled. He knew what was up: they were going hunting!

Cler looked around for Dennis. A camp robber swooped down from a nearby birch and snagged a crust of bread left on the ground near Dennis' trailer. Just then, Dennis ducked out the trailer door, all ready, with his boots, khakis, jacket and hat on. He saw Cler, and started toward him.

"So want to go bag a moose?"

"Sure!" Cler answered cheerfully.

"Can we take my dogs?" Dennis asked. His dogs were playing with Corrie and Paxton, chasing each other around the yard.

"Are they trained for hunting?" Cler asked, patting Buddy, who wagged his tail.

"No, but they need a chance to learn, don't they? Dan, get over here! Dinah, come here, Dinah!" he called. The little black

146

and white dog made a swift u-turn and ran over, but the big pup kept going.

Dennis strode over and caught Dan by the collar, and yanked on it, nearly choking him. "When I call you, you'd better come!"

A pained look crossed Cler's face. "Say, Dennis, if he's not trained, that pup can spook a moose and get himself trampled. Why not just take Dinah and leave Dan here with the kids?"

"Fine," Dick said. "Can you kids hold onto him until we're gone?"

"You could tie him up," Cler suggested.

"He has to learn to mind, and tying him up just makes him bark his head off. Drive you crazy."

"OK, go get your pack, and let's get on the trail," Cler said, waiting while Dennis left and returned with his pack, all ready to go. The men shouldered their canvas and board packs, containing ropes and their lunches. Army green canteens dangled from each pack.

They started off, but Dennis said, "Wait a minute. Forgot my gun." He ran to his trailer and brought out his rifle. He patted his coat pocket. "Got my shells right here," he said.

Cler exhaled a calming breath. "Before we start, I just want to make sure we're on the same page. You know to always carry your rifle safely." He demonstrated with his own rifle, tucking the stock under his arm, his hand on the grip. "Barrel down," he said.

Copying him, Dennis frowned, "OK, I've got it. Now let's go!"

"Fine," Cler said, striding off across the field, while Dennis, with shorter legs, worked to keep up, and the dogs ran ahead of them. A minute or two later, Cler stopped. "Say, Dennis. Whatever you do, don't shoot *anything* down over the Bluff."

"Why not?" Dennis asked, a little miffed.

"I'm sorry," Cler said, "but I, for one, don't want to pack 1000 pounds of meat up a cliff! You shoot anything down over the bluff and you'll pack it up by yourself!"

Dennis Reilly laughed, as if Cler were joking, but he wasn't. "The other thing is, it's bull season. You can only shoot a bull."

"I suppose I can tell a bull from a cow," Dennis said, still a bit testy. They reached the start of the old wood trail, and called the dogs to heel.

"Think we can find a moose around here?" Dennis asked, gesturing with his 30-06 in his hand.

"Pretty good chance," Cler said. "Listen, we'll go toward the Bluff for a ways, then split up. I'll head east and you go west, and we'll meet back at the cabin at noon or when one of us gets a moose, whichever is sooner." They continued on, and were soon walking single file along a trail, with Dennis in front.

Cler shifted his rifle, settling it more snugly under his arm. "One thing. Be careful when you're walking down one of these animal trails. More than once I've had to step into the brush when I've heard hooves pounding, heading in my direction."

"Moose?"

"Yes. If you hear one, just get out of the way! Get in a good place by a tree while it passes, and then you can track it. It'll slow down. Moose are essentially lazy."

They trudged on, without talking. Dennis was listening for a moose that might be galloping down the trail towards them.

11

A MAN WHO SHOULDN'T OWN A GUN

Fall, 1949

The two men stopped on the trail, about a quarter mile from the Bluff. Buddy stayed alert, sticking close to Cler's left leg. Dina seemed uneasy, and stayed by Dennis. The clouds were beginning to thin, but it was still only about thirty degrees out. Dennis shivered, "Maybe I should've worn a warmer coat. It's colder than I thought."

"You'll warm up," Cler said. "So. I'm taking off here. Why don't you head west? If you do, you'll come to a little lake. I've seen moose there. If you get lost in the brush, climb a tree and look for Gun-sight Mountain; it's on the west."

"I won't get lost!"

Cler said, "If you don't see any game, head north until you come out at the bluff. There's a well-used animal trail all along the top."

Dennis took off into the brush, eager to shoot something.

Less than an hour later, Cler heard Dennis' rifle crack, echoing through the trees. Then he heard four more shots. He headed back to the place where they'd parted, and sat down on a dead tree trunk to eat his sandwich, washing it down with water from his Army canteen.

Soon he could hear Dinah barking, and Dennis rattling bushes as he apparently crashed his way through some heavy brush. Dennis emerged into the open, brushing leaves off himself and grinning like he'd discovered Christmas.

He spotted Cler. "Hey! I got a prize moose!" he exclaimed. "A big one!"

Cler stood up, swung his pack onto his back, and grabbed his rifle. "So let's go get the meat!" he sang out, cheerfully. A moose meant plenty of food for both families, and Cler was glad Dennis had been able to shoot his "prize moose."

"It should be north, and west a little," Dennis said. "I found the trail you were talking about, along the Bluff."

Cler suggested they take the wood trail to the Bluff, which they did. Dennis then led Cler along the narrow animal trail that ran along the edge. Far below, the river was a braided ribbon of gray and silver. Across the canyon, the snow-bright peaks of the Brooks Range almost blended into the white sky.

"It's just down this way," Dennis said, still jubilant at having shot his first moose.

Cler had a sinking feeling. He hadn't shot it over the Bluff, had he? *No, I was very specific about that.* Dennis led the way along the trail, shadowed by Dinah, and Cler followed behind, with Buddy at his heels.

Finally, Dennis stopped and pointed. The dogs lined up, too, looking out, and down over the cliff. Cler spied the moose sprawled on a little knoll, about fifty yards down the side.

"Damn-it, Dennis, what did I say about shooting anything over the bluff?"

Dennis looked puzzled by Cler's outburst. He peered over the cliff, to get a better look at the moose.

For a moment, Cler felt like shooting the man. "I swear, Dennis, you're going to haul that moose up here on your own back!"

150

"You don't have to get mad about it, Cler. I can help pack it up. It doesn't look all that far down."

Cler let out an exasperated sigh and gritted his teeth. "Come on, let's get started."

They found a place where they could safely scale the steep hill, without tumbling to the bottom. Digging their boots into the dirt and gravel, and grabbing an occasional willow to slow their descent, they made their way down the side. When they reached the knoll, Cler eyed the moose and slowly shook his head. He set his gun on safety, with the barrel resting in the notch of a willow, and unsheathed his machete. He was still seething, but he was in control. "You remember what I told you about shooting over the bluff?"

Dennis shrugged. "It's not a crime, is it?"

"No, but shooting a pregnant cow is!"

The color drained from Dennis' face. "I wasn't that close! I didn't know..."

Dinah and Buddy were sniffing around the dead moose. "Back, Buddy. Leave it!" Cler commanded, and Buddy backed away. His master's tone meant business. Dinah was still sniffing around. "Tie her up," Cler growled.

Dennis grabbed his dog and used a short rope from his pack to tie the dog to a small alder away from the kill. He stood by, anxiously watching, while Cler sliced open the moose's abdomen, and a baby moose, still in its sack, tumbled out. It was alive, kicking. There was another sack, and a second baby. *Twins!* For a moment, Cler considered trying to save them, but knew it would be futile. He couldn't stop the tears welling up, frustrated and sick as he reluctantly dispatched the calves to preserve the meat, and then busied himself with the cow, needing to get it bled and the meat cooled as soon as possible. He was too angry to speak, and the other man didn't say a word either, seeing Cler wielding that giant knife, with a look on his face that might mean Dennis was next.

Dennis helped by sawing off the hoofs and part of the legs with a hack saw, throwing a bone to each of the dogs, who greedily chowed down on them.

The job of skinning and quartering was nearly finished when Cler said, "Ready to pack up all the meat by yourself?"

Dennis lifted his head and stared at the top of the Bluff, which was way up there. "You must be kidding." It wasn't possible to carry all this meat up there alone. Just not possible.

Cler sighed. Unless he helped, they'd never get done before dark. Left overnight, the meat would be carried off by bears, wolves or other scavengers. He glanced over his shoulder at Dennis, who looked worried. *Good!*

"Not kidding. We're going to haul every bit of meat and bone back to the cabin. I need the meat, so of course, I'll help." He heard Dennis' sigh of relief, and continued, "Here, take this. You might as well get your pack loaded and start on up."

Without a word, Dennis lifted part of a front quarter with maybe sixty pounds of meat on it. With one hand, he grasped the sawed-off leg bone, and the other gripped a section of ribs, and dropped it onto a pack board. When he had it secured, he untied Dinah and told her to heel. She picked up the bone she was chewing on and followed him. Dennis crouched down in front of the loaded pack, shrugged his shoulders through the leather straps and, with a grunt, hefted it onto his back and staggered to his feet.

A few minutes later, Cler glanced up and spotted Dennis clinging to some willows, resting, halfway up to the top. Well, he probably wasn't cold anymore.

Cler gathered up his tools, and called Buddy, who came, carrying the moose hoof in his mouth. "Good luck getting that back to the cabin," Cler told the dog. He left the hide spread over some small alders, to cool and dry a little. When they were finished hauling the meat, he would fold the hide and pack it home, too. He shouldered his pack, and started uphill. When he got to the top of the bluff, he was winded, but he caught up with

Dennis on the trail. The man didn't look too happy, but Cler waved. "How's it going?"

Dennis grimaced. He stopped for a moment, and rested his hands on his knees, with his elbow holding his rifle pressed to his side. His face was bright red, running with sweat.

"You alright, Dennis?" Cler asked, genuinely concerned.

As soon as he could catch his breath, Dennis panted, "I'm fine! Just let me rest a minute."

"Sure. I'll meet you back at the cabin," Cler said, slipping past him, not wanting to waste daylight.

Over the rest of the afternoon, the entire moose, minus only the offal and hooves, was hauled up the bluff and back to the cabin. The bones would make soup or feed the dogs, the hide could be tanned. It was only a half mile from the cabin to the bluff, but adding the climb up and down made it an exhausting proposition. During the trek, the men were too exhausted to talk, or even think about anything except putting one boot in front of the other.

On their first arrival at the cabin, they encountered the dog, Dan, with a small piece of moose hide clenched in his jaws.

Dennis' face clouded over. "You stupid..."

Cler put out his arm. "No matter. There's plenty of hide to be had around here."

Dennis seemed too drained to pursue the dog. He and Cler tied the meat in the porch rafters to air. They gave the liver to Gwynne to cook for supper. "So you got your moose, then, Dennis?" she asked.

"Yes," he said.

"That's nice," she smiled. "Now comes the hard part," she added, "packing it home." She didn't know just how true that statement was. Without any more chit chat, the men left. It was nearly dark as they made their way home with the last load.

For supper, Gwynne dredged slices of the fresh liver in flour and spices, and fried it golden. It was delicious, but the men were almost too tired to enjoy it. Mildred tried to make conversation. "So you shot your prize moose! I'm really proud of you," she said.

Dennis gave her a haggard look. "My back aches, and I don't want to talk about it." After the Reillys left to their trailer, Cler collapsed on the couch, leaned his head back and closed his eyes.

Gwynne sat down beside him. "Hard day, huh?"

Without opening his eyes, Cler said, "Do you know what that numb skull did?"

"You mean Dan, the wolf dog?"

Cler blew out a breath through pursed lips. "I mean Dennis."

"Can't guess," Gwynne answered.

"I told him that whatever he did, he couldn't shoot a moose down over the Bluff. So what did he do?"

"Shot one down over the Bluff," she said. "I wondered why it took you so long to bring it home."

"That was why, but it gets worse. I was mad enough to shoot Dennis." Cler still had his head on the back of the couch, with his eyes closed.

Gwynne said, "Oh, Cler, that's not like you."

"It was a cow and she had twins in her."

Gwynne was shocked. She didn't know what to say.

"At least we have the meat," Cler said.

Now it was morning, a few days after the exhausting hunting trip. Dennis decided that he was going hunting, to bag a black bear, without Cler's help. Maybe it would be bigger and better than the bear Cler had hanging on the back side of the cabin, even though that bear had a beautiful white patch on it.

Dennis called roughly to his dogs, "Here, Dinah. Here, Dan! Get over here!"

Dinah came running, but not Dan, so he went looking for him. Around the corner of the cabin, he spotted him trying to snag a piece of Cler's bear skin. Dennis smacked Dan alongside the head. "Leave it alone! Bad dog!" The dog cowered and slunk away, while Dennis swore under his breath.

154

Out in the yard, sawing a log into stove lengths, Cler had witnessed the incident. "Why don't you tie him up?" he asked.

"He's got to learn," Dennis said. "If I have to beat some sense into him, so be it."

Cler went back to sawing the log.

Dennis said, "I'm going hunting this morning. Maybe get a black bear."

"There's plenty around," Cler said, without looking up.

Dennis was gone for several hours. The Oborn kids played with Dan, who was still just a big puppy, and the dog loved the kids. Buddy joined in the romp and showed the younger dog how to fetch sticks, but Dan was not a retriever.

Dennis returned without a bear. He went out again for the next three days, hunting alone. Each evening, after the children were in bed, the adults visited, played a game of Canasta, and discussed the Reilly's plans. Cler was willing to let them camp at Kenny Lake as long as they needed to, while they were looking for a place to homestead. He had his doubts about their living all winter in the small travel trailer, but Dennis would do what he pleased, and Cler didn't argue with him.

After his fourth day of hunting, Dennis came back dragging a black bear. Everyone congratulated him, and he seemed very pleased with himself. With the interested children looking on, he managed to skin it out and hang the carcass high in a tree to cure. Then he tacked the hide up on the east wall of the cabin to dry.

The wolf dog just wouldn't leave that fresh bear skin alone. He repeatedly jumped at it and tried to tear it off the wall. Dennis yelled at him and he ran away. Later that evening, the Reillys came to visit. Dennis brought a gun Cler hadn't seen yet. It was a Smith and Weston .38 revolver, and he was proud of it.

"I've practiced quite a bit, and I'm a pretty good shot," he said.

"That's a nice pistol," Cler said, "Not really a gun for hunting, but I wouldn't mind having one just for show. Where'd you get it?"

"Got it from my uncle, who used to be a police sergeant. He's the reason I like guns so much. I used to want to be a policeman, but I went to work for my dad, instead. He owned a hardware store in Mandan."

While they played cards, Dennis hung the Colt on a nail on the wall. He forgot to take it when he left.

The next morning was overcast and cold. Bits of snow fell from the white sky, so light that it was hard to tell it was snowing. Dennis had let his dogs out earlier, and when he stepped out the trailer door and called to them, they didn't come. He walked up the hill, and spotted Dan on the east side of Cler's cabin. When he got closer, he could see that the dog was busily mauling the fresh black bear skin, torn off the east cabin wall.

Dennis ran toward the dog, yelling and waving his arms, stopping long enough to pick up a stick of kindling, ready to beat him. Dan saw him coming, dropped the skin and took off.

"Dan, get back here!" Dennis hollered, but the dog ran even further out of reach.

Corrie was in the living room when Dennis slammed into the cabin, grabbed his side arm off the nail, and tore back outside. When the door banged shut, Corrie Lynne jumped up and ran to the kitchen window, to see what was happening. She was a thin little girl, barely tall enough to see out the window, but with her new glasses, she was able to see clearly. There was Dan, the friendly dog she'd played with all day yesterday, running in circles, just out of reach of Mr. Reilly, who was yelling at him. The man aimed his pistol and fired. The dog jerked in mid-stride, as the gunshot cracked, and Dan dropped to the ground.

Cler was stacking wood on the porch, when Dennis ran past him into the cabin and back out again with his .38. Cler heard the yelling and the shot, and ran out to see what was going on. As he rounded the front corner of the cabin, he saw Dennis standing over the dog with the revolver .

Paxton and Lestie were playing in back of the cabin when they heard the gunshot. Curious, they left their play and ran

156

around the corner in time to see the dog, Dan, lying on his side with blood running from his mouth.

They stopped in their tracks. Paxton said, "That guy shot his dog!"

"Why?" Lestie asked, her eyes filling with tears.

"I don't know," her brother said. as they ran back behind the cabin and hid from the terrible sight.

Cler didn't see his children as he strode across the yard. "Say, what's going on, Dennis?"

The man bristled. "Stupid dog just couldn't learn!" His hand gripped the revolver, white-knuckled, trembling. Dan was silent, but still alive.

Fearing the guy had lost his marbles, Cler was ready to take the .38 from Dennis, but he saw the red rage in his eyes, and stopped himself from reaching for the gun. For a tense moment, Cler waited.

Slowly, Dennis lowered the .38, until it pointed at the ground, loose in his hand. The crimson had faded from his cheeks and his skin was turning a pasty gray.

Dan lay still on the ground.

Cler took in a deep breath and let it out. "Better get him buried."

Dennis' shoulders drooped. "I'll get my shovel."

Cler gestured toward the big grassy field, south of the driveway. "Somewhere out there. And, Dennis?"

"Yeah?"

"After you get him buried, maybe you better head on south." He watched as Dennis turned and walked across the yard, and down the driveway, until he disappeared behind the willows.

Gwynne came outside and saw Cler over in the yard near the dead dog. She had heard the shot earlier, but assumed that someone was target practicing. Now she wondered just what had happened. From the expression on Cler's face, she knew he was upset, but couldn't read it. Anger? Grief? She approached him.

"What is it?" she asked, touching Cler's elbow.

He felt for her hand and took it in his. His hands, usually so warm, were icy. Staring off toward the far field, he said, "Dennis shot his dog. I don't understand the guy at all." He explained that Dennis was coming back to get the dog and bury it out in the field. They waited, standing vigil over Dan's body, until it was taken away.

Cler and Gwynne were still standing there when Emma's old car came rattling up the driveway and parked in the yard. Grandma George and Emma climbed out, and Gwynne greeted her friends with a hug each. Emma shuffled over to Cler.

"What you got there, Cler?" Emma asked, eyeing the bear skin. "Look like wolves get that bear skin."

With a nod, Cler indicated the dead dog, still lying where it was shot. "Not wolves; the dog tore it off the wall."

Grandma George approached, and her black eyes grew wide, "Cler! You shoot that dog?"

"No! I wouldn't do that, Mama George." He pointed out in the general direction of the lake. The Reillys had been there long enough that the Georges had met them.

"The dog belongs to that guy, Reilly. His dog wouldn't do what it was told, and he got mad and shot it."

Mama George said, "That good dog! Why he no give him me?"

"He didn't have the good sense to do that. I'm sure you could have trained him."

Mama George slowly shook her head. "Stupid Chechako," she murmured, which was the worst thing Cler had ever heard her say about anyone.

The native people of Alaska had always depended on their dogs, and treated them with respect. Grandma George had four sled dogs, and Franklin used them for hunting and checking his snare lines in the winter. Neither he nor any of his family would ever mistreat a dog.

Emma changed the subject, "We got salmon for you." She handed him the paper-wrapped package.

"That's so nice! Thank you," Gwynne said.

158

"Yes, thank you," Cler added. "I have a nice moose hide to give you. I'll bring it down later."

Emma and Grandma George grinned widely. "You good man, Cler!" Grandma George said.

While Dennis buried his dog, Gwynne walked down and knocked on the aluminum door of the trailer, making a hollow rattle.

Mildred opened the door, "Hello, Gwynne," she said, evenly, but tears filled her eyes, "I'm so sorry about all this. Please, come in."

"It's not your fault..." Gwynne hugged her friend, who was silently weeping. After a moment, they moved into the trailer and Mildred shoved over a pile of clothes on the sofa bed, so they could sit down. They sat side-by-side.

Gwynne put her arm around her friend. "Cler told me you're leaving. I'll sure miss your company; I've really enjoyed having a girl friend to talk to."

"Me, too," Mildred murmured. "This trip sure hasn't been what I hoped. I mean, it all sounded so good when we started out. Now I can't believe we thought we could make it on horseback! I mean, camping out in this weather?" Even as they were sitting there, they could see tiny flakes of snow drifting past the small window over the table.

Gwynne stared down at her folded hands. "I hope you find a good homestead, but it *is* getting late in the season. You and Dennis should probably go south for the winter. Anchorage or the Kenai."

"I guess we will. I'm just sorry about..." her voice trailed off. She picked up a shirt from the pile of clothes, and folded it, laying it in a dresser drawer that was sitting on the floor. Gwynne stood up and took part of the pile. "Let me help you." She sat down with the pile on her lap, and began folding a red flannel shirt.

Mildred said, "You and Cler have been good to us. Tell Cler thank you." Mildred folded pair of khaki pants and packed it with the other clothes. She looked up, her eyes level with Gwynne's.

"You know," she said, "I love my husband, but sometimes I just can't stand him."

After he buried Dan, Dennis loaded his share of the moose meat into a couple of boxes that he put into the trunk of the car. The weather was so cold now that the meat would be refrigerated nicely. He took the bear skin, which wasn't mauled all that badly, and left the bear carcass hanging in the tree as a parting gift. He hooked up the trailer to the car, put Dinah in the back seat, and then he and Mildred left Kenny Lake. Cler and Gwynne, and the children, watched them go, waving as if to wish them well, which, in truth, they did.

In some way, Cler felt that he'd failed. He'd earnestly tried to help Dennis, the ultimate Chechako. Helping one another was the code of the Bush, but Dennis needed help Cler couldn't give him. It was not just mistakes the man made. Anyone could make a mistake, but Dennis had a temper that bordered on insanity. Cler could not trust him around his family.

That night, there wasn't the usual babble of conversation around the table. The children were eating quietly, only breaking the silence with "Please pass the butter," or some other small request.

Inside the cabin was light and warmth, but the wilderness spread out in the dark, in all directions, with hardly a living soul besides the Oborns and the Georges, it seemed, for a thousand miles. As snow fell outside the windows, Gwynne felt the gloom that seemed to pervade the cabin. For her, it was the fact that her friend, Mildred, had left and she'd probably never see her again. Gwynne couldn't help feeling a sense of loss, but she was also worried about Mildred. Married to a man with such a temper... She glanced over at Cler. Few men had the calm, generous nature of her husband. Her gloom lifted, as she realized for the thousandth time, how lucky she was.

Seven-year-old Corrie was quiet, and her stomach hurt. She had seen something terrible, and putting it out of her mind

160

was not possible. After supper, she helped her mother clear the table, and the little kids all went to bed. Corrie went to her room, feeling anxious. Instead of climbing into her own bed on the top bunk, she crawled into the sleeping bag with Lestie, on the bottom bunk. The warmth of her little sister helped take away the chill she felt.

After Corrie fell asleep, she dreamed she was playing with Dan. He was jumping around, and she tried to pet his back, but he had wings that were stiff and hard, like the wings on a dead duck she'd found by the lake once. She woke up with a shriek, and saw that the lamp was still lit, out in the other part of the cabin. Shaking, and crying, Corrie rolled out of bed and went to find her dad, who was still sitting at the table, reading.

When Cler saw his little girl, he took her onto his lap. "Did you have a bad dream?"' he asked gently.

Corrie couldn't stop sobbing. "It was awful, Daddy. I was playing with Dan, but I couldn't pet him, because he had wings."

"It's just a dream," her father said.

Gwynne said, "Just go back to bed and say your prayers, Honey. You are letting your imagination frighten you."

Corrie lifted her head from her father's shoulder. "I saw what happened, Mama. I was looking out the window and I saw Dan get shot! He jumped and cried, and blood ran out of his mouth!" Corrie buried her face in her father's shirt.

Wrapping his sobbing child in his arms, Cler was taken by surprise. How had he missed this? Until this moment, he thought no one in the family had seen Dennis kill his dog. Cler felt his heart break. His child had been hurt, and in some way it was his fault for not protecting her. He stroked her back and cuddled her to his chest. He could do nothing, now. What had happened, had happened, and it could not be undone.

Corrie had stopped crying, and as she looked up, her father wiped tears off her cheek with his thumb.

"Sometimes awful things happen, Sweetheart. I'm so sorry you saw what you did. Instead of dwelling on it, try to picture something good, instead."

He stoked her hair, and held her close, softly singing, "There's a long, long trail a' winding into the land of my dreams, where the nightingales are singing and the soft moon beams..."

Corrie savored the comfort of her father's arms, soothed by his mellow voice. Into her mind came the sweet song of birds and the moon shining on the open fields around Kenny Lake.

Buddy

12
NATURE'S LESSONS

Winter, 1949

Buddy went with Cler almost everywhere. If a dog can conceive of love, then Buddy understood that Cler loved him, and loved Cler in return. The dog seemed willing to do anything for his master.

As for Cler, Buddy was more than a protector, a bear alarm and a fetcher of ducks. He was a companion against loneliness as Cler tromped the woods checking his rabbit snares, hunting, or cutting wood.

When Ben Pinks gave Buddy to Cler, he said, "This is the best bear dog I ever seen. He can smell a bear a half mile away, and he can smell his way back to the cabin in a snowstorm. He might just save your life sometime."

One day it was Buddy's life that needed saving.

It was a bitterly cold day in October and Kenny Lake was partially frozen, but a few ducks swam around in the middle of the lake, where there was still some open water bravely. Cler took Buddy with him to hunt ducks.

The children were back in the warm cabin playing on the floor near the drum stove. Gwynne was peeling potatoes and the lamps were lit as night was closing in.

Gwynne kept going to the door and looking out for Cler. She went back to the kitchen and added sticks to the wood-burning range. She finished peeling the potatoes and put them on the stove to boil.

About then, the door suddenly flung open and Cler came stumbling into the cabin, carrying Buddy in his arms.

Gwynne hurried to close the door behind them. Both man and dog looked soaked and partly frozen, covered with a silvery layer of frost.

"Cler! What on earth---"

Laying the dog down by the drum stove, Cler tried to take off his frozen coat, but Gwynne had to help him; his fingers were numb. With her own hands shaking from distress, she unbuttoned his wet wool shirt and peeled him out of his stiff, icy trousers. She grabbed the Army blanket off the rocking chair and draped it around him. By the stove, under the blanket, he stripped off his long underwear, letting them drop to the floor. Gwynne hurried to fetch dry long johns.

With Cler warming himself at the drum stove, Gwynne dried Buddy with a towel and covered him with a baby blanket. The dog lay shivering and limp, his eyes closed.

Celestia sat on the warm floor near the stove, with her hand on Buddy's damp head, petting him and willing him to be all right.

Her father stood shivering, his teeth chattering, so that he could barely talk. "I was d-down by the lake, away on the other side, t-trying to get a bead on a duck that was pretty n-near the shore."

Sitting just out of the lamplight, Celestia listened to the story. It came in pieces, broken by her father's coughing and

164

shivering. He said that he shot the duck and Buddy ran out and broke through the ice, disappearing under the water.

"I waited for him to come up again, but he didn't. I couldn't wait any longer, so I waded out, breaking a trail through the ice, heading to the place I saw him go under."

"Oh, Cler!" Gwynne wanted to chide him but this wasn't the time.

"I found him, but getting back to the cabin seemed like ten miles instead of maybe one." His voice shook in time with his trembling body.

Even as a small child, Lestie knew what frost bite was. One day Ben Pinks had come to the cabin to visit, and she stood nearby as he rested on the couch talking to Daddy, who was sitting in the rocking chair. Ben noticed Lestie and smiled at her, beckoning her to him. She stood by his knees and looked up at him. His face was wrinkled and dark, and he had shaggy whiskers on his chin. He showed her his hands.

"You know what caused this, little lady?" he asked.

She shook her head, noticing that he had only little stubs for several fingers.

"That there's 'cause of frost bite. Froze 'em right off when my old car wrecked one winter's day up on Thompson Pass. I lay there quite a while. Got my toes, too," he said, winking at her.

Now, watching her father trembling under a blanket, by the stove, Celestia was frightened that frost bite would eat up all his fingers and toes.

After several minutes, Cler dropped the Army blanket to the floor, standing there only in his long underwear. He opened the rear of his long-johns a crack, to let more heat in, and inched closer to the stove.

With a yelp, he jumped and grabbed his backside. He closed up the crack, embarrassed to see everyone looking at him.

Gwynne started to giggle then, covering her mouth.

Cler stared at her and then burst out, laughing, "My backside was so frozen I leaned on that stove for a whole minute before I even felt it!"

If he could laugh, Gwynne knew he would be all right.

In her place in the shadow, Lestie smiled, still petting Buddy. Under the baby blanket, the dog was shivering less. He would recover, too.

Spring, 1950

GETTING RELIGION

Emma George invited the Oborns to attend a camp meeting at her mother's cabin. A traveling preacher was coming to preach an Easter sermon, and all were invited. Gwynne decided she should at least let her children go, since it was Easter. She and Cler justified not going by the fact that Grandma George's cabin was not very big, and they thought the children should be given priority.

With hair brushed and faces scrubbed, the children trooped down the road to the George's cabins, an easy half mile. Corrie was seven, Paxton six, and Lestie was four. They could not remember ever attending church before.

It was one of those gorgeous mornings when the air shimmered, while the sun beamed like a blessing on the verdant earth, just coming alive from winter. A thousand shades of green burst from budding bushes, trees and newly minted moss in shady places.

A group of native people crowded into Grandma George's cabin. The three Oborn children were greeted warmly, and invited to join Emma's children, who sat cross-legged on the freshly mopped linoleum. The adults sat on the few chairs, or leaned against the walls. The preacher stood like a dried reed, with the cold iron stove as a podium.

Corrie, who was not quite eight, had never seen a preacher before, and this one was particularly fascinating. He was a very old gentleman, with glasses thick as Coke bottles. His skin was speckled with brown spots: hands, face and bald head. He was tall, and his frayed white shirt hung from his shoulders, as if

166

on a wire hanger. His hands were too large for his arms. To Corrie, he might have been a hundred, but his gaunt, wizened look may have been merely the effect of his many years in the Arctic, shepherding his scattered flock.

Once everyone was settled in the tiny living room, the preacher began to speak. His voice was surprisingly strong. He started with a prayer, and by the time he got to the "Amen!" there was no doubt he meant it.

The thick lenses of his wire-framed glasses magnified his eyes; to Corrie, they looked enormous, red-rimmed, faded to gray so pale that the irises were almost as white as his eyelashes. For a moment, Corrie thought he was finished speaking, because he just stood there, scanning the little group of listeners. But he was just beginning.

"My friends, since it's Easter Sunday, I've taken my text from Luke 24, verse 46 and 47. 'Thus it behooved Christ to suffer, and to rise from the dead the third day; that repentance should be preached...' It's my job to preach repentance, and so I ask you, friends, and I want you to search your hearts. Have you repented of your sins? Are you prepared to meet your Maker?"

The children stared at the preacher, open-mouthed, while the adults squirmed. All except Grandma George, who only understood part of what he said.

His voice rose a notch, "Is anyone here prepared to die?" Again, he looked over the assorted sinners. No one answered, but he plowed on, becoming more enthusiastic the longer he talked.

Corrie and the other children listened, uncomprehending, perhaps, but entranced by the drama. A few things stood out, like his repeated reference to fire. This was especially interesting to six-year-old Paxton, who, being a little boy, was fascinated by fire. The preacher spoke of the Fiery Pit, where the wicked were continually burned, but were never consumed. There was Hell Fire. Damnation. More on the fires of Hell.

When the children were walking home, Paxton said, "I liked the part about Hell Fire."

Lestie said, "I liked the Lamb, but I don't like blood."

Back at the cabin, the children were asked to report on the preacher's Easter message.

Corrie said, "We kind of liked it, but we're not sure what he meant about getting washed in the blood of the Lamb."

With a big grin, Paxton added, "I really liked the part about Hell Fire."

Cler turned to Gwynne, "Maybe we should have gone. Sounds like a good old fashioned camp meeting."

Gwynne asked Corrie, "Did he actually talk about the Resurrection?"

"I'm not sure, but there was a lot about Damnation."

With enthusiasm, Paxton said, "The wicked get thrown in a fire pit, but they never die!"

Gwynne and Cler exchanged glances. Cler said, "Well, I'm glad you children enjoyed it."

That night, Cler began reading the Bible to his children, starting with the book of Mathew. He realized he'd neglected to teach his children his own religion. He felt there should be more of an emphasis on God's Love than on His Retribution.

He and Gwynne were not perfect, but they were people of faith. They prayed, and had taught their children to pray. When the children were very small, they learned to say, "Now I lay me down to sleep; I pray the Lord my soul to keep. If I should die before I wake, I pray the Lord my soul to take." Then they added their own little prayer. "Please bless this cabin to keep us safe from bears," or "help me be a good girl or boy," or whatever came to the child's mind.

By this time, Corrie and Paxton had learned The Lord's Prayer, and recited it. "Our Father, who art in Heaven, hallowed be thy name, thy Kingdom come, Thy will be done, on earth as it is in Heaven. Give us this day, our daily bread, and forgive us our debts as we forgive our debtors. Lead us not into temptation, but deliver us from evil, for thine is the kingdom, the power, and the glory, forever, Amen." After the Lord's Prayer, they too, said their own prayers.

After a few weeks of listening to her older siblings recite the Lord's Prayer, Lestie folded her hands and knelt at her mother's knee, asking, "Mama, can I say the big kid's prayer?"

Gwynne looked down on her tousle-haired child. "What do you mean?"

"I mean, "Our-Father-who-art-in-Heaven.""

Gwynne said, "Well, certainly; if you know it."

Four-year-old Lestie surprised her mother by reciting the entire Lord's Prayer without missing a word.

BUDDY GAVE HER A DUCK

When Lestie was outside, the faithful black lab, Buddy, would follow her around and lie down near her as she played. One sunny, spring day she wandered across the grassy field to the spruce forest and found pinecones scattered on the ground. She began putting these fascinating objects into a small black purse Mama had given her. It was an old, cloth purse shaped like an oval box with a lid and it had a brown, celluloid handle.

As Lestie picked up pinecones, she followed a trail leading into the trees. The path was soft with dried needles. Buddy stayed beside her. When they came out in the clearing, Lestie saw a small lake strewn with ducks---big ducks and little ducks. Her eyes followed those fuzzy baby ducks as they paddled after their mothers and she said in her mind, "I want one of those!"

Being a dog, and perhaps psychic, Buddy's ears perked up. He bounded through the dried grass on the shore, and leaped into the water with a splash. The closest ducks scattered, and the big ducks flapped their wings, scuttling off a ways, while the tiny ducklings paddled furiously after their mothers. Buddy swam out and cleverly scooped up a baby duck in his mouth. Then he swam back to the shore and waded out of the water with his black, curly hair dripping. Lestie held out her hands and the big dog opened his mouth. Safely perched on his tongue was a little gold and black duckling, which he dropped into her cupped hands. Then he shook the water off his coat, spraying droplets into the still air.

She held the tiny creature and petted it for a moment. Then, she dumped the pinecones out of her purse and tucked the duckling into it. She and Buddy headed back down the trail through the woods.

When she entered the cool, dark cabin, Lestie spied her mother sitting on the couch. "Look Mama!" she exclaimed and opened her purse. "Buddy gave me a duck!"

Gwynne looked into the purse and spotted the duckling. "You need to take that baby duck right back to its mother," she scolded, "It will die if you keep it!"

Lestie scowled in disappointment, and slowly left the cabin with the duckling. She ambled across the field and along the trail through the woods, with Buddy faithfully following.

As she walked, Celestia remembered the black bear Daddy shot and how he'd nailed the skin to the back of the cabin. Were there more black bears in the woods? She wondered. Buddy would know if there was one.

...

After Lestie left, Gwynne heard baby Charles stir in his crib. Cler was gone hunting. He should have been back by now, Gwynne thought.

She didn't know what was the matter with her, but she had no energy. She could barely make herself get up and get dressed in the morning, and would have slept all afternoon on the couch but for Lestie waking her up. A baby duck. What was that child doing with a duck?

Gwynne lay back down again.

Charles was playing in his crib, but he wanted out. He held onto the side rail and jumped up and down. "Mama, mama, mama!"

"Corrie Lynne?" Gwynne called to her seven-year-old, who was sitting on a chair in the kitchen, reading a book.

Corrie didn't need to ask what her mother wanted. She put her book down with a sigh and went to lift Charles out of his crib. He was two now, and getting pretty heavy, but she managed. She took him potty, washed his hands and face, and set him up to

170

the table with a biscuit. Then she went back to reading her book, which she'd already read once. It was Black Beauty, and she wished she had another book on horses. She was fascinated by them, even though she had never even seen one.

PAXTON PLAYS CAPTAIN HOOK

Six-year-old Paxton was bored, looking for something to do, when he spotted his father's machete, the huge knife used for cutting up moose and bear meat.

The only other person in the house at the moment was his four-year-old sister, Lestie. She was sitting cross-legged on the floor, playing with her rag doll.

"I have an idea," Paxton said.

Lestie glanced up at him. "What?" Her brother had a lot of ideas, and they were usually pretty entertaining.

"Remember when Peter Pan and Captain Hook were on the gang plank, sword fighting?"

"Ye-es," his sister said. Their father had read them the story only a few days ago.

"Let's play Peter Pan and Captain Hook!" he exclaimed. He hunted around and handed her a paring knife. "You get to be Peter Pan because you're the smallest. This is your sword."

She took a stance, like a sword fighter, which her dad had demonstrated during his reading of the story.

It took two hands for Paxton to heft the machete from the big wooden block where it was stored. Gripping it with both hands, unlike any sort of sword fighter, he growled out the words of challenge, "*En garde!*'

Lestie just stood there, poised with her puny paring knife as the only defense against a deadly blade that was a long as her arm.

Cler strode into the cabin in time to see Paxton with the razor-sharp machete aimed at his little sister, both of them poised as if for a duel. His first instinct was to yell, but he didn't want either of them to flinch. "Hold it right there," he said, not loudly, but firmly.

The children froze; a tableau of a parent's nightmare.

In two long strides, Cler reached his son and snatched the machete away from him. His heart was still pounding from the shock of seeing what could have been a scene of bloodshed.

Lestie hastily dropped her paring knife beside the machete on the cupboard. It looked like a straight pin beside a shovel. This might be a spanking offence, she thought.

Cler looked down on two sets of eyes staring fearfully up at him. Paxton's were brown as buttons; Lestie's like pools under a blue sky. *I should punish them for their own good*, he thought, but seeing how frightened they were, he felt his resolve weaken.

"Son, you could have cut off a hand with that thing. Yours, or your sister's. What were you thinking?"

Glad his dad had asked, Paxton perked up. "We were pretending I was Captain Hook and she was Peter Pan. Like in the story. When they were fighting on the gang plank."

So that was it. Suddenly, Cler felt complicit in this mischief; he was the one who'd read them the story, with all the sound effects and gestures to boot.

"I see. Well, I'm disappointed in you, Paxton."

Paxton's face fell.

Cler took up the knives and slid them into the knife block against the wall. His children watched his every move. He crossed to the chest against the back wall, and rummaged in a drawer.

"Here," he said, showing a bone handled pocket knife to Paxton. It was dark brown, about three inches long.

"The blade comes out like this." He demonstrated by putting his thumb nail into the little slot and pulling out the blade. Snapping the blade back into place, he handed the little knife to Paxton.

"You try it."

Confused by his father's seeming change of heart about meting out punishment, Paxton fumbled with the pocket knife, until he had the blade open.

172

His father took the knife back. "Practice sharpening a stick with it. Always cut away from yourself, like this." He demonstrated the technique on an imaginary stick. He folded the blade and tucked the pocket knife into Paxton's hand.

"This is yours," Cler said, "as long as you're very careful with it. One of these days, I'll teach you how to skin a rabbit."

Lestie had watched this entire interchange between father and son without saying a word. Now she spoke up, "So do I get a pocket knife, too?"

"No! You're a girl!" Paxton said. This from a boy who'd handed her a paring knife, not ten minutes ago, and challenged her to a duel.

Her father patted her shoulder. "Maybe when you're six."

13
OUT OF THE WILD

Summer, 1950

It was a beautiful day at Kenny Lake. Lestie had been playing outside under a spreading pine tree, making piles of pine cones into designs. She stood up and dusted off her hands, looking around for a playmate, but none of the other children seemed to be around. Even Buddy wasn't outside.

Lestie felt drawn to a path that she had walked with her father a few days earlier. He called it the wood trail, because he walked back there to collect deadwood for the drum stove. This trail led to the Copper River Bluff, a half mile or so back. Silver and black remains of burned trees sometimes appeared through the green leaves, looking, for a moment, like wolves or bears, but she'd seen them before, and wasn't afraid of the dark shapes.

Today the woods were sunny, and the path drew her along. The air was silent, except for a meadowlark that seemed to be singing, "I just love..this pretty little place," over and over.

Lestie stopped when her eyes caught sight of something up in a birch tree. Curious, she approached, and looked up into the leaves. There was a large cat-like animal lying on a fat branch. It had tufts of white fur sticking out of its ears, and its spotted coat shone in the dappled light. She didn't know it, but it was a lynx, a small wildcat. Fortunately for the little girl, the lynx was not interested in dropping out of the tree on top of her. It was more likely waiting for a rabbit.

She passed the cat, and continued down the trail. Around a bend she caught sight of a hulking form only a few yards away. This was something huge; It was a brown bear, and it was tearing apart a rotten log. It seemed not to have noticed her yet, but she didn't wait around. She took off, her little legs barely touching the ground, as she flew back to the cabin.

174

She tugged on the heavy door, and yanked it open. Her father stood up from where he was shoving a log into the drum stove, when he heard the door slam.

"What is it?"

"Daddy! I saw a big kitty in a tree. And then I saw a bear!"

He shut the door to the drum stove.

"Where?"

Lestie was still out of breath. "On the wood trail. Not very far, Daddy. I didn't go very far." She was expecting to be scolded for wandering into the woods, but her father didn't even look at her as he crossed to the door. He stopped, "What color was it?"

"It was brown. And it was really big…"

Cler grabbed his 30-06 and a box of shells. He threw back the bolt and loaded a shell, slamming it into place, and dropped the rest of the shells into his pocket.

Paxton asked, "Dad, can I go?"

Cler shook his head, "Stay in the cabin. Come on, Buddy." The dog leaped to his side.

Gwynne said, "Cler, be careful."

With his heart pounding, Cler took long strides across the field, and into the trees, keeping to the trail. He was angry, sick to think of Lestie running into a bear. He strained to hear any sound in the brush. He had to restrain Buddy, taking hold of his collar. "Heel, Boy."

Buddy quivered, excited, like he knew exactly where they were headed. "Heel, Boy," Cler repeated.

Rounding a corner, Cler stopped in his tracks, grabbing hold of the dog. Buddy strained at his collar, and growled low in his throat. It was a large, brown bear, about twenty yards down the trail, with its back half turned. Lestie was right. It was huge. The bear was occupied, tearing up a rotten log, feeding on ants and grubs.

The dog growled, and the bear lifted its head, sniffing the air.

Cler held onto Buddy, weighing his options. Unlike Ben, he didn't hate bears; he thought they were superb creatures, and he had never killed anything for sport. This was not sport. Only a few minutes ago, he had sped out of the cabin impelled by adrenalin, ready to assassinate the wild animal that could have mauled his child. Why was he hesitating?

In those few seconds of inaction, the bear whirled around. Rising to its full height, its black, pig-eyes focused first on Buddy. Cler released the dog; Buddy knew his job. He barked once, to get the bear's attention, and then dropped into a sort of crawl, with his head forward, eyes locked on the bear's, showing his own canines, challenging his foe to a snarling duel. The bear shut his snout, temporarily mesmerized.

Cler willed his heart to slow, and raised his rifle, snug against his shoulder. He took a bead on the bear's eye, held his breath, and squeezed the trigger. The gun exploded with a concussion that echoed through the trees. Without waiting to see where the bullet hit, Cler jammed another shell into the chamber. The bear shook its head, stunned, as Buddy barked and snarled, dodging forward, springing back.

The bear roared, furious. Dropping to all fours, it heaved itself after Buddy, who flipped around, dashing away, drawing the animal toward the brush.

Cler took careful aim, hit the bear just behind the ear, and reloaded. The bear roared, confused and half-blinded. Cler just had time to reload as it headed for him. He got off another shot, and launched himself behind the trunk of a dead tree, loading as he ran. He steadied his arm against the tree and squeezed the trigger. The massive animal rolled to the ground and laid there. Buddy stayed where he was, with his legs splayed, ready to leap into action if the bear moved.

Cler's hands shook, as he set his gun against the tree, and leaned beside it, letting his heart slow down. He watched for a moment, eyeing the bear. It was crumpled on the ground, like a piled rug. He felt a pang of regret for having killed it.

Still a bit winded, he hiked back to the cabin. Cler thought of his little Curly Locks. No, if he had it to do again, he'd definitely shoot the bear.

In the still cabin, Gwynne and the children had heard two shots crack through the air. They waited, and then heard two more shots, close together. Gwynne knew Cler was reloading like crazy to be getting that many shots off so quickly.

A short time later, Cler slammed through the door. "I got 'im," was all he said, as he hurried back outside.

This time, the children followed to see what their father was doing. He put his gun in the jeep, and then threw some long, heavy ropes onto the wood wagon, which he hooked up to the jeep. The winch was already bolted to the front bumper. He jumped into the jeep and took off across the field, pulling the wagon behind.

When he returned, the whole family went out to see the bear. It lay heaped in the wagon like a furry mountain. One huge paw dangled over the open end. Its claws were like knives, curved, black, and at least six inches long.

"Look at that!" Paxton exclaimed. "How much do you think it weighs, Dad?"

Cler stood surveying the animal. He shook his head, "I can't say for sure, but maybe five or six hundred pounds. I had to use the winch to lift it and drag it onto the wagon. Hey, shut the dog in. I don't want him wallowing in guts."

Paxton grabbed Buddy's collar and hauled him into the cabin.

Over the next hour, both Corrie and Paxton watched their father winch the bear out of the wagon, and tie it to the cross pole on the swing, hanging by its front paws. The sturdy pole was braced on thick branches, and nailed between two spruce trees.

He laid a canvas underneath, and neatly sliced open the abdomen, careful not to nick the stomach or intestines, with his freshly sharpened machete. Paxton and Corrie were interested in watching the gutting and skinning of the bear. Paxton, because he wanted to learn how to skin a bear, and Corrie because she wanted to be a doctor when she grew up, and was fascinated by the inner workings of both humans and animals. She had a book that showed the different layers of muscle, organs and bones in a human body. Watching the way the bear was put together was very interesting, she thought. She watched her dad separate out the liver and heart, which could be eaten fresh.

The rest of the family retreated into the cabin. While Cler was working, his friend, Don Goodman, came bumping up the drive in his pickup truck. He stopped and jumped out.

"Mighty fine looking bear, you've got there, Cler," he said. Cler laid his machete on the wagon and wiped his hands on a rag, as Don approached.

"Where'd you find him?" Don asked.

"Right in my back yard," came the answer.

"No kidding? Tell me about it."

Cler and Don moved further away from the bear, and leaned against the fender of the truck.

In Alaska's interior, men swapped bear stories in order to learn about bears and their habits, rather than merely to entertain each other. Bears were considered the nemesis of every man living in the Bush. The more you knew about them, the better were your chances of surviving an encounter.

Cler said, "Well, it took four shots with my 30-06."

"Only four shots?"

"Yup."

"Looks like a pretty big fellow to go down in four shots."

"I was lucky, I guess. I was so close I could see the gray whiskers on his snout."

"That close, I can't believe you had time to reload. You're lucky he didn't get you, first."

Cler grew serious, "Don, did you ever shoot a bear you didn't want to?"

"Last week I shot a black bear that got into my shed. I didn't think much about it, one way or another. Why'd you ask?"

Cler stared at the half-skinned animal hanging from the pole by its giant paws. "Well, he's just such a giant of a bear. Like a trophy hunter's dream."

Don said, "I know you have no patience with trophy hunters, but Cler, it was a threat to your family. And you need it for food. There's a difference."

"I know there is, and you're right. We need the meat."

"Well, I'd better let you get back to work." Don climbed into the pickup and gave a wave as he drove off.

Cler took the hide and half the meat down to Grandma George. She said she'd make him a bear rug in return for the meat.

When Cler returned home, Buddy met him at the door and stood trembling with anticipation, alerted by the smell of him. Cler handed him a piece of meaty gristle. "Here you go boy," he said. "Good job helping me today."

On the enclosed porch, Cler peeled off his bloody clothes, dropping them into the wash tub. He poured cool water into the basin, and soaped up a rough rag, scrubbing himself all over.

He shut Buddy on the porch, where the dog would easily hear and smell any animal that came around in the night. Cler had tied the half-carcass up on the swing pole to cure.

Wrapped in a towel and barefoot, Cler almost stumbled to his room, where Gwynne was still awake, reading by lamplight.

"All done?" she asked. She got a whiff of bear mixed with the fragrance of lye soap.

"I'm bushed," Cler said, stepping into one leg of a clean pair of long johns. "I can't believe what I've done today."

He dragged up his long johns and hunched into the top half. Pulling the gaping front together, he fumbled with the buttons, his fingers feeling stiff and sore.

"Need help?" Gwynne asked. Without waiting for his reply, she scooted up in bed and reached to fasten the button at his navel. He managed to get the bottom three done, while she finished the rest.

He made his way around, shoved back the sleeping bag, and fell into bed. The steel springs squealed, groaned and shuddered until he settled himself.

Gwynne reached a hand and brushed back his dark curly hair, still damp from washing. He had a faint odor, but it wasn't bad. She turned and blew out the kerosene lamp. They lay in the darkness, listening to the still house.

After a few moments, Gwynne said, "You haven't told me about killing the bear."

He sighed, "Well, that's about it: I killed him. For the size of him, it's a miracle he went down in four shots."

"You must be kind of proud of yourself."

Silence ticked by, and then Cler said, " To tell you the truth, I have mixed feelings about it. He was so huge; a magnificent animal."

"But we need the meat," she said.

"Yes. We need the meat."

Cler and Gwynne worked hard to make sure their children were fed. During times of scarcity, food was usually adequate, but not abundant. The worst times for the children, was when their parents were not home and there was no bread left in the breadbox. It was one of those times, when no one was there to cook, that Paxton stood looking dejectedly into the empty breadbox. He said, "I'm so hungry, I could eat my own hands!"

Corrie frowned at him, "I dare you to do it!"

Paxton promptly went and found the butter dish and the salt and pepper shakers, and set them nearby on a chair, while he held his hands over the crackling hot drum stove, as if to roast his fingers like hot dogs. As his hands began to turn red, he licked his lips. "With a little butter and salt and pepper, they'll be delicious!"

Not willing to be left out, Lestie joined him, holding her hands as close as she dared to the stove. When she and Paxton both had red hands, they stopped to spread butter on them, which immediately melted, and Paxton shared the salt and pepper, liberally sprinkling Lestie's hot little hands. He began to lick off the butter from his own, and she followed suit. Neither child, of course, dared bite into their fingers, but just the hot butter, salt and pepper seemed extremely satisfying, and they

180

went back for second helpings, warming their hands, and spreading on more butter, salt and pepper. It was enough to tide them over, until Mama and Daddy returned home and cooked dinner.

A MOVE INTO TOWN

The early summer was bright and warm, and Gwynne tried to be outside as much as possible. Like the wild flowers that spread a blanket of color over the meadows, she also came alive in the sun. She enjoyed hanging out the clothes, and sweeping off the porch because it got her out of the cabin.

One sunny morning, Cler and Gwynne slipped away for a walk. It was still too early for mosquitoes, and the air was clear as crystal.

Cler was dressed in a flannel shirt and wool trousers, while Gwynne wore jeans and a sweater. They both had jackets tied around their waists. Even though the morning was gorgeous, the weather could never be trusted. Clouds could roll in and drop the temperature twenty degrees. They ambled down the wood trail, and passed the spot where Cler had shot the brown bear. As usual, they both kept alert for any sound or sudden movement in the brush. Cler had his 30-06 rifle in hand, pointed at the ground, as they walked. Gwynne felt perfectly safe whenever she was with him.

Cler was worried, however. He was almost out of money, with no prospect of any coming in soon, besides the stipend. He owed the hospital in Palmer, the grocer at Chitna, and prospects of making money staying here, didn't look good. He'd need to find work, but it would require a move into Anchorage. He could think of no other way. "I've been thinking, Sweetheart. We're getting low on money, and besides, Paxton and Corrie will both be in school come fall. Maybe we could go into town this summer, and I could earn some money for the coming year, and maybe even more, for the improvements we need out here at Kenny Lake."

"What would you do, Cler? Work on Base?"

"If I can get a job on base, I will. I might even build and sell a cabin or two. I've heard there's a housing shortage in Anchorage, and I will probably be able to sell whatever I manage to build. What do you think? Want to move into town for a while?"

"How soon would we go?" she asked, taking his hand.

"I think we should go as soon as possible, in order to take advantage of the summer and get something built for ourselves, that we can sell later."

"All right," she said. He apparently had it all figured out.

MOUNTAIN VIEW

Within a few days, they had packed up their clothes, tents, and other essentials into the little trailer, and moved to Anchorage. On their way into town, Cler stopped at a small store to buy some groceries and get gas. When he entered the store, a man standing at the counter called out, "Well, Cler Oborn! How are you doing, buddy?"

Cler recognized Larry Straley. He and his wife Laura were the couple Gwynne and Cler had met at the border, when they were all coming to Alaska. Cler explained that they had homesteaded out at Kenny Lake, but were moving to town temporarily.

Larry shared that he had a house in Spenard. "Why don't you and Gwynne stop by?"

"Gwynne and the kids are out in the jeep. We're pulling a trailer and I need to get a tent pitched somewhere before nightfall."

"Easy," Larry grinned. "Pitch it at my place. I have an acre in the trees. You can stay with us as long as you need to. There's not much housing around Anchorage, but there's plenty of land you can buy for a song."

Cler followed Larry's panel van back to his house, and while Larry and Cler stood out in the yard, catching up with each other, Gwynne went inside to talk to Laura. The women were as

182

thrilled to see each other as Cler and Larry were. Laura was petite and dark, in contrast to Larry's light complexion and sandy hair.

Laura and Gwynne fixed some dinner while the men pitched the Army tent. Soon, they were all sitting around the living room, discussing their lives so far in Alaska. Larry worked for the rural electric co-op that furnished power to the Anchorage area. He and Laura had just adopted a tiny, native baby named Gloria. Gwynne thought Gloria could have been Laura's, with her dusky skin, black hair and eyes.

After dinner, when the dishes were washed and food put away, Laura laid Gloria on a towel on the kitchen table to change her diaper. Laura glanced over at Gwynne, "You can probably do this better than I can," she said, only half joking, as she struggled to keep the tiny baby still enough to pin the diaper without sticking her.

"You're doing just fine," Gwynne smiled, and stroked the baby's black cap of hair. She touched Gloria's splayed fingers, as small as a doll's. The baby grasped her finger with a surprisingly strong grip, and Gwynne felt a pang of longing.

"Makes me wish I could have another one," she said, covering her heartache with a little laugh.

"I know that feeling," Laura sighed, and Gwynne felt sorry for mentioning her longing to her friend, who had been trying to have a child for years.

Laura brightened, "You could contact the Welfare, Gwynne. They always have children they need to place. You and Cler would make great foster parents."

Gwynne smiled, "I've never thought about it. When we get settled somewhere, I'll ask Cler what he thinks."

"You know, they pay you," Laura added, grinning, "It's not a lot, but if Cler is hesitant, you may want to mention it."

A few days after they arrived in Anchorage, Cler took a job on Fort Richardson, the Army base, as an electrician for the Army Guard. Now that he had a job, he was ready to buy some land to build a house on.

Larry knew a man who owned a pig farm in Mountain View, north of Anchorage. He was sub-dividing his homestead and selling the lots cheap. Cler and Larry went together to look at the lots, and when the men got back, they were excited.

"There's all kinds of land available out there in Mountain View, and the pig farmer, Aricanen, has a bunch ready to sell," Cler said, shrugging out of his coat. "The land is relatively flat, with swampy areas, but the price is cheap."

Cler made a deal with the pig farmer to buy four lots with no down payment, and payments to start after Cler began to receive paychecks, in about six weeks. The lots had been partially cleared, and had water piped to them. They were situated not far from the main highway, on a rough dirt road that had been cut through the trees with a bull dozer. Thick brush, made up mostly of willows and cottonwoods, surrounded the lots.

They pitched the green Army tent and the white tent, with the pieced-together wooden floor, on one lot, and Cler dug an outhouse. When he got a house built, he'd put in a septic tank. Since the weather was nice, they were comfortable, at least temporarily. The big Army tent made up the sleeping quarters, while the baraba was the kitchen.

Buddy kept guard on the family, and Gwynne felt safe with him around. Though they lived not far from town, she knew if anyone came around, Buddy would bark. The dog seemed to love living in the tent. At night, he curled up on the end of Paxton's sleeping bag, and kept Paxton's feet warm. Peachy slept with Corrie.

They had only been in Mountain View for a few weeks when Buddy followed Paxton into the woods. Paxton had discovered a fat birch tree to climb, and a little pond full of frogs. There was a trail through the brush, that led to the highway. While Paxton was climbing the tree, Buddy went exploring, and when Paxton called to him, he didn't come. Paxton figured he'd gone back to camp where the tents were, although it was unusual for Buddy to stray far from a child he was guarding.

184

Buddy wasn't at the lot. All day long, Gwynne and the children hoped he'd come back. When Cler came home, he was met with the children's cries.

"Daddy, Daddy, Buddy ran away!"

"Ran away? He wouldn't run away. Not Buddy. Just wait; he'll be back."

Later that evening, the man who owned the pig farm came looking for Cler. He was a large man, with a big belly, and hands like hams. He knocked on the doorframe of the white tent while Gwynne was cleaning up dinner, and the children were out in the Army tent, sprawled on their sleeping bags.

Cler answered his knock, throwing back the canvas door.

"Hello, Sam. What can I do for you?"

"Cler, can we talk in private?"

"Sure," Cler stepped outside the baraba, but Paxton, nearest the tent wall, heard what was said.

"Is your curly-haired black dog around?"

"No, he's not. Has he been bothering your pigs?"

"Oh, no. It's just that I saw a dog just like him lying by the highway. I wondered if he was yours."

Paxton heard his father say, "Well, then. Thanks for letting me know. I'll go have a look."

"Maybe it's not Buddy," Paxton whispered to his sister.

Four-year-old Lestie saw the tears in her brother's eyes, but she didn't understand what had happened to Buddy; he simply never came back.

Lestie making mud pies Summer 1950

14

MOUNTAIN VIEW

SUMMER, 1950

    Gwynne hired on as a waitress at a café in downtown Anchorage. Called the Log Cabin Café, it was part of a large, log building known as the American Legion Log Cabin. The local LDS congregation met in one end of the building, renting space from the Legionnaires for Sunday meetings. This was the first opportunity Gwynne and Cler had to take their children to church.

    Gwynne worked weekends, and on weeknights from 5:30 p.m. to 11:30. In order to get to work, she would have to ride the bus. Though it wasn't far, getting to the highway required her to walk through the woods, and the edge of the swamp. She had to cross over a small stream on a couple of logs that made a rudimentary bridge. Then she took a trail through the brush, uphill to the highway, where there was a bus stop.

Coming home, she reversed the order. Even though it was summer, daylight faded after eleven, when she got off work, so she had to carry a flashlight to find her way through the dark woods.

Soon after Gwynne started working, Cler found a little trailer they could buy with a bedroom at the back, a nice little kitchen and lots of cupboards all around. He set up the trailer on one lot, dug a septic tank, hooked up electricity and water, and installed a telephone.

The children slept in the bedroom, while Cler and Gwynne slept on the pull-out couch in the front room. Cler built a lean-to on the side, which provided Gwynne a place to do the washing. He bought her a gas washing machine with a wringer and twin tubs.

Gwynne took care of the children, while Cler worked on Base, and when he got home, she left to waitress at the café downtown. On weekends she worked days, while Cler cared for the children.

One evening she got off late, and walked to the bus stop, which was a block away from the café. It was nearly midnight, but since it was summer, the sky was still fairly light, even though the sun had dipped below the horizon. The streets were deserted. As Gwynne stood waiting for the bus, she didn't see a man approach her from behind. He grabbed her, pinning her against him, her arms at her sides, as he held a knife to her throat.

His filthy words paralyzed her with terror; she had never heard or imagined anything so vile, and she could barely breathe for the horror of it. Just then, a cab came around the opposite corner of the street. The driver slammed to a stop and leaped out of the cab, yelling. Her attacker let go of her and fled as the cab driver chased him down the street.

When the driver came back, he was out of breath. "Are you all right?" He panted. He was a big guy, with bit of a belly on him. He took off his ball cap and wiped his forehead with the sleeve of his jacket. "I'm sorry the creep got away!" Still holding his cap, he leaned his hands on his thighs, breathing hard.

Gwynne was trembling so much that she could hardly answer. "I'm all right, I think..." She felt light headed, and feared she might faint.

When he'd caught his breath, the cab driver peered at Gwynne. "Is there someone you can call? I can take you to a phone."

Still shaking, Gwynne let him drive her to a bar, the only place open at this hour, and he went inside with her, to make sure she was going to be OK. The bartender said he'd keep an eye on her, until her husband came.

As soon as she started talking to Cler on the phone, Gwynne was crying again, barely able to beg him to come and get her. While she waited, she calmed down, and decided she'd tell Cler that she was OK. If she made too big a fuss about it, he'd make her stop working, but they needed the money.

Gwynne was sitting on a bar stool when he arrived; she climbed off and met him halfway to the door.

"Are you all right?" he asked. With a gentle touch on her shoulder, he drew her closer to him.

"Yes," she said, giving him a kiss, and trying to smile. "It's just that there was this creepy guy at the bus stop. He tried to grab me, but a cab driver came by and scared him off. I'm fine, now. Thank goodness for that nice cab driver!"

Cler put his arm around her as he walked her to the car, "You should call me if you have to work late again. I'll come get you."

"If I have to work late, I'll call. But I hate having you leave the children in bed, alone," she told him. "I'll still take the bus, but I'll be more careful."

She sat close to Cler on the bench seat of the car, feeling the warmth of him through her thin coat. She still felt cold to the bone.

They arrived back at the trailer to find the children all asleep, the girls cuddled together in one sleeping bag, and the boys in another. The bed on the fold-out couch was ready and waiting for her, the covers thrown back, the way Cler had left them. The impression of his head was still on his pillow.

While Gwynne undressed and slid into bed, Cler took off his own clothes. He rolled in beside her and drew her into his arms. "I love you," he whispered.

"I love you, too," she said softly. "Thank you for coming to get me." A few silent moments passed. "One thing I didn't tell you is that the man had a knife."

Cler leaned up on his elbow. "What? The man who tried to attack you?"

A rush of guilt washed over her, and she was sorry she had told him.

"Why didn't you tell me?" Cler asked sharply, as if he read her thoughts.

"I was ashamed," she said.

He lay down again, pulling her to him, wrapping her in his arms. "No, don't be. It wasn't your fault."

"I should have watched out better. He came up behind me."

"Hey," he said, stroking her shoulder and arm, "Listen to me. It was not your fault."

"You sounded mad."

"I was just shocked. I should have been there to protect you."

"You can't protect me every moment."

"I know," he whispered. "But would that I could."

Gwynne pulled away a little and lay on her back. "Anyway, I'm fine. I really will call if I need you."

"Good. That's good," he said, snuggling up to her shoulder.

Gwynne lay staring up in the semidarkness. Her eyes traced the wavy lines of wood grain in the trailer's ceiling. The light coming through the small window was getting brighter, as the sun rolled closer to the horizon. She needed to get to sleep, so she could get up and take care of the kids when Cler left for work.

She closed her eyes and tried to fall asleep, but nervous energy played across her chest. She lay there trying to slow the beating of her heart, mouthing silently, "I'm all right. I'm all right. I'm all right."

Cler's soft breathing turned to a deeper, slower cadence, that was not quite snoring. She listened to the familiar rhythm of it and felt herself drift away on the sound of safety and peace and Cler's love that had an almost magical ability to calm her.

On Sundays, Cler took the children to church. After church, the family walked to the nearby café where Gwynne worked. Sometimes they all had a dish of ice cream before going home. To the children, seeing their mother dressed up in a little white apron, with lipstick, and her name pinned on her neat cotton dress, was at first like encountering a stranger. After a while, however, they got used to the idea that mother was sometimes a waitress who served people in a café, rather than only the mother they knew at home. She seemed to them like an important person, working out in the world. It was OK, because Daddy was there when Mother wasn't. If needed, Corrie stepped in, a back-up for her parents. She'd been doing that since she was four.

As the summer passed, Gwynne continued to work at the café. She found she enjoyed being around other people. Shy by nature, and not particularly talkative, she felt herself coming out of her shell. As the weeks passed, Gwynne had time to be alone with her thoughts, as she made her way in the clear, sweet air of summer, from the little trailer in the clearing, through the woods, to wait for the bus. It was a source of wonderment that she was coming alive, finding herself again. It dawned on her slowly, the way the sky begins to lighten to faint pink, then rises until the world is ever brighter, blue and gold.

FARMING IN MOUNTAIN VIEW

From a man in Mountain View, Cler bought a pregnant female goat named Clementine, and it wasn't long before she had two perky little kids, which Lestie and Corrie promptly named Tina and Sylvia. Cler built a small barn and pen, and also strung a wire for an electric fence, so his animals could feed on the thick vegetation around his property.

He made plans to buy more stock. At this time, most of the cows in Alaska were in Palmer, where the weather was more temperate than further inland. In Palmer, there were a number of farmers who had come to the Matanuska Valley from the northern Midwest under Roosevelt's New Deal. These hardy folks had succeeded to a surprising degree, farming in the Arctic. They built barns and kept milk cows and goats.

Mountain View wasn't the Matanuska Valley, but some people had managed to keep cows, so Cler believed it was worth a try. The goats he'd bought were doing fine so far.

Cler drove his truck to Palmer, where he had located a dairy farmer who was willing to sell him a weaned bull calf, and a pregnant heifer. They were black and white. The little heifer had a white heart on her forehead.

On the way home, Cler drove along happily singing a popular song. "I love those dear hearts and gentle people who live in my home town, because those dear hearts and gentle people will never, ever let you down." He suddenly knew what he was going to call his animals: the heifer would be "Dear Heart," and the bull calf, "Gentle People."

In Mountain View, he unloaded the animals into the fenced-in corral, and went into the house to tell Gwynne and the kids. "Come out and see what I've got!"

The family filed out to see the calf and heifer. Paxton picked a handful of weeds and reached over the board fence, offering them a treat. Dear Heart came shyly to investigate, sniffing at the greens. She nibbled at them while the children petted her.

Cler outside trailer in Mountain View 1950

FALL 1950

A RIDE HOME

As fall came on, and the days got shorter, Gwynne found herself leaving the café where she worked and waiting at the bus stop in the dark. It wasn't so bad with the lights downtown, but the walk from the bus stop in Mountain View left her to make her way home through the swamp, in the dark.

One evening, as she was finishing her shift, a man, who came in regularly and had been friendly with her, mentioned seeing her at the bus stop.

"Where do you live, Gwynne?" he asked. "I could take you home, if you like."

It was cold outside, and she thought of that walk through the woods and found herself agreeing to let him take her home.

On the ride to Mountain View, the man put his arm around her. "You know, Gwynne, I'm very attracted to you." He pulled her closer to him.

She froze, unable to move away from him, and unable to speak. She felt confused. She could only think that he'd been nice to drive her home, and she shouldn't be rude to him. With his hand on her shoulder, he went on about how pretty she was, and now he was beginning to scare her. When his grip on her shoulder loosened, she moved away.

At that point, he broke off talking to her, and when they finally reached the trailer, he stopped to let her out, reaching across her lap to open the passenger door. She bolted from his car and ran to the lean-to, her heart beating into her throat.

Once inside, she closed the door and leaned against it, trying to calm herself. She felt stupid for accepting the ride, and stupid for not telling the man to take his hand off her shoulder. "I can't tell Cler about this," she decided.

As she lay in bed that night beside Cler, who was softly snoring, she began to think about her experience with the man who'd brought her home. He'd seemed so nice to her, but she wouldn't trust him again, of course. Maybe he'd come back to the café, apologize, and offer to take her home again. She'd tell him, "No," no matter how nice he seemed.

When it came to other men, she realized she had no experience to guide her. It was probably because she'd begun to date Cler when she was fifteen. He had been her only real crush, and her only love. War and circumstances had influenced their decision to get married young, and now here she was, twenty-six years old, with the experience and savvy of a fifteen-year-old! No wonder she couldn't take care of herself; she had never learned how.

Well, she was having some experiences now, that was for sure. Maybe God knew she needed to start standing up for herself. One thing was for certain, she wouldn't let anyone take her home again. She would rather deal with the darkness and the swamp.

SERIOUS ILLNESS

It was the end of September, and all the children were sick. Gwynne had to quit her job at the café, and stay home with them. The sickness started with cold-like symptoms, coughs and sore throats, including fever. After about a week of those symptoms, a red, blotchy rash appeared, and then moved down their bodies. Gwynne knew then, that it was measles.

She treated it the way her mother treated her, when she'd had the measles. She kept the children quiet, in a dark room, because their eyes were light sensitive, and measles was thought to affect the eyesight. The children slept, hot with fever, and Gwynne had to wake them up to persuade them to drink water or sweetened tea, which was supposed to sooth the stomach and replace liquids lost through their fevers. The rash lasted a few days, and then disappeared. By then, three of the children were out of bed, wanting to play outside. Paxton, Lestie and two-year-old Charles all seemed to recover just fine, but Corrie languished. She didn't stop coughing, and though her rash disappeared, her sore throat got worse.

A week before they got sick, Paxton and Corrie had started school. Corrie, in second grade, loved going to school, but Paxton had to be forced out the door every morning. Since His sixth birthday was in November, and the cut-off was the end of November, he did not start first grade as he'd hoped, but he had to go to Kindergarten. He felt too old to be shuttled into a baby classroom with little kids, and he was angry. He hated school, and his teacher wasn't all that fond of him, either. Now, after being house-bound for ten days, he was willing to go to Kindergarten, just to get out of the trailer.

Corrie Lynne was not well enough to go anywhere. After several weeks, she still had a fever, and was still coughing. Every day, Gwynne hoped she would finally get well. She kept the child on the couch during the day, so she could tend to her as she went about her housework, or did laundry in the lean-to, while Lestie and Charles played near-by. One evening, she gave Corrie Lynne a teaspoon of cough medicine. A few minutes later, Corrie began to shriek. Her mother ran to her, and saw her jerking uncontrollably.

194

Oh, I've poisoned her! Gwynne thought, panicking. "Corrie Lynne, what's wrong?"

The child kept jerking and crying as if she were having some kind of fit.

Cler was working next door, on the first of three log houses he was planning to build. Kitty and Chuck, a young couple who were going to buy a log home from him, were there, too.

Gwynne ran to the door of the lean-to and screamed, "Cler, help! Come here!" She hurried back inside the trailer, and took Corrie Lynne in her arms, trying to hold her still, but the jerking continued.

As he stepped into the trailer, Cler rushed to take her from Gwynne. "Go ask Kitty to stay with the kids," he cried, and Gwynne ran to get her.

Cler wrapped Corrie snuggly in a blanket to try and slow the jerking. She was seven years old, but so thin and light that she felt like a doll to him.

Kitty arrived at the door, "What can I do to help?"

"Just stay with the kids, please," he said. Gwynne slid into the front seat, and he put Corrie in her arms. He took off, pushing the jeep as fast as it would go.

Providence Hospital was a two-story, white-painted building on the North end of Anchorage's downtown. It was only a few miles from Mountain View, and Cler arrived in minutes. Corrie was still sobbing with frustration because she couldn't stop her limbs from jerking.

When Cler carried her into the emergency room, the admitting nurse looked alarmed, "Bring her right back," she said, rushing to open the door to the treatment area.

Before Cler had time to lay Corrie on the exam table, the doctor was there. He quickly assessed the situation, and sent the nurse to bring a needle full of sedative. With Cler and the nurse both trying to hold her leg still, the doctor managed to inject the sedative into Corrie's little thigh. In a few minutes, she fell asleep, and the twitching stopped.

"I've seen this before, but it's rare," the doctor said. He was a young man, thick through the shoulders, with blond hair cut like a soldier's, and he wore gold-rimmed glasses. "They call it Saint Vitus Dance. It's almost always a symptom of rheumatic fever when it occurs in children. Has she been running a fever for a while?"

Gwynne spoke up, "She had the measles, but she just didn't get well like the rest of our children. She had a sore throat, and then a cough that wouldn't go away." Gwynne was afraid to tell him, but felt she had to. "I gave her a teaspoon of cough medicine, right before she started jerking. Do you think..."

The doctor could tell Gwynne was troubled. "What kind of cough syrup was it?" he asked gently.

"Something the doctor prescribed for all the kids when they first got the measles. They all took it, but..."

The doctor said, "No, that isn't what caused this. Rheumatic fever is caused by a strep infection, which also causes St. Vitus Dance, which she has. From her symptoms, I'm sure she has the infection all through her system, even if her throat isn't sore, any more. I'm going to start her on sulfa drugs right away."

Corrie Lynne was admitted to the hospital, where she had to undergo daily blood draws, to determine if the sulfa was killing the infection. The medicine was bitter, but it was chocolate flavored, and she took it without fussing, which endeared her to the nurses. She was not afraid of needles, either, and had an almost clinical interest in the procedures that were done on her, asking questions and watching every move. The staff loved her, plying her with ice cream and other treats, and she soaked up the attention like a sponge.

When she was able to return home, she still had to stay in bed for three months. After being in the hospital, being home was a bit of a let-down. Boredom was the worst part. She worked on the Calvert Course, colored pictures, and read every book she could get her hands on. Sometimes she just laid there, staring up at the wood grain on the trailer's ceiling, listening to Celestia and Charles play out in the lean-to.

196

She didn't get so much attention at home, as she had in the hospital, but Aunt Ella made her a crocheted pink shawl to wear in bed, and Grandma sent her some story books.

By the time she returned to school, she'd missed so much that the principal declared Corrie Lynne needed to go back to First Grade. This frustrated her and annoyed her parents, who insisted she be tested first. She got 100% on the tests, which went up to Sixth Grade.

The principal called Gwynne and Cler in to tell them Corrie Lynne could go to Second Grade. "We were amazed," he said. "We think she is a very bright child."

As they left the school, with their little girl in tow, Cler mimicked the principal's patronizing tone, "*We* think she's a *very bright* child..." He laughed. "Of course, she is! We already knew that."

Fall 1950

IN THE FIRST LOG HOUSE

In the main room of the log house, Cler installed two big corner windows. He did this mostly to please Gwynne, but after the windows were installed, he decided the effect was so good, it would make selling the house easier, when they wanted to go back to the Homestead.

He designed a fairly flat roof that made it easy to sheet with rough lumber. Gwynne climbed up on the roof to help him. She rolled out the paper, and he stapled it down. Then with a bucket of hot tar, Cler tarred the roof.

When the log house was completed, the family moved in, and rented the trailer to a young couple who had a small baby. The husband worked on the base with Cler.

In the new house there were two bedrooms, with a set of bunk beds in each one, and a bathroom hooked up to a septic tank. The kitchen, situated at one end of the big room, had running water and electric stove and fridge. Gwynne and Cler slept on a fold-out sofa bed in the living room. They finished the house with linoleum floors and throw rugs. The black-painted cedar chest was used for a coffee table. Gwynne thought the house was just perfect.

One warm afternoon, when only Gwynne and the younger children were at home, they heard yelling and pounding on the screen door, which was latched with a hook. It was the man who lived across the road.

"Le' me in! Hey, le' me in!"

Gwynne knew right away that he was drunk again. Having been sweeping the floor, she hurried to the door, still carrying the broom. Lestie and Charles hid behind her skirt and peered out at the gray-haired, unkempt man.

"I got to see Cler!" he yelled. Through the screen door, Lestie could smell his breath, which reeked with an odor she had smelled before on a man who had come to the cabin once and talked to her daddy.

The old man kept rattling the screen door.

"You go home, Barnard*," Gwynne said firmly, "Go home!" The hook on the door bounced up, and as she was trying to lock it again, he tore it open. She beat him on the shoulders with the broom handle until he turned away.

She locked the screen, and slammed and locked the front door. She and the children watched out the window as Barnard staggered across the muddy road and back to his little house.

That night, Gwynne told Cler about the incident.

"I think he wanted money for liquor or something," Gwynne said.

"I'd better check on him," Cler muttered, peering out the front window. "Last time I went to check on him, I caught him drinking rubbing alcohol! Sometimes I think it would be kinder to buy him beer."

Cler left and was gone only a few minutes. He came back and took a loaf of fresh bread and a can of tomato juice from the cupboard. He cut the loaf in half and wrapped one half in a dish towel, while Gwynne watched.

He paused before he opened the door. "Barny's drunk up all the vanilla and lemon extract the store will sell him. He says Joe, the storekeeper, won't sell him liquor anymore. I talked to him about staying away from my house when I'm not home. I don't know what else to do."

Gwynne asked, "Will the police do anything?"

He shook his head. "Nah. The police have enough to worry about." He left, carrying the sack of food.

Cler didn't drink alcohol himself, but he was kind and patient with those who did. Alcoholism was an enormous problem in Alaska, because of the cold, dark and isolation, and it was not unusual for Cler to help those who were impaired, who crossed his path.

Gwynne and the children had been there when Cler encountered a slow, weaving car, and drove up beside it, forcing it to pull over. He'd get out and go talk to the driver. Several times, he got in the driver's car and drove him home, while Gwynne was left with the children, to follow and pick up their father at the stranger's house.

While Cler was gone helping Barnard, Lestie sat on the floor playing with her rag doll, thinking about her dad helping a drunk person. When Cler returned, Lestie asked, "Is Barnard a bad man, Daddy? He scared us."

Cler shook his head, "No, Curly locks, but he's a sick man. He won't bother you anymore; he promised me."

Gwynne raised her eyebrows and looked sideways at Cler, "Let's hope so."

BLACK SATIN

It was raining and cold when Cler found Dear Heart and her newborn calf out in the grassy enclosure. The calf was lying on the ground, wet and shivering. He picked it up and carried it to the house. With the calf in his arms, he kicked against the front door, and Corrie let him in. "What's wrong Daddy?" she asked, as

199

he brought the calf over by the stove. The other kids gathered around, while Gwynne rushed to fetch a blanket, and a towel.

"Dear Heart had her baby," he said. "Paxton, go shut Dear Heart in the shed, will you? This calf is a little cold, so I'm trying to warm him up." He briskly rubbed the calf's wet, black coat with the towel, "Come on, little guy. You can make it."

Corrie said, "He sure is pretty. Can we name him Black Satin?"

"Sure." He kept rubbing.

When the little calf was dry, he seemed to perk up. Cler picked him up from beside the stove. "OK, Black Satin. Want to go get some milk from your mama?"

Out in the barn, Cler encouraged the calf to nurse. He squirted a little milk into its mouth, and in a few minutes, Black Satin was nuzzling his mother for more.

Later, before Cler went to bed, he checked on the cow and calf in the shed. Black Satin was lying stiff on the hay, dead. The only thing Cler could figure was that the calf wasn't warm enough when he took him outside.

Weather in Anchorage continued cold and rainy. Everything seemed damp, and the chill went right to the bones. It penetrated coat, hat and long underwear. Probably because of this damp weather, it was only a few weeks before Gentle People, the bull calf, died.

Cler didn't want to take a chance on losing Dear Heart. He loaded her up and hauled her to Palmer to Mel Sanders, the farmer who'd sold her to Cler. Mel agreed to keep her in his barn, through the winter.

15

FOSTER PARENTING

WINTER 1950

After they moved into the log house with the big windows, Gwynne found a way to earn some income, without working at the café, and at the same time help ease the empty spot she had in her heart. She signed up to take a foster child. Mrs. Wade* (not her real name), the social worker, came to the log house to interview Cler and Gwynne, and see about what kind of living arrangements they had.

Mrs. Wade was a short, dark woman with a slightly hunched back. She was very blunt, to the point of rudeness, but she said she approved of Cler and Gwynne as parents and admired their snug home and attractive, polite children. She soon brought to them a little native girl, named Becky. Gwynne could tell that Mrs. Wade had a special relationship with Becky, a beautiful child, with black hair and eyes. Gwynne loved her right away. Mrs. Wade explained that the child had been given up by her adoptive family, because the young couple who had her couldn't deal with her.

The social worker explained that Becky's problems came from the many things the child had gone through, including having Meningitis when she was two, which had rendered her deaf. Now she was four, coincidently the same age as Celestia.

Gwynne soon realized she had her hands full: Becky wasn't potty trained; she was a fussy eater; she tore holes in her mattress; had had no discipline; and threw the most violent temper tantrums Gwynne had ever seen. Still, the child responded to being held, and liked her baths. Becky was put in a baby crib in

201

the girls' room, where Corrie and Lestie could get help for her if it was needed.

At first, Lestie didn't like the new situation. She was her daddy's little girl, and he should appreciate the fact that she didn't throw tantrums. It irritated her that he had another little girl to hold on his lap, and that Becky was such a brat.

It wasn't too long, however, before Becky's tantrums diminished, and all the children, including Lestie, enjoyed playing with her. Becky was soon potty trained, and eating better. She became more responsive to others. When someone wanted to get her attention, they had to stomp on the floor and Becky would turn toward the vibrations. She also looked up when a plane flew over. In these small ways, she became acquainted with the world beyond her limited hearing.

When Cler turned on the radio, Becky would put her hand on it to feel the music; she'd get a faraway look in her eyes as if she remembered hearing music before she became deaf. Gwynne decided that most of Becky's problems came from frustration in not being able to talk.

With other children around and discipline, Becky blossomed. She learned to eat better, to wait her turn, and to play with others. Her tantrums decreased, and Mrs. Wade was thrilled with her progress.

One morning after breakfast, Gwynne was holding Becky on her lap, brushing her dark, shiny hair. "I always wanted a brown-eyed girl," she said. "Now I guess I have her!" She kissed Becky on the cheek and the little girl smiled, showing her tiny white teeth.

Lestie watched this from her seat across the table. Mother had often sat Lestie on her lap and brushed her hair like that. She felt a little stab in her heart. She asked, "Mama, do you like black hair best?"

Gwynne continued to brush Becky's hair. "I like it, too," she said, not looking up.

Lestie was satisfied with that.

202

It was raining when Gwynne loaded all the children into the car and drove to the Welfare office downtown, where she had to take care of some business involving Becky's medical bills. The children waited in the car while Gwynne went in. Becky kept rolling down the car window and Paxton tried to make her stop, but she kept doing it, so he slapped her hand.

It happened that a woman coming from the building saw the incident and turned right around and stormed into Mrs. Wade's office, reporting that Becky was being abused. The next day, Mrs. Wade, who had a hot temper, appeared at the Oborn's house and demanded Gwynne turn Becky over to her.

Gwynne was devastated. She tried to explain what had happened, but the woman wouldn't listen, so she sadly packed Becky's things.

Perhaps Mrs. Wade had cooled down after she thought things over. At any rate, she showed up the next day with a fat little Aleut baby, named Donny. This baby was going to be adopted, but they needed someone to care for him while he was having treatments in Anchorage, to burn off a large strawberry birthmark on his head.

"Will you take him?" Mrs. Wade asked, sounding a bit humble, Gwynne thought.

Of course, Gwynne was delighted, and Donny was loved, cuddled and shamelessly spoiled by the whole family for the next three months.

Eight-year-old Corrie Lynne was well aware that somewhere there was a couple who intended to adopt little Donny. As the birthmark faded over time, she knew it would not be long. When she knelt on her bunk bed each night to whisper her prayers, she'd always add, "And please make the people decide not to adopt Donny."

Corrie was at school when the day came and a young man and woman arrived with Mrs. Wade to pick up the baby. Two-and-a-half-year-old Charles watched Donny being carried out the door in a strange woman's arms.

"Why can't we keep my baby brother?" he asked, sorrowfully.

As Gwynne closed the door, she turned to look at her little boy with tears welling in his big, brown eyes and she stooped to hug him. She hadn't realized how the loss of Donny might affect the child closest to him in age. He wasn't the only one who felt terrible: she did, too.

When Corrie came home from school she ran to check the crib in her room, and Donny was gone, but she still had hope.

"Mama, did the people want Donny?"

"Oh, Honey! What do you think? Of course, they loved him right then. As soon as they saw him."

Corrie could picture the chubby baby waving his little arms in greeting. His bright smile, dimples and big, brown eyes. She knew for certain the people would not be bringing Donny back, and her chest hurt like something was trying to squeeze the breath out of her.

Gwynne hadn't meant for it to happen: you weren't supposed to "get attached" to a foster child. But they had all bonded to the baby, and they all felt the loss.

When Cler got home from work, he was engulfed by his children, "Daddy, Daddy, they took Donny away!"

Gwynne was at the stove stirring something in the big iron kettle. Smelled like beans with tomatoes and onions. She put down the spoon. Cler could tell by the stricken look on her face that she was hurting.

"I'm sorry," he said, stooping to kiss her.

He addressed the children, who gathered around, waiting for a word from Daddy that would make it better.

He only stated what Gwynne had told them earlier. "We knew when we took him that we'd only get to have him for a little while."

"But we wanted to keep him," Corrie said, distraught, taking her father's hand. "I prayed and prayed."

Her father squeezed her hand. "We'll all miss him."

204

That night, as Gwynne and Cler lay on the bed in the front room, and the chatter in the children's rooms had died away, Gwynne lay facing the wall. Cler felt the bed shake and put a hand on her back. She was silently crying. He was surprised she was taking this so hard. They'd only had Donny three months, and she'd always known he wasn't theirs to keep.

Cler sighed, wondering what he should say to her. "You really got attached to the cute little guy, didn't you?"

He heard her sniffle and she turned over onto her back, staring up at the ceiling, lit dimly by the starlight coming in the corner windows. She wiped her eyes on the edge of the sheet.

"I don't know why I'm so devastated," she said. "What's the matter with me? I guess being a foster parent is too hard! I don't think I'll take another child."

Cler said, "I think you've done an amazing job. Think of how you helped Becky. But you've been able to have four babies of your own."

In her mind, she heard the word *five. I might have had five.* A sob from deep inside erupted from her throat in a gasp, and Gwynne tried to shut off the tears that flowed again, running down the sides of her temples. She sat up, hugging her knees. She pulled on the sheet so it could reach her eyes, and wiped at her face. After a minute, it came to her: the reason that letting Donny go had hit her so hard.

She lifted her head from her knees and said slowly. "Cler. There's something...I want to tell you. I should have told you already, but, well, I think I felt ashamed, like I'd done something wrong, but I didn't know! The truth is, I wasn't consulted."

Cler sat up on the bed, scooting so his back was against the wall. In a low voice, so as not to wake the children, he asked, "Gwynne, what are you talking about?"

She glanced over at him, sitting beside her in the dim light. She could just make out the shadows where his eyes were, and the little glint in them from the window. She put her head back on her knees, unable to face him.

"I'm talking about the operation I had in Palmer...when... they took everything out. I didn't know! Not until I woke up from the ether and I heard the nurse and doctor talking." And then it came out in bits, and Cler read the rest in the pauses between sobs. He had known she was depressed and sad after the operation, but he'd always believed it was only because she could never have another baby. Now he learned that part of it, a very important part, was that she'd been pregnant at the time, without knowing it.

"Doctor Graham told me that another baby might kill me. But what if he was wrong, and it really wouldn't have? I should have jumped off that operating table and run out of the hospital!"

She was crying again.

Cler thought of the old doctor, overworked until his heart gave out. He took Gwynne in his arms, murmuring, "It's nobody's fault. Sweetheart, just let it go." There was nothing more to say, so he just held her, but his own heart was aching.

BACK TO CIVILIZATION

In mid-December of 1950, Cler ordered a Jeep Station Wagon from a local dealer. The cost of the vehicle was greatly discounted if he picked it up in the States, instead of paying to have it shipped to Alaska, so he asked for the new vehicle to be delivered to Ogden, Utah.

Cler arranged for the couple in the trailer to take care of the goats while he was gone, and paid them by giving them a month of free rent. They could milk the goat and have it for their baby. Other than that, there wasn't much work to do, except keep an eye on the log house, and throw the goats some hay every day.

The first part of the journey took the Oborn family from Anchorage to the Port of Valdez. On the way, they drove over Sheep Mountain easily, as the road was freshly plowed. On to Glenn Allen, past Copper Center, past the road to Chitna. At this point, Cler told all the kids to wave hello to the Homestead, which, of course, was ten miles away, down the Edgerton Cut-off.

From the intersection of the highway and the Cut-off, it was another eighty miles to Valdez, over Thompson Pass.

This was only the second year that Thompson Pass was not closed during the winter. The Pass had been considered impossible to keep open, as it often filled up with thirty or forty feet of snow. The winter of 1949-50, a private contractor had proved it was possible to keep the road open. This year, the Road Commission took over maintenance, and the Alaska Steamship Company was taking advantage of this access to the interior of Alaska by offering travel to the States out of the Port of Valdez. Cler's intrepid little jeep drove up the winding pass with only a little slipping on the ice where the ascent was steepest.

To Corrie, it was like driving in a white tunnel. She peered out of the jeep's plastic windows, but the wall of snow on both sides, cut through by the plow, was so high she couldn't see the sky.

Soon the family was safely up and over the mountain, and headed down to the coast.

Valdez was a small port town, established in gold and copper mining days. From the turn of the century to the late thirties, Copper ore, mined in the mountains around Chitna, was carted by narrow gage rail to the coast, smelted down, and shipped Outside from Valdez. Copper was first discovered there by two prospectors, who sold out two years later to big mining interests. It wasn't long before violent disputes had erupted between rival mines over special timber needed for the smelters. The only good timber grew on the coast and the mining companies fought viciously over the available supply.

A roadway had been cut, with great difficulty, through Keystone Canyon and over Thompson Pass, allowing access to the interior of Alaska. This was the only other access from the coast, other than the narrow gage rail, which took a different route. The road through Thompson Pass became a freight route between Valdez and points inland. It also serviced the mines near Chitna, via the Edgerton Cutoff. For wagon drivers, the pass itself became a deadly running of the gauntlet, as hired gunmen from different mining companies waited in the rocks, to shoot their rivals, as they maneuvered their wagons through the narrow pass.

Later, in the first decades of the twentieth Century, railroad barons fought over building a railroad through Keystone Canyon and over Thompson. It never happened. By 1938 the mines at Chitna shut down. when shipping the ore became unprofitable.

On their trip to the States, the Oborns stayed in an old hotel in Valdez that hearkened back to mining days. It was two rickety stories tall, its siding weathered silver, and it stood across the street from the wharf, where the steamship, Baranof, was docked, getting ready to take passengers and freight to Seattle.

Inside the hotel, an elderly clerk greeted the family and checked them into a room. Cler carried two large suitcases, and Gwynne carried Charles. Corrie and Paxton both toted boxes tied with ropes for handles. A worn stairway lead up to a narrow hallway, where the floorboards rippled with age. A half dozen faded, wooden doors marched down both sides of the hall.

Cler unlocked the door to their room with a large, iron key.

While her parents were busy settling into the room, four-year-old Lestie wandered down the hall, and spied a door ajar. She peered into the room; her eyes stopped on the belly of a long, white creature standing on four stubby legs. She was shocked to see it had big claws on its feet!

Running down the hall, she cried, "Daddy, Daddy! I saw a big white monster!"

Cler took her hand to go see the "monster" and when he spied it, he burst out laughing.

"Honey, it's just a big bathtub!" He led her into the bath room, "Here, just look at it."

Clutching her father's hand, Lestie stood on tiptoe to see over the monster's side. "Oh," she said. It wasn't alive.

Cler was still chuckling as he led her back to their room. "Well, it's high time we got back to civilization," he told Gwynne. "Lestie doesn't know what a bathtub is! You know, it's been a while. I believe I'll take a towel down the hall, and avail myself of that hot water!"

Cler had arranged for a man to buy the jeep. He left the room to meet the man and returned a few minutes later with the money. Corrie Lynne stopped playing on the bed to watch her parents counting out a pile of bills on the table, in the corner of the room.

"It's not a fortune," she heard her father say," but it'll have to do. When we get to Utah, we can borrow a little from my dad, if we have to."

The next morning, it was overcast and beginning to drizzle as they walked a few hundred yards from the hotel to the water, where fishing boats dotted the harbor, and the steamship was docked. From where they stood on the dock, they could only see the side of the huge ship; it looked like a black mountain rising up beside the wharf. They waited in line, with their baggage, along with many other passengers, as the purser checked tickets and stewards took away their luggage. When it was their turn, the family walked together up the gangplank.

Corrie, who seemed to know a lot for an eight-year-old, took her sister's hand. "This ship is going to take us back to Civilization," she said.

"What's that?" Lestie asked.

Corrie thought for a moment, "It's not Alaska," she said.

The Baranof was a fine, large ship, one of five passenger ships owned by the Alaska Steamship Company. They had a booming business during the Yukon Gold Rush, freighting passengers and supplies. During the reign of Kennecott copper mining, they made a fortune hauling ore, and freighting for the canneries that sprang up all along the coast of Alaska.

When the second World War started, Alaska Steamship Company had a virtual monopoly on Alaskan shipping. The government took over fifteen ships for the war effort, but let the Company run them. After the war, the company's freight business slowed, due to loss of government subsidies, rising fuel prices, and competition with the Alaska Highway. They decided to focus their efforts on luxury passenger ships, and by the time Gwynne and Cler took their voyage on the Baranof, the Company owned four other steamships. (The Oborns were fortunate to have the opportunity to take a ship to Seattle. In 1954, the company suspended passenger service, and reverted to container shipping.)

The Baranof could hold two hundred passengers, with accommodations ranging from steerage to luxury cabins with their own bathrooms. Ticket prices varied, depending how much money one was willing to shell out. Even with cabins in steerage, passengers had access to all other areas. The ship featured a formal dining room, ball room, observation rooms with floor to ceiling windows, and a children's area. The two rooms Cler had reserved were modest, with a bed and two bunks in each room. As soon as they boarded ship, the little family trooped after a steward, who led them down red-carpeted hallways with brass handrails, until they reached their cabins. Cler and the boys would sleep in one room, while Gwynne and the girls would sleep in the neighboring one.

A friendly young man in a white uniform brought their suitcases on a trolley and Gwynne busied herself unpacking and stowing clothing, while Cler corralled the children in the other stateroom. When they heard the ship's horns blast, they hurried to the deck for the "bon voyage."

By now, snow was falling. As a tugboat pulled the ship away from the dock, the crowd gathered at the rail, huddled in coats, where cold spray wet their faces. Wrapped in her father's arms, Celestia put her shoes on the rail and watched the shadowy green coastline slip by, ghost-like in the falling snow.

The ship was slated to travel down the Inland Passage along the coast, and then out to sea. The night they left port, Cler and Gwynne put the children to bed, and then went to the Bon Voyage party in the ballroom. Too soon the ship was rocking on the waves, and Cler brought his wife back to her stateroom.

When they came in the door, Gwynne stumbled to her bed without even taking off her dress.

"What's wrong with Mama?" Corrie asked. "She looks sort of pale."

Cler grimaced, "She decided she'd look good wearing green make-up!"

Gwynne moaned, "Very funny, Cler." The purser brought sea-sick medicine to the room, but for Gwynne, it was too late.

The next morning, Cler and the kids went down to the dining room for breakfast. The tables were set on pristine white cloths, with sparkling crystal glasses, and gold-rimmed china plates.

Gwynne had made Cler promise he make the children use their best manners. "Use your napkin," she told Corrie and Celestia before they left their mother in the room.

After they left, Gwynne couldn't help thinking of her own mother, who had taught her, an only child, how to be a lady. She sighed to herself. Being a lady, she knew, was not a useful survival skill in Alaska, but being on this ship reminded her that the niceties of civilized life were still being practiced somewhere.

When the ship reached the open sea, it began to roll from side to side on the waves. Hours passed and the storm worsened. Gwynne stayed in her room, seasick, and soon Corrie and Paxton joined her in their staterooms, where they moaned in bed, each of them keeping a basin close by.

At lunchtime, Cler took Lestie and Charles, and made his way to the dining room, with his children clinging to him, while he kept one hand on the rail, to avoid from being thrown into the walls. In the big dining room, the tables were bolted to the floor; they tipped and rolled with the ship. At first, the dishes mostly seemed stuck to the thick, white table cloths. Cler chose a table just as the ship lurched and a plate crashed to the floor. At this point, the stewards dashed around, grabbing china, goblets and other items off the tables, stacking them on wheeled carts. The purser announced over the commotion that meals would be served in the staterooms to those who desired it. The few passengers at the tables abandoned the dining room and Cler led his children back to their own staterooms.

"Do any of you want some lunch?" Cler asked, opening the door to the room where Gwynne and Corrie were in bed with the lights off.

He heard only moans in reply to his question. Cler shut the door softly and stumbled to the next room, leading his two children.

Cler told Charles and Lestie to be good, while he laid himself down on the bunk opposite Paxton, looking pale.

"We're hungry," Lestie complained.

"Be patient!" Cler murmured, closing his eyes.

When the steward knocked on the door, Celestia opened it.

"Will you be ordering lunch?" the man asked, holding onto the door frame to steady himself against the rolling of the ship.

Lestie ordered for Charles and herself, "Yes. We want chicken and potatoes and gravy, please!" She heard her father groan. As soon as the door closed, he put his pillow over his head.

With most of the family staying in bed, Charles and Lestie were left to enjoy the novelty of wandering around by themselves on the ship. After downing their lunches, they sneaked out of the cabin and ran in the halls, laughing out loud as they careened from one wall to the other. A young purser in a spotless white uniform caught the children literally bouncing off walls, "Please, children, hold on to the hand rails!"

They found their way to an observation lounge, and stood with little faces pressed against the cold glass. There was no sea or sky; only the gray of rain sheeting the windows, and waves crashing, turning into white foam on the deck. The same purser who'd caught them running in the halls approached the children.

"Hi," he said, stooping down beside them, "Where are your parents?"

Lestie looked directly into the man's eyes that were clear as ice, but friendly. "They're all sick," she said. "Throwing up. It's yucky."

212

The man smiled, "There's a lot of that going around. Hey, tell you what. If you'll be good, I'll take you to the children's activity room. Then I'll tell your Daddy where you are."

The activity room had small tables and chairs, a bookcase of children's story books, bins of paper and crayons. There were no other children there.

"I'm going to turn on a show for you," the purser said, leading them to a corner where a small box sat on a stand. The stand was bolted to the floor, and the box was strapped to the stand.

The purser fiddled with buttons and knobs, and a green window on the front of the box flickered into pictures. A low humming sound turned into music and a high-pitched voice called out, "Hey, kids! What time is it?"

A bunch of children shouted out, "It's Howdy Doody time!" and then burst into a song using the familiar tune of "Tah ra ra boom de ay!" Lestie recognized the tune; her father used to sing it as he cooked sometimes. The children in the box were singing, "It's Howdy Doody time! It's Howdy Doody time!"

Charles, being not quite three, was mesmerized by the moving pictures.

Lestie asked the purser, "How can they all get in the box?"

The young man laughed. "You've never seen one of these, I guess. It's called television. Have you ever seen a movie?"

Lestie shook her head.

He said, "Well, it's like a storybook come alive. We have a special set-up on the ship, just for this television. Amazing, isn't it?"

"Amazing," Lestie echoed. As she watched, she figured out that Howdy Doody was a freckle-faced puppet and he had a grown man friend, named Cowboy Ted. Cowboy Ted was a doughy looking man in a cowboy outfit, and he wore a cowboy hat. It seemed to her that he was wearing a really funny costume, and he was very silly.

16

BACK TO CIVILIZATION

December, 1950

Seas grew calmer as the ship traveled south, into warmer waters, and once again the family was up and around. Lestie and Paxton wanted to go outside, so Cler had them bundle up and he took them out on deck. The air was cold, and the sea was brighter, but still under overcast skies. There was nothing to see out there but waves and an occasional sea gull, so the children went back to the reading room to look at books.

There were activities on the ship for everyone. In the movie theatre, the family saw "She Wore a Yellow Ribbon," an exciting western with John Wayne and Ben Johnson, who was Gwynne's favorite movie star, she said. There were cavalry men, stampeding horses, and beautiful women who needed rescuing from an impending Indian attack. This was the first movie the Oborn children had ever seen, and even Charles was mesmerized by the action and drama playing across the big screen.

The adults attended a dance in the ball room with a live quartet, and one night there was a Silly Hat contest. Passengers had to make a hat out of whatever was available. Gwynne concocted a wonderful bonnet made from a coat hanger, a roll of toilet paper and various fruits from the fruit bowl in the cabin.

Cler couldn't help laughing when he saw his wife sporting her crazy hat, but he shut up and bowed like a gentleman, "May I escort you to the dance, my lady?" It was no surprise to him when she won the prize for "most creative."

Early one morning, the low, sad sound of the ship's horns woke up Lestie. She slipped out of bed and opened the door to the hallway. Her father was just leaving his room next door. He spied his daughter and took her hand.

214

"That sound means we're approaching land. Let's go see!"

He led her to the windows of the dining hall, where they stood and watched the dim coastline begin to take form. At first there was a faint, gray line along the edge of the lighter gray sea. Then the wavy line seemed to grow higher, filled in with darker shapes. The shadows became a forest of rectangle shaped buildings that grew larger and larger.

Cler said, "Look, Curly Locks! That's the Port of Seattle. Did you ever think buildings could be so big?"

She stared, trying to fathom the approaching buildings, which grew, slowly filling up the view. The ship slowed, approaching the wharf. Here, other ships were docked. Cler explained the scene, as best he could, to his little girl. He pointed out warehouses that stored things unloading from the ships, and canneries where salmon were processed for distribution in cities all over the country. All kinds of boxes and people crowded the docks, and tall cranes pointed into the sky. Nearby, where the Baranof was easing up to the wharf, they could see a crane dangling a huge box on a chain, loading a ship next to theirs.

"We'd better go wake up the family," Cler said, suddenly excited to be back in the States. The trip to Civilization had taken only four days.

The train ride to Utah took an additional day, with most of the journey taking place at night when the children were asleep. For the night, porters transformed the space where two bench seats faced each other, into two sleeping bunks, pulling shut a set of heavy curtains to separate the bunks from the aisle of the train. In the morning, the family took their turns in the tiny bathroom, washing up in a little round aluminum sink. Then Gwynne fed the children bread and cheese that she'd packed in a canvas bag, along with other rations for lunch. They expected to be in Ogden before dinner.

"Come on, Curly Locks!" Cler took his daughter's hand, lifting her into the aisle. "Want to go for a walk? I'd like to see more of this train."

"Cler, be careful!"

215

"She's fine, Gwynne," he assured her, leading Lestie ahead of him down the aisle toward a door at the rear of the car. Cler had to push hard to open the door on the end, and then he helped his daughter step over the rumbling spaces between the trains. The air between train cars vibrated with bumping and clacking over the rails, so loud Lestie could barely hear her father sing out, "Upsy-daisy!" as he took firm hold and swung her across the shifting gap. Looking down, she glimpsed railroad ties whizzing below the iron links that connected cars.

They repeated this maneuver from car to car, until they were excluded from entering the caboose by a sign saying, "No admittance!"

Cler read the sign, they turned around and repeated the swinging, lumbering walk from car to car, down each swaying aisle, until they were back to Gwynne. She glanced up from reading a book when she heard Cler exclaim, "Well, Lestie, that was an exhilarating walk!"

Once the family reached Utah, Cler's parents were supposed to pick them up at the Ogden Depot. The huge stone building, with its central arch over the main room, echoed with the sounds of porters calling out for passengers, announcements over the loud speakers, people talking and babies crying. To Celestia, it was a vast, strange world of confusion. She clung to Corrie's hand as they navigated benches, luggage and strangers, trying to keep up with their parents. At one point, they lost sight of them. Lestie looked up to see Corrie's eyes wide and scared behind her glasses, and Corrie squeezed her sister's hand so hard it hurt. The fact that Corrie was afraid, too, worried Celestia. She let go Corrie's hand and put her arm around her, pointing, "It's OK, Corrie. Mama and Daddy are over there, see?'

Sure enough, the rest of the family was gathered over near the huge doors, where they were talking to a short, older man in a brown winter coat. He had a red, knitted scarf around his neck and a fedora, and he wore glasses. Corrie peered at where her little sister pointed.

"It's Grandpa!" she exclaimed.

216

In Ogden, there were all sorts of relatives to visit. There were, of course, the two sets of grandparents, other aunts and uncles, cousins, and even the children's two great-grand mothers.

Cler's mother, Gwendolyn, fussed over little Charles, repeating how much he looked like Cler as a toddler.

Charles was a sturdy, solemn little boy, with his father's tawny complexion, and brown eyes. It wasn't easy to get him to smile, and he didn't say much, but one thing he liked was to eat. He wasn't used to the bounties of Grandmother's house, and when he could, he'd stuff food into his pockets for later.

Grandma was a neat little woman with snow white hair, skin the color of creamy coffee, and almost black eyes that tended to sparkle. She discovered she could get her little grandson to smile when she gave him a cookie, so she gave him several more. She didn't realize that he stashed the extras in his pockets, just in case he got hungry. She discovered this, when she went to wash his clothes. The first time, she found half a dried-out hamburger, complete with bun. Then she started finding cookies.

She took Charles on her lap, "You can have as many cookies as you want, dear boy, but you must not put food into your pockets. Just ask Grandma if you want something to eat!" The idea that food was so plentiful didn't quite register with the child. He continued to carry food around in his pockets, along with a few rocks, rubber bands, and marbles.

Cler's father, Ernest Oborn, worked for Utah Power and Light. He was an accomplished organist, with aspirations of playing someday with the Tabernacle Choir in Salt Lake City. On Saturdays, he taught piano lessons in his home. He had taught his children to play, as well. Musical talent ran through the family, and trickled down to many of his grandchildren.

Ernest and Gwendolyn had raised three boys: Willis, Frank, and Cler, and a daughter, Ella.

Ella was married to Andrew Morse, who was some years older than she was. She had a teenage son, Ernie, by her first husband. She and Andy had two children; David, who was seven, and Susan, five. Another daughter, Andrea, had died during Cler and Gwynne's first year in Alaska.

On their second day in Ogden, Cler and his father went to pick up the new Jeep from the dealership. Cler was so pleased, he couldn't stop smiling. He ran his hand over the smooth, maroon fender, "Not a scratch or a speck of dust on her!" he exclaimed. When he climbed behind the wheel, he grasped it with both hands, sitting up straight. There was plenty of headroom.

His dad slid into the passenger seat, "How do you like it, Son?"

"I feel like a kid at Christmas," Cler said, grinning.

When they got back to the house, the whole family emerged to look at the new Jeep. "Hop in," Cler said, pushing open the passenger door for Gwynne. The kids scrambled into the back. Waving to Grandma and Grandpa, they drove over to Ella and Andy's little frame house in North Ogden. Andy had five acres of land, mostly taken up with a garden, a field and a small orchard.

When they drove up the hill, and into the yard, Ernie came out of the house to greet them. He was a big kid, tall and soft muscled. He had only been eleven when Gwynne and Cler left for Alaska, and at fifteen seemed to have grown a foot. He waved, "Come on inside. Mom has lunch ready!"

The aroma of frying onions and potatoes greeted them as they entered.

Ella came from the kitchen, wiping her hands on a dishtowel. She reached up and stood on tiptoe to hug her brother, "Oh! It's good to see you!" she said, releasing him, and then giving Gwynne a hug. Ella was pink-cheeked and fair-skinned like her father, Ernest, and her hair was prematurely gray. She was a masterful cellist and a grade school librarian. Her husband, Andy, worked on the railroad as a fireman, and had the run to Carlin Nevada, something he'd done for twenty years.

The adults talked over the babble of children, as food was dished from the stove, in the tiny kitchen. With plates of potatoes and gravy, boiled cabbage, and thick slabs of homemade bread, the adults and Ernie took their plates to the front room. The six children stood around the little table, wolfing down their lunch, and then escaped to the attic, where their cousins had what seemed like a horde of toys.

Meanwhile, Ella and Andy asked questions about living in Alaska, and Cler did his best to answer them.

Ernie wasn't saying much, but he was interested.

Cler addressed him, "I could sure use some help on the homestead. Maybe one of these summers, you can come up and stay with us."

Ella and Andy exchanged glances. Ella turned to her son, "Is that something you'd like to do?"

Ernie was surprised; he hadn't even considered it. "I guess so. Yes, I think I would!"

It was almost Christmas, and the grandparents on both sides did as much as they could to make the visit memorable for the children. Grandma Oborn had made sister dresses for Corrie and Celestia out of red and white striped cotton.

On Saturday, the girls were excited to put on their dresses and go to town with Grandma Paxton. She picked them up in her long, black Studebaker.

Cheryl, Gwynne's little sister, was sitting in the front seat, looking like a doll in a red wool coat with a black fur collar and matching bonnet. "Hello, hello, hello!" Cheryl said, cheerily. She was a petite ten-year-old with silky brown hair that came to her shoulders, and blue eyes that seemed too big for her little heart-shaped face. Lestie and Corrie piled into the back.

In town, they stopped at Keely's Drug store. It was a long, narrow store with one big window littered with signs declaring, "Watson's Vanilla Sold Here! Hire's Root Beer; Weber Dairy Ice Cream." Once inside, the three little girls climbed onto round stools that were covered in red vinyl with chrome plated sides.

Cheryl said they should order ice cream sodas with chocolate syrup, whipped cream and a cherry on top. Gwynne suggested Corrie and Lestie share one. The girls ordered, and then stared, fascinated, as the skinny boy behind the counter

219

concocted their treats in mere seconds, plopping scoops of ice cream into tall, frosted glasses, adding a squirt of soda to each, a swirl of whipped cream, and a drizzle of chocolate, topping it off with a bright, red cherry.

Cheryl picked up a long handled spoon, and took a big bite of whipped cream, skimming off the cherry at the same time. She popped it into her mouth, and politely chewed and swallowed before she drawled, "Dee-licious! Come on, girls, dig in like a dog!"

Grandma gave her a look that might have meant, "don't be uncouth," but Corrie followed Cheryl's example, taking a bite that included the cherry. "Dee-licious! Try some, Lestie," she said, and Lestie did.

It wasn't bad, she thought, but she would have preferred a nice stick of squaw candy, the smoked salmon like Grandma George made. They'd only been gone for ten days, and already she was homesick for Alaska.

Oborn Family in Ogden, 1950

CHRISTMAS 1950

Santa Clause came to Grandma Oborn's house, where Cler and Gwynne and the children were staying. There was a little decorated fir tree in one corner of the living room. It had shiny, colored glass ornaments. Some were painted by hand, with little snowmen or a pink-faced angel. Lestie longed to touch the ornaments, but she'd been warned they could fall off and shatter. She had never seen anything prettier.

There were several packages under the tree, wrapped in brown paper, tied with red string. On Christmas morning, the children were finally allowed to open them. Grandma gave all four children mittens she'd knitted from different colors of yarn. Paxton and Corrie received story books, and Celestia got a vinyl doll with black braids, and a doll quilt made by Grandma. Charles was happy with a wooden toy that clattered when it rolled across Grandma's wood floor. It was filled with colored balls that looked like gum balls, inside a cage of wooden bars. Paxton wanted to disassemble the toy to see if the balls were gum, but of course, he didn't try it, at least, not then.

After opening presents, the family drove over to the other grandparent's red brick home, a few miles away. Cheryl let them in, "Hi! Want to see what I got for Christmas?"

Grandpa was sitting in a chair in the living room, and he stood up to hug Gwynne and shake hands with Cler. The children greeted Grandpa and followed Cheryl into the dining room, where there was a decorated tree and presents piled on a sideboard. Grandma was in the kitchen, and she came out wiping her hands on a red and white striped apron. "Hello, dears," she said, "Would you like a glass of cider? Cheryl can help you in the kitchen." She left to greet Cler and Gwynne.

After cider, which was tangy and delicious, the children were allowed to open their presents: a teddy bear for Charles, rag doll for Lestie, wool coats for Corrie and Paxton. Cheryl proudly showed off new twin dolls in a little bed. They had cunning faces, with glass eyes, half opened, like newborn babies. Lestie was not allowed to touch them.

One of Grandpa Oborn's cousins owned the Ogden Standard Examiner, and Grandpa called him up to tell him about his son being home for a few days, from Alaska. The day after Christmas, a reporter and photographer showed up to interview Cler and Gwynne about their adventures homesteading in Alaska.

Before the interview, the photographer posed the family with their new GMC wagon, which sported an Alaska license plate, saved from the old jeep. In the picture, there's snow on the ground, and they're all wearing coats and boots, but it doesn't look like anyone is cold. After all, they seem to say, we're

Alaskans! It is a perfect family portrait, but it also reveals something about each individual.

On the left, Cler is so tall that he has to lean sideways, bracing himself on the fender. He's wearing his Army Air Corps bomber jacket, looking proud. Corrie, in neat braids and a new dress, is the only child caught with a grin. Charles and Celestia are solemnly studying the photographer. Paxton is trying to look grownup, and Gwynne's barely-there smile reveals shyness at having her picture taken. The photograph is haunting in its honesty, capturing the family in one shining moment of time.

Having thoroughly visited their kinsfolk, and becoming somewhat celebrities in their old home town, Cler and Gwynne packed up and left for Alaska. They had a new suburban and a little money in their pockets, and they were anxious to get back to Alaska, hoping the worst of winter would be over.

Driving the Alaska Highway was actually easier in the winter, because the gravel was plowed and graded flat, and the road was frozen solid. Tall banks of snow took the place of guard rails, and the trip was actually not bad, with a good heater in the new Jeep and new tires that held the road. There was no dust to choke them, or mud to slow them down. Sometimes the road was icy, but for most of the way, temperatures kept the snow the consistency of chalk.

Since it was winter, they had to stop at road houses each night, but with all the travelers on the highway, such places had sprung up at regular intervals, and they always found a room for the night.

FEBRUARY 1951

A TODDLER NAMED BUTCH

Once they were settled back in their log home in Mountain View, Gwynne again applied for a foster child. When a tiny, malnourished toddler was brought to her, she took one look at him and her heart melted. "You've brought me a baby," she said

223

happily, as she ushered in Mrs. Wade, the frank, almost rude little woman who had brought, and taken away, the other two foster children. Gwynne showed her to the sofa.

"His name is Howard Mahle, and he's almost three years old, but his development is arrested," Mrs. Wade said, brusquely, seating herself with Howard on her lap. "He's part native and will have benefits through Native Services."

Sitting nearby in the rocking chair, Gwynne watched Howard stare up at the light bulb on the ceiling, while Mrs. Wade talked. The child didn't cry, but neither did he smile. His eyes were blue, his dark hair had been shaved off, revealing several scars on his scalp, and he was so thin that his stomach was swollen. She noticed other small scars on his face. Mrs. Wade handed him over, and Gwynne lifted him onto her lap.

With her hands on his sides, she could feel his rib bones. She settled him on her knees, with one hand on his chest and one on his back, as he was wobbly, but she wanted to look into his face. Howard continued staring at the light bulb.

Mrs. Wade said, "He's mal-nourished, and has brain damage from encephalitis. He doesn't walk, talk or crawl, and he has rickets. You can read more in his file. Do you still want to take him?"

"Yes," Gwynne said, "Of course." She was still trying to make eye contact with him. "Hello, little Howard," she said softly. He stopped looking at the light bulb, and focused on Gwynne's face. He stared at her for a moment, and then he smiled, and it was as if someone turned on the sun.

"I guess he likes you," Mrs. Wade said. "You seem to have a way with this type of child..."

Gwynne thought, what type is that? She cuddled him closer. To her, Howard was just a child who needed to be loved.

Cler began to call Howard "Butch" because "Howard," he said, was too much name for such a little kid. After that, he was always Butch, or Butchy.

When he was bathed or fed, Butchy responded with a smile, but Gwynne worried that he didn't eat enough. She fed him oatmeal, and formula made with canned milk and Karo syrup. He liked bread and jam, canned peaches and applesauce. Little by little, he gained weight, but he stayed the size of a two-year-old.

He slept in the crib in the girls' room, and Corrie often put him to bed or got him out of the crib in the morning. To her, he was a baby to dress and play with, and as he grew healthier, he began to crawl. He was soon walking, and then running all over the place.

Gwynne could tell Butchy's hearing was not affected by the encephalitis, because he turned to look at people when they talked to him, and he loved to listen to music on the radio. He was still very distractible, but he engaged with the other children, giggling and laughing as they all played together. It wasn't long before he began to say "Mama" and "Dada."

As they grew to love him, Gwynne wanted to make him a permanent part of the family. She talked it over with Cler, and he agreed that if things worked out, they would try and adopt Butch. As for the other children, they just assumed he was one of them, there to stay.

AIR RAID

The Korean War was going strong, and since Alaska was strategically located, there were mandatory air raids and blackouts of the city. With Elmendorf Air Force Base, as well as Fort Richardson close by, the civilian population was at risk. With Pearl Harbor only six years earlier, and with Alaska so close to Russia, no one doubted such an attack could happen.

When the sirens howled, everyone was supposed to pull their heavy "black out" curtains and turn off all except emergency lights indoors.

One winter night in January, while the sirens were blaring, the Oborn family gathered in the dark living room waiting for the "all clear" to sound. Cler peeked out the edge of the curtain and muttered under his breath. "I'd better go see what Barny is up to," he said, shrugging into his coat.

The man's front yard was lit up by a large Christmas tree that had been on for days. Drooping strings of colored lights lit up the darkness, reflecting off the deep snow that filled the yard. They had most likely been strung in years past, when Barnard was feeling more chipper. Cler crossed the street and knocked on his door, calling out to him.

"Hey, buddy! You know we're having an air raid? OK if I turn off your Christmas tree?" When there was no answer, Cler found the extension cord under the tree, and pulled the plug.

At that moment, Barny answered the door; he leaned against the door frame, wearing only his union suit and old slippers. He was definitely not sober. "Hullo, Cler. Now, what was it you wanted?"

"It's all right, Barnard. Just go back inside, it's cold out here."

A week later, on a bitterly cold night, Cler had a feeling he should check on his neighbor. A few minutes later, he came back, and Gwynne met him at the door.

"Everything all right?"

He spoke in a low voice, but Lestie was sitting at the table coloring a picture, and she heard what her father said. "Oh, Gwynne, Barny's dead. Criminy! I wish I'd checked on him sooner."

"That's awful!" her mother said. "What happened to him. Alcohol, do you think?"

Cler shook his head. "I don't know. He was stretched out on his bed on top of the covers. The house is like an iceberg. Maybe he was too drunk to notice his furnace was out. I really wish I'd gone over there sooner." He was standing by the phone, which hung on the wall in the kitchen, and he dialed a number. "Hello, I want to report a death. It's my neighbor. I found him when I went to check on him a few minutes ago. I think he may have frozen to death." He gave his name and address, as well as Barnard's. When he hung up, he noticed Lestie.

"Why aren't you in bed, Curly Locks?"

"I was coloring," she said. "Is that man dead, Daddy?"

226

His dark eyes were troubled. He stepped over to her and ruffled her hair, "It's not something you need to worry about. Now go on to bed."

She slid off her chair and stood there, looking up at him. "But I heard you say he was dead."

She barely came up to his pants pocket, so he stooped to kneel on one knee, in front of her. "Yes," he said. "He froze, because he had no heat."

"We have heat, don't we?"

"Yes we do. Now go on to bed."

She went to bed feeling uneasy. Out by the road, there was a frozen, dead raven lying on top of the snow. Its wings were huddled around it, and its eyes looked frosted shut. When she saw it today, she didn't care about it, but now she couldn't get that image out of her mind.

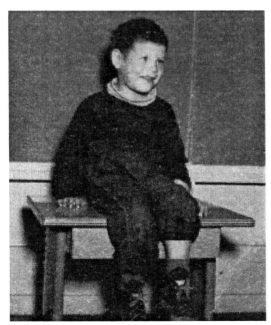

BUTCHY

Butchy always seemed to be a toddler, even as the others grew taller and went to school. He was a few months older than

Charles, but remained the baby in the family. He loved to give and get hugs, and he had an infectious giggle. Though he didn't say many words, he seemed to be always glad just to be alive and he never sulked or cried in anger. He was hyperactive, always in need of supervision, but at the same time, he was a little ray of sunshine.

Butchy liked to follow Celestia and Charles around the yard and play in the sawdust or any pile of dirt that happened to be handy. They made little roads in the dirt and built pine cone towns with rocks and leaves for cars and people. Of course, Butchy couldn't keep from touching everything, and he liked to mess up the roads and towns better than to watch the others build them, but it was all part of the game.

It was raining outside and the little Oborns had more energy than usual. Gwynne had a headache, and she ignored them as she washed the supper dishes in a pan in the kitchen. Butchy, Charles and Celestia were running around the oil stove giggling and chasing each other: first through the living room, into the kitchen, past the table, past the doorway to the back rooms, back into the living room, in a circle.

Gwynne was thinking she'd let the running go on for two more minutes and then she'd call a halt to it.

Only seconds later, Butchy collided with the copper boiler, which was sitting on the floor near the stove, with its lid on. As he hit, the lid tipped in, and Butchy's arm and shoulder fell into the scalding water. He screamed and jumped, dripping water. In a second, Gwynne had grabbed him. She ran, carrying him under one arm, to the sink, where she dipped his arm into a bucket of cool water.

"Go get your dad!" she yelled to Paxton who had materialized from a back bedroom. He took off out the door and brought Cler in from the barn.

Trying to assess the situation over Butchy's screams, Cler called for the petroleum jelly, and grabbed a pair of scissors to snip off Butchy's white, long-sleeved undershirt. He worked as carefully, but quickly as possible, trying to spare the skin, but

228

some skin came off with the wet shirt. Gwynne handed him the big jar of petroleum jelly, and he gently smeared it over Butchy's red and quickly swelling arm and shoulder. He found more burns on Butchy's back, where the water had run down. Having covered all the burns with a thick glaze, Cler loosely wrapped a clean cotton dish towel over the arm and shoulder, and then left with the little boy in his arms, wrapped in a blanket. He drove as fast as he could to Providence Hospital.

Hours later, when they returned, Butch was in bandages over his shoulder, arm, half his torso and upper back—more than a quarter of his tiny body. His cute little elfin face, however, had been spared, and his burns eventually healed, leaving scars only on his back. The scars reminded the family how precious he was to them and how close they came to losing him that day.

Oborn Family 1951

17

SPRING 1951

DEAR HEART

One day in the early spring, when the snow was melting into mud puddles on the road, and fields of dried grass from last summer were almost bare, the family drove to Palmer to visit Mel Saunders and his family. While they were there, Mel's wife served a fine meal of fried chicken, mashed potatoes and boiled turnips. After dinner, they all went out and looked at Dear Heart in her stall in the big barn.

"She's going to have a calf," Mel said.

Cler grinned. "That's fine. Just what I hoped." He said he'd be back in a week to take Dear Heart home to Mountain View.

A few days later, Mel called to tell Cler that Dear Heart had died. "I'm sure sorry," he said. "I let the cows out to pasture, even though it's a little early. I think maybe she ate some frozen clover, but I don't know what it was for sure that bloated her. I found her lying on her side and stuck her to relieve the gas, but she up and died, anyway. I can't tell you how sorry I am."

Cler sighed, "I had high hopes for that little heifer, Mel, but I don't blame you. I just appreciate your keeping her for me. I'll pay you the barn charges anyway."

"Hey, don't worry about it. At least I was able to save the meat, and if you want to split it, we can call it even," Mel said.

"You've got a deal."

"I'm just proud we all made it through the winter," Mel said. "This country sure is hard on man and beast."

"It sure is," Cler said. After he hung up, he told Gwynne and the kids what had happened to Dear Heart.

"Why do all our animals have to die?" Corrie asked, sorrowfully.

"Everything dies sometime," he said. "Anyway, the goats are still with us, and we still have Peachy." He was just as devastated as anyone, but he had done his best, and couldn't blame anything except the weather.

Later, he drove back to Palmer to get the frozen and cut-up beef from Mel. That night, Gwynne fried up some steaks. Corrie, who never seemed to miss a thing, eyed her steak. She could tell it wasn't moose meat, because it was not as dark as moose usually was, and it had almost no smell to it. Moose meat had a delicious, woodsy aroma. She stared across the table at her dad, who was savoring a big bite of steak.

"Is this Dear Heart?" she asked.

A pained look spread across her father's face and he stopped chewing for a moment.

Gwynne spoke up. "We traded Dear Heart for it."

Cler's eyebrows went up, but he finished chewing his bite of steak. Corrie didn't feel very hungry.

RAIN AND ELECTRICITY

231

In Anchorage that year, and all along the coast, spring and early summer weather was either overcast, about to rain, or raining. The land around Anchorage, and Mountain View especially, was a typical Alaskan swamp, which was called muskeg. In summer, the muskeg could thaw, and there was no telling how deep the swamp could become.

In the early spring, Cler had purchased a war surplus ambulance for a very cheap price. He thought it would be great for hauling things. It needed some work, but he intended to get to it as soon as the weather warmed up. He parked it on the edge of his property, on a flat, snowy place by some willows, which seemed like a stable enough spot. As spring came melting along, the ground began to thaw, and, unnoticed by anyone, the ambulance began to sink.

There were willows growing between the house and the ambulance, which is why Cler didn't notice that it was slowly disappearing into the bog. One warm day he walked back to check on it, and it was sunk up to the door handles. It took three men and a winch to get it out.

"Thank goodness I checked on it! A few more days, and it would have sunk out of sight!" he told Gwynne, who, along with the children, all their friends, and a few other neighbors, stood in the rare sunshine, watching the rescue of the ambulance.

Gwynne stared at the mud-covered old vehicle. "That thing sinking out of sight may not have been all bad," she grinned.

"Hey!" Cler said, "this is a good truck! I have plans for it. OK, fellows, let's pull it on over here into my yard."

The yard itself was a sea of mud, but Cler knew from having parked his other vehicles there, that his front yard was not a bottomless bog.

That summer Anchorage got enough rain to inspire Ark building. The Oborn children went outside whenever it was not pouring down. Merely drizzling was as good as overcast, and overcast was as good as sunshine, by comparison. Other houses dotted the area, hidden back in the trees, along newly cut roads. In the swampy areas, blueberries grew in abundance. On high, cleared places, like berms at the side of the dirt roads, wild roses and raspberries flourished. Mosquitoes also flourished, with plenty of standing water to breed in.

It had been raining for a week, and when the rain finally stopped, Corrie, Lestie and Paxton ran out of the house, glad to be outdoors. Everything was wet: the tall grass in the yard bowed with water droplets, dirt in the dooryard was sticky mud, leaves on the willows dripped.

Lestie was about to give her baby doll a bath in the rainwater on top of a fifty-gallon barrel, when she looked up to see Paxton standing on an upturned water bucket. Just above him, a low-hanging electrical wire ran from the shed to the power pole. Paxton teetered on the bucket, reached up and grabbed the wire to keep from falling. Something banged and sparks sizzled as he froze for a moment and then fell to the ground, limp as death.

Lestie screamed and ran to get Mother. By the time she reached Paxton, he'd begun to moan. Gwynne helped him roll over, and walked him into the house.

"You're just an accident waiting to happen," she scolded, as she checked him over. He was pale and weak for a few minutes, but he quickly recovered.

His mother was right about his accidents. Only a few days earlier, she had been doing the laundry, with the wringer going. As she lifted wet clothes from the washer with a stick, and fed them to the rollers, Paxton touched the clothes. His arm was sucked in up to his armpit before Gwynne could get the wringer popped open and stopped. He lost some skin under his arm, and the bandages were still on, when he almost electrocuted himself.

When Cler returned from work, Gwynne told him what happened with the electrical wire. "I don't know what we're going to do with that boy," she said.

"Aw, he's just a curious youngster. He wants to know everything about everything. You know the story about my riding my bike on the big water pipe, across Ogden Canyon, don't you? I was twelve..."

Gwynne put out her hand like a policeman, "Stop. I know the story, and I don't even want to think about it!"

With animals to feed, a goat to milk and a job, Cler was a busy man. Gwynne worried about him keeling over from exhaustion, but all she could do was help when she could, and take care of the family.

During the summer, Cler started still another project. With a housing shortage in Anchorage, and more people streaming north every day to find work, he wanted to take advantage of the lots he owned. On one, was the trailer and lean-to. The new log house they lived in was on lot number two. Now, he began to build another log house on the third lot, working on weekends and evenings.

Cler's houses were simple to build, and of his own design. The walls were made of logs, cut flat on three sides, so they fit tight. With a generous bead of glue between logs, no other insulation was needed. The plumbing was simple and drains were hooked up to a septic tank buried in the yard. Electrical wiring was strung to lights in all rooms, with outlets for the stove and refrigerator, as well as two extra outlets in the kitchen. The ceilings and floors were made of rough lumber, cut and hauled from the homestead, in a used dump truck Cler had bought, trading in the ambulance. The floors were finished with linoleum.

With demand for affordable housing so great, Cler believed he could sell three log houses and the trailer, if he could just manage to get them built.

WILD ROSE MAGIC

Much of the Anchorage bowl was either covered in swamp (called muskeg, because it was underlain by permafrost) or what locals called "brush." Brush was a tangle of bushes and skinny trees that grew so thickly that it was difficult to make one's way through it. Wherever there were cleared areas, like on building lots or dirt roads, raw dirt never remained bare for long. Grass, fireweed, and flowers of all kinds grew quickly and soon covered

234

the dirt with vegetation. It took only a little longer for wild raspberry bushes and rose bushes to spring up. The summer of 1951 there was an abundance of wild rose bushes growing like a hedge around the Oborn's yard.

As soon as the rains stopped, and the sun came out, sweet, pink blossoms appeared like magic over the mounds of dark green. All the buds flowered at once. One of those first sunny days, Cler stepped outside to change the oil on the jeep wagon, and smelled the sweet fragrance of the wild roses. He thought of how Gwynne seemed to be feeling low this morning, in spite of the sun finally coming out. It might take a while for the light to work its magic, but the roses were beckoning. He took out his pocket knife, put on his leather gloves, and cut a bouquet for Gwynne. He stepped through the door, holding the bouquet behind his back.

Gwynne was sitting at the table, trying to get up the energy to clear the dishes and put the milk away. Lestie and the little boys were running around the house, still in their pajamas. They all stopped when they saw their father come in.

"Sweets for the sweet," Cler sang out, and then, like a magician, he whipped out the bouquet with a flourish, "Ta da!" and the children giggled with delight.

Gwynne couldn't help but smile. She stood up from the table and gave Cler a kiss. She kept on smiling, as he placed the roses in a jar of water, and she inhaled their sweet fragrance.

Cler began to clear the table.

"Thank you," she said, "but I will do the dishes. You go on back outside. I'll be fine."

FRIENDSHIP

The Oborn children were used to relying on their siblings for companionship, but now there were other children living in houses and trailers scattered through the trees, and down the road. The pig farmer who lived at the top of the hill had a daughter, Diane, who was Corrie's age. As the weather got nicer,

235

the girls spent time together playing at Diane's house, which had a real lawn, a barn and a swing. Lestie wanted to play, too, and tried to follow the older girls around, but they teased her, "Tag-along too, Lou, tagalong too, Lou," they taunted, making her leave them alone.

This was a sad time for Lestie, who wanted to be with her sister. She had no one to play with, except her brothers, who were not little girls.

In June, Gwynne took Celestia to register for a half-day kindergarten held in a small church, not far away, but on the other side of the woods from home. In the large basement room, where class was to be held, Gwynne met another mother, Mrs. Earles, who had two little boys in tow, while Gwynne had Charles and Butchy. Mrs. Earles' daughter, Joyce, was the same age as Lestie. The two mothers struck up a conversation, while the children were being tested for school readiness.

A nurse in an Army uniform was doing the testing, assisted by a young blond woman who was going to be the teacher. One of the tasks was to walk barefoot across an army blanket on the floor. This was, perhaps, to enable them to spot gait problems. Lestie stood at the edge of the blanket, frowning. It was her turn, but she had no desire to cross that blanket.

"Go ahead," the nurse prompted, tapping her on the shoulder.

Lestie started across. Hating the feel of the rough wool against her bare feet, she walked with legs apart, like a cowboy just getting off a horse.

Her mother met her on the other side. "What's the matter with you? It looked like you had on a full diaper!"

Joyce's mother laughed and Gwynne shook her head. "I never know what she's going to do next."

When it was her turn, Joyce fairly skipped across the blanket. "My Joyce is such a responsible child," Mrs. Earles crowed. "She's the oldest, and really a lot of help to me."

Gwynne found out the Earles lived near her, in a trailer just through the trees. "I wonder if our girls can walk together," she said, corralling Butchy between her knees. He was a little escape artist. Gwynne glanced over at Celestia, whose attention was focused on something outside the window.

Lestie was actually studying a blue jay, that had landed in a tree branch. It had cunning little black eyes, and a tuft of blue feathers that looked like a hat. She heard her mother say, "My little girl tends to daydream and I'm afraid she'll be watching squirrels or getting lost, instead of getting to school!"

Lestie felt insulted. She never got lost! And what was so bad about watching squirrels? Nevertheless, the mothers arranged for Joyce to walk with Lestie to school. They strolled through the woods, trekked across a log over a creek, and walked on to the little white church. On the way, Lestie entertained Joyce by pointing out interesting objects, like fungi growing on a tree, a squirrel nest in a black spruce, and various small animals they caught sight of. She told Joyce about her little play places on the homestead, the time Buddy gave her a duck, and the bear she saw, that her daddy killed. They enjoyed the walk, and they always made it to school on time.

Now Lestie didn't follow Corrie and her friend, Diana, around anymore, to annoy them. Lestie had a friend of her own.

August 1951

A BOY NAMED ARTHUR

One Sunday afternoon, Cler was scouting out the fourth lot, which bordered a little creek that ran through the woods. He wanted to make sure the fourth lot was dry and suitable for the next house he wanted to build.

In the woods, he spied a pup tent, and a young man filling a pail from the creek. Dressed in Levis with a denim shirt, he bent over, balancing on one knee. All Cler could see was the top of his long, shiny black hair.

"Hello," Cler called, and the boy jumped. "Didn't mean to startle you," Cler said, making his way to the log that crossed the creek. The boy watched as Cler nimbly crossed the log in two steps, and stood beside him.

"I just thought I'd get acquainted. I'm Cler Oborn, and I live through those trees over there."

He can't be more than sixteen or seventeen, Cler thought.

"My name's Arthur Lopez," the young man said with a grin. He was brown as a berry, with black eyes, and he needed a haircut. When he smiled, deep dimples appeared in his cheeks.

"Do you own this property?" he asked. "I was just camping here for a day or two, until I can get a job and find a place to stay."

Cler liked the openness of the boy. He couldn't be more then eighteen, he thought, considering the smooth look of his cheeks. Cler stooped, resting on his haunches, "As a matter of fact, I own the property on that side of the creek, but not here, where you're camped. Where are you from, Art?"

"Well, I came up from Pasadena, California, but I was born in Mexico. My family lives in Pasadena. The job situation is bad down in the States, but I heard there's jobs up here."

Cler laughed, "I guess there are, but it's not Shangri La."

"I found that out, already," Art said.

"How did you get to Alaska?" Cler asked.

"Hitchhiked," Art grinned. "If I don't get work, I can always hitch my way back home, I guess."

Cler liked this boy. "So what do you do? What kind of work are you after?"

Art grinned, "I'll try just about anything, if it pays. Anything legal, I mean. "

"Well, that's a relief!" Cler laughed. "How'd you like to help me build a log house? Do you know anything about carpentry?"

"No, but I'm a quick learner," Art said, standing up. His knee was getting soaked in the wet grass.

Cler stood up, too. "I'm working on a building just over through those trees. If you have a few minutes, maybe you'd like to come and take look at it; see if you can help me out."

238

"I've got all the time in the world," Art said, with a smile that lit up his face. He set his bucket down. "I can come right now, if you want."

He followed Cler back through the woods to the partially built log house. It was a shell, with outside walls, a floor of new lumber, and a roof, but no interior walls, windows or doors yet. Cler showed Art how he wanted interior walls built on the lines he'd penciled on the floor. "These walls will divide the bedrooms and bathroom from the main room. You can see how I've got this one done, over here."

Art asked, "Are you going to work on it today?"

"No, it's Sunday. But can you come in the morning? I'll get you lined up before I go to work.

Early on Monday morning, Art showed up at the building site, and Cler showed him how to cut eight-foot 2X4's for studs, and how to build the walls on sixteen inch centers, with top and bottom plates. Art said he could do it.

When Cler got home from work, he nervously headed over to the site to check on what his little friend had accomplished. He was proud to see three nice, straight walls framed and nailed in place. The only mistake Art had made was that he had nailed studs over the bathroom doorway. "We'll have to take those studs out," he said, "That was going to be a door!"

Art looked stricken, "I'm so sorry!"

Laughing, Cler patted him on the back. "I should have been more clear, my friend. This is not a problem."

Gwynne fed Art right along with the family, and then he and Cler returned to the job site. About nine, when Cler and Art were finishing installing a window, Cler said, "Isn't it getting a bit cold in that tent of yours?'

Art flashed Cler his usual dimpled smile, "I'm a pretty tough guy."

"I really appreciate your help," Cler said, "and it would be in my best interests to give you a better place to sleep. I wouldn't want my help to turn up frozen stiff some morning."

Art looked at the floor, embarrassed. "Well, I was wondering if I could stay in that little barn of yours with the goats. The hay looks like it'd make a pretty good bed."

"I can do you one better," Cler said, dropping his hammer in the wooden tool caddy. He picked up the caddy, "Let's go in the house and see what's left from supper."

When they opened the door, they were greeted with blessed warmth and the smell of roast moose mixed with lye soap. Gwynne was at the sink, scrubbing out the roasting pan. A rush of cold air came in with the men, and the door slammed shut again.

"Hello," she called over her shoulder.

"Anything left from supper?" Cler asked.

"Some roast moose. I can make you a sandwich."

Cler and Art exchanged glances and answered in unison, "Sounds good!"

After they'd eaten, Cler couldn't bear to send Art back to his tent. He turned to Gwynne, "Is it alright if Art gets his bag and bunks in with the boys tonight?"

"Of course he can. I'll bet it's getting nippy out there during the night," Gwynne said, giving the boy a gentle smile.

"Take a flashlight and go get your things," Cler told him. "I have a folding army cot out in the shed, and I'll set it up while you're gone." It was decided that Art would sleep on the top bunk, which was a bit bigger than the cot, and Paxton agreed to sleep on the cot.

So it was that Arthur Lopez found a job and a place to sleep, as well.

Cler couldn't have hired a better helper, and every day he lined out work for Art, and checked it when he came home, often working for a few hours with him, after supper. Besides helping build the log house, Art helped take care of the three goats and milked the nanny goat.

Art Lopez and Lestie on haystack 1951

He fit right in with the family. He was polite and funny, and he took a special shine to Lestie, who was the same age as his little sister, Juanita. She lived with his parents in an apartment in Pasadena. When he had earned a little money, Cler had him make a long distance call to let his parents know how he was doing, and reassure them he was safe and employed.

Funding for the job on the Air Force Base had run out, so Cler took a job with a moving company called Shaw's. He liked it because he worked fewer hours, allowing him to work more on the houses he was building. He and Art soon finished the log house and Cler sold it to Chuck and Kitty Vandewater. Then, he and Art started on the forth log house. It would face South Flower Street. When they finished building that house, Art hoped he'd have enough money to go home.

Though they were simple structures, the log houses were sturdy and well-built. Fifty years later, the house on South Flower was still occupied.

18

BACK TO KENNY LAKE

October 1951

It was October 31st. It had been snowing for two weeks, and snow was up to the window sills, but inside, it was cozy. The oil stove was blowing heat, and sun streamed through the corner windows.

Since it was Saturday, the kids were home from school. Celestia and Corrie were at the table making clothes for their paper dolls. Scissors, crayons, and scraps of paper lay scattered on the table as they worked. Paxton was playing with the little steam engine he'd gotten for Christmas the year before, and Charles was watching. The toy had a water chamber heated by a tiny gas flame. It had arms that chugged back and forth, moving little metal wheels. It was not a train engine, but something that could pull a belt to work some kind of machine. Such engines might be used to move a derrick and drill a well, or run a combine. As a toy, it was enough for a boy to watch the wheels go around, and make it whistle when he pulled a lever.

Arthur was outside, shoveling a path, more like a canyon, from the driveway to the front door. When he stomped into the house, knocking snow off his boots, he announced, "It's Halloween, you know. We should go Trick or Treating tonight!"

Paxton turned off the burner to the toy engine. It chugged for a few seconds and then the wheels and gears quit moving. "What's Trick or Treat?"

"Don't you Alaskans celebrate Halloween?" Art asked.

He had Paxton's attention. "We made some paper jack-o-lanterns in school yesterday, and put them in the windows."

Art said, "Where I come from, the kids go door to door and ask for treats, and if they don't give you something good, well, you get to play tricks!"

242

Gwynne was wiping off the table. She paused with the rag in her hand and focused on Arthur. "I don't think my kids are old enough to go around playing tricks on people at night. I know how teenage boys used to run around tipping over outhouses and putting rotten tomatoes on the street car tracks. Cler used to do that, too, but it's too cold for that sort of nonsense in Alaska, and it's a good thing."

"Aw, Gwynne, I wasn't planning on doing any real mischief, honest. Can I just take the kids out to get a little candy or something? We'll take a bar of soap, that's all. Someone doesn't give them a treat, we'll just soap their windows."

Gwynne relented, "Well, I guess so. For a little while."

It wasn't long before the sun was low, behind the trees, and everything was touched with gold. In mere minutes the sun had sunk out of sight, and the flaming sky faded to charcoal. Gwynne watched the children scramble into snow pants, coats, hats, scarves and mittens.

"Bundle up. There's a lot of snow out there. And don't stay out too long, I don't want anyone getting frost bite." She went to the cupboard and pulled out a ten-inch aluminum flashlight. "Here, Art, you'll need this." Charles was too little to go, she said, because the snow was too deep. Even five-year-old Lestie might have a problem with it.

Paxton toted a little cloth bag for the loot they hoped they'd get, and soon they were all out in the woods, swimming through the deep snow, to a street on the other side. Lestie was floundering in snow up to her chest.

Art gallantly picked her up and carried her on his shoulders. When they reached the yard of a little trailer, he set her down, and thumped his mitten-covered fist against the aluminum door. There was a light on inside, and he pounded again. A woman came to the door.

"Trick or treat!" Art called and the children echoed, "Trick or treat!"

The woman looked over the young man in his fur hat, and the bundled children, hardly visible in the light cast from her open door. She closed the door with a thud.

Art stepped to the small window on the side of the trailer. "That deserves a trick," he said gleefully. He took out a sliver of soap from his pocket, and scribbled a swirly line on the glass. "Now, on to the next house!"

Having come out onto a road, they were able to easily approach a half-dozen houses. One lady gave them each a sucker, and a man gave them a handful of pennies. They came to another small trailer, and a young woman answered the door. By now, even Lestie knew the drill, "Trick or treat! Trick or treat!"

The woman said, "I'm sorry. I just got home from work, and I don't have a thing to give you. I'm sorry." She closed the door. Art said, "Time for a trick," and pulled out his soap.

"Let's don't trick her," Corrie said, "I feel sorry for her."

Art put the soap away.

They made their way back to their own house, by following the street around until it connected up at the top of their street. They stopped at the pig farmer's house on the hill, and said hi to Corrie's friend, Diana. Her friend gave them each a couple of pieces of salt water taffy, which they'd never tasted before. They each unwrapped a taffy and chewed on it the rest of the way home.

The little band of trick-or-treaters trooped into the log house with rosy cheeks, chattering with excitement. They kicked off their boots, wrestled out of coats and snow pants, and dropped snow-clotted mittens, scarves and hats on the floor, where snow melted into little puddles of water.

"Hang up your things!" Gwynne called to them from the kitchen.

While the others were hanging coats and piling the rest of the wet clothing on a bench to dry, Paxton hurried to the table and dumped the communal sack of goodies. The cellophane wrapped suckers scattered, the pennies tinkled and rolled. "Look what we got!" he called to the others.

Art sat down on a kitchen chair and just grinned, watching the excitement of the children. Paxton and Corrie divvied out the loot. There were three suckers each, and five pennies. When Butchy got a purple sucker, his face lit up. Gwynne grabbed a dishtowel and tied it on him for a bib before he ate it, to keep his shirt from being dyed purple by his slobber.

Even Art got some candy. He licked a sucker and thought wistfully of his little sister, wishing he were at home, taking her trick-or-treating. Down in Pasadena, the roses would be blooming. There was only a little more to be finished on the inside of the house he was helping Cler build, and then he planned to go home to his family.

Cler sold the house on South Flower street, right away. He kept the mortgage on that house, and the buyer promised to pay him monthly, until he could pay it off.

18

BACK TO KENNY LAKE

Spring 1952

As spring approached, Cler and Gwynne decided it was time to go back to Kenny Lake. If they did, they could prove up on the homestead by September. They arranged for a renter to move into their log house when they left, in May. One problem with moving back to the Homestead was that Corrie, Paxton, and Celestia would need to go to school in the Fall, and there was still no school at Kenny Lake.

Counting his own children, Cler figured there could be a dozen potential students, including two of Emma George's and her sister, Ina's kids, who had never attended school. Cler had personally recruited two families, the Ennises and Santinis, from Palmer and Anchorage, and if they followed through and moved out to the area, that would add five more school age kids. With enough kids, Cler thought they were sure to be able to have a school by next fall.

He wrote to the Territorial Department of Education, requesting them to send materials and a teacher to Kenny Lake in the Fall. He received a letter saying that if he could provide a place to hold school, the Department of Education would send all the necessary materials, including desks and blackboards. A teacher, they said, would be arriving in September.

Cler made a trip back to Kenny Lake, even before school was out. He'd purchased a little light plant to provide electricity, and wired lights in the cabin. There was a new well down the road, so he hauled some water in a wagon full of fifty gallon barrels, and set up a barrel with a spigot, on a stand. There was a hand pump in the kitchen, but the little well he'd dug would not provide all the water they needed. As necessary, he could also haul water from the lake.

Over the two years they'd been in Mountain View, Cler had made several trips to Kenny Lake for logs and lumber. He had improved the sawmill east of the cabin, which sat on open ground beyond the outhouse. He intended to help his neighbors and make a little money, too, by selling lumber. He could do it even more cheaply if they brought the timber.

He made one trip to take the goats, and returned for his family, loading up the dump truck with household goods. Paxton and Charles rode with their dad, and Gwynne followed with the other children.

Cliff Kirkland heard Cler was back, and dropped in to see him. He'd lived in the area since before the Oborns moved to Mountain View. Cliff climbed out of his tan pickup, just as Cler emerged from the cabin. They shook hands.

"It's great to see you, buddy!" Cliff said with enthusiasm. He was a bit shorter than Cler, with a receding hairline, and his eyes always seemed to sparkle with good humor. He and Cler stood around for a while, talking, and got onto the subject of the sawmill. Cliff wanted to be part of the enterprise, he said.

At one point, Cler said, "What do you think about trying to cut some timber down in the river bottom?"

Cliff scratched his chin. "I know there's some good timber down there, but we'd need to make a road to get it."

"That's what I've been thinking. I thought if we used your bull dozer, we could follow the existing trail, and make a road through my property to the bluff and then on down. There's a nice moraine, straight back there, that goes down to the river bottom."

"Let me think about it," Cliff said. "Anyway, we'll have to wait till the ground dries out."

On the 21st of June, Cler and Gwynne began writing a journal, which they hoped they could keep up. They started by listing the names and ages of their children: Corrie Lynne, age nine-and-a half, Paxton, eight-and-a-half, Celestia, six, Charles four, and "Butch," also four.

They listed their animals: Tippy, the cocker-mix, Peachy the black tom cat, Clementine, the mother goat, Tina, and Sylvia, goat kids.

Cler wrote:

I had to start the little light plant and it took off with only three pulls. I felt as proud as a new mother, and with about as much justification. (The reason is that) the drill motor overheated, because of a short brush, and I had to overhaul it, re-solder the commutator (a switch that periodically reverses the current), undercut it and make a new brush out of a flashlight battery.

After supper I went out with Paxton and Gwynne, to put up a few studs on the barn. The mosquitoes were mean, but bearable for a change. The oats are up about an inch. They were planted the sixth of June.

Cliff brought timber to saw into boards, and Cler traded him the labor for the slabs (the bark-covered boards that came off the logs first). Cler wrote in his journal that for a week the men worked together, cutting out about 2000 board feet of lumber.

Cler used the slabs to build a barn for the goats, and for various other purposes, like building a new outhouse, and he used the scraps for firewood.

One afternoon, Cliff decided to drive over to the Oborn's to check out the spot where he and Cler had talked about making a road back to the Bluff. He thought he knew where Cler had meant they would start the road. He drove across the field, but it was still wet out there, and when Cliff tried to turn around, he got his truck stuck in the mud. He tried to get out, but the more he poured on the gas, the deeper he sank into the slick mud. He left the truck where it was, out in the field, and walked to the Oborn's cabin.

He knocked on the cabin door and Cler answered it. Leaning against the door frame, Cliff had a sheepish look on his face. "Say, can you come help me for a few minutes? My truck's sunk about a foot in the mud over in your field."

"Sure," Cler said, grabbing his coat. Once they were outside, he could see Cliff's flatbed truck. "What are you doing out on the airstrip?"

"That's an airstrip?" Cliff asked.

"It will be, if I have my way," Cler laughed. "Let's take some slabs over there with us and see if they'll do the trick. If not, I'll go get my truck, but I'd risk getting it stuck, too."

Cliff and Cler with Cler's dump truck

The two men got the truck out of the mud by shoving slabs under the tires, until Cliff could get enough traction to drive onto drier ground. Cler hopped into the cab with Cliff and rode back to the cabin. Since it was spring, there was still plenty of daylight left.

When they reached the yard and parked, Cliff said, "How about helping me weld on those stake pockets we talked about, while I'm here?"

"You got it," Cler told him. He loved to use his welder, and an excuse to weld and help his neighbor was too good to pass up.

Stake pockets were square iron bands, welded along the sides of the truck's iron bed, to hold square wooden stakes upright. When they hauled logs, the stakes would help hold them in place. The men worked together, laughing and talking, until Gwynne stuck her head out the door, to see why Cler hadn't come in for dinner. She saw the sparks from the welder flying, and how much fun the men were having, welding steel and laughing together, that she just shook her head and decided to feed the children and leave the "boys" to their play.

On the twenty-third of June, Cler described his twenty-ninth birthday in the journal:

Today Cliff and I slaved all day to get out some rotten logs. They looked beautiful, but after they were felled the butts were loaded with dry rot; quite a disappointment. I didn't get home 'til 9:30...

The children welcomed me at the door with shouts of "Happy Birthday!" Corrie gave me her "Book of Egypt" that she had made last year in school, Paxton had a chipped record of "Mockingbird Hill" that he surrendered title to in a burst of generosity. Thank goodness it wasn't his real favorite, "Wave to Me My Lady." Celestia offered a green bow tie made from a quilt scrap, and Charles gave a Tiny Golden Book entitled, "The Baby Giraffe Wants to Play."

Altogether a very touching array of gifts. Gwynne made a deep apple pie with "29" written in crust. This was my first birthday of the Return to Kenny Lake celebrated.

GROWING PAINS

Cler believed that a thriving community would mean a better school for the children, friends and neighbors to help each other, and an improved standard of living for all.

One family Cler enlisted to homestead at Kenny Lake, were the Ennises* (not their real name), who, when he first met them, lived outside of Palmer, in Chickaloon, a ghost town left over from a mining operation in the area. The Ennis family originally came from Oregon.

Cler had met Ted Ennis the previous Fall, in Palmer, when they were both doing some business with the dairy farmer, Mel Sanders. Ted and Cler got to talking over supper at Mel's, and Cler told him about Kenny Lake, where the country was beautiful, there was plenty of prime land available to homestead, and hunting was the best in the Territory. "It's the perfect place to raise a family," he said.

Ted invited Cler to come out to Chickaloon and meet his family. He said he wanted to know more about homesteading at Kenny Lake. A few weeks later, Cler and Gwynne made the trip to see the Ennis family. Ted was a big man who had the deep voice and hearty demeanor of a lumberjack, which he was. He was broad shouldered, and broad across the forehead, with unruly brown hair and skin that was like leather, from working outdoors.

His wife, LaVerne, was a tall, lanky woman who wore her brown hair in a pony tail. She dressed like her husband, in a plaid shirt, Levis and lace-up boots. The Ennises owned a few acres at Chickaloon, where they raised goats and chickens. They had a teenage girl, Julie, some younger girls, a little red-headed boy just older than Charles, and a baby on the way.

The adults talked about the advantages of homesteading, while Corrie and Julie got acquainted, and the younger children ran through the bushes chasing each other. Dinner was a noisy affair out on a picnic table, where the kids came and went at will, filling up on fried chicken and mashed potatoes. By the time dinner was over, Ted and LaVerne were excited to file on a homestead at Kenny Lake. Ted said they'd be ready to move in the spring.

While Cler and Gwynne were still in Mountain View, and Cler was working for the moving company, Cler met Enzo Santini* (not his real name. All names in this family have been changed). He and his wife, Zoya, had come to Alaska from the Midwest, and they were renting a trailer in Mountain View. Enzo was first generation Italian, having moved to New York with his family when he was a boy. He was intelligent and hard working, and Cler liked him right away.

Enzo had a thatch of black hair with a white streak in front, and a beaked nose that didn't detract from his darkly handsome face. He was short and hard muscled, and looked like a guy you wouldn't want to meet in a dark alley.

While they were working together one day, Cler mentioned the fact that he planned to move back to his homestead in Kenny Lake. This led to a discussion about

252

homesteading in general. Enzo had never considered it. He had come to Alaska for the job opportunities, and didn't know anything about homesteading. The first conversation was followed by other chats, and the men discussed the advantages of Kenny Lake over other places in south central Alaska. It wasn't long before Enzo had made up his mind.

He and Cler were sitting on a packing box after loading a truck, just taking a breather. Enzo said, "Well, Cler, I've talked it over with Zoya, and we want to move to Kenny Lake and take out a homestead. We think it'll be good for our boys, teach them to work hard; get them out of the city."

Enzo didn't have much good to say about cities, and he considered Anchorage to be as bad as any, even though it was hardly a city, in the usual sense of the word. Anchorage had grown from 3,000 in 1940 to 35,000 in 1950. People were scattered through the woods and hills, with almost no paved roads, even downtown. Still, it had a hospital, stores, police force, Rural Electric Association, and city government. It was a center of operations for the military in Alaska, the hub of the Alaska Railroad, and a neighbor to the Matanuska Valley with its farming and mining operations. The more people who came to town looking for jobs, the more like a city Anchorage became. Enzo said he wanted peace and quiet out in the Bush; the kind of life that homesteading offered.

Cler thought it would help both Enzo Santini and Ted Ennis to get in touch with each other as they looked into homesteading at Kenny Lake. Maybe take a trip to scout out available land. This is exactly what the two men did.

At the same time that Gwynne and Cler arrived back at the Homestead , Ted Ennis took out his own homestead about two miles down the road from Kenny Lake.

A few days later, the Santinis filed on a homestead next to the Ennises. The men figured that close proximity would make it easier for them to help each other. They intended to work on their cabins together and pool their resources. Maybe plant a communal garden.

As Ted came to know Enzo better, he found out that Enzo was a man who could be depended on if you were in a tough spot, but he was also impatient, opinionated, and had a hair-trigger temper. It wasn't long before Ted Ennis, a gentle sort of man, realized he had made a mistake in choosing to live so close to Enzo Santini.

Enzo's wife, Zoya, was Russian. She was very short and round, and never said much. LaVerne tried to be friends with her, but they had little in common. Zoya was devout Russian Orthodox, and even in her tent she had Icons of the Virgin Mary and Saint Peter hung on the canvas wall, and prayer candles. To LaVerne, this was a form of sacrilege, as she was a very conservative Protestant.

The children of the two families were also so diverse in sex and age that they didn't become friends. The Santinis had two school age boys who worked beside their father like men. They were a couple of years younger than the Ennises' oldest girl. The only Ennis boy was Dallas, a four-year old, and they had three little girls, all younger than Alina Santini, who was six.

Santini ruled his family with an iron hand, while Ted and LaVerne were more laid back and didn't believe in corporal punishment. The two families were so totally different, that it was only a matter of days after they'd pitched their tents and started building their cabins, that minor disputes began to arise. Where Ted was a friendly, outgoing soul, he was also easily offended, and Enzo was the kind of guy who had to be right all the time. It would be an understatement to say that the men had difficulty communicating. For instance, while Enzo was helping build an outhouse, Ted said, "Why don't we dig the outhouse over there?"

Enzo replied, "I think that will be too close to your house."
"No, I think it's a good spot."
"Well, I don't."
"I do, and it's my outhouse."
Enzo picked up his shovel and stormed off, "OK, you can just dig the danged thing by yourself!"

It wasn't just trying to work together. It was a lot of little things, or so Cler gathered when he listened to the men complain about each other. It might be that Ennises' goat wandered over to the other homestead and was found eating the garden. Maybe it was the incessant barking of the Santinis' dogs, a sound that would easily drift across the still night air and keep a guy awake. Whatever the root of it, in a very few weeks, the feud was in full swing.

Cler heard something about the problems from one or the other of the men every time they showed up to buy some lumber from Cler's saw mill, buy some gas, or borrow tools. By the time the men had cut the timber and hauled the logs for their cabins, Enzo and Ted were barely speaking to each other, even though they lived within stone-throwing distance. No actual stones had been thrown, perhaps, but Cler figured it was only a matter of time.

One day, near the end of June, Cler took Paxton with him to help Enzo on his cabin. The families were still living in tents, and their cabins had to be finished during the short summer. Cler found that instead of both men working together on the same cabin, they were each working on their own, and Cler had to choose which man to help.

The Santini boys were quick learners and hard workers. The oldest boy, called "Little Enzo," had the sharp features and dark good looks of his father. He was ten years old, and his brother, Sal, was eight, as was Paxton. Cler wanted the boys, Paxton included, to learn that there were ways of solving problems, other than getting into heated arguments. There was such a thing as listening to what the other guy had to say, and compromising to make things work, even if you didn't get everything you wanted.

As he, Paxton, and the Santini boys all grabbed hold to lift each heavy log into place, Enzo fitted and spiked them at the corners. Cler pointed out to the boys how much easier it was when they all worked together.

It happened that the morning after Cler and Paxton had been over helping build Enzo's cabin, Ted stopped by, as Cler was just finishing up cooking some of his famous sourdough hotcakes. "Come in and have some breakfast," Cler invited. He poured the rest of the batter onto the hot griddle, filling the whole thing.

"Don't mind if I do," Ted said, and Paxton scooted over on the bench at the table to give the big man room to sit down. The other kids and Gwynne had already had their fill, and had left the table.

Paxton was eating regular-sized pancakes, about four inches across. "Those sure smell good," Ted grinned, "I'm so hungry, I think I could eat about ten of those."

"Shall we make it a bet?" Cler called, flipping the griddle-sized pancake over.

"Sure," the big man said, without looking.

Cler slid the giant pancake onto a plate and brought it over to Ted, who stared at it. He gulped, "Looks delicious," he said, pouring on syrup. When he got to the last bite, it was obvious he was stuffed full.

Cler asked, "Want nine more of those?"

Both men broke out laughing.

Cler grew serious. "You know, Ted, I've been thinking about the problems you and Enzo are having. When you two talk, it's like this conversation you and I just had: you were talking about regular pancakes, and I was talking about a whopper. We think we know what the other guy is saying, but sometimes we don't."

Ted frowned, "You're saying Enzo and I don't communicate, like we don't speak the same language. Well, geez, Cler, he's Italian! We sure as heck don't speak the same language!"

Cler said, "Now, Ted, you know Enzo speaks English. What I'm saying is, even if you both speak English, you don't understand one another. Now, I think you're a reasonable guy, and I know Enzo can be stubborn..."

"As a mule," Ted inserted.

256

"As a mule," Cler said. "But, here's the thing. Neither one of you is going to change, so there has to be another solution. I had an idea that came to me in the night."

Ted frowned, "You were up in the night thinking about us?"

"I guess you could say that. I mean, listen, Ted. You guys start going at it, and one of these days, somebody might start shooting."

Ted leaned his elbows on the table, with his chin in his hands. His clear blue eyes were troubled, "I don't want that to happen, but I don't know any solution, other than packing it in and going back to Palmer."

Cler sat down across the table. "You would both be ahead if you worked together. You know that, don't you?"

Ted looked down at his plate. "I know. Enzo's got boys, and all I have is girls to help me. But it's easier working alone than getting into it with Enzo! I don't know how we're going to stand living so close to each other."

Cler folded his hands and leaned forward on his elbows. There was a sparkle in his eyes. "That's where my solution comes in! What if you and LaVerne moved to the other side of the lake? It's still on your property, and your homestead includes plenty of land over there, too. You're only partway done with your cabin. Take it apart, and move it! I'll even help you do it. We can use my dump truck to haul the logs."

"It's a thought," Ted said. "I'll talk to LaVerne."

So it happened that the Ennis family moved to the other side of LaVerne Lake. Enzo Santini perked up as soon as he heard they were moving, and he and his boys even helped Ted dismantle his partially-built cabin, and haul the logs. Ted reused all the logs, hauled some more, and built a two-story cabin, a barn and a chicken coop. LaVerne, who was one of the hardest working women you'd ever run into, helped build the chicken coop, and immediately went back to raising chickens and goats, as she had in Chickaloon.

For a while, things settled down between the families, and they got their cabins built, and wood piles stacked for the winter. The two men even went out together and bagged a moose, and split the meat, without incident.

The Oborn children were delighted to have friends on both sides of LaVerne Lake. Paxton and the Santini boys became buddies. All the boys worked hard with their fathers, and they all couldn't wait to own their own guns. Alina became Lestie's best friend. They played dolls, and climbed trees, and made little play places under the trees.

The children were friends, but for Enzo and Ted, LaVerne Lake wasn't always big enough to keep the two men from annoying each other. When conflicts became heated, Enzo or Ted continued to call on Cler to mediate their disputes.

Even as new homesteaders settled down the road, Cler was like the unofficial mayor of the community. All sorts of people came to him, whether they needed information about the local area, the best places to buy land or homestead, or if they had problems of one kind or another, he was always glad to help. The one thing that he said gave him gray hairs was his two friends, Enzo and Ted, arguing with each other over seemingly inconsequential things.

One day, Cler stomped into the cabin and threw his knit hat on a chair. "You know, Gwynne, I'm tired of being the umpire around here! I wish Enzo and Ted would just get along!"

Gwynne was slicing bread for lunch. She looked up as Cler dropped down on his chair at the table and ran his hands through his hair. "Well, why do you let them drag you into it?" she asked.

Cler sighed, "I'm trying to prevent all-out war. They've got guns, and they know how to use them."

19

GROWING PAINS

Summer, 1952

Curly locks, curly locks, wilt thou be mine?
Thou shalt not wash dishes nor yet feed the swine,
But sit on a cushion and sew a fine seam
And feed upon strawberries, sugar and cream.

That was a nursery rhyme Cler recited to his curly-haired youngest daughter. It made Lestie smile.

She had never had a haircut, even though Mother often called her mop of reddish blonde curls a rat's nest, as she struggled to brush it. One night while Gwynne was combing tangles after a bath, Lestie sat on her lap wearing a white nightgown.

Corrie was watching. "She looks just like an angel," she said.

"Yes, she does," her mother replied.

Of course, being a normal child, Lestie was not an angel. Her father sometimes recited another poem to her, which started off nicely, but ended on what felt like an insult, even to this small girl who didn't know exactly what it meant.

Cler would ruffle her hair and recite, "There was a little girl who had a little curl, right in the middle of her forehead. When she was good, she was very, very good, but when she was bad, she was horrid!"

Then one hot July day, when Lestie was six, that bush of curly locks met up with Mother's sewing scissors. The temperature at Kenny Lake was soaring toward ninety and sweat ran down the back of Lestie's neck, under her thick mat of hair. When her mother called her into the dim, cool cabin, Lestie gladly obliged.

"You need a haircut," her mother said, without any preamble. "Sit up on the stool and try not to fidget."

With a towel pinned around her neck, Lestie perched on a stool near the kitchen window, where there was plenty of light.

Gwynne took her sewing scissors and began to cut. Long curls fell onto the linoleum below. She snipped and snipped. Sitting still felt like punishment and Mother was taking a long time.

At one point Gwynne paused for a moment and murmured, "Oh, dear..." but then she kept cutting. Finally, she pronounced, "all done!" She unpinned the towel and Lestie hopped down off the stool, while Gwynne reached for her broom and dustpan. Lestie ran out of the dark cabin and into the sunshine. She felt lighter, and there was a nice, cool breeze on the back of her neck.

The other kids weren't anywhere nearby, so she went looking for them. She wandered down the hill towards the lake, where she saw a car and trailer parked on the grass.

"Oh, boy! Campers!" She ran down the driveway and across the gravel road, where Paxton and Corrie were engrossed in conversation with a man and woman.

At almost ten, Corrie was not shy of talking to strangers, and today was no exception. She felt it was her duty to warn campers and would-be fishermen that there were no fish in Kenny Lake. In addition, it was always fun to find out about the travelers; where they were from and why they were in the area.

As Lestie ran up to the group, Corrie stretched out her hand dramatically, "And this is my little brother, Charles," she said. "We call him Charles B. B. because he has two middle names."

Lestie skidded to a stop in the dust. "I'm not Charles, I'm me! I'm Lestie!" She reached up and felt her head. There was not much hair there.

Corrie stared at her. "What happened to your curls?" Turning to the two strangers, she added lamely, "Well, she used to be a girl."

260

Lestie turned around and ran home. Bounding into the cool cabin, she stopped before the dim image in the mirror on the wall. Her sister was right—she used to be a girl, but now she looked like a boy!

She stared. Maybe it would grow back. Hair did grow back, didn't it? She wasn't sure, but she really hoped so. Maybe by the time it was cold outside. She'd need some hair to keep her head warm.

TRIP TO TOWN

In July, Cler took Paxton and Corrie with him and drove into Anchorage with a load of lumber. He was going to fix up the log house in Mountain View. While the renters were there, in May, there had been a fire in the kitchen, and a wall had been set ablaze. The renters had moved out, and now Cler needed to replace that wall.

He and the kids spent the night in the log house, which still smelled strongly of smoke, but Cler left the screen door open, and it wasn't too bad. Early in the morning, he rousted the kids out of their sleeping bags. "Up and at 'em! Rise and shine! Let's have some breakfast, and then we'll get busy."

The sun was shining, and the birds were chirping in the trees surrounding the little clearing. Mountain View wasn't a bad place to live, Cler thought, as he worked on his leather gloves, and began unloading the lumber.

It took all morning to brace the roof and saw out the scorched and half-burned logs. Paxton and Corrie hauled the pieces away, piling them up by the old goat shed.

When they stopped at noon, the three dropped wearily onto the pile of new lumber to eat the tuna sandwiches Corrie Lynne had made.

For a while they said little, concentrating on their lunch, listening to a magpie chattering in a tree nearby.

"Maybe he wants a bite," Paxton said.

"Try throwing a crust over there, and see what he does," Cler told him.

Paxton broke off a bit of crust, and chucked it under the tree. The magpie eyed the bread, but stayed in the tree.

Cler said, "It might take another day to replace the wall, but with any luck, we'll have it done even sooner. I'm going into town to pick up the fire insurance check. You kids want to come with me?"

"We'll stay, unless you're going to buy ice cream," Corrie said.

"I'm broke. But if they give us the check, I'll buy ice cream for supper." As Cler opened the door to the cab, ready to climb into the truck, out of the corner of his eye he saw a black and white blur. The magpie swooped down and snagged the bread in his beak, flying back to his branch. It made Cler laugh out loud.

Cler left the kids picking up scraps of lumber, while he drove off after the check. He was hoping he could buy some supplies with the money. They were running low on everything back at the Homestead, and they expected a lot of company this summer.

He parked the dump truck in front of a small frame house with a sign in its window, advertizing "Fire, Flood, Life Insurance."

The secretary, a little blonde, looked up as a bell tinkled and Cler came through the door. "Hello, Mr. Oborn. What can I do for you?"

"I just wanted to pick up that check for the fire," he said.

"Oh, I'm sorry. I put that check in the mail a couple of days ago."

Cler exhaled. "That's all right. I'll just watch the mail for it, then. Thanks."

He returned to the log house, feeling a bit down. For the next few hours, he concentrated on building the wall. There wasn't much for Corrie to do, so she walked up the hill to see if her girl friend, Diana, was home. Paxton stuck with his dad and handed him nails, or whatever he needed.

262

The kids went to sleep around nine-thirty, tired out from helping, and cleaning up sawdust. With daylight until eleven, Cler was able to finish the wall. He stashed his chain saw and other tools in the cab of the dump truck, and took a cool shower before he climbed into the sack.

The next morning, Cler and the kids rolled up their sleeping bags and left. With luck, the house would be rented soon. The boom was still going on, with more people coming to Anchorage every day. No available house would be vacant long.

With no money in his pocket, Cler drove to the Stop & Shop, the little store owned by his friend, Joe Karschevyk. Joe was Hungarian, a crusty old guy with salt and pepper hair that stood up like a rooster comb on top his head. He was muscular, heavy around the middle, with the attitude of a bull dog, but a heart of gold. He'd come to Anchorage after the war, and set up a store in Mountain View. He was the storekeeper who had tried to ban Barnard from buying alcohol, for his own good.

He greeted Cler with a hearty handshake, "Long time, no see," the storekeeper laughed. "You been up to no good, Cler?"

"Just the usual, trying to survive; maybe get a little ahead..."

Cler told him about the house fire, and the insurance check that was in the mail. "I can't go back to Kenny Lake without some groceries, though."

"What you need, I'm gonna give you and you pay later. Now, what you gotta have?" He let Cler charge all the supplies he needed, and even helped him load the boxes into the truck.

"I'll send you the money when I get the fire insurance check," Cler promised.

"No problem," Joe said. "People don't trust nobody these days, but me, I trust you."

After he left the Stop & Shop, Cler decided to check how much he had in the bank. Maybe there was enough to buy the kids some ice cream. He was amazed to find out he had 750 dollars! He talked to the banker and found out that the man who'd bought the cabin on South Flower had paid off the mortgage.

Cler was whistling when he climbed back into the truck. He grinned at his kids, "What say we all stop for ice cream before we head home?"

NO GHOST OUT TONIGHT

In mid-summer, when the sun set at Kenny Lake, the sky faded to gray, but never got really dark. The sun just bumped along below the horizon, leaving the sky pink and gold, and then it started coming up again. For children, this semi-darkness made the trip down the path to the outhouse less scary, but it also made running around outside, playing tag until bedtime, great fun.

That summer, Gwynne and Cler invited the neighbors, especially the Santinis and Ennises, over. They didn't hesitate to invite both families at the same time, hoping that as time went by, Enzo and Ted would learn how to communicate with each other.

Often, the adults played cards around the table, while the mob of children chased each other around outside.

There were all sorts of games to be played, including hide and seek. It was easy to hide under a pine tree or in the barn, or even in the tiny duck house that Lestie managed to squeeze into once. For the game of "Kick the Can," they ran through the grass trying to tag each other before someone on the other team ran out and kicked the tin can.

Sometimes, Gwynne made fudge for a treat, but most of it was for the adults. The fudge pan was given to the children, along with several spoons, so they could share the sugary scrapings.

As summer passed, daylight dwindled and the children's games became more raucous, and delightfully scary, as the nights grew darker. In one game, an unfortunate child would wander around saying, "No ghost out tonight. Not ghost out tonight,"

264

while the others hid in the shadows, and each took a turn at jumping out with a "boo!" that scared the "it" child silly.

When they tired of chasing one another, the children laid down on a blanket, and looked up in wonder at the stars.

Meanwhile, the adults were inside talking and laughing together. The children could hear their laughter drifting outside into the quiet night. It seemed like a very good thing.

HORNETS!

In the Bush, without proper medical treatment, even small injuries could result in serious illness or even death. Both Gwynne and Cler were surprisingly competent at treating the mishaps that occurred while they lived in the Bush. They kept emergency medical supplies on hand, along with all the simple remedies they might need.

One sunny day Corrie, Paxton, Lestie, and a few neighbor kids were playing down by the lake, pretending to be wild horses. The inspiration for this game came from the book, Black Beauty, which Corrie had read several times. All the kids chose to be different breeds or colors of horses, as they galloped around, prancing and neighing to each other.

Lestie, who'd been assigned to be a Pinto pony, was keeping up with the herd pretty well, even though she had bare feet. She pranced over the dry grass and right into a nest of hornets. The hornets were naturally enraged by this intrusion on their home in the grass, and began to sting feet and legs, hands and face without mercy.

Lestie circled the lake shore, leaping and swatting futilely, until she reached the road, but the hornets kept after her. She ran screaming back to the cabin, and crashed through the door.

"What on earth is the matter?" Gwynne jumped up from the couch, and met her in the kitchen.

Lestie couldn't stop crying, and the stings didn't stop hurting.

Gwynne helped peel off her daughter's jeans, dislodging two hornets trapped against her leg. Sobbing and breathless, Lestie collapsed in a little heap on the floor.

The next thing she knew, she was lying on the sofa, with a cold, wet cloth on her face. She could smell vinegar. She moved the wash cloth to peek out, and saw her mother dipping a rag in a small bowl sitting nearby, on the floor. With the vinegar rag, she dabbed at the stings.

Her mother saw her peeking out. "Better now?"

Lestie pouted, "I guess so, but I don't feel very good."

"Just lie there for a while. We'll show your stings to Daddy when he gets back from Anchorage, tomorrow."

Gwynne squeezed out her cloth and folded it, laying it neatly over the side of the enamel bowl. She let out a short breath, pausing to think. "I'll tell you what. How would you like to wrap up in my blue blanket, and sleep on the porch tonight, where it's cool. Would you like that?"

Lestie thought of her mother's soft, blue blanket, a luxury no one else in the family had. They all slept with rough, wool Army blankets and sleeping bags. "The blue blanket would be nice," she said.

Several times, Gwynne applied more vinegar to the stings, and that night, she wrapped Lestie in the soft blanket. It was like being wrapped in Mother's love. She fell asleep contented, in spite of the aching pain over her whole body.

PLAY PLACES NATURE MADE

Summer meant a lot of work for their parents, but for the children, the sparkling woods and fields were like a wonderland. They spent nearly every day of summer outdoors.

The older children had chores to do, such as washing dishes, feeding animals, or carrying in wood for the stove, but there was still plenty of time for play. There were no stores to shop, movies to see, lawns to mow or little league teams to occupy them. All they had to do was soak up the endless light and dewy air of summer.

A fat cottonwood tree stood sentinel at the outer edge of the circle driveway. Its thick branches offered purchase to a child's small feet, and a ride, high in the sky, swaying with the wind.

When the children roamed the homestead and surrounding woods, they never ran out of places to explore. They christened many of their favorite places with special names.

The area was mostly flat, but on the east side of the homestead was a clearing, where a gentle, grassy slope allowed a child to lie down at the top, parallel with the slope, and roll, giggling all the way to the bottom. This place they named "Roly-poly Hill."

"Fairy Meadow" had been a lake in its former life, but now it was a damp meadow carpeted with flowers: blue bells, forget-me-nots, daisies and more. In high places, at the meadow's edge, the fireweed bloomed, tongues of pink against the white of aspen bark. The tall, green stocks began to bloom along the lowest part of the stalk, while the rest was covered only with red buds. As summer passed, the buds opened, inching their way to the top. The buds at the tip bloomed in fall. Fireweed, like a living calendar, crossed off the days of summer, and when all the buds had opened, and the flowers had turned to silk, it was Fall, and winter would be coming fast.

SCHOOL ON THE PORCH

Cler had not stopped nagging the Territorial Department of Education for a teacher and supplies. At one point, they sent a polite letter back, asking if there was a building available where school could be held. He wrote back, "I have a small addition on my cabin that will be sufficient for holding school. It is large enough for the twelve students we anticipate will be attending."

The addition was the porch. It spanned the width of the cabin, and was about eight feet deep. The windows were covered

267

in translucent plastic, and it had a screen door, but now he built a solid door. This porch was meant to shelter his winter's wood supply, but now it would become a school room. He went to work emptying it of wood, and then he laid the floor with rough lumber he cut himself, on his sawmill. He also installed a small iron stove.

Two black boards and other supplies arrived, and Cliff Steadman, the new mailman, delivered the bounty to the Oborn's front porch. He and Cler stacked the desks and supplies at one end. It was summer, and the porch was still needed for other things, like hanging meat to cure.

Later that week, Gwynne received a letter from her best friend in High School, Carolyn. She and Gwynne had kept in touch over the years, through letters. Now she wrote, "Dick and I are making a trip up to Alaska in August. I was wondering if we can come to Kenny Lake and visit. Dick's interested in applying for a teaching position up there somewhere, but we want to see if we like it, before we make any rash decisions!"

Gwynne wrote back and told her to come. She and Cler would be delighted to see them.

The porch with plastic windows

20
ROPES, GUNS, AND GRIZZLIES

Summer, 1952

On two sides of Kenny Lake, there was a dark wood of very large spruce trees, part of an old forest not burned in the fire of 1926. While Paxton and Lestie were exploring one day, they walked down the road, crossed it, and followed an animal path south, through the brush. At one point, the trail split and led off in two directions, so Paxton tied his red bandana to the top of a willow. It was a marker to help them know which way to go, when they returned to the spot. They kept following the animal trail through the brush, and reached the stand of spruce trees on the west side of Kenny Lake. They decided to walk through the forest until they reached the lake, then go home by way of the trail along the edge.

The ground beneath the giant trees was carpeted thick with dead needles that muffled their footsteps. After walking for a while, they discovered a dark path that led deeper into the woods. The atmosphere was solemn and mournful as a graveyard.

They continued following the path, until they came to a small clearing shadowed by the great trees, where nothing had grown. The floor of the clearing was raw dirt, sprinkled with dry needles.

"This is kind of a creepy place," Lestie whispered, as if speaking louder would disturb unseen residents. She looked up, where Paxton was staring. Hanging from a heavy branch, was a faded, tattered rope. It was tied in a special knot both children had seen before, when their father had shown them how to tie different knots. They had learned sheep shank, square knot, and granny knot. This type was harder, made by coiling the rope and forming a loop.

It's a hangman's knot," Paxton whispered. "And look how it had a loop, but it's been cut. It must have been a hangman's noose."

"How do you know that?" Lestie whispered.

"It's pretty obvious," he said, studying the grayish, frayed rope. The unusual knot was remarkably intact.

"It looks very old," she said.

He stepped closer, staring up to study the rope. "Yeah, it's old alright, but it's still here, because it's been protected from the weather by these giant trees. The branches are like umbrellas. No sun, no rain down here."

"So what was it for?" she asked.

"A hangman's knot? I'm guessing some miner or trapper got hanged here. They used to hang horse thieves, I know that much. And they used horses around here during mining days."

The huge tree had sturdy branches. Paxton pondered how best to reach the rope, which seemed like a rare piece of history, and he wanted it. He jumped, grabbed a thick branch, and pulled himself up.

"What are you doing?" Lestie asked, horrified that he'd try to climb the tree, the site of a hanging. It was like stealing something from the little painted houses in the Russian grave yard

270

at Chickaloon, something they'd never do. They'd visited it once, and had seen dishes and other trinkets left for the departed. Their father had made it perfectly clear that nothing should be touched.

"Let's go; let's just get out of here!" She begged.

"I'm going to get the rope, and show it to Dad," he grunted, grasping the branch with the rope, while he stood on the limb just beneath it.

She backed out of the way, watching him saw the rope off with his pocket knife. It fell to the ground. Paxton wriggled back down the tree in a few seconds. He and Lestie studied the knotted rope as it lay on the ground. There was a murmur somewhere up in the tree, that sounded like a person.

"Did you hear that?" Paxton whispered.

Lestie had heard it. She was too frightened to speak, so she just nodded. Paxton grabbed the rope. "Let's get out of here!" He took off, and Lestie was right behind him. They ran all the way to the fork in the trail, and retrieved the red bandana. For a minute, they stopped, panting for breath, their hearts beating hard.

"We're just scaring ourselves," Paxton said.

"Don't you believe in ghosts?" she asked.

"Sure, but why would they hurt us?"

"For stealing their rope?"

"Not likely," Paxton said. "Why would they want the rope that hanged them?"

This seemed like good reasoning, and they were out in the sunlit willows again, so they followed the animal trail to the road, and walked the rest of the way home. When they reached the cabin, they spied their father out in the yard. "Look what we found, Dad." Paxton waved the hangman's knot at his father.

"Where did you find that?"

"Out in the spruce forest, west of the lake," Paxton said, handing the rope to him.

Lestie added, "It was hanging from a big tree."

Cler examined it. It was certainly old, and it was definitely tied in a hangman's noose. "What do you think it is?" he asked.

Paxton said, "I think somebody got hanged with it, like a miner or a trapper that stole somebody's horse. Probably a long time ago."

Cler thought about what he knew of the history of this place: the road house, the freight wagons and the horse barn down by the lake. Bloody feuds over timber; miners, gamblers and adventurers. Who could say that nobody had been hanged back in that forest? He handed the dusty souvenir back to Paxton.

"I think you may have a real historical artifact, son."

"What shall I do with it?"

"Start your own Museum of Kenny Lake History," his father said.

On the porch, Paxton tacked the hangman's knot high on the inner wall. It became a conversation piece for visitors, and for students who would later attend the first Kenny Lake School.

DUCK HUNTING WITH DAD

Paxton was a big kid for his age, strong and smart. He'd been his father's right hand man since he'd helped put out the grassfire, when he was only four. Cler had taught him many things, as the two of them trekked through the woods together, checking rabbit snares or hunting ptarmigan, the Arctic version of sage hens.

At six, he'd been allowed to hold the .22, and to shoot it with his father at his side. Now he was eight, soon to be nine, in November, and he wanted a gun of his own.

One day, Cler called Paxton to his side. He reached into the rafters of the cabin and took down the twenty-two rifle that had been more or less gathering dust.

"I think you're old enough to learn how to use this gun," Cler said, checking the chamber. Finding it empty, he handed the gun to his son.

Paxton's eyes grew big. He fondled the smooth stock, wiping off some dust, and ran his hand along the blue barrel. "Really, Daddy? Really?" he couldn't believe it. His own gun!

272

"I want you to go outside and practice shooting tin cans." He gave him a box of shells. "Be careful where you aim, and always carry the loaded gun pointed toward the ground. You know all this," Cler said.

For the next few days, Paxton practiced shooting his twenty-two whenever he got the chance. It was August, and ducks were thick on the lakes around the homestead. Rabbits were also plentiful. "When can I go shoot something for dinner?" he asked.

His father said, "Get your gun, and let's go duck hunting this morning. It looks like a perfect day for it. He called Tippy, the Springer spaniel. He was a good retriever, and would fetch birds or ducks, though he was not the all-purpose dog Buddy had been. There would never be another dog like Buddy.

Carrying rifles, father and son tramped through the stand of spruce trees, east of the air field, to Scotty's Lake. This was where Scott and Maxine had built a cabin, and it had burned to the ground. Now, grass and weeds had almost obliterated the old cabin site.

When they arrived at the lake, Tippy quivered with eagerness. He wouldn't have far to swim, because Scotty's Lake was barely more than a large pond. At their approach, the ducks scattered into the reeds along the shoreline, trying to hide.

"You go around to that side, and shoo them out of the reeds," Cler instructed, pointing to the south side of the lake, "while I go over to the other side."

Paxton waited until his dad reached the opposite side of the lake. Cler was ready with his gun, as Paxton started yelling and kicking at the grass, and a half-dozen ducks paddled furiously out of the reeds. Cler shot a couple of ducks and Tippy retrieved them, as the scattered birds fled back into the reeds. Again, Paxton yelled and flushed out ducks. One big mallard swam lazily behind the rest, and without hesitating, Paxton raised his gun, took aim at the slow duck, and pulled the trigger. The bullet missed the duck, skipped like a rock on top of the water, and ricocheted toward his father.

"Stop shooting! Stop!" Cler madly waved his arms and ran around the shore toward Paxton.

"You almost killed me!" he yelled, running up to his surprised little boy. "I felt that bullet fly past my ear!"

Paxton had seen the white mark as the bullet had ricocheted off the water. He didn't know a bullet would do that. "I'm sorry, Daddy, I'm sorry!"

"We have enough for today," Cler said, going back for the two he'd already shot. When they returned to the cabin, Cler laid the dead ducks on the kitchen counter. Then he took the rifle from his boy. He reached overhead and wedged it in the rafters.

"You can have this gun back when you're nine," he said.

GUNS AND SAFETY

With children around, Cler was always conscious of gun safety, and tried to teach it to his kids. Corrie and Paxton had both been checked out on the .22, and had been allowed to shoot targets, but only under supervision. One day six-year-old Lestie was admiring the 30-06, while her father was cleaning it. "That's a pretty gun, Daddy. Can I shoot it?"

"May I," her father corrected, "Whether or not you can, remains to be seen."

"May I?" she asked. She'd never shot a gun, but she'd been around them so much that she thought it would be easy.

Cler hefted his thirty-ought-six. It was heavy. "You want to shoot this?"

"Yes," she said. "Corrie and Paxton get to shoot the twenty-two."

"Well, OK... Put your coat on and come with me." He led her out into the yard.

"I want you to understand the power of this gun," he told her. He led her away from the cabin, and told her to wait, while he set an empty tomato can on a stump. When he came back, he dropped to one knee, behind her, and wrapped his arms around her, helping her hold the heavy weapon.

274

"Look through that notch and we'll line up the metal piece on the barrel with the notch. We're aiming at the can. See that? Just look, but don't put your cheek against it."

She looked, and lifted her head again. "I think it's aimed right," she said.

"OK, then. Now just squeeze the trigger."

She found the trigger and pulled on it. The gun exploded with a sound that deafened her ears and she let go, falling backward, as he father held on to the 30-06. She was too stunned to cry.

"I'm sorry," her father said, as he lifted her, one hand still holding the rifle. "Are you OK?"

"Yes," she said. Her fanny hurt, but she was too embarrassed to tell him.

"Now you know why you mustn't touch my firearms, unless I'm there to help you."

She decided it would be a long time before she asked again to shoot a gun.

FISH CAMP AND DADDY'S BEARD

One summer morning Cler took Lestie with him to visit their friends, the Georges, down at their fish camp on the Copper River. When they arrived at the camp, the people were busily filleting and smoking fish.

Cler parked the dump truck and they both got out. Her father said, "Don't get in the way or fall in the river."

"I'll be careful," she promised.

"I'll only be a minute." He headed off to talk to some of the men. One of them was just snagging a huge King Salmon from the catch box, using a hooked spear. Cler approached him, and he brought it to the truck and flipped it into the iron bed with a thump. Cler handed him some money. When Lestie got a good look at the man, she realized he was Nick Lincoln, Ina's husband. Though Grandma George's daughters had married, the entire family was always referred to as "the Georges."

Grandma George spotted Lestie and shuffled over to hand her a long strip of dried, smoked salmon. "Thank you, Grandma!" Lestie grinned, running back to climb into the truck.

Cler finished talking to Nick, and then he slid into the cab and started the engine. "Are you going to give me a taste of that squaw candy, Lestie?"

She tore off half, and gave it to him.

With his mouth full of fish, Cler said, "Good stuff! Nothing like it."

She nodded, her own mouth occupied.

They rode together in silence. The dump truck bounced and banged noisily over ruts in the dirt road. When they reached the main road, they passed the little settlement with its cabins and caches, and Cler said, "You know, Lestie, we probably owe our lives to the Georges."

For a while, she studied her father's face, wondering what he meant. "Do we have to pay them back?"

"We can only be good to them, like they are good to us," he said. "And sometimes, the only way to pay back a good deed, is to help someone else. It's the way the world works."

Thinking about paying people led Lestie to think about money, which was a fairly precious commodity in her family. She had once mistaken a nickel for a quarter and embarrassed herself by offering the storekeeper a nickel for five candy bars. Now she was thinking of pennies, as she studied her father's profile. He had a mass of curly hair, a smooth, high brow and what she thought was an attractive nose, and like the profile on the penny, he even had a beard, of sorts. He had grown it since they'd been back at Kenny Lake. It was rather sparse and surprisingly red, even though his hair was dark brown.

"I think you look like the man on the penny," she said when they arrived home. Cler took her hand and helped her jump down from the cab.

"Abe Lincoln? I guess you like my beard!" he laughed. She followed him to the back of the truck, where he grabbed the King Salmon by the gills and hauled it toward the cabin.

276

Once inside, he dropped the fish onto the split-log table. Gwynne already had the pressure cooker steaming, with the lid sealer, and a large number of new tin cans lined up, ready for canning the fish. They set to work. Cler began cutting up the salmon, while she stuffed the pieces, bones and all, into cans.

"Say, Dear, do you like my beard?" Cler asked.

Lestie watched as her mother set aside the can she'd just filled, and stared at him. "I like you in a beard; I love to run my fingers through it, but I guess yours could be fuller."

"Lestie thinks I look like Abe Lincoln." He chuckled a bit self-consciously.

"Nah," Gwynne said, leaning over to kiss his cheek, "You're not hairy enough." His smile disappeared and she said quickly, "But hairless is much more handsome!"

Cler looked hurt. "Hairless? I thought I'd managed to grow a pretty good beard!"

The truth was, Cler was not a hairy man, at all. His basic hairlessness must have come from his Indian forebears. At any rate, back in High School he took Gwynne to swim at a hot springs, and they were sunbathing by the pool, when she noticed he had two hairs on his chest. She reached over and plucked one out.

"Ouch!" he said, "What did you do that for?"

She frowned, "You had two hairs on your chest. Now let me pluck out the other one!" This was a story the children had heard their mother tell, and they thought it was very funny when she teased Daddy.

Now Gwynne said, "I think your beard would look better trimmed. That's all I'm saying."

A day or two later, at dinner, which happened to be spaghetti, Gwynne looked up from her plate; her eyes landed on Cler's face and stayed there for a few moments. He noticed her staring at him.

"Like how I trimmed my beard?" He asked, turning to show his profile. He'd shaved his cheeks, and all but a tuft of red, curly hair on his chin.

"It looks like you have spaghetti on your chin," she smirked.

Cler smacked his fork down on the table. "That's it! I might as well shave the whole thing off!"

Corrie squinted at her father. "Shave what off, Daddy?"

GRIZZLY!

It was desperate blatting of the goats in the barn that woke Gwynne. The springs complained with a series of squeaks, as she rolled out of bed. Cler woke up.

"What is it?" They could hear Tippy barking on the porch.

"I don't know, but we'd better go see, I guess." Gwynne slid her feet into her slippers and made her way down the hall to the main cabin. When she opened the door to the porch, Tippy stood his ground, barking and growling at something outside.

"Cler!"

He was right behind her, shrugging into his bomber jacket. He reached for his 30-06, and shoved a shell into the chamber. "If Tippy's that upset, it's not just a moose."

He stopped at the screen door, where the spaniel had braced himself with four legs spread, his head down, growling viciously. He restrained the dog and pushed open the door, leaving Tippy inside. "I'm sorry, boy, but you're not a bear dog."

It was high summer, and fairly light outside, though the sun hadn't yet rolled above the horizon. Out in the barn, the cow was making a racket, and the goats were frantically bleating. It had to be a bear. Cler tried to see where it was.

While he was still standing in the yard, Tippy stopped barking, and the cow and goats quieted. Cautiously, he made his way to the barnyard, and stooped to examine the ground around the barn. In the damp sawdust, he could see prints. They were like a very large man's hand, only with claws that dragged furrows in the dirt, where the fingers would be. This was one big bear...

The tracks led around the barn, as if the bear had been trying to find a way in. Cler followed the tracks, as they angled off toward the trees, keeping his eyes open for a dark shape, or movement in the brush. He ventured into the trees and followed a thin trail for a few minutes. The bear would have taken the trail, rather than trying to break his way through the thick willows and alders. He heard the crack of a branch breaking at the same moment he spotted the bear, not ten feet away. With a woof! it rose to its full height, maybe eight feet. Its fur was dark, glossed with silver tips; its massive head was wide and flat. A grizzly!

The grizzly focused on Cler, its little black eyes glittering with malice. Cler's mouth went dry as he took a couple of steps back, and then braced himself, feet planted against the recoil; he sighted in on an eye and pulled the trigger. The explosion thundered in his ears, slamming the butt of the rifle into his shoulder.

Not taking his eyes off the bear, Cler grabbed a shell from his jacket pocket and reloaded. The grizzly shook its head as if it had been stung by a bee. With its great paws half raised, the animal swayed like a cobra measuring its prey. Cler sighted his rifle again, on the other eye, just as the grizzly roared, the shot hitting it in the mouth. Its face streaming blood, it reeled, and dropped to all fours. Cler reloaded, slamming a shell into the chamber. He shot again, hit it in the neck, and reloaded. It was still coming. Before he could get off another shot, the bear lunged for him. With a swipe of its giant paw, it knocked the gun from his hands, sending it flying, as a claw ripped the arm of his bomber jacket, slicing into his flesh.

The next thing Cler knew, he was up a tree and the grizzly was down below, roaring at him. For maybe five minutes, the bear furiously shook the cottonwood, which was no more than eight inches through the trunk, while Cler wrapped his arms around it, and hung on for dear life. Then, as if suddenly deciding to take a nap, the bear collapsed and rolled over onto its side.

Cler was breathing hard, his heart still beating like thunder in his chest. He studied the giant animal, slumped on the ground below. One forearm was extended, with the paw open. Its claws

279

were at least eight inches long, curved and black, the ends needle-sharp, lethal. The paw twitched, and Cler's heart jumped, but that seemed to be the grizzly's last bit of adrenalin. It looked dead, but was it? He waited. If he climbed down, he'd have to almost step on it to reach the ground. He'd wait a while longer, until he was sure. From his vantage point in the tree, he searched for his gun. He couldn't see it, but it had to be somewhere over there in the bushes.

Finally, certain the bear was dead, he shinnied down the tree. It wasn't until his feet were firmly on the ground, that he noticed the rip in his leather jacket, along the length of his right forearm. He examined the jagged tear and touched a sticky ooze of blood. It was only then that he felt searing pain. He unzipped his jacket partway and lifted his wounded arm with his left hand, easing it into the opening of the jacket, so the zipper could act like a sling. He'd look at the wound when he got back to the cabin.

He sidestepped past the carcass, and moved to the bushes, where he thought his gun had flown. He spotted it caught in willow branches, grabbed it with his good arm, and made his way home, to get his machete.

Back at the cabin, Cler sat on a chair in the kitchen, while Gwynne washed the gash in his arm. It wasn't very deep, but it had torn into the muscle. Thank goodness his arm had been protected by his leather jacket, she thought, as she poured sulfa into the wound, and closed it with butterfly strips of adhesive tape. When his arm was all bandaged, and resting in a sling, Cler said, "Thank you, Sweetheart." He reached for his machete, in the knife block.

"What do you think you're doing?" Gwynne asked.

"I'd better get back there and bleed that grizzly."

"Oh, no, you don't. We have a phone, and we have friends. Call Cliff or Ted. They'd be more than happy to go take care of that bear for you."

Cler called Cliff, who brought his truck, and Ted showed up right behind him. They hauled the bear out of the woods, and winched it up to hang from the swing pole. By this time, it was full

280

daylight, though only about four in the morning. "We're happy to help," Cliff said, as he and Ted set about skinning the bear. "And don't think you need to give us any of the meat. Next time one of us has been mauled by a bear, you can return the favor."

"I hear you," Cler laughed, and then winced, because he'd moved his arm wrong. "But you fellows are still getting some of this meat. There's going to be way too much for just my family. While we're at it, let's take some down to the Georges, too."

QUACK-QUACK THE DUCK

With stores, roadhouses and gas stations few and far between, the Oborn's cabin was the place where people stopped by on a regular basis. Friends and strangers alike stopped, either just to visit, or with some need.

Cler kept extra cans of gasoline, with the thought in mind that he ought to open a gas station. As it was, he would sell or give the gas to those in need. Whether someone was in need or just visiting, they were always welcome, and the coffee pot was always on.

One afternoon, a friend that Cler had worked with at the moving company in Anchorage stopped by. Cler was going out to chop wood for the stove, when Hal drove up in front of the cabin, and parked his panel truck.

"Well, this is a nice surprise," Cler said, shaking Hal's hand, and then Rita's. "I didn't recognize your truck. What brings you folks up this way?"

Rita grinned, "We came just to see you!" She was small and slender, while Hal was a hefty man, with a barrel chest and big shoulders. Working for the moving company, he built a lot of muscle, and could lift an oak dining table by himself.

Hal laughed, "Actually, we're on our way up the road, to the Chain Lakes. We heard they're teeming with grayling about now."

"It's good fishing," Cler told him. "You can catch 'em using a bent pin and piece of line on a stick!"

"No kidding? So what do you use for bait? We have plenty of flies."

"Flies work, but you can use a bit of bacon or cheese. They're not picky."

At this point, the rest of the family wandered out of the cabin, a few at a time, wanting to see the "company." Cler introduced his family to them.

"Hal and Rita, this is my wife, Gwynne, and these are my children: Corrie and Paxton. The little ones are somewhere around here." He turned to Gwynne, "Hal and I worked together at Shaw's."

"Come on inside and we'll get you something to drink," Gwynne offered.

"Thanks, Gwynne, but first, we brought you folks a present," Hal said. "Knowing how you're starting your farming operation here, we thought your kids might like this." He winked at Corrie, who was standing nearest to him.

"Be right back." Hal went to the back of his truck, grabbed a door handle, and the rear doors swung open from the middle. He took out a small cardboard box. Inside, was a little yellow duckling. Hal held it in the palm of his hand, and it just sat there, looking around with its beady little black eyes.

"On our way through Palmer, we stopped at the State Fair and I ended up with this little duck," Hal said. "I won it in the shooting gallery, believe it or not! I thought your kids would get a kick out of it."

Corrie Lynne was standing closest to Hal as he held out the duckling on his meaty palm. She adjusted her glasses and took a better look. It was love at first sight. "Can I have him?" she asked Hal.

He grinned down at the little girl. She was wearing a plaid flannel shirt and baggy jeans that seemed too big on her slender frame, and her hair needed brushing, but behind those glasses her blue eyes sparkled with intelligence. "I'm sure you will take good care of him," he said, "that is, if your folks say it's OK…" he looked to Gwynne for the verdict.

282

"Of course!" she said. "Corrie Lynne is a great little mother! Now, why don't you come on into the house?"

Corrie thanked Hal for the duck, and lifted it reverently from his hands. The baby duck made a tiny sound, "Peep, peep."

"I'm going to name him Quack-quack," she said.

The big man grinned, "Can't think of a better name for a duck!"

DICK AND CAROLYN ARRIVE

In August, Gwynne's friend from high school came to visit. Carolyn had written to Gwynne earlier in the summer and asked if she and Dick could come up to Kenny Lake because Dick was interested in teaching school in Alaska. The couple flew to Anchorage, rented a car, and arrived in Kenny Lake for a week-long visit.

Dick was a slim, handsome man with carefully groomed black hair and a California tan. He wore black, horn-rimmed glasses, and a khaki shirt and pants that made him look like a civil servant. Carolyn was blond, blue-eyed and shapely. She wore no makeup, and her eyebrows and lashes were light, but the natural look suited her. There was a softness about her that couldn't be disguised by blue jeans that fitted her figure, a green flannel shirt, and leather lace-up boots. She and Gwynne greeted each other with warm hugs. It had been a decade since they'd been together. Cler and Dick immediately took to each other, as if they'd been friends as long as their wives.

On their second morning, Dick and Carolyn wanted to go fishing. Cler and Gwynne packed up the kids, along with a picnic, and they all drove down the road to the Chain Lakes to catch grayling. These lakes were carved out by a glacier. They were deep and cold, and they came right up to the edge of the road. Dick and Carolyn drove their own car, and parked beside Cler's jeep wagon on the gravel lot that had been created when the road was built. In order to fish, they would have to sit on one of the tumbled boulders dumped there by the crew that had built the road through the canyon.

The Oborn children on a rock at Liberty Falls 1952

Dick and Carolyn were avid fishers, and they were thrilled to discover the Chain Lakes. They caught one little lake trout after another, barely getting their hooks in the water, before a fish took the bait. Even the children fished. Cler cut poles from nearby willows that had grown up among the rocks lining the road. He gave them a short piece of line to tie onto a stick, and they baited the hook with a small piece of cheese. Celestia and Charles both caught a good-sized grayling, while Corrie and Paxton, who had the patience to sit longer, caught several.

Gwynne didn't fish, but spent the time visiting with Carolyn while trying to keep Butchy from falling into the water. They all stopped fishing long enough to eat a picnic in the parking lot, since there was no other place they could gather. After lunch, Cler and Dick gutted the fish at the water's edge, and they packed them in a cooler Dick brought along.

Cler didn't have time to play all day. Summer was too short. So, Dick and Cler spent the afternoon hauling deadwood for the winter's wood supply, and the hour before dinner sawing it into stove lengths and splitting some for kindling.

When they all sat down to a supper of fried graying and new potatoes, Dick was almost too tired to eat. "This is delicious, Gwynne," he said, "but I'm so bushed, I can barely hold my head up." He turned to Cler, "You have to work pretty hard around here to get by, don't you?"

Cler finished chewing and swallowing a bite of tender fish, "Oh, but it's worth it! Where else can you find scenery like this, and live on fish, fresh out of the lakes and rivers?"

Dick savored another bite of his fish, "You're right, of course. We put in a long day, but it's not like you have to go for wood every day, is it?"

"Of course not. We spent the morning playing, didn't we?"

Carolyn said, "We surely appreciate your taking the time off to take us places."

"We love company," Gwynne told her. "It makes us feel a little less isolated here in the wilderness."

Cler laughed, "Oh, Honey! We've never been isolated. We have each other!"

While the Lyndsleys were at Kenny Lake, the family also went on an outing to Liberty Falls, which was only about six miles up the road. Carolyn took pictures of everything. "I think the scenery around here is just spectacular. It feels like one could live on the view, alone."

"I've felt like that myself," Gwynne told her, "many times. These summer days just soothe your soul. It's even beautiful in the winter."

"I'm sure it is," Carolyn murmured. When she and Dick left to go home, they promised to keep in touch. Cler reminded Dick that there was an opening for a school teacher right here in Kenny Lake.

THE FIRST SCHOOL

Fall, 1952

Summer was flying by, and Cler was beginning to worry. It didn't look like the Territorial Department of Education was going to send a teacher by September, when school should be starting.

There were more people moving to the area, with more children. Gwynne and Cler took the children and went to visit the Clements*(not their real name) who had recently moved a trailer onto some property down the road. Their thirteen-year-old daughter, Dot, would be going to the Kenny Lake School.

George Clements and his wife, Jean, were both large people, heavy through the middle, and their daughter looked just like them. George and Cler had already met, when they were both at the store in Chitna, and George had invited Cler to bring his family and come for a visit.

The children, except for Dot, played outside. while the grownups talked. Dot remained in her room, with a trunk load of comic books that she promised to share later, if the kids would leave her alone.

George leaned back in his chair, with his arms crossed, resting on his stomach. "It's horses I love. Had a small ranch outside of Butte, but I sold out and came up here, thinking this area might be a lot like Montana. I want to bring some horses up here. What do you think?"

Cler told him he'd need a good barn, since the winters were so extreme, and plenty of hay, because there would be nothing for the horses to eat.

"I know cold," George said, "I've seen it thirty below some winters. The horses do need shelter, but a small stable will do."

Cler said, "I guess there's not much difference between thirty below and sixty below; cold is cold. The difficulty comes when you run out of feed. Winter comes, and it doesn't go away any time soon, George. Doesn't let up for six months."

"You say, sixty below?"

Cler nodded. "But some people do have horses in this country. Just make sure you have a warm barn and plenty of hay, that's all I'm saying. I hope it works out for you."

Dot came out of her room and addressed Gwynne. "If your kids want to come in and look at my comic books, I'll let them take some home, if they want to."

"Thank you," Gwynne said, "I'll go get them."

The children crowded into Dot's bedroom and were amazed to see a whole trunk full of comic books. It was like a gold mine of entertainment. She let each of the children choose two comic books, if they promised to take care of them and bring them back.

When they returned home, the children became engrossed in the comic books, and they all read until bedtime. Their father sat down with them, and read one comic book after another. There were so few opportunities for him to just sit back and relax, that it was noted in his journal. "Wasted a whole evening reading comic books, but I have to say it was a break from my worries, and it was pretty entertaining."

The next day, Cler was out on the porch adding an extra layer of plastic to the windows. The front porch was nicely closed in now. He nailed up the blackboards, and tried out the chalk on one, writing, "Kenny Lake School, Opening September 15, 1952."

Gwynne stepped out on the porch. "Getting ready for school, I see."

Cler smiled, "Just trying to get ahead of the game. You know, with the Newton girl, and three of our own, I count eleven or twelve prospective students, depending on whether I can convince Franklin to attend." The boy had never gone to school, and he was pretty shy about it. He was fifteen now.

"I sure hope we get a teacher," Cler mused.

"If they don't send one in time, why don't you do it?" Gwynne asked. "You'd make a great teacher. Don't you think your military training would count?"

"It might," Cler said. "I guess I could try and get a temporary certificate or something, just in case a teacher doesn't show up. I wouldn't mind teaching, just until someone qualified arrives. I guess they'd pay me to do it, and we can sure use the money."

As it turned out, his military schooling did count, since he'd gone to officer candidate school and graduated. All he had to do was pay a small fee to the Territory of Alaska, Department of Education, and he was provided with a temporary teaching certificate.

August ended, and the Department of Education sent a letter officially agreeing to pay Cler to teach the school, until they could send someone. Cler asked Cliff Steadman to spread the word as he delivered the mail, that Kenny Lake School would be starting the second Monday in September.

SCHOOL ON THE PORCH

Cler welcomed his students, and made it clear that he would be called "Mr. Oborn" during school hours. This surprised his own children, to whom he was Daddy, but they soon got used to it. It was like a game to remember to say "Mr. Oborn" on the porch, and "Daddy" everywhere else.

The students began each day with the Pledge of Allegiance, and a patriotic song. They learned "America the Beautiful" and the "Star Spangled Banner." No one but Mr. Oborn could hit the high notes, and he sang an octave lower, but it was the spirit that counted.

After the pledge and song, Cler read to his students from a children's classic, such as Tom Sawyer, and Swiss Family Robinson. As usual, his dramatic reading kept the children on the edge of their seats.

288

Using the method suggested in his teaching materials, Cler set the older students to a task, as he taught the younger ones. Then he left the younger grades to do work according to their level, and saw to the rest of his class. In this way, each child was taught reading, writing and arithmetic at their own level.

When a child needed to practice a sum or write a word on the blackboard, Cler would say, "Go back to the back black board." It always struck his students as funny, and they all tried to repeat it, seeing who could say it the fastest.

When it came to science, Cler was in his element. He loved to teach about the stars, and planets. For science and history, the grades all got in on the same lessons.

After a lesson on the constellations, he suggested the kids go outside that night, and try to spot the ones they were learning about. That night, the Oborn children trooped outside, and found the north star, the Bear, and the Dipper. From there they could locate Cassiopeia, the beautiful, but vain lady of Greek Mythology.

The children learned about animals that lived in the woods and streams around them, and could name many of the plants that grew in the Arctic. They also performed simple chemical experiments, such as mixing vinegar and soda, and learned the three states of water, by dropping ice onto the hot stove and making steam.

Celestia started first grade that year, and the first thing she learned was how to spell her whole name, including her middle name, Alice. She had watched Corrie doing her Calvert courses, making large, round letters on wide-lined paper, and had memorized the way words looked, without ever actually trying to read. Now she took to reading and writing as easily as drawing and coloring, which she'd done since she was two.

Cler enjoyed teaching his students poetry. He could recite long poems by heart, and the words to dozens of songs. He wanted his students to love these things, too.

The younger grades learned simple poems like "Ode to a Cloud," or "Trees," while the older ones memorized "Paul Revere's Ride," as part of a history lesson.

Celestia was distracted from her own work by the reciting of the older students, and before long she had their long poems memorized, too. But she hadn't done her arithmetic, which was her least liked subject. If she needed help on subtraction, however, there was always her older brother nearby, to help her. These were the delights and the advantages of a one room school.

Even for Gwynne, the first days of winter sped by. On her front porch there were a dozen children singing, reciting, laughing, taking part in learning. The porch was a hive of activity.

Gwynne sometimes left the door open a crack so she could listen to Cler read to the class, or sing a ballad. Four-year-old Charles crept onto the porch and participated in art lessons, or observed the second graders reciting their poems. "I think that I shall never see a poem as lovely as a tree..." He, too, began to memorize poetry, and it wasn't long before he could read.

A BOY AND HIS GUN

Paxton turned nine in November, and as Cler had promised, the boy got his .22 rifle back. He reached into the rafters, and took down the gun, wiping dust off its stock with his sleeve. Then he took down a box of .22 shells, placing them on the table.

Cler said, "I want you to remember the rules we've talked about. Never kill anything that you don't intend to eat. Never point a gun at another person, even if it's not loaded."

"I'll remember, Dad!" Paxton was so excited, he stood on first one foot and then the other, waiting for his father to hand him the gun.

"Go outside and practice," Cler told him, opening the chamber to check for a bullet. Paxton rushed to grab his winter coat, a heavy, duck cloth affair that hung down to his knees; something his dad had picked up at Army Surplus. Jamming on his Arctic hat, the one with furry flaps over the ears, he stood ready.

Cler said, "Practice on some tin cans first. Then go find supper for us. There are a lot of rabbits in the woods; see if you can bring back a couple. Still got your pocket knife?"

Paxton slipped his hand into the pocket of his baggy wool pants and pulled out his little knife. "It's sharp, Dad," he said, proudly, flipping open the blade, which was shiny, looking well-honed.

"Good! When you get the rabbits, bring them home and skin 'em out. Keep the skins; your mother's making a blanket. And no gut shots." One hand under the stock, and the other under the barrel, Cler offered the precious gun.

The boy took it with both hands, and then tucked it against his side, holding it barrel down, as he'd been taught. His dad gave him a box of shells.

"Go," he grinned.

THE DEPARTMENT OF EDUCATION FAILS THE GRADE

It was November, 1952, and still no teacher had arrived from the Territory's Department of Education. Cler enjoyed teaching, but he had so many other things he had to do. He had to feed the animals, for one thing, and there were now three goats to milk. Teaching school, he hadn't cut up enough wood to last 'til Christmas, and he worried he hadn't stockpiled enough to last the winter.

Another thing that was plaguing him was the ongoing trouble between Enzo Santini and Ted Ennis. They sent their kids to the same little school, and the kids seemed to get along, but there was tension at the last parents' meeting, when the men almost came to blows over how long the boys could miss school to go hunting with their dad.

Cler liked both men, but honestly, there were times when he wanted to shoot both of them. He didn't tell Gwynne, because she seemed to be going into a slump herself, the way she tended to do as winter came on, but he thought he was beginning to get ulcers from just dealing with so much. Teaching kids, taking care of his family, settling arguments between Enzo and Ted. He was losing a lot of sleep. And why had no teacher arrived at Kenny Lake, to replace him?

One night over a supper of canned moose meat and gravy, Cler said, "I'm about fed up with the dilly dallying of the Department of Education. Why don't we just take the kids down to California for the rest of the winter, and let them go to school there?"

"I guess we can do that," Gwynne said. "I'd never pass up a chance to miss a winter here, but do you think you can get a job? In the letter I got from Carolyn the other day, she said the jobless lines are staggering down there."

"Write back and find out if they know of anyone hiring pilots, or electricians," Cler said, only half serious.

Surprisingly, a couple of weeks later, a letter arrived from Carolyn. It included a newspaper article. Carolyn wrote, "Dick thought Cler might be interested in this article." Apparently, McClellan Air Force Base, near Sacramento, was being converted from wartime use, to peacetime maintenance of military aircraft. They needed men with skills repairing and testing aircraft engines in the new facility. Cler wrote to McClellan and by the middle of November, he got a letter in the mail. It was a job offer, to help build the new facility and work as an airplane electrician.

Cler figured they could spend six months in Sacramento while the kids went to school, and still come out ahead. This time, they decided to take a plane to the States. They bought tickets on Alaska Airlines, which was now flying out of the new Anchorage International Airport.

Before they left Kenny Lake, they took the goats to the Santinis, and Quack-quack and the dozen chickens to the Ennises, and paid them to take care of the animals over the winter.

HEADING SOUTH FOR THE WINTER

Gwynne and Cler herded their excited children up the portable stairway and into the DC-3. The shuddering take-off

292

stunned the five children into silence, but their cries could not have been heard over the roar of the engines. Corrie and Paxton, who had window seats on opposite sides of the aisle, kept their noses glued to the glass as the runway, buildings and surrounding trees shrunk away. In moments, the plane was flying over the silt-laden waters of Cook Inlet, and Cler pointed out the plane's dark shadow moving below them, cast onto the surface of the water. Tiny whitecaps, stirred up by wind, broke the surface into random patterns. The plane rose higher, and soon there was nothing to see but fluffy clouds. Winds aloft buffeted the plane, as they headed south.

Butchy became airsick, but there were white bags handy for such emergencies. A stewardess brought a wet towel to help Gwynne clean up the little boy, who cried for a few minutes and then fell asleep with his head on her lap. She petted his soft brown hair.

Heading southeast, the plane flew with the sun, until night overtook them. The engines droned steadily on, engulfing the plane in a cloud of noise. The children slept, tucked around with blankets and little pillows, leaning against each others' shoulders.

When they arrived in Utah, Cler's dad, Ernest, picked them up at the airport. With hugs and happy exclamations, the grandparents were thrilled to see their "little Alaskans" again.

At the Oborn grandparent's brick house, Lestie and Paxton crept down the steep steps into the basement, which they remembered from their previous visit. They knew that down there in the gloom there was a stash of old toys: a rocking horse, wooden blocks, some heavy iron cars, and even a train set.

Aunt Cheryl, Celestia and Corrie Lynne Thanksgiving, 1952

It was the week of the Thanksgiving holidays. Cler and Gwynne had decided to spend a few days in Ogden, buy a used car, and then leave for California, to stay over the winter. They purchased an old Nash, which had loads of trunk space, and was supposed to get good gas mileage.

For the two days before the holiday, Lestie and Paxton stayed with their cousins, at Aunt Ella's, while Corrie stayed with Cheryl. For those two days, they went to school as "visitors." The school was two stories of cut stone, with aged wooden floors and tall windows that rose up almost to the high ceilings. When Ella came out of the principal's office, she gave David a note for his teacher, and the boys headed for David's classroom upstairs, while Ella took the girls down the hall to Kindergarten.

Lestie felt uncomfortable. She was a first grader now, and yet she was being demoted to kindergarten. When she saw the huge classroom, however, her fears vanished. There were pint-sized tables and chairs and shelves loaded with books and toys. "After while, we get a snack," Susan told her. "Graham crackers and little bottles of milk." Lestie decided she was going to like it here.

Meanwhile, third-graders Paxton and David arrived upstairs. A pleasant, round-faced teacher greeted the boys and accepted the note from the principal.

"Well, hello, Paxton. I'm Mrs. Marsh. So you come from Alaska? That's so intriguing! I hope you'll tell our class all about life in the Arctic."

Paxton smiled. He wasn't sure what he was supposed to talk about, but if he had to, he'd think of something. He was given a seat near the door. He glanced around, figuring if he hated it here, he could easily escape. After the bell and all the students were seated, the teacher put a hand on his shoulder, "Class, this is Paxton Oborn, from Alaska."

She showed them a large map, and pointed to Alaska. "It's an American Territory, and it's very big, as you can see. It goes from the eastern panhandle, (this part, see, that looks like the handle of a pan) which is farther west than any point in the United States. See that? And if you keep going west, you have the Aleutian Islands..."

Someone tapped Paxton on the shoulder, and he turned around to see a freckle-faced kid, who whispered, "Do you live in an igloo? Have you ever seen a polar bear?"

"Well, of course!" Paxton whispered back. This was going to be fun. When Mrs. Marsh gave him the floor, he spent a half hour describing his own version of life in Alaska, complete with dogsleds, igloos, polar bears, and man-eating wolves. Of course, he mentioned, modestly, that he had a pocket knife, owned his own gun and he was a pretty good shot.

A HANDFUL OF CLOUD

The family loaded into the Nash so early on Friday morning that the children snuggled into the pillows and blankets in the back seat and slept for two more hours. The rest of the luggage was tied onto the carrier on top.

It was late when they arrived in Reno, Nevada, "the biggest little town in America," or so the marquee exclaimed. The main street was lit up in garish colors of neon, and sported several gambling casinos and cheap motels. Cler pulled into a motel that advertized "vacancy." It was a low, frame building running parallel to the street, with parking in front of each room. From what they could tell by the signage, a couple could get a quick divorce for only $10, right across the road.

The room had two double beds. Cler and Gwynne slept in one, putting the girls and Butchy in the other. Paxton and Charles slept in a corner, in sleeping bags.

The next morning, they reached the top of the pass over the Sierra Nevada Mountains, near Truckee. The road was windy and narrow, and the drop-off over the cliff was so far down, that Cler figured a person would have time to sing "Nearer My God to Thee" clear through before they hit the bottom.

They started the steep descent; there was a patch of cloud lingering over the mountain, and the road seemed to disappear into it. Cler said, "Look, kids! Roll down the window and you can grab a handful of cloud!"

Paxton rolled down the window, and he and Lestie reached into the cloud and tried to fill their hands with it, but of course, they couldn't.

"Oh, Daddy!" Lestie laughed, "Is this really a cloud?"

"Of course it is. We're in the clouds, but it's hard to hold onto one, isn't it?"

296

Paxton cranked the window up, because the cloud was cold. He rubbed his wet hand on Charles' face, "Here you go, wash your face in a cloud!"

Charles just giggled.

They were down the mountain before they knew it. Cler followed a map and drove straight to McClellan Air Force Base, which was now a depot for maintaining military equipment and aircraft. He checked in with the provost martial, who directed him to the officer who was in charge of Cler's unit.

Gwynne and the children stayed in the car, with the windows rolled down. It was warm, maybe 65 degrees outside, and the air felt balmy compared to Utah. While they waited, Gwynne passed out cheese and crackers to the kids.

She watched the door of the two-story metal building, expecting Cler to reappear any moment, but he didn't come out. She sat there waiting, watching the door. It had been painted dark green once, she thought, but now it was faded to a pale green with a chalky surface. All the buildings looked like they were left over from the war, which they probably were.

Butchy was sitting on the floor at Gwynne's feet, fiddling with the buttons on the dash. She glanced down at him. "Oh, no, Butchy!" He'd managed in just minutes, to unscrew the knobs on the heater, unscrew some nuts and bolts, and pull wires out from under the dash. She pried his little fist open and extracted the handful of wires, and lifted him onto her lap. "Here, have another cracker!"

Finally, she saw Cler coming around the side of the building. He took long strides, covering the distance in mere seconds. He looked happy, excited. He pulled the driver's side door open and slid in.

"I start on Monday. I'm really going to like this job. I met some great guys I'll be working with."

"What are you going to do, Dad?" Paxton asked.

"I'll be helping to build a large building, and maintaining airplanes, Son. I'm the guy who'll fix the electrical systems."

"I'm glad you'll like it," Gwynne said. "Now, can we go find a place to stay? These kids are ready to get out of the car. Oh, I almost forgot. Do these wires go to anything important?"

She pointed to the wires hanging down by her feet.

Cler eyed them. "What happened? Those probably go to several things: heater, headlights..."

"Butchy was entertaining himself," she said.

Cler shook his head. Butch hadn't a clue he'd done anything wrong. The little guy's crooked grin and bright blue eyes showed he was just thrilled to be noticed.

"You little monkey!" Cler said. "Let me make sure this thing starts, so we can get to Sacramento before dark. I might have to fix the headlights!"

The car started, since Butchy hadn't actually disconnected anything but the heater. Just outside of Sacramento, they pulled off the highway at the Blue Moon Motel, a cinderblock structure laid out in an old orchard. It was painted an intense shade of turquoise, while the doors were flamingo pink. They paid for a room, and bought a newspaper. In the room, Cler poured over the ads, while Gwynne put together supper from the cooler.

Cler was looking for a little trailer to rent, but he found something else. "Here's just what we need! Listen to this, 'Truck house, furnished. Sits on flat bed truck. Runs great." It gave an address where they could view the item, and it was only a few miles away.

While Gwynne and the children stayed in the motel room, eating supper, Cler just had to go see the "truck house." It turned out to be a cargo container, with windows and an aluminum door on the side. The man who was selling it had bought it from the military, and it had been used, he said, as temporary living quarters on base during the War. It was fitted out with a kitchen and tiny bathroom, a couch across the front that made into a bed, a fold-down table, and a tiny bedroom on the back with a set of bunk beds. There was a small stove at the back, that burned coal.

Cler checked out the flat bed truck that the container sat on. The engine started right up, and ran smoothly. The vinyl was torn on the bench seat in the cab, but otherwise, the whole outfit looked clean and perfectly suited for Cler's purposes. He figured that his family could live in the truck house over the winter, and travel up to Alaska in it come spring. In Alaska, he was sure he could sell it for a profit. He arranged to come back the next day to pay for it and pick it up.

After an hour or so, Cler returned to the motel, enthusiastic. "It's going to be perfect! It's just what we're looking for! Want to go see it?"

Of course, the kids wanted to go see it, but Gwynne was tired. "Let's get the kids bathed and put to bed," she said. "We can get a good night's sleep, and go pick up the truck in the morning."

As soon as Cler sat down on the edge of the bed, he felt the energy seep out of him. Gwynne was right; he'd been running on adrenalin. He smiled sweetly at his wife, "Is there anything left in the cooler? I think I forgot to eat."

The next morning, they bought the truck house.

22

November, 1952

SACRAMENTO

Cler drove the truck and Gwynne followed with the car, until they reached a neat trailer park, where they rented a space. As soon as they were in place, Cler hooked up the electricity, water and sewer, while Gwynne and the children checked out the new living quarters. Corrie, Paxton and Celestia bypassed the combination kitchen-living room, and went down the hall. There was a closet on one side and a bathroom on the other, and a little bedroom at the rear. The bedroom had a set of bunk beds and a round coal stove by the back door. Paxton crawled up onto the top bunk.

"Get off! We girls get the top bunk!" Corrie yelled.

Lestie ran to the front room. "Mama! Paxton won't get off the top bunk and Corrie says *we* get it!"

Gwynne called down the hall, "The girls can share the top bunk, and you three boys get the bottom."

Paxton rolled off the bunk and brushed past his sister, demanding, "Why can't the boys have the top?"

"Butchy can't sleep up there, that's why," his mother said "He might fall off."

Paxton muttered. "I don't think it's fair."

His dad heard him. "I'm surprised at you, Paxton. Fair isn't just getting what *you* want. It applies to all involved."

Somewhat deflated, Paxton walked back to the bedroom and lay down on the bottom bunk. He knew his father was right. It wouldn't be fair to Butchy to let him fall off the top bunk. As it happened, Celestia rolled off the very first night, and cracked her head on the stove. She wasn't seriously injured, but she learned not to sleep so close to the edge.

The park had rows of trailer houses and a central cement building that provided restrooms and showers, as well as coin-operated washers and dryers for the tenants. It was neat and clean, not far from a grade school and only ten miles from the Base.

Gwynne got a job selling a line of fine china, which was marketed like Tupperware, which means it was sold at home parties by women who got a cut of the product sold at the parties. To be a "distributer," Gwynne had to buy her sample case of three-inch china plates. She had always loved beautiful dishes, and this line of china appealed to her artistic senses. It had a dozen lovely patterns, and it was famously stronger than similar-looking china. When she first brought home the sample case, Cler tried the demonstration suggested in the seller's manual, while Gwynne held her breath and the children watched with interest. He set a fragile-looking, three-inch plate face down on the floor and stood on it. The dish remained unharmed. Amazing! Being sold on it herself, Gwynne hoped she'd be able to sell it to others, and make a little money.

She took care of Butchy and Charles during the day, but in the evening, after Cler got home, she left to sell china, dressed in her nicest gabardine skirt and blouse. She was nervous, to the point of being sick to her stomach, by the time she left home.

She found the house where the party was to be held. It was a white brick home in a neat neighborhood with well-lit streets and paved driveways. She parked on the street and slid out of the car, standing for a moment on the end of the walk. She strode confidently up to the house, the heels of her pumps clicking purposefully on the cement. *I can do this.*

Gwynne did make some money selling the porcelain plates. Her circle of customers grew, as women from one party invited their friends to their own houses, and those women in turn, held their own parties. It was a way for her to get out and meet people, and she was able to help buy groceries and gas.

Cler at Dick and Carolyn's house

DICK GETS THE TEACHING POST

Soon after arriving in Sacramento, Cler and Gwynne made a trip to see their friends, Dick and Carolyn, who only lived about an hour and a half away, in Vallejo. They left Sacramento and headed south on Route 40.

After traveling through the lush vineyards of the Napa Valley, they reached the little city of Vallejo, and stopped at a gas station to call and get directions. They found the Lyndsley's pink stucco house in a neighborhood of similar houses, all painted like Easter eggs. Red azalea bloomed profusely on bushes that nearly covered the front of the little house. A pomegranate tree dropped fruit on the driveway. Cler parked at a slight angle to avoid smashing pomegranates. He and Gwynne climbed out of each side of the car, stretched, and let the children out.

"What are those, Daddy?" Corrie asked.

"They're pomegranates. Leave them there and I'll ask Dick if he wants you kids to pick them up."

"You need to be good," Gwynne warned.

"We're always good," Corrie said.

Dick greeted Cler at the door, with a hearty handshake. "Come on into our humble abode!"

Carolyn and Gwynne hugged each other. "Wow! You look great," Gwynne said.

Carolyn grinned. Her blonde hair and red lipstick were perfect, and she wore a slim black skirt and fitted blouse.

302

Dick said the kids were welcome to pick up the fallen fruit and take it in the garage, where he had a box to put it in. After they picked up the interesting fruit, Dick told them to take the box out to their car so they could take it home. "We're getting sick of them," he told Cler.

After they put the box in the car, Corrie and Paxton and the other kids sat around on the floor, trying to be quiet, while the grownups talked. Gwynne anchored Butchy on her lap, but he tried to wiggle away.

"Why don't you bring him into the kitchen and we'll find him a cookie?" Carolyn offered. "We can get something for everyone to drink, too." The two women left, with Butchy stumbling in his awkward little gate, clinging to Gwynne's hand.

Dick said, "Carolyn and I have some news. We liked Alaska so much when we were there last summer, that I applied to teach at Kenny Lake, and believe it or not I got the job!"

"That's great!" Cler said. "When are you going?"

"We'll be leaving in a couple weeks, in time to start after Christmas. I was just wondering about where the school is going to be held."

"It'll be on my porch, I guess, the same as it was when we left. I actually taught school myself, for a couple of months, but I was just waiting for a teacher to get there. I taught up until Thanksgiving break."

Dick clicked his tongue, thinking. After a moment, he said, "Well, I was kind of hoping they'd built a school house by now."

Cler laughed, "That's the plan, but it'll have to be for next year. Since Gwynne and I will be here until spring, you and Carolyn are welcome to live in our cabin while we're gone."

"That's great!" Dick said. "So we go up there, you come down here, and it all works out. I'm so excited to get there!"

Meanwhile, the women were having a lively conversation in the kitchen, punctuated by giggles. They were fixing lemonade, while Butchy was tied to a kitchen chair with a dishtowel around his waist, so he wouldn't fall off. He was crumbling a cookie in his hands, and eating the pieces off his lap.

Gwynne squeezed half a lemon into a bowl. "You don't know how good this looks and smells," Gwynne exclaimed. "One thing I've missed is citrus. I can't seem to get enough since we've been here."

Carolyn said, "When we go to Alaska, I plan to take along a whole crate of lemons!" She laughed, a bit nervously. "Dick is so set on going to Kenny Lake...I'm a bit worried..."

Gwynne looked up from cutting the last lemon in half. "I think you and Dick will be fine. There are some good people out there at Kenny Lake."

"I know it'll be great, but it's so far out of town, I'm worried about what I'll do if I have to see a doctor..."

"They have a clinic and hospital now at Glenn Allen, and some new doctors in Anchorage, Carolyn. We like Cal Johnson."

"Dr. Johnson? Does he know about female troubles?"

Gwynne smiled, "He seems to know about as much as any doctor, I guess."

Carolyn poured a small amount of lemonade into a clean glass, and took a sip. "Needs more sugar." She spooned more sugar into the pitcher, and used a long-handled wooden spoon to stir it. "I just worry too much, I guess. " Again, she poured a little and tasted it. "Just right!" She arranged glasses on the table and filled two for Cler and Dick. "How much do you want the kids to have?"

"Better make those half full. I'll take the cookies in." Gwynne untied the dishtowel that kept Butchy on the chair, and used it to brush crumbs into her hand. She threw the crumbs into the trash can. Butchy slid off the chair and ran back to the front room.

Gwynne said, "I don't want to give you the idea living in the Interior is easy, Carolyn. Kenny Lake is pretty remote, but there are plenty of people around if you need them. And Anchorage is only half a day's drive."

Her friend took a deep breath, and put an arm around Gwynne's waist, giving her a gentle hug. "You've managed, so I guess I can... Thanks, Sweetie. You're such a treasure!"

304

A few weeks later, Gwynne got a letter from Carolyn. "We're settled in the cabin, and school is in session. Dick says to tell you the kids are great, and thanks for leaving so much wood to burn. We're doing fine. I'm just a little surprised it's so cold already, but they say our blood is thin from living in California and it will thicken up after awhile. I certainly hope so!"

A LESSON IN COMPASSION

A little girl named Alice lived next door to the truck house, in a small trailer, with her eight-year-old brother, Jack, and their parents. Alice was in Lestie's first grade class at school. At first, Lestie didn't like her very much, because "Alice" was Lestie's middle name, and that name, she thought, only belonged to her.

After a few days, Lestie got used to the fact that different people could have the same name. The girls played in the trailer court together, washing doll dishes in mud puddles and taking turns riding Charles' tricycle.

In Sacramento, the winter was cool and rainy. Corrie and Lestie walked through a large, grassy field to get to school. They wore long cotton stockings with garters to hold them up, and a nice wool sweater over their dresses; the sweaters and dresses were presents from Grandma Oborn and Grandma Paxton.

Alice wore the same ragged dress and sweater every day to school, something Lestie barely noticed. One day she did notice how Alice's shoes looked on her bare feet. Her heels flattened the backs of her shoes and hung over the end. Lestie thought it was an interesting way to wear shoes; kind of like slippers.

One day at school, she and Alice got into an argument on the playground. Alice could be bratty at times, but then, so could Lestie, for that matter. It was a childish argument, something about a ball.

"It's my turn!"

"Is not!"

Lestie slapped her on the shoulder and Alice cried to the teacher, "Celestia hit me!"

The teacher scolded harshly, shaking a finger at her, "You mustn't hit poor little Alice! You should be ashamed of yourself!"

The bell rang and both girls filed into the classroom with the other children, but Lestie wondered why the teacher had become so angry.

That night, lying in her top bunk, staring out the tiny window across from her bed, Lestie saw a flashing red light coming down the street and in a moment, the trailer court lit up, as a police car stopped in front of the trailer next door.

Cler said, "There they are!" The truck house trembled as the door swung open and closed again with a soft metallic thud.

Lestie continued to peer out the window. Two policemen were knocking on Alice's door and Daddy was out there talking to the police. She could see Mother at the side, wrapping her robe around herself against the chill.

The policemen disappeared into Alice's trailer. A moment later, one came out carrying the little girl in her ragged dress, and the other led her silent brother by the hand. Both children were placed in the back seat of the patrol car and taken away.

Gwynne and Cler thumped up the steps; the aluminum door opened with a whine and banged shut again. Lestie heard her dad say, "I feel bad calling the cops but what else could we do? Some people shouldn't have kids."

Lestie slid off her bed, and padded in her bare feet out to the front room. Her parents were sitting on their bed. They looked surprised.

"What are you doing up, Curly Locks?" her father asked.

"I'm wondering why the police arrested Alice and Jack."

He pulled her closer, against his knee, "So you saw that?"

"I was looking out the window."

"The police didn't arrest them or anything like that," he said, "The problem is that their parents haven't been home for three days. The police are taking them to Social Services, so someone can take care of them."

"You mean, their mother didn't feed them?"

306

"Yes, among other things," he said. "It's kind of like when we got Butchy. His own mother didn't take care of him, so we got to keep him. Now we love him, don't we?"

Her father kissed her and sent her back to bed; she didn't fall asleep for a while. The more she thought about it, the more guilty she felt for hitting Alice. She suddenly could see Alice as she was: a little girl in a ragged dress, because that was all she had. A little girl who didn't have parents who loved her. Lestie felt overcome with remorse for hitting Alice. She lay there in the dark, with tears soaking her pillow.

Cler, Gwynne and the Oborn children with Nan.
Bill and Nan's house in Hollywood Hills 1952

MEETING GROUCHO MARX

Cler's brother, Bill, invited the family down for a weekend, and they made the trip a week before Christmas. Bill and Nan lived in a ranch-style, white brick house, with a red tiled roof. It was surrounded by lush vegetation, situated in the rolling hills south of Los Angeles.

Bill was now the producer of a TV show called, "You Bet Your Life," with the comedian, Groucho Marx. Groucho and his three brothers, Chico, Harpo, and Zeppo, were a family act popular in Vaudeville, on Broadway, and in motion pictures from 1908 to 1949.

As the producer of Groucho's TV show, Bill was able to arrange for Clermont, the Alaskan Homesteader, to make a guest appearance on the show.

Groucho was a funny guy with a black moustache and eyebrows that looked like wooly caterpillars. His head was mostly bald, and he wore round, horn-rimmed glasses. Those unique features were copied and sold as a gag. All you had to do to look like Groucho was put on the fake glasses, complete with eyebrows and mustache attached to them.

With butterflies in his stomach, Cler stood behind a podium, in front of the camera. Someone dabbed a powder puff in his face to douse the shine on his forehead. Above his head, a cartoon duck with glasses and mustache like Groucho, was suspended on a string. If, during the show, the guest said the "secret word of the day" the duck would descend in a flurry of weird quacking and the guest would win a prize.

The show began, Groucho greeted his audience, and a side-kick announced, "Ladies and Gentlemen, meet Clermont Oborn, from Alaska!" The audience burst out cheering, clapping and whistling, but a guy was holding up a sign that said, "Applause," so Cler didn't take it seriously.

"We'd like to get to know you, Cler," Groucho said, in his funny, lilting accent. "It says here you're an Army Vet turned Alaska Homesteader, is that right?"

"I am," Cler said. "We live two-hundred and thirty miles north of Anchorage..."

"Wa-aa-y out in the boon docks, I take it? "

"That's right.."

Groucho glanced at a card, "Says here you sent your wife into town with the mailman, for an important event."

"She was going to have a baby," Cler said, straight faced.

The audience broke up.

Groucho wiggled his caterpillar eyebrows up and down, "Did you go along?"

308

"Oh, no," Cler replied, "I had to take care of the other six kids in the cabin. I trusted the mailman."

The audience roared.

Cler didn't win any money, but being with his big brother, and on TV to boot, was a reward in itself.

The next morning after breakfast, they packed up to leave for Sacramento. Nan and Bill followed them out the door, and the two families stood around on the concrete driveway, enjoying the December sunshine. Nan had Kathy, their pretty, dark-eyed toddler on her hip, and she set her down. Little Kathy, in a white dress and diaper, toddled across the fresh-cut lawn, after a brown rabbit that hid under a bush, bowed low with azaleas.

Gwynne was admiring the pink flowers, when Butchy slipped away and scampered after the rabbit, too. The bunny disappeared through a hole in the board fence, behind the bushes, and the two children knelt at the fence, with Butchy trying to coax the rabbit back through the hole. "Bee bee," he called.

"That's Henry, " Bill said. "He adopted us when he was just a tot. Been hanging around our yard ever since."

"I love all these flowers," Gwynne said, leaning to smell a yellow rose.

Bill said, "Say, you ought to go to Pasadena for the Rose Parade. You've never seen anything like it! Float after float of nothing but flowers!"

"New Year's day, isn't it?" Cler asked.

"Yes. You'll be off work, so go see it. I'm sure your little Alaskans will not believe their eyes."

"Maybe we will. Hey, it's been wonderful seeing you, Bill." He hugged his brother, and glanced over at Nan, who was holding Kathy again. "And your beautiful family."

"Flattery will get you everywhere," Nan laughed.

They filled up with gas before they left town, and took the highway north, through the desert, rather than the longer route along the ocean. Cler was a bit worried about the miles he was putting on the car. McClellan Air Force Base was ten miles from the trailer court, so he was putting twenty miles on it every day, at least. Gwynne added miles, whenever she went out to sell china. He just hoped the old Nash would hold together until spring, when he could sell it.

TRUCK HOUSE CHRISTMAS

It was Christmas Eve, but Gwynne and Cler were saving every penny they could for a grub stake to take back to Alaska. They had bought some candy and nuts for the stockings, but that was about all they dared to spend. Still, it was Christmas, and there was one thing Cler thought of, that was free.

As they gathered around the little table for a simple supper, Cler said, "Hey, gang, after supper, let's go for a ride and see the Christmas lights! I've passed by some really terrific displays; houses all lit up!"

The children hurried to finish their bread and soup. Talking and giggling, they loaded into the old Nash. With the back seat down, open to the trunk, there was extra room for the four children to snuggle together in the back. Butchy sat up front on Gwynne's lap.

On the way to see the lights, Cler stopped at a corner, and noticed two small boys beside the road, selling a two-foot pine tree.

He rolled the window down, "What do you want for it?" he asked.

"Fifty cents," the taller boy said.

Cler handed them two quarters. Then he climbed out and opened the trunk, angling the tree in; a sweet, woodsy smell filled the car. The children bounced with excitement, letting the little branches tickle them.

"Be careful," Gwynne said, "don't break the branches!"

As they drove off, Cler started singing, in his clear baritone, "O Christmas tree, O Christmas tree, how lovely are your branches." Gwynne joined in more softly, and the children sang,

310

whenever they knew the words. After that, they sang "Jingle Bells," in spite of the fact it was beginning to rain outside.

In the rain, Christmas lights shimmered on palm trees and houses, making rainbow smears of color. With rain increasing, Cler cut the excursion short and headed back to the trailer court.

When they arrived back at the truck house, rain was pouring down, and everyone hurried to get inside. Over the kitchen sink, Cler shook water off the little tree, and then he stood it in a small bucket, using rocks to stabilize it. He set it on the table, and asked Gwynne if she had any empty tin cans.

She rummaged around and found several, which she washed and dried. Meanwhile, Cler retrieved leather gloves, pliers, and tin snips from his tool box in the truck. He sat down at the table and used a can opener to remove the lids and bottoms of each can. With his tin snips, he cut a pointy silver star from each round of tin. He used needle-nosed pliers to turn the edges of the star, so they wouldn't be so sharp.

Cler glanced up to see four little faces focused avidly on the finished star in his gloved hand. "Don't touch these stars or the metal leftovers, he said. "The tin is sharp. But isn't this pretty?"

"It looks bootiful," four-year-old Charles said, eyeing the star.

Cler used a nail to hammer a hole in one point, threaded a piece of string through it, and hung the star on the tree. While he was working on ornaments, Gwynne took out white paper and scissors. She made glue, by mixing a little flour and water in a cup. "Come and help me make paper chains for our tree," she called, inviting the children to kneel around the orange crate that served as a coffee table.

Fortunately, Butch had fallen asleep in the car and had been put to bed. If he'd been up, he would have been getting into everything.

Gwynne had only two sets of scissors, so she and Corrie cut paper into strips, and then they all made paper chains by gluing one strip into a circle and looping the next one through it, then gluing that one. This kept the kids busy and out of Cler's hair, while he was working with sharp pieces of tin.

When each child had made a chain as long as they were able, Gwynne took all the chains and linked them together. Cler finished hanging the stars, Corrie cleaned up the glue, and Gwynne looped the paper chain around the Christmas tree. As a final touch, she wrapped a red dish towel around the bucket, to give it a festive air. The children gathered, admiring the tree. "Wow, that's a super tree, that's pretty," the children said, and Butchy echoed, "Pity!" Cler sang "I'm dreaming of a white Christmas," and began telling them the story of the first Christmas.

"Joseph and Mary had to take a long trip to go back to where they were born and pay taxes. This wasn't an easy journey, because Mary was going to have a baby..." While he told the story, the children stared at the tree. To them it was beautiful with white paper chains like snow, and silvery stars hanging on it. Outside there was drizzling rain, but inside the little truck house it was Christmas.

Suddenly feeling weary, Gwynne sat down on the couch and leaned back, resting her head. She remembered last Christmas, when they were in Ogden with their families. The brightly decorated trees, the turkey with all the trimmings. She was raised an only child, and there were always beautifully wrapped presents under the tree, and most of them had been for her. Then she remembered one Christmas when she was eight, when she had learned a lesson. It was during the Depression, and many people were suffering, but her father was never out of work. One present appeared under the tree, but she had always gotten lots of presents, so she wasn't worried.

"Now don't peek at that present," her mother told her. A few hours later, when her mother was visiting a neighbor, Gwynne had carefully pulled off the ribbon and opened the box. Inside was a little sewing machine, along with a pair of scissors, ribbons, spools of thread and squares of cloth; everything a little girl would need to sew doll clothes. It was a wonderful present.

She carefully put it back together and set it under the tree. On Christmas morning, there was still only one present: the box with the sewing machine, and because she had peeked, she didn't even have the joy of being surprised. She hid her disappointment and hugged her mother and father, thanking them. It dawned on her that they had done the best they could to give her Christmas. Now, she wished that she could give a better Christmas to her children. There would be no presents under the tree for them to open, only some candy and nuts in their stockings. Somehow, she knew her children would be happy; they all took delight in very simple things.

Gwynne sat up, "It's bedtime, children. Cler, can we have prayers now? I'm really tired."

Cler offered a prayer and reminded the children to say their own. He sent them to bed and gathered his tools, to take them to the tool box, out in the cab of the truck. When he came back, he whispered, "The kittens are fine. I gave them some milk." Gwynne smiled. She'd forgotten; there would be two little presents under the tree, and the children would love them.

On Christmas morning, the children rolled out of bed early and found their stockings hanging on their beds, full of nuts and candy. They exclaimed over the candy, and stole to the front room to find a nutcracker so they could eat the nuts. To their surprise, there was a small cardboard box on the table, under the tree. Daddy was sitting on the couch with Mother, drinking a hot drink.

"Look in the box," he said. Corrie opened the flaps, while the others watched. In the box were two tiny kittens. One was white and the other was golden yellow.

"Looks like Santa stopped by. Take turns and you can hold them," Mother said.

Corrie picked one up first and Paxton picked up the other. "What shall we call them?" he asked.

"Scotch and Soda!" their father suggested, wryly.

"Oh, Cler," Mother said, thumping him on the shoulder.

"I get it!" Corrie exclaimed. "This one looks like butterscotch candy and that one is white, like baking soda."

"See how smart our daughter is?" Cler laughed.

ARTHUR, JUANITA, AND THE ROSE PARADE

After Christmas, Cler called Art Lopez, who was living with his parents in Pasadena. He invited the family down to watch the Rose Parade. "Our apartment's on the second floor, and the parade goes right down our street. We have a great view. Do you think you can come?" he asked.

"I'm tickled you asked," Cler replied. "We'll be there!"

On New Year's Day, they made the trip to Pasadena, encountering heavy traffic, with miles of the main street closed to cars, and more barricades going up. They drove around until they found Art's apartment complex and a parking place in visitor parking, off the alley. They located the Lopez apartment, up a flight of stairs, and knocked on the door. In a moment, they were greeted warmly by an Hispanic man, who looked a lot like his son, Arthur, with the same slight build and dimpled smile.

"Buenos dias, Senor Cler y Senora," he said, shaking their hands with enthusiasm. "Come in, come in!"

Senora Lopez, a round little woman, rose from her chair, and stood shyly beside her husband, smiling, "Buenos dias!"

Art hurried out of the kitchen. He had a towel tucked at his waist, and was wiping his hands as he came.

"Hello!" He shook hands with Cler, and hugged Gwynne. Then he saw Lestie, and swept her up in a big hug, "Little sister!" When he set her down, he said, "My other little sister is in the Parade, and we're so excited! We'll see her go by."

Art's mother said something in Spanish, and Art said, "This is my mother, Theresa, and my father, Armando. They speak more Spanish than English, but they want you to know they're so happy to meet you. Mama wants me to say, and this is embarrassing, but she's grateful you took care of me in Alaska." He grinned at his mother.

314

She smiled at Gwynne, "Gracias."

Art said, "I'll point Juanita out to you when we see her. She's about this high and will be twirling a baton, with a bunch of other girls, in front of the Pasadena High School Band."

Art's father indicated that they should all sit down, and Art headed back to the kitchen, saying, "I'm in the middle of making some chile rellenos to celebrate your coming! We'll eat in a little while."

When he came back to the living room, the grownups were all seated on chairs facing the open windows, and the smaller children were peering out to try and see where the band music was coming from. So far, they couldn't see anything but a couple of policemen trying to clear the street and keep the crowd back.

A troop of airmen in dark blue dress uniforms came marching, with Old Glory in the front, and the people in the crowd grew quiet. Hands moved to hearts, as the flag passed by. The adults and children in the Lopez apartment also rose to their feet and put their hands on their hearts. Cler was touched to see Art and his parents saluting the American flag, looking just as proud as he felt.

They had a wonderful view of the festivities. Pretty girls in prom dresses waved as the flower-decked floats moved slowly past. There were marching bands, sailors in white bell bottom uniforms, a hay wagon with Old Time Fiddlers, and more. The Oborn children had never seen anything like it. The music, colors and passing spectacle were so overwhelming, they didn't know where to look next.

"There she is!" Art exclaimed, his black eyes shining. His mother and father leaned out the window to get a better look at their little girl. She was the smallest and she was strutting along, out in front of the other girls, all dressed up with her black hair in a ponytail, wearing a little red jumper and white shoes and socks. She twirled her baton without missing a beat.

Corrie and Lestie watched, fascinated, as tiny Juanita strutted by, down on the street, while the crowds of people on either side cheered. When she had passed, Lestie leaned over to Corrie, and whispered, "Don't you wish you could be in the parade, and twirl a baton?"

Corrie thought about it, "No, not really. I think it would be exhausting."

SCOTCH AND SODA

The day after the older children went back to school, Butchy and Charles were playing outside with the kittens. When they came inside for lunch, they left them in their cardboard box, and Charles tucked the lid over them, but when they returned, the box was open and the kittens were gone.

"Mama, Mama," Charles cried, "come see!"

Gwynne stepped onto the porch and shaded her eyes from the sun, looking down at the empty box. "They must have climbed out and run away. Maybe they went home," she said.

Charles wiped his eyes. "Let's go get our kitties," he said, as if it were that simple. Gwynne decided that maybe it was.

She took Butchy by the hand and the three of them walked down the row of trailers to the one where Cler had bought the kittens. There, curled by the steps, was a mother cat and four kittens, two yellow and two white.

Charles could tell which ones were theirs, and he scooped up the kittens, one in each hand. Gwynne rapped on the aluminum door, and a woman in a tatty bath robe answered, scowling through the screen. "What?" She didn't seem completely sober.

"I see my kittens escaped and came back here," Gwynne laughed, trying to make light of it.

"Your kittens? They're my kittens," the woman said.

"No, look," Gwynne said, as nicely as she could, "Charles, bring me Scotch and Soda."

The woman scowled. "You want a drink?"

316

"No, no! That's what we named them. I know these are our kittens. See? Scotch has this tiny black spot on his nose, and Soda here is fatter than that other white kitten."

The woman's eyes were so bloodshot they looked like roadmaps. "You want them kittens, it'll cost you fifty cents."

Gwynne reached into her apron pocket. She had three dimes she'd forgotten to give her kids for milk money. "Thirty cents and it's a deal." The woman opened her screen door and took the dimes.

Walking back to the truck house, Charles said, incensed, "That lady cheated us, Mama. Santa Clause gave us those kittens for free, and now you had to pay for them!" His mother smiled. When they got home, she took Scotch and Soda into the truck house and found a fountain pen. On each kitten's furry back, she printed in large letters, "Scotch" and "Soda."

1953 Cler, Butchy, Gwynne, Lestie, Corrie and Charles in front of Truck house. Just before heading back to Alaska

23

BACK TO ALASKA

Before they left Sacramento, Cler bought a female Peking duck for Quack-quack's mate. Corrie named her new duck Jerusha, from a storybook that repeated the line, "Quack! Said Jerusha, I think I'll lay an egg!" On the trip to Alaska, Jerusha would live in a cardboard box, and whenever possible, she would be let out to eat weeds and bugs.

They drove over the mountains and crossed Nevada, to Utah. In Ogden, they stopped to pick up Ernest, Ella's son, who'd agreed to go with them to Alaska, and help Cler on the homestead. At sixteen, the boy was almost as tall as Cler, and outweighed him by thirty pounds. He was thick around the shoulders, with straight, brown hair shaved to an even fuzz over his head. He had his mother's clear blue eyes, and calm demeanor. He brought along his pup tent, so he had a place to sleep when they stopped for the night, and he had a driver's license, so he could take a turn driving the truck house.

Cler bought some goats in North Ogden, on the way out of town. The goats were black and white Alpine, a nanny and her male kid. The nanny was already named Cleo, and Cler named the little male, Chechako. During the trip north, the goats would ride in a large wooden box in the kitchen, placed so it was possible to walk around it. The box had a hinged end that could be dropped to let the goats out.

Cler and Ernie loaded in the goats, and secured the box. Gwynne double-checked to make sure all the children were settled, and then she took Butchy up front with her. They headed on to Alaska, fully loaded with supplies and passengers that included two adults, one teenager, five children, two goats, two kittens, and a duck. The children rode in the back, where they could play and sleep as they wanted to. Ernie took his turn driving. Cler insisted they keep a regular schedule, which included stopping for the night.

Each morning, Gwynne filled a wash basin and put it out on the fender, with soap and towel, for some of them to wash up, while others used the bathroom and kitchen sinks in the house. After everyone had washed and dressed, they'd eat breakfast outside, if the weather was nice. Beds were made, clothes picked up, and the place generally straightened, before everyone piled in and they continued on their journey.

The roads were good through Idaho and Montana, and in three days, the family reached the Canadian Border. Cars and trucks waited in a long line at the check point. It seemed a lot of people were on their way north; it looked like a parking lot. One by one, each vehicle was checked by red uniformed Mounties. They asked why the drivers were entering Canada, whether or not they had anything to declare, and if they had adequate money to pass through the country. Canada and America were close allies, but their economies were still struggling, and Canada didn't want to get stuck with indigent travelers. Also, firearms and live animals had to be accounted for, and alcohol was prohibited.

The truck house stood out among the more ordinary cars and pickups. With some curiosity, a fresh-faced young Mounty approached the cab, and Cler rolled down the window.

"Good morning. What kind of vehicle is this?"

"We call it a truck house; it's a flatbed with a container on it, fitted out with living quarters."

"Excuse me," the Mounty said. He left to confer with another, possibly more senior, officer and the two of them walked around the outside of the vehicle. In a few minutes, the first officer returned.

"Where are you folks headed?" he asked.

"We're going to Alaska, to our Homestead," Cler said.

The Mounty spied Gwynne sitting on the passenger side of the cab, with little Butchy on her lap. Gwynne noticed the officer looking her over, and color came to her cheeks. She hadn't braided her hair this morning, she was wearing the same cotton dress she'd worn yesterday, and she felt disheveled.

Butchy grinned and waved, "Hi!" and the Mounty smiled, "Will you folks please step out of the vehicle?"

Getting out, Gwynne carried Butchy, who clung to her like a little monkey. Cler opened the aluminum door on the side of the truck house, and pulled down the retractable steps, "Everyone out!" Assorted children appeared and scrambled down the steps. The Mounty made a note on his clipboard.

"Anything to declare?"

"Livestock," Cler answered.

"Livestock?"

"In the house." The Mounty didn't look like he was going in, so Cler said, "We can bring them out, Sir." He motioned to Corrie and Paxton, who climbed inside. Paxton came out carrying the baby goat; Corrie had Jerusha in her arms.

The officer wrote on his clipboard. "Is this all?"

Just then, Ernie stuck his head out the door, looking a bit groggy. He'd been asleep in the back bedroom.

"Almost forgot Ernie," Cler said.

The Mounty asked, "Family member?"

"Nephew. Ernie, can you go get Cleo?"

"Sure." Ernie ducked in and came back leading the nanny goat on a rope. She clattered down the steps, bleating loudly, tugging on the rope to get over to Chechako. Paxton let him run to his mother, where he butted against her, attempting to nurse.

The Mounty looked at the ground, trying not to laugh.

After a moment, he checked his clipboard, and asked, "Is that all you have to declare? Any guns or alcohol?"

Cler said, "I have a rifle in the cab." The Mounty followed him to the cab, where Cler retrieved his 30-06 from the rack, and broke it open. The Mounty placed a seal on it, and told him not to remove the seal until he left the country. Cler put the gun back in the cab and returned to his family, who were all milling around, most of them trying to control an animal. Cleo was blatting at Chechako, who was running away, with Paxton chasing him, trying to lasso him with his belt. Jerusha was also struggling to get out of Corrie's arms, quacking her displeasure while Corrie wrapped her in her arms.

"Now," the young officer asked over the hubbub, "Is this all? No other guns or alcohol?"

"That's it," Cler said.

"No it isn't," five-year-old Charles piped up, "What about Scotch and Soda?"

The Mounty's shoulders sagged. He looked weary. "Scotch?"

Paxton had lassoed the baby goat, so Cler took hold of the belt, nodding toward the door. "Scotch and Soda. Go!"

'Sure, Dad!" Paxton thumped up the steps and through the door. In a moment, he came out carrying the kittens.

Cler took each of them by the scruff and held them out to the officer. Although they'd grown a bit, their names were still visible, printed across their backs.

"There you are," Cler said, "Scotch and Soda!"

The Mounty read the names, and burst out laughing. He quickly sobered up. "Is this all?"

"Yes," Cler said, equally sober.

"You're certain?"

"Yes."

The young man asked, "Mind if I take a look inside?"

"No, help yourself," Cler said.

The Mounty was only gone for a few moments. "Wow! That's a nice set-up! Hey, good luck to you folks." He watched as all the animals and people were loaded in. When Cler was ready to drive off, the Mounty resumed his professional demeanor and waved them through the gate.

In Canada, the roads weren't too bad, and they made as much as three hundred-fifty miles a day. Spring was on the way, but the further north they went, the more snow they saw along the road, and the trees went from leafy, to pussy willows, to winter-dead, over the passes. At Dawson Creek, they started on the Alaska Highway, and it was slow going. It had rained, and there was a bridge washed out, which delayed them a day, and in many places rain and melting snow made the highway into a mud bog. Cler managed to maneuver the truck through the worst places, but of course, they didn't make good time. Where the road was gravel, frost heaves bounced the truck, and riding over the rough roads rattled the bones. Everyone was grateful when they stopped for the night.

The road seemed endless, as it twisted and turned through miles and miles of brush and tundra. Once, Corrie and Lestie were riding up front, when their father began to get sleepy. They were several miles from White Horse, Canada, and he wanted to get there before they stopped. He must have fallen asleep for a second when he slammed on the brakes, crying, "A white horse in the road!"

Cler decided to find a place to pull over and stop for the night. He went to bed, still seeing the road ahead, every time he closed his eyes.

Most evenings, they'd camp, and if they were in a low place, where the snow was gone, the children played outside, while Gwynne made supper. Cler staked out the goats, and Corrie let Jerusha feed on new sprigs of grass, under her watchful eye. When they reached the border, the officials took the seal off Cler's gun, and he put it back together.

That morning, when they were not far into Alaska, they stopped at a large hot springs. There was no snow near the steaming water, and someone had built boardwalks leading into the willows, where there were several hot pools. They noticed a sign, "Beware of Bears," so Cler took his gun with them to the pools, which were quite a ways back. They all kept an eye out, but they didn't see any bears. They chose a pool that wasn't too hot for the children, and they all got a bath.

Warm, clean and refreshed, the children put on dry clothes and they all hiked back to the truck, where the parents changed their own clothes. They gathered around the table for a lunch of canned beans and wieners. From the hot springs on, the road was graveled and graded, and they arrived at the Homestead that evening.

May, 1953

HOME AGAIN, IN KENNY LAKE

The sun had disappeared behind a bank of clouds. The fields were faded beige with last year's grass, and snow lay in dispirited patches here and there. The road was a muddy track, and so was the dooryard.

Dick and Carolyn must have heard the truck rumbling up the drive way. They and their two boxer dogs were standing in the yard, and the dogs barked at Cler as he climbed down out of the cab. Dick grabbed the dogs' collars, while Gwynne and Ernie exited the cab, and the children spilled out of the truck house.

"Welcome home!" Carolyn greeted them all and gave Gwynne a warm hug. "It's wonderful to see you!"

Dick shook hands with Cler, "How was the trip?"

"It wasn't bad," Cler said. "We had an extra driver. Ernie, meet our good friends, Dick and Carolyn Lyndsley. This is my nephew, Ernest Passy."

After the introductions, Ernie went to work unloading the goats from the truck house. Corrie brought out Jerusha, and carried her to the little slab barn. She found the hens' watering dish and filled it from the water barrel beside the barn, which still had some water in it from last fall.

The other children ran around getting reacquainted with the old homestead, as if they hadn't been there for years. Celestia and Paxton raced each other to Old Climbing Tree and hugged it like a long-lost friend.

In the cabin, Gwynne and Carolyn caught up on each others' lives while they got supper on. They discussed the hard winter, and particularly Carolyn's health problems. " I went to see a doctor in Anchorage, but he recommended I see a specialist down in the States," she said.

Gwynne gave her a hug, "I'm sorry, Honey. You've had a time of it, haven't you?"

Meanwhile, Cler and Dick were having a heart-to-heart talk on the front porch, in the school room. "We're more than ready to go home to California," Dick said, perched on the edge of the teacher's desk, as he probably did frequently while teaching.

Cler sat down on top a student desk, nearby. He was disappointed. He liked Dick, and dreaded trying to find a replacement for him. It had seemed like a miracle when Dick had agreed to take the school at Kenny Lake.

"Won't you consider staying another year? You could live in the truck house. It's not bad. It was a little crowded with five kids, but for just you and Carolyn, it would be ideal. I'd let you live in it for nothing."

Dick shook his head, "I appreciate the offer, and we're grateful for your letting us use your cabin. I was really hoping we could make Kenny Lake our home, but I have to tell you, Cler, it's been a tough winter."

He looked Cler in the eyes, "I don't know how to say it without sounding like a pantywaist, but I can't take another year of this. Maybe I'm just too much of a Californian. I thought this would be an adventure, but it was an unrelenting trial, as well. I don't have to tell you, the cold is brutal. The porch never heats up. I mean, the stove could warm me on the front, but my back would be freezing. The kids had to wear coats and mittens during class in January, or they would have gotten frost bite!"

Cler knew winter and felt one just had to deal with it. When it was forty below and the car wouldn't start, you simply didn't go anywhere. If you absolutely had to go somewhere, it was possible to start a car, even at forty below, but it better be worth the risk. You could heat the engine block with a blow torch, and pray you didn't blow up the car.

Cler said, "I hear you. I felt kind of guilty basking in the California sun while you were up here freezing your tail pipe off!"

324

Dick laughed, "Very funny. Seriously, Cler, the kids were great, but some of the parents...I don't know how to say this, but what in blue blazes is wrong with those people?"

The smile slid off Cler's face. "I think I know who you're talking about..."

Dick said, "Santini and Ennis. Seriously. You know those guys better than I do, but they seemed to think that since I was living in your cabin, I should be able to solve their problems. Anyway, one day Santini really lost it! He almost shot Ted Ennis! Criminy, Cler, we almost had a murder here!"

Cler leaned forward, surprised, "I'm guessing Ted's still alive, but what was that all about?"

"I think it started over Enzo whipping his boys."

"Oh. Well--" Cler began.

Dick cut in, "I'm not talking about a spanking. This was only a couple of weeks ago. I was calling roll, and Little Enzo was missing, so I asked Arlo where his brother was. He said Little Enzo had been caught by his dad, smoking a cigarette, and had got a whipping, with a cat-o-nine tails, no less! He said it in front of the whole class, like he was proud of it!

"'My brother's tough,' he said. 'It's no big deal.' I was shocked. I don't think a kid should be whipped with a torture device!"

Cler sighed. "You didn't say anything, did you?"

"No, of course not!"

Dick ran a hand through his black hair, messing it up. He seemed troubled. "In retrospect, I don't think Ted actually said anything to Enzo, either. Ted's kids probably told their dad, and Ted made a comment that got back to Enzo. Like, maybe Ted said Enzo was a bully, or something. Whatever happened, Enzo stormed over to Ted's waving a rifle, threatening to shoot him if he interfered in his family business again!"

Cler was trying to make sense of it. He hoped the problem wasn't ongoing, or he'd get dragged into it.

Dick went on, "Ted told him he didn't know what he was talking about, and Enzo left, but then Ted came running over here

325

to tell me, and he was furious. He wanted to know what to do. I told him for Heaven's sake don't confront him! Just avoid Santini for a while. Believe me, I laid low, too."

Shaking his head slowly, Cler said, "Now I remember why I was getting ulcers before I left. So, between the cold weather and the feuding neighbors, you've about had it."

"Yeah," Dick said, "I've had it."

Cler stood up, "Well, I'd better go get some wood for the kitchen stove. The girls will need it for cooking supper."

He went out to the wood pile and picked up the ax. The kitchen stove needed smaller pieces of wood than the logs Dick had sawed for the drum stove. As he chopped up the kindling, Cler thought about his friend, Enzo Santini. He was pretty certain Enzo wouldn't have actually shot Ted. It was more about saving face. He was a proud man. The idea that his method of discipline had been called into question by his neighbor, and possibly the whole community, must have shamed and embarrassed him. Maybe he'd think twice before he used that whip on one of his kids again. You couldn't tell Enzo what to do, but if you left him alone, he could learn. Cler had seen it happen. Enzo was not an evil man, merely a flawed one, like everyone else.

Cler had seen the whip in question. It was old, Italian leather, with a worn, woven handle, and nine strips of leather with knots on the ends. Enzo said once that it belonged to his father. It hung on the cabin wall, along with Zoya's Russian icons. A family memento. *We learn how to be a father from our own father*, Cler thought.

He remembered his dad had a leather belt that he occasionally threatened to use on a wayward boy's behind (he had three sons), but Cler couldn't remember his dad actually using it. Cler had rarely spanked his kids, and if he had, it was for direct disobedience. Most folks spanked their kids, but he'd read somewhere that the usual swat-on-the-butt kind of corporal punishment doesn't do much to change behavior. If a child has done wrong, and gets a spanking, the article said, it merely evens the score, relieving the child's conscience, and allowing them to forget about it. *That's why I don't remember any spankings,* Cler thought with a wry grin.

He had chopped a nice armload of kindling, so he picked it up and carried it into the cabin.

Gwynne and Cler stayed in the truck house for a few days, while Dick finished some school-related paperwork for the Territory, and Carolyn packed up their things. They'd be driving to Anchorage and flying home to California.

On the day after the Oborns were back in Kenny Lake, Cler took the dump truck, and Paxton and Corrie with him, to retrieve his animals. He stopped first at the Ennises, and sent Corrie with Julie to get Quack-quack, and the chickens, while he visited with Ted. They talked about how the winter had been, what was happening in the community, but there was no mention of the incident with Enzo and his gun.

Julie Ennis, a lanky girl with glasses, who was a couple of years older than Corrie, took her out to the chicken coop. All over the yard, chickens were pecking at the new, green grass, or eating bugs. Inside the hen-house, there was a big, white duck, in place of the half-feathered duckling Corrie had left in November. There were a couple of dozen chickens roosting, and Quack-quack was perched on a low wall, in what must have been an attempt to roost along with the hens. He wobbled a bit, and flapped his wings to regain his balance. Obviously, his webbed feet were better suited to swimming. He spotted Julie and Corrie as they opened the door, and greeted the girls with enthusiastic quacking.

"Ever see a duck roost?" Julie laughed, sweeping the big duck up under her arm.

"No," Corrie said, "I wonder how he learned to do that."

Julie handed her the duck, with his wings pinned to his sides. "I guess it's because he grew up with chickens. He seems to think he's a chicken!"

"Well, I hope he learns he's a duck," Corrie laughed, "I brought a wife for him, all the way from California!"

Cler gave LaVerne an envelope of money for feeding the duck and chickens over the winter. Most of the hens were loose in the barnyard, but it was easy to tell which were the Oborns'. LaVerne's hens were either black, or speckled black and white, while Gwynne's were red. There were nine of them.

The girls and Paxton lured the red hens with grain, caught them, and loaded them into a couple of cardboard boxes. They put the boxes in the back of the dump truck. The kids got in, and Cler drove on down to the Santinis to pick up the three goats.

At the Santini homestead, Enzo was out in the yard, splitting firewood. He lit up as he saw Cler arrive. He waved and hurried over as Cler, Paxton, and Corrie climbed out of the cab.

"Hello! You're back! We missed you!" His dark eyes shone as he heartily shook Cler's hand. His face seemed more deeply lined, and the streak on his black hair seemed to have turned whiter over the winter.

"Glad to be back," Cler said. "So how's the family?"

"Good. Zoya had a little girl."

Cler was taken by surprise. He'd had no idea Zoya was expecting. The woman was naturally so round, who could tell? "Congratulations! When was she born?"

"April first. In Glenn Allen. The tent hospital."

"So you didn't have to go clear to Palmer. That's good."

Corrie asked, "Can we go see the baby?"

Enzo nodded toward his cabin, "Sure. Inside."

Corrie and Paxton knocked on the door and Alina, the seven-year-old girl, opened the door and welcomed them into the cabin. "Hi, Corrie! Paxton! Wanna see my sister?"

Zoya was rolling out dough on the table. "Hello! You want some vastedda?" That's what she called her scones. It was a traditional Sicilian fried bread. Hers were famous in the community for their tender, mouth-watering goodness.

"We came to see the baby, but I'll take one, please." Corrie grinned.

"Me, too," Paxton said, his mouth watering as he watched Zoya use a slotted spoon to lift a golden brown rectangle of fried dough from the bubbling oil on the stove. She set it on a clean, white cloth, and when she had all the fried bread out of the oil, she dropped in some more. She sprinkled a little sugar over the brown vasteddas, using a small shaker.

"Let them cool a minute," she said, and began cutting more rectangles of dough.

"While we're waiting, can we see the baby?" Corrie asked.

"Sure," Alina said, "Nika is over here." She proudly showed them the baby, who lay in a small wicker basket in the corner of the room. They peered at Nika, who was fast asleep. She had a mat of black hair and rosy, milk-chocolate skin that looked soft as a flower petal.

"She's beautiful," Corrie whispered.

Out in the barnyard, Enzo and Cler were looking over the goat herd. Along with Cler's goats, there were three nannies and a Billy calmly nibbling at the new leaves and last year's weeds. All of them were black and white, except Cler's Clementine.

"The goats look good. Fat." Cler said.

Enzo smiled, "I'm throwing the stud fees in for free!"

"That reminds me," Cler said, "Here, let me pay you and then I'll take them off your hands." He pulled an envelope out of his jacket pocket. "We agreed on seventy-five dollars. Does that still seem fair?"

Enzo lifted his hands, palms out, as if to stop him. "It's too much. I made money selling your goats' milk to the other homesteaders. We're even."

"No, Enzo. You fed my goats your hay, and I need to pay you."

Enzo countered. "I need some boards cut for an addition on my goat shed. I'll bring some logs over to your sawmill, and we can call it even."

"I promised you cash." Cler said.

"Fifty bucks," Enzo replied, "and I'm not taking a dollar more."

Cler counted the money and handed it to him, "OK, thanks. You can take the rest out in boards." Cler wanted Enzo to have the cash. He figured with a new baby, there was bound to be a hospital bill.

While the men were talking, the boys herded the goats up a makeshift ramp into the back of the dump truck, and secured the tail gate. Corrie came out of the cabin with vasteddas (which the kids called "wahstedies"), and they polished them off on the way home.

"I'm not saying these are better than Gwynne's scones," Cler said, after savoring the last bite of sweet, warm bread, "but these are really, really good!"

The nanny goats, Tina, Sylvia and Clementine, were unloaded in the yard, near the slab barn. They seemed right at home, and began grazing on spring grass. Cleo and Chechako were immediately accepted into the herd. For herd animals, the more there are, the safer they feel.

When Corrie put Quack-quack in the barn, Jerusha waddled over to greet him, but he sidled away from her, watching her with suspicion. Every time she approached, he waddled away. "What's wrong with you, Quack-quack? This is your new girl friend. She's just like you, a Peking duck!"

It took a few minutes before he let the little female come near. He didn't know he was a duck, so maybe he didn't know what she was, either, but he figured it out soon enough. Quack-quack and Jerusha lived with the chickens for a few days, until Cler built a duck house for them, and before long, Jerusha laid fourteen eggs, and faithfully sat on them while Quack-quack stood guard. Twenty-eight days later, there were thirteen baby ducks.

It wasn't long before Tina, Sylvia and Clementine had babies, too. Tina and Sylvia had twins, and Clementine had triplets, but the smallest one wasn't very strong, and it died. The baby goats were soon running around the homestead, following the children all over the place, trying to imitate everything they did.

Gwynne took pictures of the little goats hanging over the swing, running up the slippery slide and sliding down with their black ears flapping. They even followed the human kids into the

330

cabin, their little hoofs drumming on the wood floor. It seemed like someone had to constantly shoo them out.

By this time, Butchy was allowed to play outside, without constant supervision, although some other child was usually enlisted to keep an eye on him. He ran after the baby goats, who knew how to get away from his hugs and kisses, and he'd sit in the dirt with a spoon and play for hours. It was not a good thing when he discovered how to open the latch on the duck house.

Lestie found her little brother gripping a duckling.

"See?" he said, as if showing her a prize he'd won.

"No, no, Butchy, you can't hold the baby ducks!" she scolded. She managed to unlatch his little fingers and take the duckling away from him, but its head flopped to one side. She hurried to show it to Mother, hoping something could be done to revive it.

Gwynne didn't even have to feel for a pulse. She just shook her head "Oh, dear. I guess Cler had better figure out a better way to lock the duck house." It wasn't Butchy's fault when a couple of other ducklings disappeared. It may have been any of the predators that lived around Kenny Lake, including weasels.

Butchy came in the back door of the cabin one day, with a muskrat gripped around the middle. At least, Lestie thought it was a muskrat. It might have been a weasel. "What in the world is that?" she called to him.

Butchy brought it over, "See Kitty!"

Lestie eyed the long, furry creature. It was still soft and wiggly, so it must have just quit breathing. "Come on, Butchy," she said, leading him outside. "Let's put that kitty in the garbage pit." Out the back door, away from the cabin, Cler had plowed a pit suitable for burning trash. Butchy's weasel, or muskrat, was buried with the refuse.

Of fourteen baby ducks, nine grew into lovely white Peking ducks.

24

COMING TOGETHER

Summer, 1953

The community was growing. Other homesteaders moved in, and it was time to build a school. The Oborn's front porch just wouldn't do. One afternoon in early June, Cler called a meeting of the parents in the community. They crowded into the schoolroom, and everyone managed to take a seat by sitting either in, or on a desk. Cler stood in front.

"We need to decide what we're going to do with our kids in the fall. As I figure it, there'll be too many for this room. As many as twenty."

"We can't afford to buy land, Cler," Ted Ennis said.

"We're all in the same boat," Cler replied. "but I'll set aside ground for the school, if you people want to build it down below my circle."

"OK by me," Enzo said.

Ted said, "I guess we'll need another teacher, since Dick Lyndsley left."

"I'm hoping we'll get another teacher from the Territory by the time school starts. If no one comes, I'll do it. No matter what, we have to build a school, regardless. A log building; nothing fancy."

Cliff Kirkland said, "We all have a lot to do, getting ready for winter, but if we each donate a few days to building the school, we can get it done. For starters, I think we should stockpile some logs."

Cler said, "Any of you who can get some timber off your own property, I can bring my truck and help you haul it. We'll get started on the foundation next Saturday."

Ted Ennis spoke up. "I have to clear some land for a barn, myself, but I'll cut a dozen extra logs and bring 'em over."

Not to be outdone by his neighbor, Enzo spoke up, "I'll do the same."

"Thanks, Ted, Enzo. We can cut some boards on my saw mill, for the floor." Several other men raised their hands and offered logs.

"How's that sawmill working, Cler?" Ted asked.

"Fine."

"I'd like to buy some lumber when I build my barn, if you got the time," Ted said.

"Sure thing. Talk to me after," Cler said.

The meeting was a success, as every man with kids agreed to help with the school. As for those who hadn't showed up at the meeting, Cliff Steadman said he'd inform them of the decision to build a school, and enlist their help. He'd be stopping by to give them mail, anyway.

ERNIE

With nowhere else to put him, Ernie was consigned to the top bunk in the boys' room and Paxton took the bottom bunk. Charles got the Army cot, and Butchy's crib was moved to Cler and Gwynne's bedroom.

Paxton and Charles admired their cousin, and liked him. To his younger cousins, he seemed like an adult. For one thing, he had a driver's license.

One morning, Cler took Ernie with him to Anchorage, to get supplies. He let the boy drive the dump truck and noticed he was a capable driver. Too bad he doesn't have anything of his own to drive, Cler thought.

While they were at the grocery store, Cler saw an ad posted on the bulletin board, that caught his eye. "1948 Ford pickup. Best offer." He borrowed the store's phone, and contacted the owner of the truck.

On the way home, he and Ernie stopped to look at it. Ernie didn't know Cler was thinking of buying the truck for him.

The little Ford pickup was green and looked to be in pretty good shape, but the owner admitted it needed some engine work, and was willing to make a deal.

Cler asked, "Does it run? Can I try it out?"

"Sure it runs, but the muffler's about to fall off. I got it wired up, and the engine runs rough. Go ahead. Check it out."

Cler couldn't resist. If the truck needed fixing, that was OK. He and his nephew could work on it together. It would be fun!

Cler left the dump truck and keys with the pickup's owner, while he and Ernie went for a drive. The engine was burning oil, and with the bum muffler, it made a racket, but Cler made the guy an offer, and he took it.

Cler smiled as he handed the pickup keys to Ernie. "Want to drive it back to the Homestead? I'll have to follow you, in case there's a problem, but I think it'll make it there just fine."

Ernie climbed behind the wheel, more than happy to be able to drive it, but he still didn't know it was going to be his. They made it back to the cabin in good time.

When he opened the front door, Cler called, "Come out and see Ernie's truck!" Paxton was off the couch and out the door in three seconds flat.

"*My* truck?" Ernie asked.

"I bought it for you! Now you can run errands and do all sorts of things for me," Cler joked. Of course, Ernie was thrilled. What teenage boy wouldn't love having his own truck? Even if it meant running a few errands?

Ernie enjoyed working with Cler. He and his step-father had never been able to work together like this, Ernie thought. When he and Cler worked together, they didn't have to say a lot, and since Ernie was a boy of few words, this suited him fine. In fact, sometimes it seemed like he and Cler could communicate perfectly, without talking at all.

One Saturday, for instance, they were working together on the pickup. Cler was lying on the ground, underneath the engine, and Ernie stood by to hand him tools. When he finished with one tool, Cler would reach out and give it to Ernie, and without either of them saying a word, Ernie would hand Cler the tool he needed next. It went on like that for several hours. The young man cherished that experience.

School had always been a struggle for Ernie, who had dropped out his junior year. At Cler's suggestion, he sent away for a correspondence course from the Territory. He didn't want to go to school, but was willing to try and finish his GED while he lived with Cler and Gwynne. If he needed help, they were more than willing to give it. However, Ernie would much rather chop wood, milk the goats, or do any of a dozen other chores, than sit at the table, torturing his brain with school work. He didn't make much progress on the correspondence course.

CRACK SHOT

Near the Homestead, down over the Copper River Bluff, there was a large stand of mature spruce trees. They had escaped the fire that had swept the plateau twenty years earlier. One day in June, Cliff Kirkland stopped by to give Cler back some tools he'd borrowed. He and Cler sat on the saw horse, chatting about how the community was growing, and about the school they'd begun to build.

"I have an idea, Cliff," Cler said, chewing on a stalk of new grass. "Remember we talked about harvesting some timber down in the river bottom, if we could get to it. We need to build that road."

"That's just what I've been thinking. The ground's dry now and we ought to try it. You thinking I'll come and drive my bulldozer?"

"Hoping that would be the case," Cler said.

Cliff laughed, "Of course I will!"

Cler said, "I know another guy who'd be willing to bring his small dozer: Enzo Santini." He said he'd enlist the help of Santini and Cliff agreed to call Ennis. Scott McDaniel was back, living in a tent on a new homestead he'd filed on, across the road from his burned cabin. Cler decided to ask him, too. He knew Scotty needed logs and lumber for building his new cabin.

It was a sunny Saturday, when the men gathered at the end of Cler's airfield. Cliff arrived on his big Allis Chalmers bull dozer, a relic from building the Alaska Highway. Enzo brought his smaller dozer, also an Army surplus item, and all the men carried guns. Ted and Scotty brought chainsaws. Ernie carried Cler's ax, and his shotgun.

Nine-year-old Paxton watched the excitement as the men and machines gathered. "Please, can I go, Dad?" he begged.

"I don't think so, this time," Cler said. "We'll be clearing brush, cutting down trees. Better stay back at the cabin."

Cliff, sitting on the seat of the big bull dozer, with the engine off, heard the boy begging to go. "If you want to let him, he can ride up here with me," he offered, and Cler relented.

When the road-building party started off, Paxton proudly sat up on the bull dozer, grasping the steel bar that constituted an arm rest, with his .22 tucked down between the bar and the seat. Behind the big machine, came the smaller one, driven by Enzo. The chain saw crew followed along behind.

Engines roared, trees crashed, men shouted to each other, as Cliff cleared the way, pushing through the brush, uprooting trees, clearing willows, leaving piles of roots, dirt and quivering branches. Enzo pushed aside the piles with his small dozer, and the other men finished up by sawing off branches from the uprooted trees, and stacking the logs along the sides of the newly cleared road. During all this excitement, Paxton clung to the arm rest, his boots on the fender of the grader, having the time of his life.

When the road crew arrived at the Bluff, the vista opened like a magnificent painting before them. The men turned off their engines, savoring the silence, and the view. The Wrangle mountains, Sanford, Drum and Blackburn, rose solid and dazzling white against the blue sky; birches, aspen and willows, in every shade of green , blanketed the sides of the great canyon, and down below, the silver river braided around sandbars, dotted with buffalo that looked like tiny, black beads from where they stood. Just to the right, a moraine jutted from the top of the cliff, and down to the valley floor, like the tail of a prehistoric beast. The moraine was made of glacial silt and rock, grown over with bushes and small trees.

Cliff climbed down from the bull dozer. Cler walked over to him, and they both looked at the moraine. "What do you think, Cliff?"

"I think some of us better walk it, before I try taking my dozer down there," he said, scratching his chin. "I'll go down with you. Scotty, you want to go with us?"

"Sure," Scotty said.

"We'll just sit here and have some lunch," Ted said, dropping onto a fat log. He set his gun to one side, and reached for the cloth bag that was tied to his belt.

With his .22 in hand, Paxton scrambled down from his perch on the big dozer. "Hey, Dad, I want to go, too!"

"No, just stay here and have some lunch," his father said.

"I won't be any bother, Dad. And I can eat my sandwich while we're walking."

Scotty was standing nearby. "Hey, Paxton. You think you're a pretty good shot with that rifle of yours, don't you?"

"I guess so..." he answered.

Scotty was something of a teaser, and he loved teasing Paxton, who always took himself so seriously. "Tell you what," he said, lifting a small vial from his shirt pocket. He shook a wooden match from the vial. "If you can light this match, from, say twenty-five yards, we'll let you go with us." The other men chuckled, except for Cler, who watched with interest.

Scotty paced off the yards, and wedged the match in the crack of a dead tree, so it stuck out sideways. He returned to stand near Paxton. "There you go," he said.

The boy lifted his rifle, steadying it against his shoulder, and took careful aim. He squeezed the trigger. Bang! Whoosh! The match lit.

"Well, I'll be…" Scotty said. He ran and retrieved the burning match before it started a fire in the brush. He brought it back, still flaming, and blew it out in front of the men, who were stunned to silence.

"I guess the kid gets to go," he laughed.

Proud of his son, Cler couldn't help asking, "Any of you fellows want to try the match trick?" There were no takers.

Cliff, Cler, Scotty and Paxton trudged off to scout the moraine. The top of it was lightly wooded, mostly with willows, and it seemed wide enough for the big bull dozer, all the way down. It was an easy hike down, but a bit tougher going back up. The men were winded by the time they made it to the top of the bluff, but Paxton skipped along with the boundless energy of a little boy. Breathing heavily from their hike, Cliff, Cler and Scotty dropped onto a log to rest. The men who hadn't walked the moraine approached them.

"So, how was it? Shall we keep going?" Ted asked.

"Well," Cler said, "Looks like we can make a road, but let's do that another day. For now, we'll just harvest logs up top."

FARM ANIMALS

Cler took the dump truck to Palmer and returned the next day, with a large, red, milk cow in the back. She was a cross between a Canadian breed and something else hearty enough to survive a winter in the Interior, or so Cler had been told. He arrived when all the children were playing out in the yard with the kid goats, running around, helter-skelter. They were playing an unusual game of tag, with the children trying to avoid being tagged "it" while also avoiding being tagged by any of the baby goats.

Cler parked the truck and improvised a ramp of heavy boards at the back. He staked it in place, so it wouldn't move, as the cow walked down it. Before he removed the tail gate, Cler called out to the children. "Hey, come see our new cow!" The children came running up, with the goat kids right behind.

338

"Well, kids—and children-- this is our new milk cow. Her name's Rowdy, and from what I already know about her, she's earned the name. You'll have to stay away from her, and don't try to pet her. See that broken horn? That's from butting something with her head. But don't worry; we'll gentle her over time, I hope..."

Cler told everyone to stand back while he removed the tail gate, but the cow didn't move. He climbed up on the outside of the wood rails, and caught hold of the rope tied around the cow's neck, and tugged on it, trying to get her to back out of the truck. She let out an aggravated "Moo!"wedged her massive haunches against the side boards, and wouldn't budge. He managed to get Rowdy turned around in the truck, and pulled on her lead; she moved to the edge, where she could see the ramp, but she refused to get close to it, let alone step on it. Edging around the cow, Cler tried pushing her from behind, but she merely backed up, nearly crushing him into the cab. He responded by giving her a heavy smack on the rump.

 "Get out, Rowdy; get!" With a leap and a bellow, she launched herself over the back and jumped off, landing halfway down the ramp.

Most cows want to be milked, because a full udder is uncomfortable. They will come of their own accord at milking time, standing patiently while they are milked. Rowdy was not one of those cows. The problem is, if a cow's udder isn't emptied fully, and regularly, her milk will dry up. Rowdy acted like that was her plan, but it wasn't Cler's plan for her. He'd bought a milk cow, and he intended to milk her.

He built a sturdy stanchion with an opening to put her head through, and two boards that closed on either side of her neck. This kept her head steady. After she kicked the bucket a few times, he had to clamp irons on her back ankles, like a prisoner headed for jail.

When she wasn't being bothered, Rowdy seemed content. She roamed around eating grass and all the juicy weeds her big cow heart desired. All summer, Rowdy and the goats fed on the bounty of vegetation around the homestead, but when snow fell and temperatures dropped, they'd need hay to eat. Cler had built a pretty good barn, even before he got Rowdy. He made it even warmer, now, by covering the inside with boards and filling the walls with sawdust. He stapled layers of heavy plastic over the small window, and made a stout door out of boards that he said would stop a bear from getting to the animals. He did all this because Rowdy was going to have a calf.

A FULL HOUSE

Gwynne's parents were middle-aged by the time they had their second daughter, Cheryl. Now, she was eleven, and they were both over fifty. At this time of their lives, they should have been able to relax, but having that darling, energetic child in their home was never relaxing. Henrietta wrote and asked if Cheryl could spend the summer at Kenny Lake.

"What do you think, Cler?' Gwynne asked, when she'd read her mother's letter. "Mother wants Cheryl to come stay with us. I mean, we already have Ernie here..."

Cler didn't hesitate. "Oh, let's have her come! Cheryl can sleep with the girls, and Corrie will have someone to pal around with! No problem."

Cheryl arrived at Kenny Lake like a little whirlwind. She was dressed like a doll, in red shorts and a matching flowered blouse. She was cute as a button, with energy to burn and the personality of a mischievous elf. Corrie didn't quite know what to feel about her coming. She had always visited Cheryl at Grandma and Grandpa Paxton's house, but now Cheryl had invaded Corrie's personal space. For starters, Corrie had never felt cute, and she wasn't particularly outgoing. She liked her solitary pursuits. She was thin, with straight, unmanageable hair that hung about her shoulders, and all her life it seemed that all people could say about her was, "What an intelligent, responsible child!"

However, Corrie was wise enough to know that cute wasn't everything. She had a place of power in her family, as the

340

big sister, the boss of her siblings, and most of the neighbor kids. She knew how to make bread, skin a rabbit, shoot a .22 (she was a pretty good shot) and in fact, among her siblings, she called the shots.

When Cheryl swept onto the scene that summer, Corrie's ordered world was threatened. It wasn't long, though, before Cheryl's infectious sense of fun had her nieces and nephews, including Corrie Lynne, following her around to see what she'd think of next. One of the first adventures Cheryl orchestrated was the mission to protect Rowdy's calf from ravaging wolves.

The summer night was balmy, even for Kenny Lake, and the cabin seemed too warm. "I have an idea," Cheryl said, as she and the girls were getting undressed for bed, in the tiny "girls' room." "Why don't we ask if we can sleep outside tonight? It's bound to be cooler out there, than it is in here."

Corrie was a bit hesitant. Sure, it would be cooler out there, but there would also be swarms of mosquitoes.

Cheryl stepped back into her jeans and went to ask Gwynne, "Would it be alright if we took our sleeping bags and camped out tonight?"

Gwynne was relaxing on the sofa, while Cler was still out with Ernie, taking care of the livestock. "I guess," Gwynne said, "If you want to. You can sleep out there in the circle, where you're still close to the cabin. Keep Tippy with you and you should be fine."

In a jiffy, Cheryl was back in the girls' room rousting out Lestie and Corrie. "Come on! Get dressed and grab your sleeping bags. We're going to camp out!" She flew down the hall to the boys' room, "Come on Packie, your mom said we can all sleep outside tonight!" Even Charles, who was five, went with them. Within minutes, the little group of campers had lugged their pillows and sleeping bags outside into the dim twilight, and were making their beds on the ground. The children were dressed in long sleeve shirts and jeans to help protect against mosquitoes, particularly if they had to answer a call of nature during the night.

Everyone settled into their beds, but no one stayed there for long: there was a lot of struggling out of their sleeping bags, moving rocks or sticks that had been poking them in the back, and climbing in again. This went on for some time.

Rowdy the milk cow was grazing only a few yards away from the children's camp, and Tippy was curled up on the end of Paxton's sleeping bag. The night was quiet, except for the far away call of a loon on the lake.

"What's that?" Cheryl whispered. "It sounds like someone's dying."

"Just a loon. It's like a duck, only smaller." Paxton said.

"Oh." Silence again. The children lay staring up at the sky; there were a few high clouds still tinged with faint pink, but it wasn't dark enough for stars. Being midsummer, the sun had not even dipped below the horizon. The only sounds were the whine of mosquitoes, which had discovered new blood in the form of children sleeping out in the open. Instinctively, the kids all pulled their heads into their mummy bags, like turtles. Then, a wolf howled.

Tippy whimpered in his sleep, but he wasn't interested. One wolf's howl was answered by another. The sound seemed far across the lake to Paxton, who had been living around wolves for most of his life, and wasn't worried.

Cheryl sat straight up. "Listen! Wolves! They sound hungry!"

Corrie just burrowed deeper into her bag.

Cheryl pounded on her shoulder, "Where's Rowdy?"

"She was right over there by the driveway," Corrie groaned. "Just go to sleep."

But Cheryl was having none of that. "Rowdy's gone, and she's probably having her calf right now! The wolves can smell the blood! Paxton! Come on! We need to go find Rowdy and protect her calf!"

Paxton poked his head out of his bag. "Fine. Let's go find her, but I'm pretty sure she's OK."

Not wanting to be left out, Corrie crawled from her bag and slid her feet into her tennis shoes. She picked up her sleeping bag and draped it over her arm. In a moment, Lestie and Charles were out of their bags, ready to follow.

Paxton led the search, because he knew Rowdy's habits better than anyone in the group. The girls and Charles tagged after him as he headed down the drive, across the road, to the shore of Kenny Lake. There, quietly lying in the grass and chewing her cud, was Rowdy. Her fat belly told Paxton she hadn't had her calf yet.

"Look at that!" Cheryl pointed to the cow, who ignored the human children approaching her. "She's in labor. We'd better sleep here so we can watch out for her. If she has her calf, one of us can go get your dad."

"OK," Paxton said, "but I think she's fine." He was tired, ready to go to sleep.

They found a grassy slope, far enough from the lake that they were out of the reeds, and spread out their bags and pillows again. After they snuggled down, Cheryl said, "I brought along my little alarm clock. I'll set it for a half hour. We'll each take a turn watching. Paxton, you can take the first watch."

"Why me?" Paxton moaned. "I just want to go to sleep."

"You're the man of the company. If there's trouble, you can handle it," Cheryl told him.

Thirty minutes later, the alarm went off, waking everyone including Rowdy, who rose up and hoofed it a little further from the kids.

Paxton reset the alarm, and handed it to Cheryl, "You're next," he said.

For whatever reason, the alarm didn't go off again, and the next thing the children knew, the sun was baking them in their down sleeping bags. Rowdy didn't have her calf for another month.

25

MAKING HAY WHILE THE SUN SHINES

Summer, 1953

In Lower Tonsina, there was a meadow where a freight company, working for the mine, had cut hay for their horses back in the twenties. There was nothing there now, except a sod-roofed cabin, and some rusty implements left from the haying operation. The store and land around was still owned by Kennecott Copper, but the man who ran the store at Chitna worked for the mine, as a kind of caretaker of the area. He had already given Cler the rusty, horse-drawn hay rake and mower that were parked in the meadow, and now he gave permission for Cler to cut the hay there.

Cler refitted the hay rake and mower from horse-drawn implements to ones the tractor could pull, and sharpened the mower. He pulled the implements down to the meadow and spent a couple of days mowing the tall grass, leaving it to dry under the hot sun.

A few days later, he woke up very early, and saw the rosy sun coming through the curtains. *Another hot day. Perfect for turning the hay.* As he rolled out, the bedsprings squeaking of metal on metal woke Gwynne. Cler leaned over and whispered, trying not to disturb Butchy in the crib. "What say I take the kids down to the hay meadow today? They can have a picnic, while I rake the hay. What do you think?"

She whispered back, "I think it's a lovely day to get out of the house. I'll pack the picnic, and we'll all go!"

Ernie volunteered to stay and do the milking. Cler didn't think he'd need him at the hay field, but invited him to come down in the pickup, for the picnic, or just relax for the rest of the day, if he wanted to.

344

The children were like little birds, popping awake when the sunlight came through the windows in their rooms. They had been just lying there, wondering what they were going to do for fun, when their dad told them to get ready to go on a picnic! They jumped into shorts and t-shirts and, after wolfing down their oatmeal, they were ready to go.

Gwynne took Butchy onto her lap in the cab, and the rest of the children climbed into the back of the dump truck. It had a steel bed, with sides made by heavy two-by-twelve boards, held in place by vertical posts. The rear of the bed was open. The children milled around up there, waiting for the truck to start down the road, until Gwynne hollered, "You kids sit down back there, and don't get up, do you hear me?" They quickly sat down in a row, with their legs out in front of them, and backs against the cab. Lestie had a feeling that if Daddy got going fast enough, they would all slide over the slick steel bed and right out the back of the truck. She held on to Corrie.

"OK, we're ready!" Paxton yelled, and Cler started down the driveway. The hay meadow was about six miles away. The truck bounced along the rough road, jouncing the kids, and giving them plenty of road dust to breathe, along with the fresh air. Between the roar of the engine, the steady grind of tires against gravel, and the banging of the side boards against the iron truck bed, the kids could barely hear each other's shouts and laughter.

At one point, a side board bounced up, just as five-year-old Charles accidentally slid his foot under it, and it came down hard, smashing his big toe. Charles yanked his foot out, "Ow, ow, ow, my toe, my toe!" Corrie hastily pulled off his tennis shoe as blood oozed, soaking his sock. Cheryl pounded on the window to get Gwynne's attention and in a minute, Cler pulled over and stopped the truck. He jerked on the emergency brake, and left the engine running, as he ran back to see what was going on.

"Charles smashed his toe!" several kids cried out.

Cler took hold of the top of Charles' blood-soaked sock, and rolled it off his fat little foot. He assessed the damage, and saw it was limited to the one toe. "Might lose that toenail, but it'll be all right." He strode back to the cab and jumped in.

"That's it? That's all he's going to do?" Cheryl was incensed that Cler had not made a big enough deal of the injury. The engine roared, the truck jerked, and they were headed down the road, but Cheryl didn't let it drop. She yelled to her assembled audience, "What if his toe gets infected, and green pus comes out? What if he gets gangrene? What if his whole foot falls off?"

Charles paid no attention to her. He was no whiner. He put his sock and shoe back on and sat quietly the rest of the journey.

The grassy meadow was bright and full of sunshine, smelling of new hay. Cler attached the rake behind the tractor and in a short while, he was combing the scattered hay into neat rows that stretched the length of the visible meadow and curved off into another part of it around a clump of trees. Charles and Lestie got bored watching their dad on the tractor, and wandered across the road, where they found a little stream, and followed it into the willows. Soon they were barefoot and wading in the icy stream, running in and out, laughing and screaming with delight. Then they sat on the bank, picking up pretty colored stones. Charles' injured toe seemed all the better from being washed and iced in the stream.

While Charles and Lestie were off playing in the stream, the older kids were running around the meadow. At one point, Cheryl watched Cler on the tractor, heading away from them. "Hey, I have an idea!" she called to Corrie and Paxton. "It looks like your dad's finished down at this end, so let's play hide and seek in the hay. Corrie's it!"

Cheryl and Paxton buried themselves, while Corrie closed her eyes and counted to fifty. While she was counting, Cler made a turn at the end of the row, and was now headed their way. Corrie spotted Cheryl's red shorts showing through a pile of hay, "I see you!" Then she noticed the sound of the tractor getting louder, and her father on it, coming down the row.

"Get out, get out of the hay!"

Cheryl heard the tractor and poked her head up, dried grass falling over her face and sticking in her hair. Scrambling to her feet, she and Corrie saw Cler yelling, waving his arms, though he couldn't be heard over the putt-putt of the engine. The girls ran out of his way, and stopped to watch the rake, stirring the hay up with its curved tines, throwing it into a row behind it. The tractor passed, and Paxton's head popped out from the pile of hay, where he'd cleverly buried himself. His dad didn't see him, but Paxton saw round, three foot tines of the rusty rake passing, and turned pale. He'd come pretty close to getting raked up with the hay.

After lunch, Corrie and Cheryl flopped down on a blanket in the shade, beside Butchy who was asleep. They tended him, while Gwynne rested in the truck's cab. The sun had given her a headache.

Still full of energy, Lestie and Paxton went exploring, ending up at the old trapper's cabin. It was low at the eves, with a sod roof covered in abundant grass, with tiny blue and white flowers. There was a low door and one small window. They peered through the dusty window, into the dark interior, and spied a stove made from a rusted kerosene can, with the chimney missing, and a log bed frame nailed to the wall. There was no mattress, but they saw ropes strung across the frame, to hold one.

On the outside of the cabin, along one wall, there was a weathered-silver sluice box, that was basically a long, rough box slanted at a slight angle, sitting on board legs. It was used to separate gold from sand, by shoveling in gold-laden sand, and pouring water through it. Paxton had seen one before, in Chitna. He explained it to his sister: the heavier gold would fall to the bottom, while the sand washed away. Assorted rocks were collected on a shelf along the side of the sluice box. Lestie picked up a big one that was yellow and sparkled.

"That's fool's gold," Paxton said, "It's a worthless rock that looks like gold, but isn't." he picked up a gray and white rock. "Now this one has a little gold in it," he said, turning it this way and that. "See those little flecks sparkle in the sun? Gold. But it needs to be crushed, before you can get it out." He put the rock in his pocket.

In a few days, Cler took Paxton and Ernest with him and returned to the field, where they forked the dried hay into the dump truck. It was Paxton's job to tromp down the hay, as it was thrown onto the pile. Cler attached the tail gate, to keep the hay in, and they kept piling it onto the stack.

When they returned home, fully loaded, Cler backed the truck over to the board enclosure beside the barn, and removed the tail gate. Ernie forked some hay from the truck into the stack yard, while all the children watched.

Cler could have dumped it out; it was a dump truck, after all, but he wanted the kids to have some fun unloading the hay . He called out, "OK, kids, it's all yours! A slippery slide made out of hay!"

The children gleefully climbed up and crawled over the cab, into the hay. When they reached the unstable back side of the load, they launched themselves off, bringing down mounds of fragrant hay onto the pile below. The baby goats joined in the fun, bounding up over the cab, sliding down the slope of hay with their ears flapping in the breeze. After one slide off the hay, Paxton had had enough. He'd been stomping hay all day, and he was worn out. He went into the cabin and slept like he was dead, not even waking up for supper.

The next day, Cler, Ernie, and Paxton returned to the meadow. They brought back several more loads of hay. Around the stack, Cler and Ernie built the fence higher with slabs, to keep the goats and Rowdy out. The animals would need every mouthful of that good hay when winter snow put a stop to foraging around the farm.

BERRY PICKING

In high summer, the fireweed bloomed, the days were long, and berries were abundant. As always, Gwynne enjoyed

348

being outdoors during the summer, and she loved few things more than going berry picking with her friends, Ina and Emma, and Grandma George. Different berries ripened at different times, but Grandma George and her daughters knew exactly when to go.

Sometimes the women went alone, with one of them carrying a rifle slung over her back, but the summer Ernie was there, he was often commandeered for guard duty. Since he had a pickup, he was also the chauffeur. Grandma George was given the soft seat in the cab, but it was really more fun for the younger women to ride together in the back, talking and laughing. They all wore scarves tied over their hair, with long sleeves and pants to protect from mosquitoes, which could get thick in the swampy areas where blueberries grew best. They also wore rubber boots that came up to their knees. It was not only humans who were drawn to the berry patches. The bears also came to feast.

While the women were picking, Ernie guarded them with Cler's shotgun. He felt rather proud, being asked to stand guard duty, even though after a few hours, he grew tired of carrying buckets of berries to dump in the wash tub, and in between doing that, he was bored enough to fall asleep in the cab of his truck. Sometimes, however, things got more exciting, like when he spotted a brown bear and two half-grown cubs, plus a black bear, all feasting on berries at the far end of the patch. The bears were so contented, it seemed, that they ignored the humans. As long as they kept their distance, Ernie, and the women, ignored the bears. Nature intended her plenty for all. Ernie never did have to shoot any bears, and he was glad.

SUN AND SAND, AND THE PLAGUE

A few days after the hay had been brought to the stack, the sun was still beating down, and it was not even cool in the cabin. Gwynne was dumping flour into the big bowl for bread dough, and Cler was helping her, but otherwise, no one seemed to have the energy to do anything. Cler told the kids, who were sitting around the cabin, complaining of the heat, that they should all go swimming.

"Where?" asked Cheryl, who was up for anything that sounded like fun.

"Kenny Lake," Cler said.

Corrie grimaced, "Yuk! It's full of shrimp and lake weed, and other nasty stuff."

"Well, the ducks like it," Cler chuckled. "Actually, there's a little sandy beach about half way around the lake, on the west side. You could swim there. I'll bet the sand even goes out into the water for a ways. You can blow up the air mattress and float on the lake, if nothing else."

"Let's go!" Paxton cried, jumping up, "I'll get my shorts!"

"We get the air mattress first!" Corrie and Cheryl hollered in unison, heading to their bedroom to change.

Now, Cler was busy kneading the bread dough. Gwynne had been suffering from arthritis in her wrists and she would do all the rest, but she needed him to work the big lump of dough.

"Hey, Ernie, why don't you take a break and go with them? You can be the life guard." Cler called across the room, where Ernie was sprawled in the rocking chair. He'd already been working, chopping wood for the kitchen range. Even though it was hot, food had to be cooked, and Gwynne had to use the oven to bake bread.

"Life guard? I can do that," Ernie grinned. Paxton brought out the air mattress, and he and Ernie took turns blowing it up.

Charles couldn't swim, but he could play in the shallows. He was allowed to go because Ernie promised to watch him. At seven, Lestie couldn't swim, either, but she could take care of herself.

With Ernie carrying the air mattress, the kids marched along the trail in single file, where the tall reeds had been beaten down by moose or other animals, following the edge of the lake. They came to a little beach of white sand, that was strewn with dried lake snails. As their dad had said, the sand extended five or six feet into the water. It was perfect; the water was cool but not cold, the sun was hot, and mosquitoes were scarce.

Corrie and Cheryl asserted their dominance as the two eldest, and hogged the air mattress. They intended to float out on the lake, without touching the slimy lake moss, or the black muck on the bottom. Side by side, they clung onto the air mattress, kicking their feet and splashing, propelling themselves further and further from shore.

Finally, they looked behind them. "We're too far out," Cheryl said, "The air mattress is leaking! Listen."

Corrie listened. She could hear a tiny hiss coming from somewhere in the rubber mattress. "It *is* leaking!"

"We'll never get back before it runs out of air!" Cheryl cried, "I barely know how to swim!" Of course, this was an exaggeration, because Cheryl was a pretty good swimmer.

Corrie yelled, "Shut up! I can't swim, either. Help! Ernie! Help, the air mattress is leaking!"

"We're going to die!" Cheryl cried. The other children stopped playing in the shallows and watched the big girls with interest. Ernie just waved at Corrie and Cheryl, flailing and kicking out on the water, ignoring their cries for help. Finally, their kicking brought them back to shallow water.

"Fine life guard you are," Cheryl said, giving Ernie a dark look, as she and Corrie clung to the air mattress, which was now dragging on the sandy bottom.

"You weren't in any danger," he said. "Now give someone else a turn." He dumped the big girls off, and called Lestie over, "Want a ride? Hop on!"

She laid down on the rubber mattress with her feet sticking over the end, while Ernie took hold of her feet and steered her out into deeper water. He was up to his chest, when he tried to steer the mattress around, and Lestie fell off.

Down she sank; into the murky water, past weeds and black soil bubbling up toward the surface. She was sure she was drowning! The next thing she knew, Ernie carried her back to shore, while she coughed up water and bawled. "You're OK, now," Ernie kept telling her. "I never let go of your ankles!" She dropped onto the sand and kept crying.

"Just go home," Corrie said, heartlessly.

Getting to her feet, Lestie stopped coughing and walked away, dejected. She had almost drowned and nobody cared. She met her father on the trail, and tried to tell him her troubles, but he just patted her wet head and passed on by to check on the others.

On the walk home, Lestie stopped crying, but now she had started itching. She looked down at her arms: they were red and blotchy. Scratching just made it worse. By the time she opened the cabin door, the lake water had dried on her skin and she itched all over her body. Her mother sent her into the bedroom to change. She peeled out of her bathing suit and called, "Mother come here and see me! I'm all rashy!"

Her mother came and checked it out. Lestie was covered, head to toe, in a fine red rash.

"Good grief! There must be something in the water that you're allergic to!" She filled the wash tub with warm water, and told Lestie to climb in and lather up, hair and all. Then she rinsed her off by pouring clean water over her as she stood in the tub. After Lestie was rinsed and dried, her mother made a paste of vinegar and soda, and spread a thin film of the paste, over the worst of the rash. She wrapped a towel around her, "Now, don't scratch! If you need more paste, ask. Go put on one of those cotton dresses Aunt Ella sent you."

Having her mother take care of her made Lestie feel loved; proving that her mother noticed her in the crowd. She got dressed and went out to sit in the rocking chair. After a while, the other swimmers returned, and Ernie came inside.

"We've got a problem, Gwynne," he said, violently scratching at his arm.

"Try not to scratch," she warned. "It'll just get worse!"

"You know what this is?" Ernie asked, his face writhed with discomfort.

352

"Not exactly," she told him. "I've already seen it on Celestia, though. There must be something in the water. I'll make some soda paste to put on it."

Corrie, Cheryl, Paxton and Charles trooped in. "All of us have a rash," Cheryl declared. "I hope it's not the measles, although I think I already had them, along with Chicken Pox and three-day measles." She made her voice low and spooky, "Maybe it's the Black Plague!"

Gwynne said, "Oh, for goodness sakes, Cheryl!" She addressed the motley group of swimmers. They were dry now, covered in white scum, scratching, and jerking around like Mexican beans. "Hey, why don't you all go outside and rinse off, using the water in the barrel. Here," She handed Ernie a sauce pan. Go pour water over each other until you get the scum off. Wash all over, even your hair."

Cheryl saw the partially full wash tub sitting on the kitchen floor. She demanded, "We want a bath!"

"That water's already been used," Gwynne said, "and it's probably full of whatever made you all develop a rash. It's only good for mopping the floor, now." She stepped over to the kitchen sink and got a bar of Ivory soap. "Here, lather up outside. And be sure to rinse yourselves well, even if you use up the whole barrel of water!"

Apparently, that water's still cold, Gwynne thought, as she heard the squealing, screaming, and laughing going on out in the yard. She continued mixing vinegar and soda paste.

Dripping wet, the boys and Ernie trooped in. Gwynne handed them a cup of paste. "Smear this on the rash," she said. They headed to their room to doctor the rash and then change into clean clothes.

Corrie and Cheryl came in, dripping. Cheryl stopped in the kitchen, "Can we at least have our own towel?"

"I know where they are," Corrie volunteered. Gwynne gave them a cup of paste. "Spread some of this over your rash," she said.

"Eew! This smells disgusting!" Cheryl sniffed at the cup.

"Do what you want," Gwynne sighed.

Wearing a clean cotton dress, Celestia sat in the rocking chair, with her feet curled under her. She watched her aunt and sister pass, shivering, to the back bedroom. She felt a little smug; she'd received the royal treatment, with a warm bath, and Mother's tender care, while the others had to settle for cold showers, outdoors.

As for the mysterious rash, it was caused by a tiny water creature that hatched out in the middle of summer, according to Cliff Steadman, the mail man, who'd been a victim of the same bug; it was common knowledge, he said, that you shouldn't swim in these lakes after the first of July. Now they knew. After that Day of the Plague, as Cheryl named it, swimming in Kenny Lake lost its appeal. The rash disappeared in a few days.

When Cheryl went home, the whole place seemed suddenly too quiet, the way you feel after a brief, but lusty rainstorm passes: the excitement and noise stops, with rain no longer beating joyfully on the roof.

26

THE WELL

Summer, 1953

After Cheryl left, there was still some summer to be enjoyed, and Lestie returned to her usual solitary wanderings around the fields and woods that encompassed the Homestead. She loved the smell of the hot sun on the dry grass, and when she walked down to the lake and stood on the shore, she savored the mossy smell of the lake. She memorized the way the fluffy summer clouds reflected on the lake, which was like a mirror, nearly the same blue as the sky, with slightly darker versions of the same fluffy clouds. At the lake's edge, she stooped and looked for the tiny snails that lived in the black soil under shallow water, and pulled back the grass to expose tiny frogs, which she often caught, and then let go again. She wandered back across the road, and into the tall grass that grew up in the field. It was there that she found the old well.

Nearly hidden in the grass she came upon some silvery boards, speckled with orange lichen. They had been there a long time, she thought, because that's what old boards looked like after years and years in the sun and rain and snow.

One board was split. She took hold of the narrow piece, and with effort wrenched it to the side, peering into the dark space underneath. She scratched at the other piece of the board, which was nailed down, with rusted, iron nails. She took hold of the board, and yanked on it. The rusted nail-heads broke off, and the board shrieked, as she ripped it off.

The hole was rectangle shaped, fitted around the sides with weathered boards. It was dark down there. She dropped a rock, and caught a glimmer of water as it splashed, and then

355

heard it thump on the bottom. She dropped another rock and listened; a splash and clunk, at the same time. This meant the water wasn't deep, but it would be bad for someone like Butchy to fall in there. She shoved the boards back over the hole, and was walking back to the cabin, when she encountered Ernie. He was headed to the barnyard.

"What are you up to?" Ernie asked.

"I found a hole that might be an old well," she said.

Ernie stared at her, "What? Where?"

"Down in the field, by the main road."

He frowned, looking almost angry. "You stay away from there! Wells are dangerous. Don't you know that?"

"There's only a little water in it." Her lip quivered; she was sorry she'd told him.

Ernie could see her discomfort, and softened. "Listen. I had a little sister named Andrea; your cousin. How old are you?"

"Seven."

"Well, Andrea was five. Anyway, one day, she went missing and they found her drowned. In a well." Ernie patted Lestie on the shoulder. "You stay away from that well you found, OK?"

"OK," she said, watching as he headed toward the barn. It was time to milk the goats. After he left, she felt dizzy, as if she were falling. She had to sit down in the grass, right where she was, and put her head on her knees and as she did, she saw in her mind a little girl with golden hair, standing in the air above an open well. Lestie felt sadness rush by her like a breath of cold wind. She opened her eyes and blinked at the sunshine, but a tinge of sadness remained as she stood up and walked back to the cabin, where it was cool and dark inside.

Corrie was reading a book by the light of the living room windows, curled on one end of the couch. Lestie sat down and scooted closer. "Did you know we had a cousin, named Andrea?"

"Yes, I used to play with her," Corrie said. She closed her book, keeping her thumb between the pages. "She was my age; we were both about four, when I last saw her."

356

"Did she have gold hair?" Lestie asked, thinking of the girl she'd seen in her mind.

"Yes, in fact, she was a little like Shirley Temple, with curls, and she loved to tap dance, too."

"Ernie said she drowned in a well."

Corrie chewed on her lip. "We left for Alaska before that happened. I heard about it, though, and about her funeral. I remember Aunt Ella sent me a box of her things: little dresses, mostly, and a pair of leather shoes. In the box was a piece of satin and some other fluffy, white material. Also a satin ribbon with "Andrea" stamped on it, in gold. Mother told me the cloth was left from making Andrea's burial dress. The ribbon was on her casket."

"Did it bother you to wear her clothes?"

"I don't think I understood—about her being dead, you know."

"It's sad, though."

"It is. I haven't thought of this for a long time, but once, I heard that Andrea might have been tap dancing on the well cover, and it slid, or tipped or something. They had a lot of people looking for her, before they found her."

Corrie flipped open her book, and then paused, "Back then, I didn't understand about all that stuff: caskets, funerals, death..."

"You do, now?"

"Yes," she said. "It's pretty simple: you die and your spirit goes to live with Heavenly Father. Meanwhile, they have a funeral for you; it's like a meeting where they tell about your life. I've read about it, but I've never been to one." She went back to reading her book.

Corrie was done talking, but Lestie still had questions. She studied her nails; they were dirty, from dragging up boards on the old well. The image of the little girl standing in the air above a well was still clear in her mind. What she'd seen made more sense now. Maybe Andrea's spirit waited around for a while. Just until they found her.

Ernie talked to Cler, and that afternoon they shoveled a pile of dirt into the back of the dump truck, and then hauled and dumped it into the well, effectively filling it in.

A LOG SCHOOL IS BUILT

Cliff, Enzo Santini, Ted Ennis, Cler, and several other men had been hauling logs off and on all summer. They had stockpiled the logs on the Oborn's field, just beyond the circle drive. There the first Kenny Lake school building was going to be built.

Scotty and his wife had decided not to stay in Kenny Lake, but to go back to Anchorage, where Scotty could own his own beauty salon and sell his paintings on the side. He gave Cler permission to dismantle his partially built cabin and use the logs for the school. This was a great boon to the school project.

The men in the community had agreed to donate materials if they could afford it, and hours of work, if they couldn't. Some preliminary work was done during June. Cler's sawmill had churned out rough boards for the school's floor and roof, and the green lumber had been stacked and tied to help it dry out without warping.

The foundation logs had already been laid. The base logs and floor joists were oiled and laid on a base of tarred logs, placed vertically in the ground. The building would be 24 feet wide, and 28 feet long.

The plan was to elevate the building two feet above ground, so when the snow was deep, it would create an airspace under the floor, and help keep the school room warmer.

On the morning of the Fourth of July, members of the community and their families began to arrive at the building site for a community work day, picnic and celebration.

The school site was a beehive of activity; sawing, hammering, loud talk, and laughter filled the air. Six men worked to lay the floor. Some used the two man buck saw, others chainsaws and axes to cut notches in the logs that would form up the walls. Women peeled bark off the logs and the men hammered them into place with ten inch spikes. Little by little, the walls rose, and finally, timber trusses were lifted into place, using man power, pulleys and the winch on the dump truck.

At dinner time, they all ate salads, sandwiches and blue berry pie, and then worked some more on the school. Before the sun slipped behind Gun-sight Mountain, work ended, and the homesteaders gathered for a short patriotic program.

The grown-ups sat on logs, and the children gathered in little cliques on the soft dirt. Celestia, Alina, and Vivian would all be in second grade. They whispered and giggled, excited at the prospect of being in school together; able to see each other every day. Arlo, Paxton and Little Enzo nudged and shoved each other, establishing rank.

Cler led everyone in a ragged rendition of "My Country 'tis of Thee." Apparently there was more enthusiasm than musical talent in the group. Ted Ennis prayed, and Enzo Santini read the Preamble to the Constitution, becoming a bit choked up before the "Life, liberty and the Pursuit of Happiness." He was born in Italy, but had lived in America most of his life, and he considered himself an American.

By ten-thirty the sky was a dim, gray-blue, considered dark enough to shoot off some fireworks over the lake, and pass out sparklers to the kids. Cler lit the first sparkler, and the kids lit each others'. They swung the little wires around, making circles of light in the half-darkness.

"Be careful!" their mothers warned, "Don't burn each other and don't catch the grass on fire!"

Kenny Lake School Winter, 1953

ONE ROOM SCHOOL

The log school was finished. Some men took a day to tar and paper the roof, others put together a drum stove, and installed it in the back of the school room. From scraps and donations, a winter's wood pile grew outside the building. More books and desks arrived from the Territory, and the blackboards were tacked to the front of the room.

In September, a teacher arrived. She was young, but she had five years of experience in Minnesota, she said. Her name was Miss Burnham* (name has been changed), and she had only been in Alaska for a week. having flown to Anchorage, and driven to Kenny Lake in an old Ford she'd purchased in Anchorage.

Cler showed her the school, explained the drum stove and then pointed out where the outhouse was. He took her down the driveway to the place where he'd set the truck house on blocks and dug a septic tank for it.

"Does it have running water?" she asked, checking out the kitchen.

Cler was so glad she'd come, that he was feeling pretty jovial. "Yes, there's running water," he joked, handing her a galvanized bucket that had been sitting on the drain board. "You just have to run down to the lake and run back!"

Miss Burnham was not impressed. She got right back in her car and left for Civilization. The living conditions at Kenny Lake were apparently too primitive for her. Cler was sad to see her go, but wished her well. Perhaps she could find a job in Anchorage.

The Department of Education agreed to pay his salary, and Cler stepped up to fill in again, just until the officials could find someone else. He organized the books and materials, and enlisted help from Ernie, Scott, and Ted Ennis to move the old piano from the Oborn's cabin to the school, a temporary loan. As long as he was teaching, music would be part of the children's education.

The officials agreed to subsidize a vehicle to be used as a school bus, and Cler found one for cheap. It was a 1950 Chevy windowed van, with two bench seats behind the driver's. Since no one else wanted it, Cler took the contract to drive the school bus. Of course, it was in his interest, as the teacher, to see that all his students got to school. The best way was simply to pick them up himself.

This year, Franklin decided to come to school. He was 17, now. "I can teach you how to read and write, and do numbers," Cler promised. "I'll do it while I'm teaching all the others. You won't have to be embarrassed. Wait and see. If you don't like it, you don't have to come back."

Cler had an idea of how to keep Franklin coming to school. "I really need a janitor," he told the young man. "That's a guy who helps around the school. I'll pay you to arrive early and start the fire in the drum stove. You attend school, and then, after school, you stay and sweep the floor, and clean the black boards. Things like that. How about it?"

Franklin nodded gravely, suppressing his delight, but it showed clearly in the sparkle of his black eyes. As for learning to read and write, that would be more difficult for him than building fires. Cler put him in third grade, which sounded better to Franklin than first grade. His dignity was further preserved by his having a job and earning real money. Money was not something Franklin knew much about. His family had subsisted for generations by living off the land, and as life around them changed, they adapted by using barter, trading fish or furs for things they needed.

To teach Franklin how to count money, Cler would take a handful of coins out of his pocket, and have him count his wages. The boy saved his money and added up what he'd saved. When he had a few dollars, he traded Cler for dollar bills. These were skills he'd need in the wider world that was encroaching on his traditional way of life.

Kenny Lake School now included first to eighth grade. Charles was five and should have been in kindergarten, but he was allowed to go to first grade because there was no kindergarten, and only one other first grader.

On the first day of school, most of the students arrived early. On their best behavior, the children entered the open door of the neat room with its rows of wooden desks, each with a matching chair. The smell of new lumber greeted them, and the comforting aroma of wood smoke from the drum stove that crackled in the back of the room. Rows of windows, on opposite walls, let in the morning light and illuminated the face of their teacher, Mr. Oborn, their tall, lean neighbor, whom most of them knew. He perched on one corner of his desk, at the front of the room. He looked unusually sharp compared to the way most men looked out here in the Interior; clean shaven, so his cheeks fairly glowed, his curly brown hair neatly parted and combed. He wore khaki pants and a red flannel shirt, neatly tucked in and belted. He looked solemn, but friendly, and definitely in charge.

Lestie found a desk on the right side of the room, near the windows, and sat down, warily watching the man who was the teacher and her father at the same time. Here in this new school, he seemed bigger, more important than when he taught on the porch of their own cabin. He looked like someone she barely knew. He noticed her staring at him and winked at her, without smiling, but it was as if they shared a secret. She saw the familiar sparkle of humor in his brown eyes, and knew he was still Daddy. He was just maintaining order, as was appropriate on the first day of school.

Mr. Oborn said, "Come in and hang your coats on the nails at the back. Find a seat. I'll rearrange you once you're all here." When they'd all arrived, Cler said, "Well, here I am again. Mr. Oborn. I'll be your teacher for a while, at least, until the Department of Education sends another." He made a few more remarks, and called roll. He asked questions, and made sure everyone knew everyone else. He said, "Isn't it nice to have this new school? For those who were here last year, let me just say that this school should be much warmer than my front porch!"

A few students murmured agreement. Apparently, the porch school had been pretty cold in the middle of last winter, but of course, the Oborn children were not there to share in the discomfort.

"So, now we'll arrange you according to grade level. Charles and Dallas, why don't you two come up front and sit in this row on my left."Dallas Ennis was a first grader, while Alina Santini, Vivian and Celestia were all second graders. They were all seated behind Dallas and Charles, in the first row. And so it went until all had a place in the classroom, with the oldest and tallest students in the back. Franklin George, the only third grader, was already seated in the last desk nearest the drum stove. He was ready to add a log to the fire when it needed it.

After the big shuffle, and everyone had settled into their seats, Mr. Oborn said, "Let's establish some rules for our classroom. Give me your ideas. What rules do you think we should have?"

"Raise your hand to be called on!" a thin, lanky boy named Clarence yelled out.

"Good idea." Mr. Oborn said, writing it on the blackboard. Apparently, no one saw the irony, but after Clarence's outburst, other students raised their hands to be called on. As more rules were offered, Mr. Oborn wrote them on the board: listen to the teacher, no swearing, be kind, do your best, do your work. After a brief discussion, the rules were adopted. Then Mr. Oborn said, "Since it's such a beautiful day out there, what do you say, shall we go on a field trip?"

For a moment the children didn't respond. Then, Alina, Enzo Santini's daughter raised her hand, "Mr. Oborn, what's a field trip?" she asked.

"It means...Well, going somewhere outside the schoolroom. In this case, we'll be going into the woods to find a flag pole!"

Amid smiles all around, Clarence raised his hand. "You mean we're going to cut down a tree?"

"Exactly. We need a flagpole, don't we, for our new school? Everybody get your coats on!"

The children scrambled to don their coats and then hurried outside, into the golden autumn. The sky was blue, and the air was crisp, but the sun warmed them as it fell on their faces. Cler led them down the dusty driveway, to his cabin, where he stopped to pick up an ax, the cross-cut saw, and his 30-06. He never went into the woods without a gun.

As they left the yard, the students formed a ragged line, chatting as they followed their teacher. Across the field, along the wood road, into the sunny woods, eighteen assorted children and Mr. Oborn went looking for a flagpole, a perfectly straight birch or aspen. A carpet of fallen leaves in shades of gold and yellow crunched under foot; the woods were transparent now, with only a few yellow leaves twisting on the bare branches of the aspen trees, their black and white trunks exposed to view.

"Keep your eyes peeled for a nice, straight pole," Cler called to his troops.

"And for bears!" Paxton added, only half joking.

"That, too!" his dad answered. "You kids be sure and make lots of noise!"

Most of the students were used to the fact there were bears in the woods, but some of the newcomers were worried.

Thirteen-year-old Dot made her way to the front of the line. "Mr. Oborn, do you think it's safe for us to do this?"

Cler held his rifle loosely in his hand, aimed at the ground. He glanced around, and then smiled, "You know, Dotty, with so many noisy kids tromping through the trees, we're pretty safe. What self-respecting bear would want to take all these hooligans on?"

Dot tried to smile, "Well, would it be all right if I walked up here with you?"

"Of course!" He turned toward the troop behind him, "Hey, let's have a little more noise back there!"

Little Enzo spotted the perfect tree. It was a straight birch, about four inches in diameter, without a bend or twist in it. Paxton and Little Enzo used the cross-cut saw to cut it down, and Franklin wielded the ax to hack off the branches. All the boys, including Charles, proved their muscle by grabbing hold and marching the pole out of the woods, to the school yard.

Back at the school, the fun wasn't over. The girls took turns peeling off the bark with the curved blade made for that purpose. Franklin painted the bottom of the pole with tar, and others helped dig a posthole. Before they raised the finished pole, Cler attached the eye bolts and rope, making it into a real flag pole. He called to the scattered children, some of whom were off playing tag by now, having lost interest.

"We'll raise our flag tomorrow morning. Right now, I want you all back inside. After lunch, I'm going to pass out your grammar work books." Groans all around. Cler grinned, "You thought school was going to be all fun and games, didn't you?"

The next morning was cool and clear. Once everyone had arrived at school, they filed back outside for the first flag ceremony around the new flag pole. The children grew still. In the breeze, dry willow leaves rustled like tiny pieces of paper.

"This is a sacred ceremony," Cler reminded the assembled children. "We'll raise the flag in silence, with our right hands on our hearts." All, except Charles, copied their teacher. Charles was left-handed, and naturally put his left hand on his heart.

"Right hand," his dad whispered. Charles looked confused, so his dad moved the left hand and replaced it with his right, lovingly patting it in place.

Little Enzo and Paxton had already been instructed on proper folding and unfolding of the flag. The boys proudly raised the flag, as all eyes watched it rise against the clear blue of the morning sky. Once the flag was secured at the top of the pole, Corrie Lynne led the class in the Pledge of Allegiance.

Cler's heart swelled. This was the first flag raised over the community of Kenny Lake, and he was enjoying every minute of the ceremony. He wanted these children to remember this morning, and all the mornings after, when they raised the flag and pledged their allegiance to the United States of America.

For many Alaskans, even among the veterans, America was far away. Patriotism and ceremony seemed to take a back seat to the exigencies of everyday life in an inhospitable wilderness. For Cler, these pristine meadows and rugged mountains were America, and they inspired his love of country, just as much as Plymouth Rock, Valley Forge, and Washington DC might inspire others. He wanted the children to understand that they were Americans, and feel the same love for their country that he did. After the pledge, the young veteran/ teacher led the children in singing "America, the Beautiful." Their sweet voices rang through the air, caught on the breeze.

It wasn't the first time Celestia had sung the hymn, and she knew it by heart from last year, but she would never forget this morning around the brand new flagpole, surrounded by the green and gold of Kenny Lake in the fall. She looked up at the flag waving against the blue sky, and sang with the other children, "O beautiful, for spacious skies, for amber waves of grain; for purple mountains' majesty above the fruited plain." Her eyes rested on the snow-covered mountains and she thought they were the "mountains majesty" of the song. "America, America, God shed His grace on thee, and crown thy good with brotherhood, from sea to shining sea!"

She sang of purple mountains in a landscape of white peaks, of waves of grain, when she knew only brush, and grass and wild flowers, but the words that stood out were grace, and good, brotherhood and shining. She felt it: love, and tenderness, and a sense of place. She was an American!

Corrie Lynne and Celestia in front of the school bus 1953

THE EFFECTS OF GOOD LITERATURE

Cler had been reading Tom Sawyer to his students every morning as they gathered around the drum stove at school. The students thought Tom's exploits were hilarious. Today they'd listened to the chapter in which Tom Sawyer explained how to get rid of warts. Lestie and Paxton each had a couple of warts, so they were especially interested. They approached their father after school. He was erasing the black board, while Franklin was sweeping the floor.

"Can we try to get rid of our warts like Tom Sawyer?" they asked.

Cler glanced over his shoulder at them. "Well, I don't see why not. Just decide which method you'd like to try."

According to Tom Sawyer, getting rid of warts was simple: all you had to do was wet the warts with "skunk-water" from a soggy tree stump. It sounded good, but Paxton said there were no skunks in Kenny Lake, or probably all of Alaska, for that matter, so there could be no skunk water.

Paxton said, "We can try that other way, though. Remember? You have to prick your wart with a needle, and put a drop of blood on two halves of a dried bean. Then you have to go alone to a crossroads at midnight and bury half the bean in the middle of the road."

"What do you do with the other half?"

"I don't remember. Keep it under your pillow or something. Want to try it?"

"Sure," Lestie said.

After supper, Corrie and Lestie had to do the dishes, and then the little boys went to bed. Corrie sat at the table reading Black Beauty, while Lestie and Paxton sat around the living room, waiting for midnight.

"It's ten o'clock," Gwynne said, looking up from her embroidery. "And it's a school night." She turned to Cler, who was parked in his rocking chair under the gas lantern, studying something for tomorrow's lessons.

Gwynne asked, "Don't you think ten o'clock is late enough for this experiment of theirs?"

Cler tossed the question to his two children, "Is ten o'clock close enough?"

Paxton said, "Sure, let's do it!"

Gwynne left her sewing and located some dry beans. She sterilized a needle over a candle, and the pricking began. With his blood spotted bean ready, Paxton chose to go first. Since the nearest real crossroad was probably Tok Junction, he had to settle for the place where the driveway met the main road. "It's sort of a cross road," he told Celestia. "The tracks that go down to the lake are across from the driveway."

A few minutes later, he ran back into the cabin, out of breath. Apparently, he'd run all the way. "OK," he panted. "It's your turn!"

Lestie donned her coat and headed for the door.

"Better take Tippy with you," her mother said. She didn't add *in case of bears*, but Lestie thought it. Her faith in this exercise was weak, since she was breaking rules: it was not midnight, there was no crossroad, and if she took Tippy, she would not be exactly alone. Still, she left the warmth and light of the cabin and crept down to the road in the cold moonlight, with Tippy following. A breeze rustled the bare willows, and she heard a loon cry down on the lake. Kneeling in the middle of the main road, she dug a shallow spot in the gravel and buried half of the bean. Then she ran all the way back to the cabin, her heart beating for fear of bears in the dark.

Did Tom Sawyer's wart remedy work? It was hard to tell what exactly cured the warts. A few days after burying the beans, Uncle John Burt came to visit. He was a ranger, working for the Forest Service, and he was checking on the big fire up in Chitna. He wore the khaki uniform of a forest ranger.

He and his wife had moved to Anchorage not long after Gwynne and Cler had come to Alaska. John was Henrietta's brother, actually Gwynne's uncle, which made him the children's great uncle. He was slender, with salt and pepper hair, like his sister Henrietta, and he was a friendly man, with rosy cheeks and sparkling blue eyes.

"Look, Uncle John," Lestie said, showing him a wart on the back of her hand. "I tried to get rid of my wart, but it's still there."

John bent to inspect her hand. "How did you try and get rid of it?"

"I buried a bean in the crossroads at midnight, like Tom Sawyer said, but my wart didn't go away."

John stifled a laugh. Then, straight-faced, he reached into his pocket and pulled out a quarter. "I know how to get rid of that wart. It's simple: I'll buy it from you!"

With a wink at Corrie, who was watching the exchange with interest, he offered Lestie the quarter, and she took it. "There!" John said, "Now it has to go away, because it's not yours anymore."

"I have another one," she said, showing him her elbow.

He chuckled, reaching into his pocket again. "Well, as long as I'm buying your warts, I'd better have them all!"

Celestia forgot about her transaction with Uncle John until a few days later when she looked down at the back of her hand and realized the wart was gone. She felt for the one on her elbow. Also gone. Amazing! She never had another wart.

Partially built gas station, Kenny Lake 1953

HUNGRY TIMES

Winter settled over Kenny Lake, the school, and the cabin, blanketing the landscape in white. Snow upon snow. The spruce trees wore coats of fluffy white, like giant trolls dressed in ermine.

Moose waded up to their bellies, eating the tender ends of willows for food. They dragged their hooves to clear a bit of moss or dried grass to munch on, and grew lean. They wandered into the yard and nibbled at the bark slabs on the barn.

When a moose was around, Tippy had a barking fit, warning of danger, but the huge animals weren't fazed by the dog

370

barking. They seemed placid, ignoring the children who walked to and from school, but the children kept away. Moose could be startled for no apparent reason, and in their confusion, were as likely to run over a person as to run away.

Rabbits were plentiful that winter. They were light enough in their white fur coats to hop over the crust of snow, and they left their tracks everywhere. They survived by eating willows, like the moose. Winter was a hungry time for animals. Humans fared better, but only if they had prepared well enough.

In the Oborn's cabin, supplies were adequate, though simple. Cans of moose meat and salmon were stacked against a bedroom wall. There were flour and sugar, dried beans and chilies, lard and cocoa. In the little cellar under the kitchen, potatoes and cabbages were stored, and would be edible until Christmas. Gwynne believed in vegetables with supper, and served the family canned varieties of green beans, peas, carrots, okra, and beets.

The children liked all of them, except the beets. It wasn't long before all of the other vegetables had been eaten up, except the beets, and then there appeared beets for every supper, every night. There were some complaints, but food was food, and unless they wanted to go to bed hungry, the children had to eat what was placed in front of them.

Gwynne was praying for an early spring, when fresh greens would sprout along the outside of the barn and cabin walls, where the ground was warmest. Lamb's quarter and dandelion greens would give the family a break from what the children considered the accursed beets.

A staple of life, one that meant real contentment in the wild, was fresh bread. For this purpose, Cler kept a healthy sourdough starter going all the time. The "start" bubbled in a cloth-covered jar, a living mass of yeast and flour. Each day, after using part of it as leavening for pancakes or bread, he fed it by adding more flour and water, and a pinch of sugar.

It was a source of pride to have a great-tasting starter, and considered a neighborly gesture to share one's "start" with someone whose own starter had died, or who hadn't brought any with them into the wilderness.

ONE ARCTIC NIGHT

In early December, a system of Arctic air seemed to stall over the Copper River Valley. The skies cleared, there was no precipitation, and no wind, and temperatures dropped to forty below zero. It was a dangerous time for animals, as well as people. In the little slab barn, Cler and Ernie threw extra hay to the animals. Rowdy sheltered her calf, named Veal Cutlets (Cler's idea, though the children didn't know what it meant), and the goats huddled together to keep warm. Inside the cabin, the children stayed toasty around the drum stove, as Dad stoked it up until the fire roared and the back of the stove glowed cherry red.

One night, when it seemed to warm up a little, Gwynne and Cler got a call from Ted Ennis. He invited them over to his cabin for an evening of Canasta. Cler used a torch to warm up the engine block, in order to start the Jeep wagon. Twelve-year-old Corrie was asked to babysit. "You can sleep on the floor by the drum stove," Gwynne said. That way you'll be all together."

Ernie had been invited to go, but he said he'd rather go to bed, as he'd had a hard day cutting wood and taking care of the animals in the frigid cold.

As the children dragged their sleeping bags into the front room, the darkness and cold outside seemed to seep through the log walls of the cabin. Corrie brought a sleeping bag for Butchy, and bedded him down next to her. They all squirmed as close to the stove as they dared, and snuggled next to each other. Cler turned off the gas lamp, and gave Corrie a flashlight. "Now you kids mind Corrie Lynne, and if you need to, you can wake up Ernie, or call Ennises. We'll be back in a couple of hours," Cler told them. Then he and Gwynne left.

The fire hummed and occasionally popped, but it was no longer roaring. It was banked for the night, which meant Cler had added a log, but shut down the damper, so it wouldn't burn out

372

before morning. It was still good and warm. The grate was open a tiny bit, and flickering light was thrown onto the floor in front of the stove. Otherwise, the cabin was dark.

'I'm scared," Charles said, snuggling down into his sleeping bag.

"There's nothing to be afraid of," Corrie said. "I'll tell you a story."

"Tell about Candy Land!" Charles called out, his voice muffled by the down bag. This was his favorite story. It was a tale about all the children falling down a hole, in succession. Inspired by Alice in Wonderland, the falling down a hole was where the similarity ended. The land the Oborn children discovered was a world of good things to eat. Sometimes, depending on Corrie's imagination and perhaps her appetite, the story was called, "Good Thing to Eat Land."

Corrie began the story, "One day, Mama told us all to get out of the cabin; it was a nice day and she didn't want us under foot. So we decided to go for a walk. Corrie led the way, then Paxton, then Lestie, then Charles, than last came Butchy, following along. They walked for a while and then Corrie turned around and said, 'Where's Butchy?' He had disappeared!"

"'Let's go back and try to find him,' Paxton said. But as they marched back along the trail, suddenly Charles disappeared!"

This went on, until finally, Corrie fell in the hole, and landed on a mattress. There she discovered all her other siblings. She was shocked to find Paxton munching away on a stick, but it turned out to be chocolate!

In this wonderful place, there were lemonade fountains and licorice trees, cookie policemen and a jail made of bricks of ice cream. They were all put in jail for eating some fried chicken fence posts, but they escaped by gobbling down some of the ice cream bricks in the wall of the jail.

At this point, back in reality, a wolf howled, and it sounded pretty close to the cabin. Farther off, another howled in reply. Tecane, the big collie puppy, trembled and tried to crawl into

Charles' sleeping bag with him, but he was too big and had to settle for a soft spot on the foot of the down-filled bag. Tippy, the little cocker spaniel, leaped onto the couch in front of the window and barked angrily.

"They're after the calf!" Paxton whispered. He wasn't being imaginative, like Cheryl would have been. This was real. "Maybe I should get my .22 and go out and see," he said.

Corrie, as the babysitter, was in charge. "No, she said, "It might be a bear, and a .22 will only make a bear mad! We'd better wait for Daddy."

"We could wake up Ernie," Lestie said.

"No," Paxton said, "I'm sure Dad locked up the barn good and tight. Probably, no wolves can get in."

Lestie said, "Unless they chew the plastic window out."

"Why would they do that? Anyway, don't you think the window is too high for a wolf to reach?" Corrie asked.

"Yes, it is," Paxton said. "I think so, anyway."

After a while, in spite of wolves howling somewhere off in the spruce trees, the younger children fell asleep. Tippy had jumped down off the couch and was now asleep on the end of Paxton's sleeping bag. It seemed a long time that Corrie and Paxton waited in the darkness, listening to the wolves howl, their cries fading ever further away.

The next sound they heard was the jeep station wagon putting into the yard. In a moment, the front door groaned open and with a rush of cold air, their parents stepped into the cabin. Cler stopped in the kitchen to light the kerosene lamp, and brought it over to the pile of sleeping bags, to check on the children.

Paxton spoke up, "Dad, we heard wolves."

Cler asked, "Are you kids still awake?"

"We were worried about Veal Cutlets," Corrie said.

Cler told them, "No wolves can get into the barn. It's good and tight. Now go to sleep!"

374

He stepped around the sleeping bags on the floor, and Gwynne followed him as he carried the lamp into the back hall, to their bedroom.

The next morning was bitterly cold, and still dark when it was time to go milk the cow and the goats. Cler shrugged into his parka, donned the black bearskin hat and bear mitts, and stepped out into the frigid darkness to milk the cow. Paxton bundled up and went out with his dad. He was ten-years-old now, and when it wasn't a school morning, he milked Clementine, letting Ernie sleep in. The other nannies had gone dry.

Carrying flashlights, Paxton and Cler followed the well-trod path that cut across the yard to the barn. The dry snow squeaked under their boots. Arriving at the little slab-covered barn, they aimed their flashlights at the reinforced plastic window, and saw that it had been shredded in one corner, and ripped loose at the bottom. For a moment, Paxton was stunned.

"Did wolves do that?" he asked.

Cler checked for foot prints under the window. The fresh snow was untouched, except for rabbit tracks. He shook his head, just as mystified as Paxton was. He lifted the board that secured the heavy wooden door, and they stepped inside the barn, which was usually warm and damp with the body heat given off by the animals. The barn was chilly, and a cold draft came from the damaged window. The first thing Cler spotted was Veal Cutlets, the calf, lying dead, underneath the window.

Cler knelt to examine him. He was stiff. There was a small piece of chewed plastic with some little green threads, in the corner of his mouth. The threads were imbedded in the plastic sheeting on the window to reinforce it. *Lot of good that did*, Cler thought. He said, "Makes you kind of sick, doesn't it?"

"Yeah," Paxton said, looking down at the half-grown calf lying stiff on the hay-strewn floor of the barn.

"If I'd checked last night, when you were worried about wolves, well, I might've caught him before he froze."

Paxton looked around, "Well, at least the others are all right."

375

Letting out a long sigh, Cler said, "Why don't you go get some more of this plastic off the porch, and fix the window, while I get started milking. Better bring a couple of boards to nail over the bottom of the window, so the goats can't stand on their hind legs and reach the plastic. They might try to imitate Veal Cutlets."

When Cler and Paxton returned from the barn with the milk, they were talking about the calf.

Gwynne looked up from stirring oatmeal on the stove, "What is it, Cler?"

"The calf got hold of the plastic covering the barn window. He chewed a hole in it."

"Is he all right?" She asked.

"No, he's dead." Cler dragged his hands out of his big mittens, dropping them onto a chair. He yanked off his hat and shook the snow off his parka, then he stood warming his hands at the drum stove.

Paxton stood beside his dad. Ever the optimist, he said, "Maybe Rowdy can have another calf next year."

Lestie, Ernie, Paxton with Tecane and Tippy 1953

28

KENNY LAKE CHRISTMAS

Winter, 1953

In early December, the days were short and the children arrived at school in the dark and went home in the dark. One night, after the kids had gone to bed, Cler and Gwynne sat at the table sipping hot Postum and talking.

"We need to have a community get-together at the school." Cler said, pouring a little more canned milk into his cup, and stirring it in. He blew on it and tried it. Just right.

"How about a Christmas pageant?" Gwynne suggested, stirring a little more sugar into her own drink. "I remember having a pageant every year when I was in school. We dressed up, sang carols. It made Christmas feel more like Christmas."

"Good idea. Music, theatre, and art. Education!" Cler said.

"And food," Gwynne added.

"Of course. The mothers will take care of that."

The next day, during the usual reading hour around the cheerfully crackling drum stove, Mr. Oborn showed his class an illustration in a book. It was a Renaissance painting of the Nativity. "Notice the costumes. They wore robes, and covered their heads with cloths or scarves. Can anyone guess why I'm showing you this painting?"

The class remained silent. Finally Corrie raised her hand. "It's almost Christmas!"

"Yes, and we're having a Christmas pageant. Everyone will get to be in it: singing carols, reciting lines, and dressing up like angels, wise men or shepherds."

The students were excited, and some of them had even been in a pageant before. Cler knew they came from a variety of religious backgrounds, among them Catholic, Russian Orthodox. Protestant, Pentecostal, and Latter-day Saints. No matter. At community gatherings prayers were said, and it didn't matter who said them.

As preparations got underway, everyone seemed to be looking forward to the Christmas pageant. It would give the families an excuse to get out of their cabins, and, of course, everyone liked a party.

Every student had a chance to take part in the play. Some were given a few lines to say or delegated to sing in small groups, regardless of whether they had any aptitude for singing.

Julie Ennis, a tall, serious girl, had both talent and experience in music. She agreed to play the piano, and teach the younger kids to sing their songs. She did her best. The little boys only had to stand still, looking like shepherds, as she played "While Shepherds Watched," and a narrator said a few lines. She practiced with them and they did all right except for the part about standing still.

Then there were second graders, Celestia, Alina and Vivian. They were supposed to learn "It Came Upon a Midnight Clear," not an easy song. To cover their discomfort, they burst into giggles every time they missed a word, or a note. Patiently, Julie would stop playing, and wait until they settled down.

"OK, start over," she'd say. One afternoon there was so much giggling around the piano that Julie slammed down the cover and stormed off. Mr. Oborn was busy helping the big boys with their math. When he heard the piano cover slam, he looked up, "What's going on?"

Celestia ran and took hold of Julie's sweater. "Please stay. We promise to be good!"

Julie returned to the piano. "You guys are supposed to be *angels*," she said, disgusted.

"My mother is making wings for me," Alina told her, proudly. "They're really pretty."

"Good luck *looking* like angels," Julie sneered, but her sarcasm was lost on the girls.

After school, Lestie found her mother lying down on the couch, and she asked if she'd make her a pair of wings. "Alina's mother made some, and Alina says they're really pretty."

Gwynne had a headache, and was not very enthusiastic. "I guess I can try." She never felt very well during the winter, but this winter seemed especially bad. She had no energy, and often went about the necessary tasks of every day, feeling as if she were moving under water. Later, when she was in the kitchen, listlessly peeling potatoes for supper, her mind seemed to clear, and she suddenly had an idea of how to make a pair of pretty angel wings. There was a piece of white muslin in her cedar chest, that would be just right.

After supper, while Corrie and Celestia washed the dishes and dried them, Gwynne found the muslin, glue, and two wire hangers. She bent the hangers into wing shapes, and made the hooks fit Lestie's shoulders. She cut the cloth to fit, and glued it onto both sides of each hanger. Then she cut out cloth feathers and attached them so they fluttered when the wings moved.

"They look pretty good, if I do say so myself," Gwynne said when she finished.

Celestia kissed her mother. "They're beautiful!" The next day at school she bragged, "My mother made me some wings last night that look so real a bird might want to borrow them!"

"That's great!" Alina said, "I can't wait to see them."

Vivian didn't say anything, so the subject was dropped. That afternoon, Lestie found her mother at the stove frying some moose steaks for dinner. "Mother, can you make Vivian some angel wings, too? I don't think her mother knows how."

Gwynne turned a steak, pausing with the big fork in her hand, "I can talk to Emma, but you might be surprised at how clever she is at sewing. Maybe she needs some material. I have plenty of muslin."

When Corrie came home, Gwynne left her with Butchy and drove down the road to the George's place. She had the wings she'd made and the extra muslin with her. She parked in the only shoveled space and knocked on the door of Emma's cabin.

Delighted to see her, Emma invited her in and the two sat and talked for a few minutes about the Christmas play and the costumes the girls needed. Gwynne held up the wings. "These are wings I made for Lestie. Did you know that Vivian needs something like this, too?"

"Vivian doesn't tell me."

Gwynne explained more about the play and gave Emma the muslin. With her usual sweet smile, Emma thanked Gwynne for the muslin, saying she would make some wings, and that Vivian had a white dress

Paxton and Little Enzo were supposed to sing "We Three Kings of Orient Are." Ernie didn't actually go to school, but he was invited to participate in the pageant, and he agreed to sing with the boys. He towered over them, but it made their efforts that much more entertaining to watch. Paxton and Little Enzo could sing, sort of, but their voices were changing. Ernie's voice was more on the order of a tractor engine. Altogether, the boys were enjoying themselves.

Corrie was hoping to be Mary, with Little Enzo as Joseph, which she considered as starring roles. She was doubly upset when she wasn't chosen, because she had to let someone else carry Tootsie, who was a perfectly lovely Baby Jesus, and breakable, besides. Instead of Mary, Corrie was enlisted to be stage manager, which her father assured her was a much more important job.

She soon decided that she wouldn't have liked being Mary anyway. All Mary had to do was walk on stage, pull the baby doll out from her robe, and lay it on the pile of hay. And kneel, of course, for quite a while, which could be hard on the knees. Stage manager, Corrie happily discovered, consisted mostly of being the boss, and it seemed right up her alley. Another homesteader's daughter, red-haired Ginny, got the part of Mary, and Arlo got to be Joseph.

One day while the sun was up, the older boys were allowed to go out into the woods with Ernie and his gun, to cut down a Christmas tree. An hour later, they came in dragging a spruce so tall that they couldn't stand it up inside the building. Cler instructed them to cut two feet off the bottom, so they could put a star on top. They stood it up and it still reached into the rafters. The kids made red and green paper chains, and paper ornaments to decorate the tree.

Julie continued helping the little groups of students practice their songs after school. Two days before the pageant, the three little angels started fooling around again, breaking into giggles every time they missed a note. Julie slammed down the piano lid, and yanked her coat on. "I'm going home!" She stormed out the door. Mr. Oborn was at his desk grading papers. He looked up after Julie left, addressing the three miscreants.

"You girls know that song well enough to sing it without the piano?"

"No," they said in unison, their eyes on the floor.

"Well, then, apologize to Julie first thing in the morning."

They agreed to apologize. After Alina and Vivian left, Celestia approached her father's desk. "The problem is, Daddy," she began, but he stopped her.

"Mr. Oborn," he reminded.

She sighed, "Mr. Oborn. Vivian and Alina don't like to sing, and it's a hard song. Why do *I* have to be the only..."

Cler cut her off. "No excuses, Lestie." The next day Julie had her apology and the last rehearsal took place after school. The stage was simply two Army blankets pinned to a rope strung across the front of the room. Desks were lined up close together and in front of them, benches made of boards and logs were placed. They were all ready for the pageant, the next day.

Christmas Eve, the cabin was filled with spicy aromas, cinnamon and ginger, as Gwynne baked oatmeal cookies. The children were scavenging around their bedrooms, looking for something resembling costumes, while Corrie tried to help them. Lestie wriggled into her white night gown and grabbed her wings and halo, intending to put them on at the school.

Paxton came out of the back hall wearing a too-short bathrobe over his brown pants, with a towel on his head, looking more like a man about to take a bath than a Wiseman. His mother fixed him up a bit, by making the towel look like a turban. She pinned it with an old brooch. Corrie and Mother helped Ernie and Charles dress up like a wise man and a little shepherd.

Soon a motley band trooped down the driveway to the school, where windows cast golden squares of lamplight onto the piled snow. Red sparks from the chimney drifted into the night. Cler was already there, and Gwynne would be coming soon, bringing Butchy, and the cookies.

The school was already crowded with people. Women talked over the refreshment table spread with goodies, at the back of the room. Benches were filling fast. A few men stood warming their hands around the crackling drum stove. Grandma George and her daughters, Emma and Ina, stood uncertainly just inside the door. They were clad in their best fur parkas, wearing brightly-colored scarves.

Cler spied them and crossed the room. "I saved a seat just for you," he said. "If you want to, you can hang your parkas over there, and here's your bench."

Franklin spotted his grandmother, and waved shyly. He had come early to build the fire, and set the damper to slow heat, because the room would get too hot with all the people crowded in. He took the broom from the corner and swept up snow left in the doorway from people's boots. Grandma George watched him proudly, as he went about his duties as the school janitor.

Julie was up front at the piano, pounding out "O Come all ye Faithful," as latecomers filed in, and found a seat or stood against a wall. An air of excitement, every bit as pungent as the smell of pine, sawdust, smoke and wet fur, filled the room. Two gas lanterns, hanging on nails in the rafters, hissed softly. The log walls still smelled of sap, and in the lamplight, looked like they were made of yellow gold. At the front of the room, above the makeshift stage, a tin-foil star as big as a plate hung on a string. It twinkled, turning slowly, in the rising heat of the stove.

The players behind the curtain tried to be quiet, but of course, the little boys squirmed and the little girls giggled, mostly

382

from nervousness. There were a lot of people out there. Some of the children had never seen so many people, all in one room.

Cler greeted the audience warmly, expressing gratitude for their support. He went over the program, giving credit to Julie Ennis for sharing her talents, and for her long-suffering and patience while teaching the other children their songs. He introduced Ted Ennis as the narrator, and then led the audience and cast singing "O Little Town of Bethlehem."

Ted Ennis was situated in front of the curtain, stage right. He had a hearty voice that matched his size. He began reading, "In those days there went out a decree from Caesar Augustus for all the world to be taxed..."

As the story progressed, Joseph and Mary, costumed in long robes and bright scarves, made their way to the little manger at center stage and Mary produced a baby doll from under her robes, laying it carefully in the box of hay. Charles and Dallas, the shepherd boys edged around the curtain and stood, while Julie played and a child recited, "While shepherds watched their flocks by night, all seated on the ground..."

A tall boy wearing a white sheet, stepped out in front of the curtain and held his hands out stiffly, posing as "the angel of the Lord," who spoke to the shepherds. The shepherds were supposed to stand still, but their wiggling made the angel of the Lord even more nervous. His name was Carl, and he was terrified from the moment he appeared on stage. It was a good thing he had no lines. He just stood there trembling, with his arms stretched toward the audience, while Ted intoned the solemn words, "For unto us a child is born. Unto us a son is given!" Cler hoped the boy wouldn't pass out. Then it was time for the angels. Corrie had been adjusting angel wings on the terrified little girls. Seeing how scared her two friends were, Celestia began to cry.

Corrie said, "Just get out there! The audience is waiting!"

That didn't help. Now all three angels had their backs up, so to speak. They huddled together, whispering, "You go first! No, you go!" Somebody shoved somebody else and Cler stepped behind the curtain to see what was holding up the show. He saw their stricken faces, and stooped to put his arms around all three, trying to reason with them, "You girls have a part to play. If you don't do it, who will?" Tears ran down their faces, but the angels had no answer, and Cler left, thinking he'd convinced them to get out there. Celestia wiped her nose on her sleeve and turned to her sister, "You wanna go do it?"

"I'm the stage manager," Corrie snapped. She shoved Celestia, wings and all, through the crack between the curtain and the wall. There was no going back. Vivian and Alina followed her onto the stage. The angels all took a deep breath and sang a shaky, but passable, rendition of "It Came Upon a Midnight Clear." When the song ended, the girls had to stay out there as backdrop for the nativity scene. *Those three little angels make a sweet picture,* Gwynne thought, gazing at them fondly.

The wise men clowned their way onto the stage, more or less chanting their song, but they were nice and loud, and the audience loved it. Soon all the characters in the cast formed a final tableau of the Nativity. There were dark children, and light children, in all sizes, dressed a bit haphazardly, as shepherds, angels, kings and the holy family. They didn't look like a Raphael painting, but they looked just fine to the audience.

There was one last song, with parents and children joining in "Silent Night, Holy Night." Julie played the piano while they sang, "All is calm, all is bright round yon Virgin mother and Child. Holy infant so tender and mild, sleep in Heavenly Peace. Sleep in Heavenly peace." Those who didn't know the words just sat there smiling. When the last echoes died away, a moment of sweetness filled the room; the kind of unity that only Christmas creates.

A NEW TEACHER COMES TO KENNY LAKE

On a frigid New Year's Eve, the windows of the little cabin were frosted over with thick leafy designs, ostensibly left by Jack Frost. The family surrounded the table, chowing down on their dinner of hot moose meat stew—thick and deliciously brown. Cler finished a mouthful and waited for the hub-bub to settle down before he spoke, "Well, I got a letter from the Territory of Alaska. They're sending a new teacher." He glanced around. His children didn't seem happy. "That means that I won't be your teacher any more. No more Mr. Oborn." He winked at Lestie, who always made the mistake of calling him "Daddy" at school.

"Is the new teacher nice?" Charles asked.

"I'm sure she is. She'll be moving into the truck house, when she comes. I'm expecting her tomorrow." Inwardly, he was hoping that this new teacher would be a hearty soul who would stick around.

As the children filed into the school building on the first day after the Christmas holiday, the temperature outside was thirty below zero. A strange brown-haired lady and her little boy stood shivering by the stove.

"Good morning, students! I know it's a little cold in here this morning but it should warm up soon. Meanwhile, I want everyone to hang up his or her coat nicely and sit in their seats." She was all business, this lady. She went to the board as the students sat down and grew quiet. She printed, "Mrs. Jones."

"My name is Mrs. Jones.* This is my son, Jeffery. He's in first grade. Who else is in first grade?"

Charles raised his hand, but he didn't look big enough for first grade. His brown hair stuck up every which way because of the hat he'd worn to school, and it appeared to have been hacked off with a pocket knife. He had chubby cheeks and bright brown eyes that made him look like a Hummel figure, but he faced the teacher with an expression that said, "I neither like you nor am I afraid of you."

Firmly, he said, "I'm five."

"Well. You should be in kindergarten, and I do not teach Kindergarten."

Corrie raised her hand.

"Yes?"

"He already knows how to read and write. Dad thought he could go to first grade."

The teacher eyed the pint-sized scholar. "Very well. I'll test him later. Are there any more first graders?"

"There used to be one, but he's home sick," Charles told her.

Mrs. Jones sighed. "I suppose you can stay in first grade with Jeffery."

The drum stove could heat the school room, at least after it had been going for a while, but that didn't satisfy the new teacher. She couldn't tolerate the soot, bark chips and sawdust that littered the floor around the stove. Franklin was no longer the school janitor. He stopped going to school when Cler stopped teaching, and Paxton was enlisted to build the morning fires. He wasn't as good at keeping the floor clean and he wasn't sorry when Mrs. Jones had the drum stove replaced by an oil heater. It turned out to be a bad idea. On frigid mornings, the new oil stove was turned up as high as it could go, but it still didn't put out enough heat, and the children were miserable. They weren't allowed to stand around the stove, and they were not supposed to keep their coats and mittens on.

Outside the little log building, the Arctic winter covered everything with snow in great heaps; it lay so thick on the trees that the branches cracked and broke under the weight. The school windows became completely coated with frost. There wasn't much to see out there, anyway, but a white world. When it was snowing, the ground and sky became one, and when the sun was shining, the snow was so brilliant it hurt the eyes.

Darkness came early, settling over the frigid landscape, and the children put on their coats and walked home through the snow by starlight. Often, the Aurora Borealis crackled, like great, ever-changing purple and green curtains hanging in the air above their heads. Mornings, the snow was so cold that it squeaked under foot as the children walked the short distance to school, entering the door so stiff and frozen that they had to pull off their mittens with their teeth; their hands didn't work right. One morning Celestia felt like she would never get warm, so she left her coat and mittens on and took her seat. The teacher called to her.

"Celestia, remove your hat and coat when you enter the building. You know the rules."

"Can I leave on my mittens?"

"It is 'may I,' and no, you may not. Please go to the coat rack; then return to your seat. You are being disruptive and I won't allow it."

Celestia did as she was told, but she was freezing, sitting right by the window. For the next hour she huddled in her seat, trying to write her spelling, but her stiff, red fingers could barely hold a pencil. The chill came through the plastic and Celestia's desk was in the path of the draft. She felt like crying. Mrs. Jones didn't care if she got frostbite and lost all her fingers! She tried to study her spelling, but her mind kept going back to those happy mornings when all the students gathered around the comforting warmth of the drum stove and listened to her father read to them.

She wasn't the only one who was cold, although some students were closer to the oil heater than others. Some of them whispered to each other, saying they wished their new teacher would go back where she came from.

One day, as they sat in their desks shivering, Little Enzo, who was 11, raised his hand. Everyone knew he was a smart Alec and hoped he had a zinger.

"Yes, Enzo, what is it?" she asked.

"Mrs. Jones, how come you are Mrs., but you don't have a husband?" This sounded like an innocent question, but he knew very well that it was none of his business.

Her friendly look faded, and she just stood there. The only sounds were a few students shuffling their feet, and the soft hum of the oil heater's fan. Tears formed in her eyes, and her nose reddened, but she didn't answer Little Enzo's question.

"You have work to do," she said. "All of you."

The students got back to work.

At dinner that night, Lestie complained. "Mrs. Jones won't let us wear our mittens in school."

Paxton added, "And she won't let us stand by the stove. We're freezing, Dad."

Corrie said, "That new oil stove doesn't put out enough heat."

The children continued to voice their complaints. Among other things, Mrs. Jones was so strict, they couldn't get out of their desks without permission, even to sharpen a pencil.

"I guess I spoiled you kids. I'm sorry," Cler said, "but no matter what, you respect your teacher and try to make her time at Kenny Lake a little better. The weather will warm up, and that oil heater will do its job. Wear an extra sweater in the morning."

Cler kept the contract to drive the school bus, and sometimes Gwynne drove it. She didn't mind, and it was an excuse to get out of the cabin, while Cler cooked breakfast for the children. They only had to walk to the end of the circle drive, so of course, they didn't get to ride the bus.

Over time the kids got used to Mrs. Jones. As the weather became milder, the oil heater was able to keep the room warmer, and the children took more interest in their school work. Going to school and seeing friends was always better than being stuck in their isolated cabins all day, with nothing to do.

TECANE

In March, Charles got a puppy for his sixth birthday. Ted Ennis' collie had puppies with the Santini's big husky. One puppy was a ball of tawny gold fur, with a white ruff and chest, and a thick tail curled over his back. Charles wanted to name him Wolf, but Mother suggested he call the puppy the Ahtna word for wolf, which was Tecane, pronounced "Tee-cah'-nee" by the children.

It wasn't long before the puppy was as big as Tippy, and he continued to grow. Before he was five months old, he was bigger than either his collie mother or husky father. Tecane was huge, but being young, he wasn't brave.

388

For one thing, he was afraid of anything that wandered into the yard at night. It might be a lynx or a moose. While Tippy would stand outside barking at wild animals, Tecane would seek refuge on the porch. More than once he came crashing through the screen door, ripping the screen out in the process. In order to save the work of fixing the screen, Cler allowed him to stay in the cabin at night. He preferred to sleep with Charles, under the sleeping bag, if possible.

Tecane didn't start out to be much of a watch dog, but he was very affectionate, he adored the kids, and they loved him back.

29

OUT OF HIBERNATION

SPRING 1954

Finally, it was spring. After an Arctic winter, nothing could feel as good as spring. The school children were restless; they wanted to run outside and shout for joy. They gazed out the windows, entertained by simply watching piles of snow melting and the icicles on the eves dripping. Mud puddles beckoned. It was time to don rubber boots, and wade in the water! Tiny sprigs of green grass made their way through the last of the snow.

As soon as school was out, Mrs. Jones left Kenny Lake. She tearfully said her goodbyes, saying she had truly loved the children, but she could not imagine spending another winter in Alaska.

The citizens of Kenny Lake got busy in the spring, energized by the longer days, and the sunlight. They had a lot of projects they'd planned during the doldrums of winter, to begin as soon as the weather warmed up. Surviving winter meant working hard all summer, fishing, hunting, building better barns, getting in a winter's supply of wood, and preserving the garden produce, wild meat and fish they'd managed to stockpile over the summer. Everyone had plans to improve their homesteads and make life a little easier. Some thought of ways to accrue cash reserves. Cash in the interior was always in short supply; barter being the more common way of obtaining goods and services.

Mrs. Ennis planned to earn money with her poultry enterprise. She purchased a hundred chicks from a farmer in Palmer. She fed them until they were big enough to run around the yard and eat weeds and bugs to supplement their feed. She always locked them safely in the chicken coop at night, because there were plenty of predators in the woods that would love to feast on chicken. There were lynx, and wolves, for starters, not to mention the Santinis' dogs. Her plan was to sell eggs to the others in the community, as well as the stores at Chitna and Copper Center.

When they were big enough, the male chickens were culled from the flock, leaving only two roosters. Two, because she might lose one before he did his duty with the hens. Her family ate the banty roosters, preserving the expensive feed pellets for laying hens.

Gwynne and Cler's plans included the sawmill, a store and a gas station. Cler put the truck house on skids, and moved it down nearer the road. He bought an old fashioned glass-topped gas pump, and began selling gas. The increasing numbers of homesteaders needed gas, as did hunters and fishermen, especially in the summer. He used the truck as his store, stockpiling everything from fishing tackle to foodstuffs, as well as kerosene, candles, first aid supplies and even water purification tablets. It wasn't long before his gas station and store were making money.

With Ernie there to help at home, Cler also spent part of that summer working for the Forest Service as a smoke jumper. In the Army, he'd learned how to parachute out of a plane. When there was a forest fire, Cler was called to duty fighting fires. Often, all they could do was monitor the fire , and later watch for hot spots that might spread to other parts of the forest. He didn't have to go often, but every time he went out on a fire, he was paid, and the job gave him more needed cash. Cler was promoted to crew chief, and his pay was increased.

LIVING OFF THE LAND

One bright summer morning Paxton, who was ten, woke eight-year-old Lestie before the rest of the family was up. "Let's go out in the woods and see if we can live off the land," he said. She was always up for an adventure with her brother, so she slipped into her jeans and tennis shoes and tied a long sleeved shirt around her waist, in case it got colder later. They intended to be gone for a long time, living off the land.

Paxton had tied up a small bundle consisting of a flannel blanket, a piece of rope, a piece of the goats' salt block, and a small sauce pan. He also carried his pocket knife. They would have taken a dog with them, but Tecane was asleep somewhere in the house. Tippy was getting arthritis in his hips and only followed them to the edge of the yard.

With their few supplies, they headed off into the woods, and ended up at a small lake, where they decided to set up camp. They tied the rope between two trees and hung the blanket over it, staking it to the ground at each corner, making a tent.

Then they set about placing rocks in a circle in which Paxton built a small fire. As the wood burned down, he picked wild rice from the lakeside and Lestie pounded it into powder on a flat rock, then mixed in some lake water and crushed sugar berries to make a sort of dough. Sugar berries grew on tiny plants low to the ground. They were pale pink with the consistency of sugar inside, but they were barely sweet. She put the rock on the edge of the fire where the "dough" was supposed to cook. Paxton filled the saucepan with water, leaves from some plant and sugar berries, to make "tea."

When the dough on the rock had dried out a bit, they ate it, though most of it stuck to the rock, since they had no grease. They tried to drink the tea, but it was bitter. Lestie added more sugar berries, but it wasn't any better. Altogether, it was a pretty skimpy lunch. They lay in the warm sun and took a nap after all their hard work.

An hour later they woke up, hungry and mosquito-bitten.

In spite of their clever scrounging, Lestie decided that the woods were not full of food for humans. Living off the land was fine for moose or bears, but not so easy for two young children. So they surrendered and returned to "civilization."

When they entered the cabin, they found no one there. Even the dogs were gone. There was a note on the table: "Paxton and Celestia. We have gone to Lower Tonsina for the day to have

392

a picnic. Since we couldn't find you, we left without you. Love, Mother."

"A picnic?" We missed out on a picnic?" They checked the bread box and found a little dried out bread. It tasted pretty good to them, after their long day of living off the land.

ERNIE TURNS EIGHTEEN

Gwynne was making sandwiches for lunch; for herself, Butchy, and Ernie. He was already sitting at the table trying to work on the course he'd been taking, but he was in despair. There was no way he'd get it finished before he turned eighteen in June.

He looked up from his books. "Gwynne, what do you think? My birthday's coming up, and I'll be eligible for the draft. I don't know what to do. Think I should just ignore it and if I get drafted, well, I get drafted?"

Gwynne brought his sandwich over to him. It was salmon with pickles. "I don't know, Ernie. With the Korean War going on, you might get called up right away. Why don't you ask Cler about it when he comes home?"

"OK, I will. Thanks."

Later, Ernie and Cler were working on the woodpile. Cler was using the buck saw to cut stove lengths. He had a log of deadwood laid across a pair of sawhorses, and was sawing away at one end of the log. For a moment, he stopped to watch his nephew splitting kindling nearby.

Ernie's muscles rippled as he wielded the ax. He would balance a piece of log on the chopping block, and swing the ax high over his head, then come down with a crack that split the log in half. He'd set up each half, and split them into fourths.

Cler called over, "You've gotten pretty good at that!"

Ernie grinned. "Thanks!" He rested for a moment, leaning on the end of the ax handle like a cane, with one hand on top of the other. "Hey, Cler, I want to ask you about something. With the war on, I might get drafted. Think I should join up first? I'm thinking about the Navy."

Cler swiped his arm across his forehead; he'd worked up a sweat. "When I was your age, there was another war on. Some of the guys waited to get called, but I joined the Army Air Corps the minute I turned 18. I wanted to fly. Unless you *want* to be in the Army, maybe you shouldn't wait too long to make your choice."

Ernie thought about it. He guessed he wouldn't mind being in the Army. He decided to put off joining up, at least for a while. The real reason was that he liked it here. He was enjoying it too much to leave.

A SUSPICIOUS FIRE

The phone rang two longs and two shorts, and Gwynne answered it. The voice on the line asked, "Is Cler around?"

"He's out with the animals," she said, "if you want to wait, I'll go get him."

"This is Jack, with the Forest Service. There's a big fire about five miles out of Chitna, on the north side of the road. Just tell him to get down here as fast as he can. It's spreading fast!"

"I'll tell him. Will he be able to find you?"

"He won't be able to miss us," Jack said.

Gwynne hurried outside and called to Cler, who was headed to the house with a pail of milk. "Jack called. There's a forest fire down near Chitna, spreading fast. He wants you as soon as you can get down there. I'll take the milk, while you go get ready."

Cler grabbed his pack. In it were his fire-fighting equipment, sleeping bag, and other supplies. Because of the difficulty of fighting fires in the Bush many were allowed to burn, unless they threatened communities.

As it turned out, the Chitna fire was accessible, so that within a couple of days, they got the fire under control. Cler came home, but he had to go back the next day, to check on some hot spots near the road. When he went back, he took Corrie and Paxton with him.

A blue haze hung in the air, obscuring the mountains, as they headed toward Chitna. Even when they were several miles away from the burned area, the air was acrid with smoke. They passed green trees and drove over a bridge, and then they saw the aftermath of the fire: acres of burned-over ground. In places, smoke drifted up from the blackened tundra, where moss still smoldered. "The fire can get down in the peat and burn for months," Cler told his kids.

They passed a group of men standing around on a wide gravel area near the road, and Cler pulled over. A temporary staging area had been established there, near a creek. Cler parked and left the kids in the car, while he went to check with the fire chief.

For a few minutes Corrie and Paxton watched him talking to the other firefighters. When he came back, and slid behind the wheel, he said, "We can go home; they have it covered." He backed around and was about to drive onto the road, when he stopped and pointed, "See that kid in the blue coat?"

Paxton and Corrie saw a teenager, with his hands in his pockets. He was short and dark with a cap of straight, black hair and bangs that nearly covered his eyes. He looked to be about Franklin George's age, around seventeen.

"That guy there?" Paxton asked.

"Yes," Cler said. "He was on my crew when we were fighting the fire. I'm pretty sure he started it. I didn't know, until I heard him boasting about it to one of his friends."

Corrie was shocked, "Why would he do that?"

Cler said, "For a lot of these guys, the money they get fighting a fire is all they earn all year." Shoving the car in gear, Cler drove up the slight embankment, onto the road, and headed back toward Kenny Lake.

Paxton asked, "If you knew that kid started the fire, why didn't you do anything about it? Weren't you the boss of your crew?"

His dad glanced over at him, "Actually, I did do something."

"What?" Corrie asked.

"I worked his tail off!" Cler said.

Fall, 1954

ERNIE JOINS UP

One day in August, Ernie got a letter from a cousin his age, who suggested they both sign up for the Navy together, before they got drafted. That evening, out in the barn, Cler was milking Rowdy while Ernie was milking Clementine. Ernie said, "I got a letter from my cousin. He says the military has a thing called the "Buddy Program," or something. Anyway, if two guys enlist in the same branch of the military together, they get to go to Basic Training together, and get deployed with the same unit. My cousin wants for us to enlist in the Navy. What do you think?"

Cler had his forehead pressed against Rowdy's massive side, and he kept his eyes focused on the milk squirting into the bucket. "If you want to join the Navy more than you want to get drafted into the Army, then I think you should do it. When do you plan on leaving?"

"My cousin says we should do it right away. So we don't get drafted first."

"Sounds like a wise decision," Cler said. The milk bucket was ¾ full, and Rowdy's bag was empty. Cler stood up, releasing Rowdy to go graze. "Rowdy's not giving as much milk as usual. I hope she hasn't taken it into her head to dry up already."

Ernie carried his bucket of goat's milk to the can, and poured it in. "We're still getting plenty of goat's milk. So you think I should head out for Utah, then?"

"I'll take you in to Anchorage on Friday, and get you a ticket. Unless you want to drive your pickup down the Alaska Highway." Cler opened the boards that held Clementine's head, let her jump off the stanchion, and urged Tina into her place. He scratched Tina behind the ears, as Ernie placed the bucket under

396

her and started milking. The stream of milk hit the empty bucket with a pinging sound, as the milk foamed up.

Ernie glanced over his shoulder at Cler. "I'm not sure the pickup would get me back to Utah, are you?"

Cler laughed, "Maybe, maybe not! But it's your truck."

"I'll leave it here, for you," Ernie said. "If I go into the Navy, what use will I have for it?"

On Friday, Ernie didn't say much, as he packed up his suitcase. He was headed out the door when Lestie stopped him and gave him a hug around the waist. "We're going to miss you!" she told him. He was surprised, as if he didn't know what to say, but he smiled in his shy way. He remained quiet as he and Cler made the drive into Anchorage.

When they reached the airport and Cler was parking the Jeep wagon, Ernie asked, "Cler, do you think I'll get sent to Korea? What if I can't get into the Navy, and end up in the Army, anyway?" He seemed worried, and with good reason. There was a war on, and everything they'd heard about it indicated it was a nasty business. For a moment, they both sat in silence.

Cler said, "To be honest, you might end up in Korea, but I think on a Navy ship you'll be hauling supplies, and they're deployed all over the world, Ernie. There's a pretty good chance you'll go somewhere else besides Korea. Whether or not the Navy takes you, you're a capable young man. Even since you've been living with us, I've seen you learning skills that will help you, no matter what you do."

"Yeah, milking goats, chopping wood, hauling water..." Ernie smiled, ruefully.

Cler shook his head. "Don't sell yourself short. You can drive a truck, shoot a gun, and make sourdough pancakes!"

Ernie laughed. "I guess you're right. I can do a lot of stuff now I never expected to do. How hard can it be in the military?"

"Piece of cake!" Cler told him. "Now, let's go in and buy you a ticket to Utah, and parts unknown."

Back in Ogden, Ernie and his cousin decided the Navy didn't offer the incentives they were looking for. They ended up joining the Air Force together. Ernie called to tell Cler his news. "After Basic Training, I'm going to tech school in Mississippi, to become an air traffic controller. I'm going to finish my GED in the Air Force. What do you think of that?"

"Well, that sounds fine! I'm proud of you, Ernie," Cler said, his voice choking up. The kid had come a long way.

A COMMUNITY FEAST

A couple arrived to teach school that fall, and Cler rented the truck house to them. Julie and Hal Waugh had been in Alaska for a while, and claimed they were prepared to last a winter at Kenny Lake.

Cler was happy to give up teaching school, but he kept the contract to drive the school bus. By the end of September, temperatures had dropped and it looked like it was going to be a cold winter. Cler did his best to get the barn and chicken coop ready, by adding a layer of plastic to the windows, and rigging a heating element in the animal's water trough. He'd hauled hay from the meadow, just as last year, and had a nice stack. He'd stockpiled as much wood as he could, stacking much of it on the porch, where he wouldn't have to dig it out of the snow.

Mrs. Ennis was worried about the coming winter, too. She had more chickens than she could afford to feed. The nights were cold, but there were still a few nice days left, so she decided she would get the community together to help her. They could all feast on fried chicken, and she'd still have a few hens left to set on eggs next spring. She had no way to keep the slaughtered chickens fresh, so the alternative was to eat what they could.

As she figured, no one turned down the opportunity to take a break from cutting wood and other jobs they were trying to finish. The Santinis, Georges, Oborns, and Kirklands all came to the chicken fry.

Some of the men dispatched the hapless hens with a sharp whack of the ax, on the chopping block. The big boys hollered with glee to see a headless chicken loosed to run around the yard.

398

The boys' job was not to cheer on headless chickens, but to drain them, neck down, and carry them to the fire. There the birds were dunked in boiling water, their feathers plucked over a wash tub, and the pinfeathers singed over the flames.

Corrie, Julie and LaVerne cleaned the birds, and cooled them in a tub of well water. Corrie, with her interest in anatomy, rather enjoyed opening up a chicken and removing the different parts inside. She reserved the liver, heart, and gizzard, slicing the gizzard open to clean out the green mass of partially processed seeds. She also became an expert at cutting the chicken into parts for frying.

Gwynne and Zoya dredged the pieces in flour and spices, and then dropped them into a large pot of boiling vegetable oil and lard.

When enough chicken was fried, everyone gathered to eat the feast. There were beans and cabbage slaw and all the fried chicken they could eat. After helping clean up, the families had to get back to their own homesteads before dark, to do chores.

Back at the cabin, the Oborns had family prayer, and then Gwynne sent the kids to get ready for bed, while Cler prepared to go out to the barn. As he dragged on his boots, he grumbled, "This country is pretty hard on a farmer, that's for sure..."

Out in the barn, he milked Clementine, and then started on Tina, Corrie's goat. While he milked, he put the top of his head against the warm flank of the little nanny, and watched the aromatic milk squirt into the bucket.

"You know, Tina," he said, "I really miss having Ernie around."

Tina bleated, "Ma-a-ah!"

"My sentiments, exactly," Cler said.

A BEAR IN THE GEORGE'S CACHE

Early one morning, Franklin pounded on the door and Gwynne answered it. "Where's Cler?" The boy seemed to be in a panic.

"He's out in the barn. What's the matter?"

"We got a bear in the cache last night, and he eat a lotta fish!"

"Cler's out in the barn, milking."

In a few minutes, Cler came inside and grabbed his gun. "I'm going to go see if I can find a bear," he said, as he reached a box of shells from the rafters and dropped them in his pocket.

Grandma George and Emma were waiting in their yard. When they saw Cler and Franklin drive up, they waved them over toward the cashes, two house-shaped log structures perched on top of posts. It was the end of fish camp, and the caches were filled with fish. A bear had managed to tear the door partway off of one cache, and scraps of dried fish and bear scat littered the ground. Cler and Franklin climbed out of the truck.

Grandma George was wringing her hands, "What we gonna do?"

"Let me look around a bit, Grandma George. Then we'll make a plan."

The bear had been there in the wee hours of the morning. It had been disturbed in its feasting by the dogs' barking. Franklin said he'd spotted the bear and had shot at it, but it ran away.

Cler followed the tracks until they disappeared into the brush. It was too late to try and track it, but it was sure to try and come back for another run at the smoked fish.

"I'll get someone to help me, and we'll keep watch tonight and see if he comes back."

Grandma George nodded vigorously. "You shoot that fella, Cler. I give you the meat."

"We'll share the meat, how about that?" Cler countered.

"Then I make you a rug," she said.

He nailed up the damaged door, and when he got home, he called Enzo and Ted, to see if they'd come help him stand watch at the Georges overnight. "We can take turns sleeping in our trucks," he said, so bring a sleeping bag and a flashlight. Whoever's on watch when we shoot it, gets to have the skin for a rug."

400

After supper, Cler did his evening chores, feeding the animals, milking, and making sure the cow, her calf, and the goats were all shut securely in the barn. He checked the chicken coop and then left for the Georges.

Ted and Enzo were already there, with their headlights illuminating the yard around the caches. When Cler joined them, Ted said, "It musta' been a big one. Those caches look pretty strong to me."

"Well, they're getting old, and the door on the one was rotting out. I fixed it, but any bear that's already been into the fish, will be back to try and finish it off."

"You're right," Ted said.

Enzo said, "I'll take the first watch. It's ten now, so about midnight suit you?"

"Fine," Cler said. "If he's not here by then, I'll go from midnight to two or three. OK, Ted?"

"Sure. If you need me sooner, just let me know."

Each man climbed back into his truck and turned off the headlights. With coats and hats on, they wrapped up in their sleeping bags without getting into them. That way, they could bail out of their trucks at a moment's notice.

It was on Cler's watch that the bear came back. Cler was dozing off around 2 a.m., when the dogs set up a cacophony of barking and howling. He grabbed his 30-06 and leaped out as the bear was trying again to break open the cache. Enzo and Ted were right behind him. The three men lined up with a couple of feet between them, and all shot at once. The bear dropped to the ground. Enzo put another bullet into his head just in case, but having taken it from all three guns, the bear didn't get up again.

Grandma George came shuffling out of her cabin in her fur slippers and night gown. She saw the fallen bear and clapped her hands together, obviously pleased.

Cler said, "I'll get this bear opened up, and then we'll skin it out. You guys want some of the meat?"

Ted said, "I think we should give most of it to the Georges. They've lost a lot of fish, and they'll need it for their dogs this winter."

Cler was already kneeling by the bear, ready to slice it open. "That's what I was thinking."

Enzo said, "Well, I'd like some of it. I have dogs, too."

By the glare of headlights on Ted's pickup, Cler sliced open the bear's abdomen as it lay there on the ground. Steam came out with the smell of putrid fish.

"Criminy! That's powerful!" Cler couldn't help turning away for a moment. When he got a breath of fresh air, he turned back and carefully began cutting away the innards, trying not to nick the stomach, or guts, which would have contaminated the meat.

"Anyone wants the liver or whatever, just take it," Cler said. "I'm thinking this guy is saturated in fish oil." The liver was one thing you could eat right away, without waiting for the meat to cure.

"I'll take some," Enzo said.

Ted sniffed the liver, "You go right ahead."

Mama George had gone inside to get dressed, and she came back out in a pair of baggy pants, a coat and rubber boots. She brought an ulu with a bone handle, and handed it to Cler. He took it and used it to separate the rest of the offal from the carcass. The ulu blade was about the size of a man's hand, shaped like a half moon, with a handle across the straight side. It was much easier to use then a machete, when it came to doing the delicate work of gutting the bear.

They got the bear ready to skin, and Mama George cleaned up the innards to feed to her sled dogs. With a heavy rope, Enzo, Ted and Cler managed to drag the bear up into a nearby tree. It would be easier to skin. Cler used the ulu, and the others used their own sharp knives, and they all went to work skinning the bear. Bit by bit they cut the heavy brown fur away.

As they worked, Ted commented, "This is the strongest smelling bear I've ever had the displeasure to meet!"

402

Enzo grunted as he cut away one hind paw. "I'm not sure even the dogs will eat it."

"Well, these people will be glad to have it all. The dogs will love the rotten fish smell."

When the bear was skinned, Grandma George came out to watch. Cler gave her back the ulu. With his machete and hacksaw, he divided the carcass into quarters, while Ted and Enzo took the meat to tie up in the smoke house to cure.

Grandma George stood watching them tie up the quarters, "You take some that meat," she insisted.

Ted glanced at Enzo, "We want you to have it."

"No," Grandma George insisted. "You take."

"We'll divide up the last quarter, then," Ted said.

When he and Enzo returned to the yard, they told Cler, "Grandma George insists we take some of the meat. I said we'd share the last quarter. Alright with you?"

"Sure," Cler said. When he came home, he was carrying a chunk of bear meat.

"Whew!" Gwynne said, "Something smells like rotten fish!"

"I know that, my darling," Cler called over to her. "Come closer, and you'll get a whiff of what I've been smelling all morning!"

She stepped away, "No thanks. What are you going to do with it? Do you expect me to cook it?"

"At least we should try it."

As it turned out, the meat was so bad that it tasted like cod liver oil, that dreaded tonic the family took in the winter to add vitamins A and D to their diet. Tecane and Tippy loved it.

As for Enzo and Ted, they, too, fed the fishy bear meat to their dogs. Cler offered them each a chance to have the rug made out of the bear skin, but they both politely declined, and he insisted that the Georges keep it.

"There's no way Grandma George is going to get that smell out of the bear rug," Enzo said, and Ted echoed his sentiment.

However, Grandma George worked her magic, and the brown bear rug became one of her prized possessions.

30

BELOW ZERO

Winter 1954

It was below zero when twelve-year-old Corrie Lynne went out to feed the ducks and chickens, and look for eggs. She ducked through the little door, which was short on purpose, keeping the place warmer. The chicken coop was dim, close and damp, thick with the smell of hay and feathers. Cler had rigged a water bucket with an electric warmer, and it not only kept the water from freezing, it also added a little heat to the body heat the birds generated in the coop.

Quack-quack scrambled off the chicken's roost and waddled to meet Corrie with a healthy quack-quack-quack! She petted him, and the female duck. Jerusha opened her beak, but only a tiny squeak came out.

"What's the matter with you, Jerusha?" Jerusha answered with a wheezing croak. Corrie tucked her duck under her arm and hurried through the cold, back to the cabin.

"Mama, something's wrong with Jerusha!"

Gwynne stopped stirring the oatmeal, and set it further back on the range. "What's happened to her?"

"I don't know! Listen to her breathe, Mama. It sounds like she's sick. And she can't quack."

Gwynne could hear the wheezing. "Sounds like bronchitis, if that's what you'd call it in ducks. Let's see if steaming her a little helps, and then we'll keep her on the front porch, so we can watch her for a day or two." She stepped over to the copper boiler and took the lid off. Taking Jerusha from Corrie, Gwynne held the duck's head over the steam, with its wings pinned to its sides. Jerusha breathed the warm vapor coming off the water. She closed her beady eyes and relaxed, as if this was just the thing she needed.

405

In a few minutes, Jerusha sounded better, so Corrie made her a nice bed on the porch, gave her some water to drink, and left her to sleep. Every few hours, Gwynne repeated the steam treatment, which seemed to be working.

After a couple of days, Jerusha was more lively, and she could quack, so Corrie took her back out to the chicken coop. The next morning, she made her way through the snow to feed the fowls, and when she stepped inside the coop, the air was cool. She checked the water bucket and saw that the warmer was off. Quack-quack ran to her to be petted, and she stroked his soft, feathery head. The chickens were huddled together in the hay, and seemed fine. She looked for Jerusha, and saw her lying on her side, stiff. Corrie felt like bawling.

She picked up her duck before the chickens could start pecking on her, and hurried to find Daddy. By the time she found him, out by the wood pile, she had tears streaming down her face. He saw her coming, cradling Jerusha in her arms like a baby. "Oh, Daddy! Jerusha's dead!"

He left the ax in the chopping block and wrapped an arm around Corrie's shoulders. "I'm so sorry, Sweetheart."

"I don't know what to do," she cried.

She felt small and thin. *Still a little girl in so many ways*.

"You loved your little duck," he said, stating the obvious, but it was all he could come up with. "We can't bring her back, but we can have a funeral for her. Shall we do that?"

She looked up through her tears, "OK."

" You set it up, and we'll all stop what we're doing and come."

"What do they do at funerals?" she asked, sniffling, while she held the stiff duck in one arm and wiped her tears on the back of her mitten. "I read in a book that they talk about the dearly departed, but what else?"

"Well," Cler frowned, "as I recall, a funeral consists of a song and a prayer, and like you said, people get up and tell about the person, in this case, the duck, who died. It's called a eulogy."

Corrie laid Jerusha on the porch, in the cardboard box she'd slept in when she got sick. She left her there, and went inside, where she sat at the table and tried to write out the funeral program. She tried to think of a song that mentioned ducks, and "My Darling Clementine" came to mind. "Drove she ducklings to the water, every morning just at nine." She wrote that down: musical selection, "Clementine." They'd sing, and then she'd tell about Jerusha's life. She began to write out the eulogy.

Bundled in winter coats, the family gathered on the porch. Cler led out on "Clementine", and everyone joined in singing, "O my darling, oh my darling, o my darling Clementine, you are lost and gone forever. Dreadful sorry, Clementine!" To Corrie Lynne, at least, the song was heartfelt, and it brought tears to her eyes.

She stepped forward, "Jerusha came into our lives to be a companion to our beloved Quack-quack. She helped him learn what it meant to be a duck."

Paxton quipped, "Quack-quack still thinks he's a chicken!" and then he broke out laughing.

Corrie gave her brother a dark look and continued, perfectly serious. "Jerusha was a good mother. She laid fourteen eggs and raised ducklings, with nine growing up into ducks."

"And they were delicious," Paxton said.

"Daddy, will you tell Paxton to be quiet?"

Cler was having a hard time himself, trying to keep a straight face. "Knock it off," he whispered.

Charles raised his hand, "Can I say something about Jerusha?"

"Yes, go right ahead."

Charles said, "We liked this duck." He looked at her lying in the box, "She's fluffy."

Paxton amended, "Was fluffy. Now, can we get on with the burial?"

Cler turned to Corrie, "Are we done?" She nodded, and her dad said, "The ground is frozen solid as rock. Give her to me and I'll take care of her." Corrie handed her dad the box containing Jerusha's lifeless body, and the funeral was over. He took the duck out into the woods, far enough that he hoped one of the dogs wouldn't bring her back, and buried her in the snow, leaving her in Mother Nature's care.

WINTER EXERCISE

That Winter, temperatures at Kenny Lake varied from twenty above to fifty below, so there were few outdoor activities for children. When the snow first fell, the kids bundled up and made a snowman or lay on their backs in the powder, creating snow angels. Once, when the ice on Kenny Lake was sufficiently frozen, but the weather wasn't too cold, Cler cleared the snow with a shovel, and made an ice rink. The little kids sat on the sled and hung on while their dad skated, pulling them behind him. He'd make the sled whirl and slide over the ice. He left them to play on the sled and push each other, while he showed off by making figure 8's and skating backward.

Corrie and Paxton had ice skates, and the rest of the children ran around sliding in their boots. This was winter recreation, but soon it was too cold for the kids to be outside longer than it took to walk to school, which was five minutes. The older kids went out to take care of the animals in the barn, but again, they weren't out long in the cold.

It was different for Cler. Like other men in the community, he had to brave the cold often, and for longer than he cared to. He had to milk the cow and goats, chop wood, and sometimes use a torch to thaw out the engine on the jeep so he could go for groceries. If it was warmer than twenty below, he'd put on his snowshoes and check his snares, or hunt for game.

In spite of necessary chores, Winter generally kept people inside, and cabin fever was a real threat to one's sanity. A lone trapper with cabin fever had been known to grab his ax and run out into the snow in only his long johns, screaming, choosing to die by freezing to death, rather than from the accursed cabin fever.

Those fared better who had families, but grownups still found it important to get out of their cabins once in a while and socialize with others. Pot luck suppers, card games and scrabble were common entertainments.

At Kenny Lake, dancing offered exercise, as well as fun for adults and children alike. Neighbors regularly gathered at the Oborn's cabin, where their windup record player furnished the music, and there was room to dance, since the bedroom addition had been added on, leaving more open area in the main cabin. Those who came to these dances also brought something to eat. Cler didn't think twice about inviting both the Santinis and the Ennis families at the same time. He figured that the more Ted and Enzo got together, the better they'd get along, and it was true, even though both men still occasionally bickered. There was, for instance, the long-running "Battle of the Slippers."

Though the floorboards in the cabin were old and worn smooth when Cler laid them, Ted and Enzo worried about getting a sliver dancing in stocking feet. Cler didn't mind letting one or the other man wear his slippers; whoever arrived first. One night, Enzo and Ted arrived with their families at about the same time. They kicked off their boots and both grabbed for the slippers at the same time.

"I get to wear them tonight!" Enzo claimed, jamming his foot into one.

Ted reached for the other, "No, it's my turn!"' Enzo got hold of the toe, while Ted had the heel and they were playing tug-of-war. There was so much talking going on in the cabin that Cler didn't notice for a moment that his leather slipper was about to be ripped in half.

"Hey, guys, them's *my* slippers," Cler laughed, purposely fracturing his grammar. The tug of war stopped, but they each still held on.

Cler shook his head in mock disapproval, and reached out his hand, "Come on, boys, hand it over!" Ted let go, and Enzo handed Cler the slipper. Clef glanced pointedly at the one on

Enzo's foot, "That one, too, please." Tonight, he'd be the one wearing the slippers.

The wind-up record player started up a lively rendition of "Roll out the Barrel," and Ted grabbed his wife and started off in an exuberant polka around the drum stove. Enzo took Zoya's hand and followed suit.

Everyone danced, even the little kids, whether they had a partner or not. The cabin reverberated with music and laughter, and the fun went on for several hours. That night, when Gwynne heard "Five foot two, eyes of blue, has anybody seen my gal?" she broke out dancing the Charleston. Her children just stared at her, but everyone else clapped to see the usually shy woman kicking up her heels. A few minutes later, a song called "Whispering" began to play, and Gwynne started tap dancing, something even Cler had never seen her do. Again, her children were amazed. She did a few fancy steps and stopped, laughing, "I was a pretty good dancer when I was six!"

There was a spread of goodies on the table, and everyone enjoyed tasting Zoya's little meatballs, LaVerne's oatmeal cookies, and Gwynne's fudge.

As the night wore on, the record player was turned down, and soothing music became a background for grownup conversation around the table. When the little Oborns grew tired, they crept off to bed. Zoya's baby was tucked into a blanket in the corner, and other small children fell asleep on the sofa.

These were times to remember; they lifted hearts during the darkest days of winter, and eased sometimes rocky relationships.

February, 1955

A RABBIT INVASION

It was the end of February, and the snow was still deep, but temperatures grew milder. The cow and goats were anxious to leave the barn, but there was nothing to eat outside. Cler was

410

worried. The haystack might not last until grass grew, and rabbits had been coming around at night, eating the hay. He nailed more slabs up around the stack to try and keep them out.

"I want you to go out every day and shoot all the rabbits you can find around here," he told Paxton. "They're getting to the hay." Because of the deep snow, all the rabbits had to eat was willows. They had chewed the red bark as high as they could reach, until the twigs were gone, and the willow stems were white, two feet above the snow.

One night, Cler went out to milk, and there were dozens of rabbits crowding to get at the hay. Tippy, the Cocker Spaniel, was on the top of the stack, barking like crazy, but the rabbits paid no attention to him. Cler kicked at the rabbits, who ran off a little way. He stopped chasing rabbits and ducked into the barn to milk the goats. Rowdy had gone dry.

When he came back into the cabin with the milk, he called to Paxton, "Grab your .22 and come help me shoot rabbits!" After he handed the bucket of milk to Gwynne, he grabbed his shotgun and dropped a handful of shells into his coat pocket. Paxton jumped up from the table, where he was doing homework, and ran to get his gun.

For fifteen or twenty minutes, Gwynne could hear the guns popping out in the barnyard. She peered out a front room window and tried to see what was going on. Cler had the jeep wagon out there with its lights shining on the haystack, and she could see rabbits running in all directions.

A few minutes later, Paxton and Cler returned to the cabin carrying two rabbits, which they laid on the counter. They laid their guns on the table.

Gwynne asked, "Only two?" Paxton set to work gutting the first rabbit with his dad's pocket knife.

Cler said, "I'm sorry. We were just trying to get rid of them. "We weren't careful where we hit them. Anyway, with this many rabbits I'm afraid some of them might have Tularemia. Paxton, check the livers on those two."

He looked carefully at the innards. "These are fine," he said. "Mother, do you want the skins for the blanket you're working on?"

"Yes, thank you. Just tack them out on the porch and I'll get to them later." Gwynne would have to scrape and dry the skins to make them ready to use. She had about a dozen rabbit skins ready to make into a lap robe. "I'll make fricassee for dinner tonight," she told him.

"What does that mean, anyway?" Paxton asked, slipping the skin off the rabbit.

"Fried, sautéed, and cooked in its own gravy," she said. She didn't know if that's how other cooks did it, but that's how she cooked rabbit. Calling it "fricassee" made it sound more exotic than "fried rabbit."

Corrie came into the kitchen, "Want me to skin that other rabbit, Paxton? I'll race you!"

Paxton said, "I'm already way ahead of you, but go ahead."

Finding a small, sharp knife in the wood block, she went to work on the other rabbit.

Cler sat down at the table with his gun oil, rag and ramrod, and broke open his shotgun, ready to clean it. "The rabbits seem to be at the height of their seven-year cycle," he said, pushing the oiled rag through his gun barrel. "Next year there won't be many rabbits around, but in seven years, the place will be overrun again."

The family had rabbit for dinner, and no one complained, but there wasn't much meat on those rabbits' bones, and what there was seemed stringy.

A few days later, Cler woke up in the darkness of early morning to the sound of frantic barking. Tippy was out in the barnyard, but Tecane was on the porch, whining and scratching at the front door. Cler rolled out of a warm bed to find out what the ruckus was. He stepped into his boots, pulled the laces tight and donned his parka. He grabbed his loaded 30-06 from the rack, guessing there was a bear out there.

When he pulled the door open, Tecane shot past like a furry streak. Once outside, Cler heard a peculiar sound in the air, murmuring, rustling. Rowdy bellowed in the barn, and the goats blatted. Tippy was still barking up a storm.

The moon had almost gone down, but its light still reflected over the snow, casting inky shadows. Cler followed his own tracks toward the barnyard. As he rounded the corner of the cabin, he froze. A sea of starving rabbits surrounded the haystack! They were piling on top of each other to scale the slab fence. Tippy was trapped on top of the stack.

Cler gripped his rifle. It seemed a waste of good shells to shoot rabbits with a bear gun, but maybe the sound would scare a few off. He took aim at the middle of the pile, and fired . Blood, fur, and live rabbits scattered in all directions. He turned back to the cabin. There was no way to do this alone. He pulled open the door, and nearly ran into his wife.

"I was just coming to find out what's going on," she said, tying her robe.

"There's a million rabbits out there getting into the hay. I'll go shoot what I can and you call the neighbors. I need some help!" He traded his rifle for a shot gun.

Paxton was up and dressed, shrugging into his oversized coat. "How can I help, Dad?"

"Grab your .22 and some shells. We'll do what we can until help arrives."

Lestie heard the commotion and slipped out of her sleeping bag. Her mother was on the phone, sounding scared. "Ted! We need some men and guns; we've been invaded by rabbits, and they're getting into the hay! OK, I'll call Cliff, if you'll get Enzo and his boys."

Paxton and his dad ran into the barnyard, through a sea of starving rabbits. They charged into their midst, whooping and hollering. The rabbits scattered, but not far. Tippy leaped off the stack and ran to Paxton.

413

"Take Tippy inside, before he gets shot!" Cler ordered. He took aim at a clump of white rabbits he could only see by their rounded shadows. The blast killed some and the others leaped into the darkness. Cler ran to his dump truck and drove into the barnyard, so that its headlights lit up the hay stack and surrounding, trampled snow. He parked, set the brake, and left the engine running.

By the time Paxton returned from shutting the dog on the porch, the rabbits had closed in on the haystack again. "Stay beside, me!" Cler called to him. "Take aim, and watch where you're shooting. Don't shoot toward the barn!"

Side by side, Cler and Paxton picked off rabbits. With each explosion of the shot gun, rabbits scattered in a mess of blood and fur. Paxton's .22 got one with each shot. The mass of rabbits would part, leaping into the shadows and in moments they would be back.

It was only a few minutes before they saw headlights coming over the rise, bumping up the driveway. Ted Ennis' pickup rattled into the yard, and slammed to a stop, parked against a snow-bank. Enzo and Ted jumped out of the cab, and two boys scrambled out the back. They all had guns.

Cler saw Ted's truck. He called to Paxton to stop shooting, just as Ted, Enzo, and the boys came trotting into the barnyard. "Holy Smokes!" Little Enzo exclaimed as he saw the rabbits scattered over the snow.

"Before anyone starts shooting, let's get organized. There's going to be a lot of men here with guns, Enzo, so I think we'd better let the boys pick up dead rabbits, while we do the shooting. Boys, don't start picking up until we tell you to."

Enzo started to object, but stopped himself. With his rifle vertical in his hand, Enzo waved at his boys, "You heard the man, go put your guns in the truck."

Cler reached out to his own son, "Paxton, take your gun into the cabin and put it up. And please bring me another box of shotgun shells." They heard an old pickup roaring up the driveway, and recognized Cliff Kirkland's rackety Ford, with one headlight out.

"Throw the rabbits in the pit over there," Cler called to Little Enzo and Arlo as they came running back from their truck."Ted, can you bring your truck over here and get some more light on the subject?" Ted hurried to his truck, and Little Enzo and Arlo ran to pick up rabbits before the shooting started again. Paxton soon joined them and the boys went to work, carrying clusters of rabbits by their ears, to the pit beyond the outhouse.

Corrie and Celestia knelt on the couch, peering out the window. They could hear the guns cracking, and see a confusion of moving shadows amid the garish light cast by the trucks' headlights. For a few moments, the shooting stopped, and the boys raced around picking up dead rabbits. The men stood still, waiting. They were lit from behind, their bodies casting long shadows toward the haystack. They stood with legs braced, guns at the shoulder, all aimed in the same direction. While the boys were gone, a cluster of rabbits moved into the light, creeping toward the hay, and then the shooting started all over again.

Corrie said, "Let's go back to bed. Can I crawl in with you?"

Lestie agreed. They were both shivering; their hands and bare feet were freezing. Lestie wriggled into her mummy sleeping bag, and unzipped it wider, so Corrie could crawl in. The bag still had a little warmth left in it. They lay there listening to the guns popping. "It's kind of awful, don't you think?" Lestie whispered.

Corrie said, "No. I hope they get all those rabbits. If we run out of hay, our goats will starve, and Rowdy will, too. You want Sylvia to starve to death just because a bunch of rabbits ate the hay?" Sylvia was Lestie's white nanny goat. She shook her head.

Now the guns were silent, and they heard the men and boys calling out to each other. Finally, a truck engine roared to life, and then another. They could hear the rumble of trucks and cars driving away, the sounds fading, until there was only silence.

The girls didn't go back to sleep. When they heard the drum stove crackling, they carried their jeans and sweaters to dress beside it. Gwynne had added a couple of logs to the fire, and the stove was putting out heat, but the cabin was still cold.

Outside the row of windows, the sky was beginning to pale, and a blush of pink caught the tip of Gun Sight Mountain. The shadows faded. The snow turned blue.

They heard the tractor start, and then the chugging of its engine as it rumbled past the kitchen window. Paxton stomped into the cabin, and kicked off his boots. He dropped his coat on the floor. "Dad's burying the rabbits, so they won't attract any wolves," he said, headed to the kitchen. Mother had the kitchen fire started. She poured the tea kettle into the wash basin, so Paxton could wash his half frozen, bloody hands in the warm water. Even though he'd worn his mittens, blood had soaked through.

His mother said, "Be sure to wash thoroughly, in case some of them are diseased." She handed him a small, stiff-bristled brush. Paxton took up a bar of lye soap and began to scrub his hands, careful to get under his nails.

A few hours later, Paxton and Celestia had put on their coats and hats, and were out surveying the mound of raw dirt covering the pit where the rabbits had been buried. Signs of the early morning carnage were all too evident. The snow was pink with blood. All around the yard, boots and tractor tires had eaten up the snow, leaving muddy tracks.

"It's sad about the rabbits," Celestia said.

"It's just part of the cycle of life," her brother told her. "Animals live and die, just like people. If we hadn't killed the rabbits, most of them would have died, anyway, from disease, but we would have lost the hay."

He was only eleven, but to his little sister, Paxton seemed very wise.

416

31

INSIGHT

The burst of energy Gwynne had at the dance didn't last. Winter dragged on. For weeks, the sky hung like lead above the frozen landscape. Lately, Gwynne had been barely able to drag herself out of bed. Some days she managed to get dressed, braid her hair, and send the kids off to school, but then she'd lie down on the couch, with a pillow and a blanket, watching Butchy play with blocks and little gadgets on the floor. He could spend all day taking apart an old alarm clock, or dismantling a broken radio.

One gray morning, Gwynne was sitting at the table, staring at an array of sticky plates and silverware from the family's breakfast. She was trying to gather the strength to clear the table and do the dishes. She wanted nothing more than to go back to bed, but Cler would be coming in from doing chores, and wonder what was the matter. Why did he keep asking her what was wrong? She didn't know the answer!

"Dear Lord," she prayed. "I don't know what to do. What's wrong with me?"

She sat there, listening to Butchy's unmelodious humming, as he dismantled, with his bare fingers, the same alarm clock Cler had put back together for him last night. Burning wood popped in the drum stove, and a tiny puff of smoke escaped into the room through some small crack around the door. In Gwynne, it set off a coughing spell that closed her airway. She rose up and hurried to the door, yanking it open, and crossing the front porch, frantic to get a breath of air. The frigid air opened her bronchial tubes and she managed to suck in a wheezing breath. After a few minutes, she could breathe normally, and returned to the cabin.

Feeling light headed, she lay down on the couch, where she curled up with her head on a pillow. She fell asleep for a while, and woke with a start. Where was Butchy? He was still fiddling with the clock. Thank goodness! She continued to lie down, and began to close her eyes again, when a thought came to her that she should get up and read her grandmother's journal. She knew it was in her cedar chest. The feeling came again, more persistent. *Go and find Alice Paxton's journal.*

The cedar chest was being used as a bench at the table, covered with a folded Army blanket, so Butchy could sit on it. Before Gwynne opened the chest, she cleared the dishes and left them to soak in the dish pan. She wiped off the oil cloth on the table, and dried it with the dish towel. Then she lit the kerosene lamp. The day outside was so gray that little light came through the kitchen window.

Opening the chest, Gwynne breathed in the scent of cedar. Right on top lay a creamy, crocheted baby shawl made by her grandmother Burt for Gwynne's own blessing day. She had wrapped Charles in this same shawl, and Cler had taken him somewhere out in the woods to give him his name and a blessing. At the time, it seemed like the right thing to do, but now she wondered, *Why did I not go with him?*

There were other items laid flat, some wrapped in tissue paper. Cler's baby dress, a pair of embroidered pillow cases, and a quilt made by her grandmother Burt that was too pretty to use in a cabin. In the bottom of the chest, she found the old ledger that Alice had made into a combination scrapbook and journal.

On the first page, in a flourish of curlicues was written, "This book belongs to Alice Norris Crosby." There were cut-outs of hearts and flowers, taken from cards, and magazines. On other pages, were black and white pictures of silent film stars, lace trimmed valentines, and fancy little dance cards embossed in gold. The dance cards were like tiny books, with pages, where a boy could write his name on a line, and reserve a dance with the girl who carried it. The cards had no dates, but must have been used when her grandmother was a young debutante. Gwynne's eyes scanned the old-fashioned boys' names: Elmer, Clarence, Albert and many more. Grandma was a popular girl. On one page, her grandmother had written vital statistics. Alice Norris Crosby, born in Auchenheath, Scotland, 14 June, 1873. Came to America on board ship with parents James Crosbie and Ellen Aird.

Gwynne knew that George Paxton had married Alice in 1902, on one of his trips home from the gold fields. He and she were both twenty-nine at the time. Gwynne also knew that George went back to Alaska soon after the wedding.

Gwynne turned pages and found entries dated during the first year of Alice's marriage. She wrote of going to town with her girl friends, and of being bored. She didn't mention her husband, but said she loathed being alone.

"I felt so out of sorts today, that I went to the picture show. I walked to town, and met my friends, Mildred Black and Mary Jane Kimball. I felt better just seeing them. We had such fun! Saw Charlie Chaplin. We laughed all the way through."

In a neat hand, Alice had penned a few lines each day for a few days, and then skipped days or weeks. There was no mention of the birth of their baby, Charles, eleven months after she was married. As Gwynne read the journal, she began to see a pattern.

"Did nothing today. My head ached when I went to bed last night, and I was still afflicted this morning. Took some medicine Doctor prescribed. It tastes foul and does no good."

A week later, Alice was off with her friends again. She wrote that she had a girl come in to "mind the baby and do some wash."

The last entry stated, "Felt blue again today. I didn't feel like getting out of bed. The girl brought me a bite of supper, but I have little appetite."

George kept going to Alaska, essentially neglecting his wife and son for six months of every year for the next fourteen years. Then he took his son to the gold fields with him, but his wife remained at home with a hired girl to help her. Alice had migraines and needed help on the days she couldn't get out of bed. She apparently didn't get any better when George came home.

In Gwynne's earliest memories of her grandparents, Alice was never well, but she was a gentle soul. Gwynne was not as fond of her grandfather. She remembered that he gave her a puppy when she was six, but later took it to the dump and didn't bring it back. He said he had to shoot it, but she never knew why. Sometimes he tried to get her to sit on his lap, but she didn't like the whiskey smell of his breath.

There was no more to Alice's journal, but Gwynne didn't need to read any more. She knew that her grandmother had taken to her bed, and stayed there for the last thirty years of her life. When Gwynne was ten years old, she began caring for her grandmother after school. She used to bring her a basin to wash her hands and face, and talk to her. She didn't smile, but she would brighten and cooperate when Gwynne took care of her, or fed her. When Grandpa George came into the room, Alice refused to look at him, or to eat what he gave her.

Alice didn't speak, although the doctor thought she could, if she wanted to. He said if there was a fire, she'd be the first one out of the house. Gwynne wasn't so sure. She believed there was something wrong with Grandma Alice that an old horse doctor, as her mother called him, didn't know about. A heavy feeling of sorrow came over Gwynne: she grieved for her grandmother's lost beauty, energy and life.

Gwynne closed the frayed and faded leather book, and laid it on the table. Tears filled her eyes; with the back of her hand, she swiped at them angrily, ashamed. It startled her to realize that she was like her grandmother! The "blue days," low energy, not wanting to get out of bed... It must be true that she had inherited her grandmother's illness, as surely as she had inherited her perfect complexion, blue eyes and wavy brown hair.

A kind of desperate fear struck her. She whispered, "Please, Dear Lord, don't let me become like my grandmother!"

Something inside her said, *You have a choice.*

A choice. She knew what choice she had: if she didn't want to end up like her grandmother, she had to *just keep getting out of bed.* But was that possible? She felt trapped by her own inadequacies. What if the day came when she just couldn't cope any longer? What if she didn't *just get out of bed?*

When Cler pushed open the door, carrying a bucket of goat's milk, he was happily surprised to find his wife at the stove, stirring what smelled like split pea soup. When he left this morning, she'd had a headache, and he had expected to find her still in bed. He came up behind her and wrapped his arms around her. For a second, she stiffened.

"You OK?"

"Yes." She relaxed a little.

"Mm, you smell good," he said, kissing the side of her neck.

She put down her wooden spoon, and turned to face him. "I smell like split pea soup," she said, bluntly.

He could tell she'd been crying.

"What's the matter?"

"I refuse to go crazy," she said.

"Well, thank goodness for that!" he grinned. But she wasn't smiling. "What can I do for you, Sweetheart?" he asked, kissing her forehead. "Tell, me, what can I do?"

"Just bring me some wild roses," she said, "I could use a bouquet of sweet-smelling flowers just now."

Tears came to his eyes, "Oh, Gwynne, if there was a single wild rose out there under that snow, I'd dig for it with my bare hands!"

"I know," she said, laying her head against his chest. "That's why I love you so much. There's really nothing the matter with me that summer won't fix. I'm just so heartily sick of winter."

30

MAKING PLANS

February, 1955

The snow was still deep the first week in March, but Cler was pleased to see that there'd be just enough hay to feed the animals until the snow was gone, sometime in May. Once the snow melted, there would be plenty of dry grass they could eat, and reeds around the lake.

There was a new teacher at the school. Her name was Julie Waugh, and the children liked her. Cler kept the contract to drive the school bus, a long van that held about a dozen kids, or more, if they crowded in. He earned a little cash, and still had time to take care of his animals and do everything else he had to do.

Since the Waughs lived in the truck house, Julie's husband, Hal, manned the gas pump and little store, down by the road. Traffic on the road had increased with the influx of new homesteaders, and he was doing quite a bit of business.

In spite of the success of their homestead farm, and the fact that generally things were going well in their lives, Cler was worried about Gwynne: she wasn't well. Sometimes he came home for lunch and found her in bed. Today, when he'd come in with a load of wood, she was sitting in the rocker, crying, with Butchy asleep in her lap. He kissed her but she wouldn't talk about what was bothering her. He determined that tonight, after the children had gone to bed, he would try to get to the bottom of it.

The kids were in bed, asleep, when he went outside for wood to bank the fire for the night. He came back in, dropped the logs beside the stove, and brushed the bits of sawdust and bark off his shirt. Then he sat down on the couch, near the rocking chair, where Gwynne sat under the gas lamp. She had a book on her lap, but she wasn't reading.

Cler searched his wife's face. She was so pale, with fine lines around her mouth, and purple smudges under her eyes. She was only thirty, but she looked ten years older. Something seemed to be killing her; he was not sure what.

"Sweetheart, I wish you'd tell me what's wrong."

"Nothing's wrong, really, Cler," she said, swiping at a tear that had spilled down her cheek."

" I know you don't feel well."

Gwynne let out a sigh. "Honestly, Cler. I don't know what it is."

"Does it seem worse now, than usual?"

"It's always bad in the winter. We know that, but it does seem to be getting worse. And today I had another asthma attack from breathing in a puff of wood smoke. Maybe my problem is just allergies."

Cler grasped at this tiny straw. "Then we'll do something about it. Whatever it takes. We could buy an oil heater."

"It might be more than that. There's some hole deep inside me, something I—I feel like it would help if we could go to Church again. That would give me a lift. And maybe I need to see a doctor."

Cler took her hand and smoothed it with his thumb. She had beautiful hands, long fingers and oval nails, but the skin was chapped from winter and washing: clothes, dishes, children. "Would things be better for you if we moved into town?"

Gwynne felt something shift inside her. She hadn't dared suggest it, but she did need town. A doctor. The Church. "Really? Are you saying you'd be willing to move again, now, when things are going so well for us here?"

He leaned forward, his mind rapidly putting it all together. "It would be just temporary; until you feel better. You could see the doctor, find out what's the matter. What do you think?"

"But you'd have to get a job, and find a house, and...it's just too much to think about."

423

"I've never had any trouble getting a job. I can sign on at the Air Force Base. There's still a war on, and..."

Gwynne's heart sank, "Oh, Cler! You can't be going off to Korea. I won't let you! Here you say you want to help me; do you think it would help me to be left with five kids while you go off--"

Cler interrupted her, "No, I'm not saying that. The military has lots of jobs right here in Alaska. I'm still technically in the Reserves, but I can choose what I get to do. I'd love it if I could fly again." It came out of his mouth without thinking. He could become a pilot. *Yes! Wouldn't it be wonderful to be able to fly again?*

Gwynne didn't look happy. "Fly!"

"I won't if you don't want me to."

"No," she sighed, "It's fine. Whatever you want to do is fine."

It was March. Signs of spring were everywhere, even though there was a lot of snow left to melt. The diamond willows had turned red with new growth. Gwynne glanced idly out the kitchen window as she washed the dishes, swirling the dishrag over each plate. She felt pretty well today. Maybe it was because of more daylight, and the promise of spring. Spring led her mind to think of Easter, the Savior, and His Resurrection. She longed to go to church, where she could mingle with her brothers and sisters in the Gospel. There she hoped to refill her reservoirs of faith and let the Spirit heal her soul. The words of a hymn came to her, "Jesus, lover of my soul, let me hide myself in Thee..."

Cler would be back today. He'd gone to Anchorage two days ago, to check out available jobs and housing. If he couldn't find what they needed, they couldn't move to town. She believed that if he was successful, it was a sign that they were doing the right thing.

That night, he returned late, after the children were in bed, asleep, but Gwynne was waiting up for him. She heard the dogs barking their greeting, and in a few moments, he pulled open the door, and shut it quietly.

Gwynne met him at the door. "How did it go?"

He kissed her and grinned, "Like it was meant to be."

"So you found what we need?" She followed him to the sofa, where he dropped down with a sigh.

"Yes. I couldn't find a house to rent, but I found one to buy."

She sat beside him. "Buy?"

"It'll cost the same as renting, and it's a nice house. You'll like it. We can sell it at a profit, whenever we're ready to come back to Kenny Lake."

She laid her head on his shoulder, "And you found a job?"

"I did. As a unit supply officer with the Air National Guard."

"That sounds fine!"

He kissed her hair, "Yes. Yes, it is." They sat up talking for an hour, while he told her all about the house, which was vacant, ready to move into, and the owners had even left some good furniture when they moved back to the States.

The next day, at dinner, the family gathered around the split log table, with Cler on one end dishing up soup, and Gwynne at the other end, slicing bread. Cler looked over his children, all busily slurping soup, or buttering bread. They were all so absorbed in eating that the room was quiet, except for the clink of spoons and bowls.

Cler said, "Your mother and I've decided that we're going to move into Anchorage for a while."

Paxton looked up from his bowl, "Will we be coming back?"

Cler said, "Yes, of course! But we're not sure when."

"When will we be going?" Corrie asked.

"Soon," Cler said. "I can start work on Monday." It was now Wednesday.

"Why?" Lestie asked. "Why are we moving?"

Her mother paused as she handed her a slice of bread. "I might be allergic to wood smoke," she said.

Her father added, "We'll get an oil heater when we come back to Kenny Lake. For now, I've found a nice house in town, on a place called Fireweed Lane. It has an oil heater, and a lot of other conveniences."

Paxton asked, "What'll we do with the animals?"

"Ted and Enzo will take them, along with the hay. I'm sure it will work out fine."

That night, after the children were in bed, Cler and Gwynne were sitting close together on the couch, discussing the move. Since it wasn't permanent, they could leave most of their things in the cabin and barn, making the move easier than completely pulling up stakes.

"So tell me more about your job," Gwynne said.

Cler told her that the Air National Guard would soon be moving from Elmendorf, to a new base in Spenard. It was not far from the house on Fireweed. "I can join the Guard, have all the benefits of being on active duty, but without going to war. As I said, they're hiring me as Unit Supply Officer."

"Sounds fine. And you're not going to fly."

He looked her in the eye, "The truth is, there's no reason I can't fly for the Guard. I really want to, Gwynne."

She felt a shiver of fear, but shook it off. "I don't know why that worries me. Certainly you need to fly again. You love it."

"I admit it," he said. There was a sparkle in his eyes. "It's all I've been able to think about since I found out. All I have to do is pass the physical!"

"Do you think you can pass the physical?" she asked, and playfully poked him in the ribs, making him jump.

"Of course I can," he laughed, "Any guy who's chopped as much fire wood as I have won't have any problem passing a little physical! Now come closer and let's see if I'm still a good kisser…"

In the girls' room, Corrie leaned over from the top bunk and asked, "Lestie, are you asleep?"

"No," she replied.

"Are you scared about moving?"

"I don't think so," Lestie said.

426

Corrie lay back on her bunk, "In Anchorage, I'll go to Junior High School."

"That'll be nice."

Corrie went on, "Do you realize that since I was three we've hardly spent Christmas twice in the same house?"

"I didn't know that."

"We haven't. When I was four, and you were a baby, we lived in Utah. Then we were here. The next Christmas we were in the little house by the river. The one that flooded."

"I don't remember that Christmas, but I remember that house."

"No, you don't. You were just a baby."

"But I remember the men coming for us in a boat. It was dark and lanterns were shining on the water."

Corrie said, "That's right. OK, but the next year we had Christmas here in the cabin. Then, let me see…"

Lestie was getting sleepy and Corrie's voice was fading. She heard her say, with indignation, "We've finally spent two Christmases in a row at Kenny Lake and Daddy wants to move again! I like it here. I don't want to go to Anchorage."

Celestia woke up a little bit, "What about Junior High?"

"I'm not sure I want to go."

Celestia said, "I like it here, too, but Mama is allergic."

"I know," Corrie said. "And we can go to church in Anchorage. Mama told me how much she misses going to church. Remember when we used to go to Sunday School, when we lived in Mountain View?"

Lestie thought about that. She did remember. "And afterwards we got ice cream!"

"That's true," Corrie said thoughtfully. She was quiet for a while and her sister had started to drift off to sleep. She jerked awake as Corrie said suddenly, "Ice cream! And boys… Well, that's something to look forward to!"

32

March, 1955

LEAVING KENNY LAKE

Cler had arranged for Ted Ennis to take Rowdy, and three of the goats, and Ted also agreed to take Tecane. The children were sad to think of leaving their big, loveable dog, who was afraid of rabbits. The Georges were happy to keep Tippy. The house Cler had purchased had no fence, and fronted on a major road. The dogs, he felt, were better off staying at the homestead for now. But Cler promised that this was not a permanent move. "We're coming back to Kenny Lake. Even if we stay in town for a year, we'll still make trips out here. We'll get Tecane and Tippy, and bring them to Anchorage, after we get a fenced yard for them."

With Quack-quack in her arms, Corrie reluctantly rode with her father to the Santinis. Enzo would be keeping her nanny goat, Tina and her kids. Little Enzo had promised to take care of Corrie's pet duck. He liked Corrie, and in fact, they'd had a crush on each other since they were both in fifth grade.

Little Enzo and Arlo came out of their cabin, as the dump truck rumbled into their yard. Cler parked, and he and Corrie climbed down. She approached Little Enzo with Quack-quack in her arms.

"Please take good care of him," she said, sadly. "I'll miss him."

The boy grinned. He was tall, and dark, and his brown eyes were full of mischief. "Sure, I will!"

"I mean it! I won't give him to you unless you promise!"

"I promise," he said, soberly saluting her.

He's getting better looking every day, she thought, and handed him the duck.

428

Big Enzo came out of the barn carrying an empty bucket, and waved at Cler and Paxton, who were unloading the goats. "Hello, how are you? Brought me some goats, I see. Still leaving tomorrow?"

"Right on schedule," Cler said.

Enzo gave the bucket to Arlis. "Go water the chickens." He turned to Cler, "I hate to see you go, Cler, but I'm glad to know you'll be coming back. My boys and I'll come down to help you load your truck."

"Thanks," Cler said. "Appreciate that. We'll start hauling things out to the truck around eight-thirty, but come at eight, and I'll feed you breakfast!"

The next morning, Enzo and his boys showed up in time for sourdough pancakes. Laughter and conversation around the table made it seem like they weren't really going away, Corrie thought. And yet they were.

While Corrie and Celestia did the dishes, the others began loading things into the dump truck. Only essential items would go to Anchorage. The children's beds, clothing, and blankets. Butchy's crib. Gwynne left her battered chest of drawers, with the bowl and pitcher sitting on it, and the old bed with its squeaky springs. There was a new bed waiting for her in the new house, and a better dresser, Cler said.

They took the guns and ammunition, and Cler's tools, but left the light plant, lanterns, ax and cross-cut saw, all stowed in the barn. They wouldn't need them in Anchorage, because they were going to live in a real house with electricity, plumbing and an oil heater. On the porch, they left the cream separator, and cases of milk bottles. There would be no goats to milk, and no milk to process and sell. Gwynne took a moment on her way through the porch to stop and look at the box of glass milk bottles she'd hand painted with a picture of a goat and the name of their little dairy: "Spayee Del Chaden," Home of the Goats. She felt sad to be leaving, but optimistic that moving was exactly what they needed to do right now.

When the truck was loaded, Enzo and his boys said goodbye to their friends. "We'll see you all when you come back!" they called out, climbing into their pickup truck.

Paxton was going to ride in the dump truck with his dad, while the others rode with Mother in the GMC wagon. Corrie was OK with this, because she got to ride in the front seat.

While Gwynne was in the cabin collecting a few last minute items, seven-year-old Charles called Tecane over to the car to pet him. Ted was coming to get the dog later. Lestie joined in, stroking the big dog's long, gold and white mane. They both kissed his soft head.

Charles opened the back door of the Jeep, and let Tecane jump in. Lestie, Charles and Butchy climbed in after, and covered Tecane up with a quilt. Corrie acted like she didn't see what was happening, and settled herself into the front seat.

The loaded dump truck rumbled down the driveway past them, and Gwynne started up the Jeep Wagon, pulling out behind the truck. The little caravan made its way down the hill and onto the gravel road. A half mile later, the dump truck turned into the Georges.

Cler got out and knocked on Grandma George's door, and Gwynne joined him, instructing the kids to stay in the car. Grandma George opened the door and greeted them. "You leaving?"

"We'll be back," Cler promised, and Gwynne said, "I'll miss you," and gave her a hug.

Emma and Ina must have heard the Oborns drive in, because they also came outside to greet them. The children watched as their parents spoke to their old friends, leaning down to hug each in turn. All the children waved and hung out the windows, "Goodbye, Grandma George! Goodbye Emma and Ina! We'll come back and see you!"

On the road again, the family continued on their way to Anchorage. After a while, Butchy began saying, "doggie" while Charles and Lestie tried to shush him. Lestie diverted his attention with the old alarm clock. They'd driven about fifty miles with Tecane under the blanket, when the dog began to whine.

"What is that?" Gwynne asked, keeping her eyes on the road.

Corrie said, "They brought Tecane."

Gwynne sighed. "Well, I guess we can't go back now. But you kids better take good care of him! Daddy says the house he bought is on a road where cars go by. We don't want him to get hit by a car, so he might have to stay tied up in the back yard."

"We'll take care of him, we promise!" Charles said.

Of course, no one could stand to leave Tecane tied in the yard and the big dog lived right in the house with the family. In fact, he lived to be fifteen years old.

Charles and Tecane 1955

ON FIREWEED LANE

Fireweed Lane had been a little street that ended in a swamp, but only a few weeks before the Oborns moved there, it

431

had been improved. It was now a wide gravel road that connected the Seward Highway to Spenard Road. A few short streets took off south from Fireweed Lane, but they ended in a marshy tundra area where there were no buildings or roads, only muskeg and blueberry bushes.

Gwynne pulled up in front of the little green house, as eager as the children were to see where they'd be living. It was a real house, with a big front window, a small porch, green siding and a peaked roof. "OK, this is it," she said.

The kids piled out, letting the dog loose. Tecane raced across the snow-covered front lawn, made a sharp turn toward the apartments across the driveway, and circled back to the cluster of children gathering by the front door. As soon as Gwynne unlocked and opened the door, the children filed in, and began exploring. Gwynne walked slowly from room to room, all the while, listening for Cler's truck. He should be here soon, she thought; he wasn't that far behind her.

The front door entered the living room, where a large window looked out on the front yard. There were smooth, varnished wood floors in both the living and dining areas. The former owners had left a gray, Formica-topped table with tubular steel legs and matching chairs, with padded vinyl seats.

Corrie encountered the kitchen at the same time Gwynne did. "Cupboards, and a sink, and running water!" Corrie exclaimed. "Look, Mama! A refrigerator, and electric stove. Isn't it great?" Corrie Lynne had spent a lot of time washing dishes in water heated on the drum stove, and cooking on the wood range. The conveniences in the new house looked like heaven to her.

On one side of the new kitchen was a back hall, and a roomy walk-in closet. Off the living room was a small bedroom and a bathroom. A bathtub, sink, toilet. What more could they ask for?

The largest bedroom would be for Gwynne and Cler. There was a double bed already there, and a spot for Butchy's crib. After Gwynne walked through the entire house, she realized there weren't enough bedrooms. The girls could stay in the small

432

bedroom, but where would the boys sleep? Cler must have a plan, but tonight she'd put the two boys in sleeping bags, on the front room floor.

Gwynne sat down at the table, and waited for Cler to arrive with the truck. She wanted to get the beds made up, before bedtime. A few minutes later, Cler drove into the driveway and gaily tooted his horn. He and Paxton came in the back door.

"We're here!" Paxton called out, rushing to get a look at the rest of the house.

Cler stopped Gwynne in the kitchen. "So how do you like it?" He asked.

"It's wonderful!" she ran her hand over the linoleum-covered counter. "Running water and an electric stove. What a treat!"

Cler took Gwynne in his arms, and twirled her around. He kissed her on the lips, and leaned her back, still kissing her, until her long, brown hair touched the floor. They were both laughing when he raised her up.

Lestie had been watching them from the dining room. Seeing her parents so happy made her smile. That night, she told Corrie, "I don't think we'll be going back to Kenny Lake very soon. Mama is really happy here."

"I know," Corrie said, "so am I."

As Gwynne had quickly realized, the house didn't have enough bedrooms, but Cler had a solution. He planned to insulate the attic space above the main house, and make a room for the boys. It could be accessed by a fold-down ladder in the back hall. With the extra bedroom, the house would be worth more money, when it came time to sell it. For now, Cler and Paxton installed the boys' bunk beds in the large, walk-in closet.

As soon as the family got settled, Gwynne enrolled Paxton, Celestia and Charles in North Star School, which was just short of two miles down Fireweed Lane. They would walk to school, but Corrie took a bus to the Jr. High School in downtown Anchorage. Right away, Cler began working at the Guard.

Aerial view of Kulis Air National Guard Base 1955

It was still cold and snowy in Anchorage, but the days were getting longer, and the weather grew increasingly milder. One morning Gwynne rolled out of bed to take Cler to work, so she could keep the car. She stepped into her fuzzy slippers and slipped her quilted robe over her long, flannel gown. As she climbed into the car with Cler, he glanced at her outfit.

"Aren't you cold?" he asked.

"Turn up the heater a little bit and I'll be fine," she told him. "I won't even be getting out of the car."

Cler shrugged as if to say, "Suit yourself" and backed out of the driveway.

Gwynne loved to see Cler in his uniform. She watched his face as the sun came up and shone on it from her side of the car. The brim of his hat shaded his eyes, but he was smiling, humming to himself as they drove to the Base.

At the gate, he rolled down the window and the guard saluted smartly, "Good morning, Sir!"

Gwynne felt proud of him.

Cler had become a second lieutenant back in 1943, when he got his wings in the Army Air Corps. Now, back on active duty with the Guard, he was made a first lieutenant.

Cler parked outside the hanger and leaned over to kiss his wife. "I love you," he said, and opened the car door.

"I love you, too," she said, sliding into the driver's seat.

On the way home, just as she was headed up C street hill, she felt a thud under her car, and then the flub-dub-dub of a flat tire. She pulled over onto the shoulder of the road, as close as she could get to the sooty snow bank. It wasn't until she climbed out to check the damage, that she realized she was standing in the snow in her slippers, wearing her nightgown and bathrobe.

Almost immediately, a pickup truck pulled in behind her, and a stout man in a fur hat got out. "Looks like you got a problem, Ma'am," he said, sounding a little too jovial for the situation, she thought. She felt like sinking into the snow bank when she saw his eyes drop to her slippers.

"Why don't you just get back in your car, Ma'am, while I fix the tire for you? Do you have a jack and a spare in your trunk?"

"I think so," she said.

The nice man fixed the tire in no time. He tossed the flat in and slammed the trunk with a thump.

Gwynne rolled down her window, "Thank you so much!"

"Happy to be of help," the man said, "You should probably get that flat fixed soon."

"I will," she said with feigned cheerfulness. She waved at him as he headed back to his truck. Gwynne decided this was the last time she'd ever leave the house again, in her nightgown and slippers.

T-6 Trainer

LIEUTENANT OBORN

Cler was thrilled to be back in the service. In May, he wrote in his journal, "I'm working for the Alaska Air National Guard as Unit Supply Officer, and a fighter pilot. Me, a fighter pilot! It was one of the biggest thrills of my life the day I checked out in the F-80 C. I couldn't sleep for hours that night." He was now a First Lieutenant in the 144th Fighter Interceptor Squadron.

The squadron was made up of a close-knit group of men who had all been pilots during the war. The former Guard Unit, situated on Elmendorf, had only been funded for a couple of years. In order to get funding, some high ranking officers in the Alaska Guard convinced the government in Washington that America needed the Guard, in order to establish enhanced security on Alaska's western borders. The squadron began with one T-33 trainer, and eleven pilots. Within a few months, they had been given more surplus trainers, planes used mainly for observation during the war.

The fledgling Unit met with tragedy. On November 16, 1954, the pilots of a T-33 trainer checked in with ground controllers at Point McKenzie. Less than half an hour later, a training flight of three F-80s, led by 1st Lt. Albert Kulis, passed in formation over the Goose Bay area, on the west side of Knick

Arm. His wing man watched as Lt. Kulis' fighter went into a steep, diving turn and vanished into a cloudbank.

The first T-33, with two pilots aboard, vanished, and neither the wreckage of the plane or the two pilots were ever seen again. Kulis' downed plane was sighted two weeks later, half sunk into the mud at Goose Bay. It sank before it could be recovered.

In the spring of 1955, a month after Cler moved his family to Anchorage, the Alaska Air National Guard moved out of Elmendorf and onto its new base near Anchorage International Airport. The men of the new 144th Fighter Interceptor Squadron voted to dedicate their new base in honor of Lieutenant Kulis. It wasn't long before the Air Force sent more trainers and a whole fleet of state-of-the-art fighter jets. The men were soon flying F-86 jets, testing the Alaskan Radar Screen.

F-86 jet

The main job of the 144th Fighter Interceptor squadron was to protect Alaska from incursions by Russian or North Korean fighters or spy planes. If an unidentified plane should come into American air space, the pilots of the 144th would be there to escort them out of the zone, or shoot them down if they wouldn't go. Cler told Gwynne that the most hair-raising part of his job was when he was enlisted to fly the "unidentified aircraft", testing the newly installed radar system.

Cler's mission was to take off and fly into Russian air space, then turn around and fly back over the line, triggering the system. Amid the wail of sirens, the other pilots, unaware that it was only a drill, would scramble their fighter jets to intercept the intruder. Cler said he could hear the radio crackling, "You are in American air space. Identify or turn back!" With no answer, the fighter pilots had to make visual contact, before they shot down the unidentified aircraft.

Cler said, "There's nothing like your heart beating out of your chest, wondering whether or not your buddies will see and recognize you, before they get overly excited and start shooting!"

He admitted that it was just as tough being the guy intercepting an unknown intruder. You couldn't know whether or not it was an enemy plane until you got so close you could see the pilot's goggles. Once, Cler intercepted a Russian plane that had managed to fly through the radar screen. When the Russian plane spotted two American fighters heading his way, he made a fast turnaround and headed back toward Russia. Another time, Cler said he saw the Russian pilot's face. "The guy looked terrified. I was relieved when he turned back. I really hated the thought of shooting him down."

SUMMER ON THE COAST

Anchorage is situated on Cook Inlet, where coastal rains and snow make everything greener and feed the glaciers that top the nearby Chugach Mountains.

This spring, every day seemed cloudy or raining as the remnants of last year's snow, a blackened, sooty mess, melted along the roadsides, where it had been piled by snowplows over the winter. The children walked home from school, with their boots coated thick with mud, and splashed through deep puddles. This stage of spring was known as "Breakup," when solid ice on the rivers cracked and broke up. The roads broke up, too, leaving potholes, cracks and puddles so deep that cars and trucks plowed through the water and splashed the children walking along on the top of the sooty snow berm.

However wet and muddy spring is, Alaskans love it. Glorious spring means respite from winter, and before they know it, it's summer. Every day of the brief summers are cherished. Daylight increases rapidly until, by midsummer, a rosy sunset over the silt-laden waters of Cook Inlet will grow dimmer, and then, in what seems like mere minutes, the sky becomes brighter again, as dusk becomes dawn.

On Fireweed Lane, robins and magpies pecked at the old, yellow grass that the melting snow exposed. The children, playing outside, watched them build their nests in the leaning, ragged trees called black spruce. The children responded to the sunlight like little birds, themselves. Early in the morning they were awake, bright-eyed, long before their parents wanted them to be. Then school was out, and Summer was here.

Very early one morning, the sun was already warming the ground when Lestie woke up and stepped out the back door onto the dry porch, in her nightgown, to see how the weather was. She breathed in the sweet air that smelled almost like the Homestead. The snow-capped Chugach mountains loomed into the cloudless, turquoise sky, reminding her of the mountains she was used to seeing at Kenny Lake.

Paxton joined her outside. He was barefoot, wearing jeans and a T-shirt. "It's going to be a hot day!" he exclaimed, his eyes searching the sky for clouds. "What shall we do?" The front yard had a bit of grass, but nothing else, and the back yard was a tangle of weeds.

"We can play in the blueberry swamp," Lestie offered, though it was too early for blueberries.

Paxton said, "I know where there's a creek. We can go swimming!"

"How will we get there?"

"We can walk," he told her, "it's just down the highway a little ways. Daddy pointed it out to me the other day. It's called Campbell Creek."

Excited now, they hurried into the house for a breakfast of cornflakes and milk. Store milk seemed thin and watery compared to the fresh goat's milk they were used to, but they drank it, anyway. Butchy was awake and so was Charles, and they joined the little group at the table.

After breakfast, Mother and Corrie left for the Commissary on Base. It would be hours before they got back, Paxton said. This fit right into his plan to go swimming, even though they had to babysit. "We'll just take Butchy with us," he said.

Paxton and Lestie packed up some bread and peanut butter and a bottle of green Kool-Aid, all in a big paper sack. They planted Butchy in the red wagon, with a blanket and their lunch, then they took off down Fireweed Lane. It was only a block to the highway. Paxton pulled the wagon, while Charles helped push it over the rough spots.

They headed south, walking along the shoulder of Seward Highway, pulling the little red wagon. Paxton soon realized that Campbell Creek was a lot further than it had seemed when he and Daddy were driving by in the car, but the little band trudged on, spurred by the reward of going swimming.

When they finally reached the creek, they were hot and tired. They turned off the road by the bridge and rolled the wagon down to the creek, where they found a spot beside the stream, surrounded by cool, green willows. Since it was early summer, the water flowed fast, but it was shallow and clear, with a rocky bottom.

In a few moments, Paxton and Charles had peeled out of their jeans, down to their underwear. Charles was the first to wade into the cold water, giggling and high-stepping. Paxton ran, slipped, and fell in, laughing. They cupped their hands and threw water on each other, screaming with glee.

Lestie rolled up her jeans and held Butchy's hand as he splashed his feet in the shallows. She decided that the water was

440

too cold to swim in, but the boys played in the water until they started turning blue. They laid on the blanket and warmed up, and then jumped in the creek again.

Butchy played in the sand, and Lestie knelt beside him, drawing patterns with a driftwood stick. She decorated her designs with red, green, white, gold and blue stones she took from the water. She and Butchy built a rock castle with sand and mud and pretty rocks.

After lunch, they all sprawled on the blanket to rest, and before they knew it, the sun had circled as high as it was going to get, and now was lowering. Paxton decided it was time to go home. They packed up the red wagon and Butchy, who curled up and fell asleep immediately. They made their way to the highway and began the long walk back to Fireweed Lane.

It was Cler who found them. He spotted the wagon and the children trudging along the highway, and pulled over ahead of them. They shuffled to the car, almost too tired to go any further. The children loaded in, as their dad wrangled the wagon into the back of the car.

He got behind the wheel and shut the door. "Do you kids realize your mother called the police when you didn't come home? We've been looking for you for hours!"

Paxton said, "We're sorry, Dad. It was so nice outside, we just wanted to go swimming at Campbell Creek. Remember when we talked about going to the creek?"

Cler drove for a few minutes without saying anything. Finally, he said, "We're not living on the Homestead, Paxton, where you know your way around and there's nobody to kidnap you kids! I'm very disappointed in you. It wouldn't be so bad, but you took Butchy! What were you thinking?"

What were they thinking? Lestie heard those words in her mind all the way home. They had only been thinking about how warm it was outside, and how nice it would be to go swimming. It surprised her that they were in trouble for taking Butchy! They certainly couldn't have left him home alone! She'd watched him carefully all day, and he seemed to have as much fun as they did. Why would they be in trouble for that?

Celestia, Corrie and Tecane   Charles and Paxton 1955

That summer, Lestie played with her friend, Joyce, the little girl she'd known in Mountain View. Her family lived on the next street. Lestie and Joyce both had responsibilities. Joyce had to tend her two little brothers, and Lestie often had to take care of Butchy. They incorporated the little boys into their play, and Charles joined them. The entire neighborhood, from the woods behind their homes, to the blue berry swamp, was their playroom. They spent most of their time outdoors, soaking up the light, getting healthy and tanned.

Butchy and Charles were both seven now, but Butchy was still very small. He called Lestie "Nonny," which she thought was his way of saying "Honey." Sometimes she got him ready for bed at night, singing him a lengthy string of songs, until he fell asleep. If he were left in bed awake, he'd get up again and find some mischief to get into. His favorite song was "O Susanna," which

Lestie improvised as "O Butchy Boy, don't you cry for me, for I'm going to Alaska with my Butchy on my knee!"

During these long days of summer, Gwynne's health improved. She made friends with the wives of other Guard members, and the women enjoyed visiting each other. Next door, in the apartments, Pat and Dick Otto lived, with their two small children. Dick was a pilot with the Air Guard. He was a captain and Cler's wing commander. The two couples spent time together at squadron socials, while Corrie babysat for the Ottos and Paxton took care of his siblings.

That summer, Gwynne also began taking some secretarial classes which met in the evenings. They were offered by the University of Alaska Extension Service. As she attended classes, working toward a certificate, her self-esteem blossomed; she mastered new skills and developed relationships with other women in the class. The depression that had plagued her in Kenny Lake, and had followed her to Anchorage, lifted.

On evenings when Gwynne was gone to class, Corrie had to make dinner. She always delegated nine-year-old Lestie to peel the potatoes. To Lestie, it seemed they had boiled potatoes every night.

While this repetitious job was inherently boring, Lestie entertained herself by studying the surprising differences in how the potatoes looked on the outside, compared to how they were on the inside. For instance, a rough, black scab that covered half the skin, might come away, leaving a white, perfect potato underneath. On the other hand, she would start cutting out a tiny blemish, only to find that the rot went clear to the center. This contradiction gave rise to what she called "Potato Philosophy," in which she began to think that potatoes and people were a lot alike. You couldn't always tell how good or bad a person or potato was from looking at the outside. She thought fondly of Grandma George, with her flat brown cheeks wrinkled like a walnut, and her little teeth, worn down from chewing skins. Her outside might not look beautiful to some people, but she was a beautiful person.

443

Just thinking of how much she missed Grandma George made Lestie's heart ache.

While Cler was busy at the Air Guard, Gwynne was equally busy at home. With the children all in school, Gwynne decided Butchy could use a playmate. Once again, she applied to take a foster child. A Welfare worker brought a curly-haired two-year-old named Hazel. She needed a temporary home until relatives down in the States could be located and given the option to adopt her. She went by the nickname "Cookie," which fitted her much better than "Hazel." With six children, the Oborns had a full house, but Cookie was only with them for two months, and then she was adopted by relatives.

Paxton, Celestia, Charles, Butchy, Cookie, Corrie 1955

Luscombe 8

33

BUSH PILOT

Summer, 1955

That summer, Cler, Scott McDaniel, and Larry Straley partnered up to purchase a small plane. It was a Luscombe 8 single-prop, a study little aircraft with tandem seats (meaning one in front of the other), with both seats having a control stick. The Luscombe was War Surplus. It had been used by the military as a good, lightweight aircraft known for its simplicity and reliability. It had thin, aluminum sheeting over an aluminum frame, with high wings on top the body of the plane, and aluminum struts.

They housed the plane in a hanger at Merrill Field, which had been built by the military during the war, and was now used for civilian aircraft. Many planes flying out of Merrill Field carried supplies into the Alaskan Bush, to isolated villages and towns. Outfitters flew hunters and fishermen into the Interior and landed on sandbars or grassy air strips. (The float plane hadn't been invented yet.)

Cler and his friends planned to use the Luscombe to go after their winter's meat, and eventually to recoup the cost of the plane by getting into the outfitting business, taking paying passengers, hunters and fishermen out in the Bush. Cler figured they had a good setup with an airfield at Kenny Lake, and the cabin, which they could use as a way station. The Copper River Valley was so beautiful people would pay just to see the scenery.

Cler took each of his children up in the Luscombe, one at a time. On a memorable Saturday, when the sky was clear and blue, it was Lestie's turn. Her dad strapped her into the co-pilot's seat in the front, and then settled himself into the rear.

The engine roared, the plane rushed down the runway, and lifted off, leaving Lestie, for a moment, weightless. It was exciting, and she wasn't a bit afraid. In front of her, the propeller was a shining circle of light, as they rose higher into the air. The engine hummed steadily, as the plane flew like a giant bird, over the densely-treed landscape. They were headed toward the snow topped mountains, when Cler hollered, "Take hold of the stick, and help me fly the plane!"

She grasped the stick.

"Just hold it steady!" The plane droned along for a minute or two, and then she heard, "Hey, Lestie! You're going to fly us into that mountain!"

She froze.

"Just let go, and I'll take over," he laughed, easing the plane into a turn. They circled over the glittering water of Cook Inlet, and cruised back to Merrill Field.

Scotty and Larry were working to get their pilot's licenses, and Cler took each of them up in the Luscombe, to get in some hours. On one such flight, Cler and Scotty were coming in for a landing, when the engine began to sputter and the plane rapidly lost altitude. Cler took over the controls, but they were too low, and coming in too fast. When the wheels hit, one of the struts

446

collapsed, and the plane spun around, screeching to an abrupt stop.

Shaken, Cler and Scotty climbed from the plane. Scotty said, "Bit of a rough landing, there, Cler!"

Cler grinned, "Guess it coulda' been rougher!"

They walked around the plane, assessing the damage. "Only minor," Cler said. "Have to replace that strut, though. Grab a hand hold, Scotty, and let's tow the old gal back into the hanger."

When Cler got home, he found Gwynne in the kitchen. "So how was it?" she asked, meaning the flight.

Cler snagged a fresh biscuit off the counter. Taking a bite, he said, casually, "Well, we won't be going out in the Luscombe for a while."

"Oh? Why not?"

"Plane's cracked up right now, but it won't be hard to fix."

"Cracked up? How'd that happen?"

"Just something of a rough landing; nothing to worry about," he said.

TRIP TO KENNY LAKE

Cler had a long weekend over the Fourth of July, and wanted to use the time to make a trip back to Kenny Lake. He had things he wanted to check on, and he wanted to pay Enzo and Ted for taking care of the animals.

It had only been four months since the children had been back home to Kenny Lake, but they were as excited as if it had been years. The family loaded up in the Jeep Wagon and made the trip in less than four hours. They took some food and clothing, so they could stay over the long weekend. Arriving at Kenny Lake, they stopped at the truck house and the gas pump. Hal and Julie Waugh were still living in the truck house and manning the gas station. Hal came outside when they pulled up to the pump.

"Well, howdy folks! Long time no see," Hal laughed, talking like a cowboy, which he wasn't.

447

"Hi, Hal. We're back for the weekend. How have things been here at the Lake?"

"Just fine! It's summer, so business has picked up. Want to fill up with gas, while you're here?"

"Sure," Cler said, and Hal lifted down the hose and inserted it in the Jeep's gas tank. He flipped a lever and the gasoline, like dark tea, filled the glass top, as the children watched. The gallon marks on the glass registered how many gallons drained into the Jeep's tank.

"Can we get out?" Paxton asked, opening the car door. "Charles and I want to run up to the cabin."

"Go ahead," Gwynne said, glad to let the boys out.

When the tank was full, and Cler finished talking to Hal, the family continued on up the driveway. Tall grass grew between the tire tracks. Cler drove past the school, closed for the summer, and up to the cabin. The dooryard and cabin looked undisturbed, and healthy weeds had grown up in the spot where Gwynne usually emptied dishwater. As soon as the car stopped, the rest of the kids piled out, happy to be let loose to run and play around the old Homestead.

When he reached the porch, Cler realized that the board he'd left nailed across the door was lying on the ground. He crossed the porch and opened the cabin door, and Gwynne followed him in. It was dim and a bit dusty inside, from sitting closed up for the past four months. Gwynne was glad to be back, but just walking into the cabin made her realize the conveniences she'd already begun to take for granted in Anchorage.

The cabin seemed undisturbed, until Gwynne entered the bedroom and found out her pitcher and bowl were missing. The spot on the dresser where it had been sitting still showed a ring in the dust.

"Cler! Someone's been in the cabin!"

He hurried to their bedroom, where he spied the empty spot on the dresser.

"Who would steal my bowl and pitcher! It was your mother's!"

448

Cler shook his head. "Better you never tell my mother," he said, but it was no joke. "Look around and see if there's anything else missing." They checked, but it seemed only the pitcher and bowl set that had been stolen. They decided to take anything else that might be valuable, back to Anchorage with them. They selected the set of classics, and several other books they liked. Looking through cupboards and drawers, they realized they hadn't left anything very valuable. Still, it was their home that had been invaded.

"I'll ask Hal Waugh to keep an eye on the place," Cler said. "Maybe leave the board off the door, and just nail it shut. Keep the old pickup in the yard, so it won't look abandoned."

Corrie and Cler took a ride up the road to the Santinis. Cler wanted to talk to Enzo about leveling the airfield. In October or November, he intended to fly up and bring Larry or Scotty to go hunting. Enzo could use his bulldozer to plow a landing strip in the snow and it would make an even smoother place to land.

Corrie wanted to see Quack-quack.

While Cler and Enzo were talking about the airfield, Corrie went seeking Little Enzo in the barn. When she stepped into the slab and log building, she smelled the familiar aroma of goats and hay. Little Enzo was balancing on a short piece of stove wood, milking one of his goats. He looked up, surprised to see Corrie.

"Well, look who's come back! Hi, Corrie. How's life in the big city? Did you like Junior High?"

"I did! And I'm looking forward to this Fall. Are you going away for high school?"

Little Enzo shook his head, "No, I guess not." Finished stripping the milk, he picked up the bucket and carried it over to the big can, where he carefully poured the milk in, and replaced the lid. "I'm going to take correspondence, I guess. My dad needs me to stay here and help him."

"I understand." She glanced around, "Where's Quack-quack?"

Little Enzo looked uneasy. "He's dead."

Corrie's heart sank. "Dead? What happened?"

"I'm so sorry," he said. "I know how you liked him. Ever since the ice melted, we were letting him go out and swim on the lake. He always came back in the evening when we called him. At night, we closed him in the barn."

Corrie was angry. She didn't care how nice they'd been to him. She wanted to know why he was dead. "So what happened to my duck, Little Enzo?'

He set the milk bucket down, and stood facing her, "In a way, it was my fault. I was here milking when I heard my dad calling Quack-quack to come. I should have gone out and got him. Well, you know my dad, he doesn't have a lot of patience. I heard a shot and when I got out there—"

"What? He shot my duck?" Corrie was incredulous.

Little Enzo took a step back, "I'm sorry!"

Corrie felt sick. She'd trusted him with her pet and look what happened: Quack-quack was dead!

The shame in Little Enzo's eyes brought her around.

"It wasn't your fault," she said, touching his arm. "I'm not mad at you. I just feel really sad." She didn't even ask what happened to the duck after he was shot. Zoya wouldn't have let that fat Peking duck go to waste.

Except for Corrie's upset over Quack-quack, the family enjoyed their few days at the homestead. On Saturday, the Fourth of July, the community held a little picnic and celebration at the lake, hosted by the school teacher and her husband.

As they left Kenny Lake, each member of the family had different thoughts and feelings. Cler still had plans to return to the homestead. He thought about his airfield, the outfitting business with Larry and Scotty. Gwynne was thinking she'd be glad to get back to hot and cold running water and a flushing toilet. Corrie had resigned herself to Quack-quack's death, but she didn't think she'd ever forgive Big Enzo for shooting him. Like her mother, she would be happy to return to civilization and indoor plumbing.

Paxton and Charles, however, talked about how great it would be when they all moved back to Kenny Lake. Celestia

450

wanted to come back, too. But she would be happy anywhere, just as long as she could be near her daddy.

INTO THE WILD BLUE YONDER

One day in July, the Air Guard held an open house and picnic for the families of those who worked on base. Food was served in the cavernous hanger. While the visitors filled their divided metal plates, they were treated to a demonstration drill. All at once, deafening sirens split the air, and four men in bulky flight suits took off running toward their swept-wing jets, out on the runway. Lestie recognized her father by his height, and by his curly brown hair, before he pulled on his helmet. Corrie did, too. "There he is!" she cried, pointing at him, as he swung into the cockpit of one swept-wing jet.

In seconds, the jets took off in a thundering roar of engines and almost immediately they rose straight into the blue sky. They rolled away from each other and tore off in four different directions. As the jets disappeared into the blue, Corrie, Paxton, Charles and Lestie shouted, "There he goes! That's our Dad up there!"

When he was flying, Cler seemed to be in his element. In September, he wrote in his journal, "Jet flying is flying at its most thrilling. An ordinary plane moves about three axis during flight and so does a jet, but the movements are so accelerated. It is bewildering at first to sit in a tiny cockpit, surrounded by hundreds of switches and dials, each one of which must function in a very precise manner, in order for you to continue to live.

"When all is ready, you press a couple of switches and move a lever and a gentle rumble starts to bring the seven ton aluminum monster to life. As the rumble increases to a roar, you button down your harness, check oxygen and radio, and taxi out for a take-off. The take off is where you realize that this machine is really different.

451

"As you sit at the end of the runway, hold the brakes and pour on the cobs, your knees shake with the strain and you want to get the hell out of there, but as you release the brakes it's too late; already the airplane is moving down the runway. 2000 feet go by and the plane is gaining speed; rudder action can now be felt; 3000 feet, you have over 100 mph and the nose will come up a little; 4000 feet, it's lifting off at 140 mph.

"The scenery outside is a blur, as you reach for the gear. When the gear snaps up your air speed jumps to 190 and you start the flaps up; 250, the plane sinks slightly when the flaps come up. Nose up trim, climb out is fantastic; before you complete your cockpit check, you are passing through 5000 feet (above the ground). Never before have you felt such performance. A normal turn almost blacks you out, the slightest back pressure and you gain about 2000 feet of altitude.

"Landings are a real hair-straightener. Landing speed at 350, a tight turn at about 2-4 g's, while you lose 200 mph, put down gear, flaps, and speed brakes, and come screaming at the ground at 150 mph. A solid plunk, let down the nose and start with the brakes as the runway end roars up to meet you."

The well-used jets the Air Force was giving the Alaska Air Guard had a few problems, and although the mechanics and electricians went over each one in detail, things could, and did go wrong.

Following the journal entry in which Cler described the rush of flying and landing a jet, he added a cryptic note, "I've had one emergency so far and that's enough. Complete electrical failure and burned up the brakes. Hope that doesn't happen again soon."

What happened was worse than his journal entry implied. After the accident, Cler called Gwynne from the base to tell her about it. "I was coming in for a landing when everything went haywire. Not much left of the jet, but somebody came and took a picture of it, and it might be in the newspapers before I get home from work, so I thought I'd better tell you about it first. Don't

452

worry, I'm fine. I'll stay here with the medic for a while, then I'll be home about the same time as usual."

"Medic? I thought you were fine!"

"Well, they had to cut me out of my harness, because I was upside down. My shoulders are a bit bruised, that's all. I'm sure I don't have a concussion. Honest, I'll be home in two hours. I love you!"

Gwynne's stomach was in knots in spite of his assurances. If she'd had the car, she'd have taken Butch and run to the Base. Instead, she made herself walk into the kitchen, where she started a moose roast for supper.

When Cler arrived home that evening, Lestie met him coming in through the door, and he stooped to hug her. He was wearing his blue uniform. He took off his hat, with the golden eagle on the brim. He held her tightly, smelling like the cool, clean outdoors.

When he let her go, he crossed the room and sank onto the couch, handing his hat to Lestie. She laid it on top of the book shelf, and returned to sit beside him.

Cler leaned forward, his elbows on his knees, and ran his hands through his matted curls. "Whew! What a day!"

Hearing him, Gwynne hurried from the kitchen. Underneath his natural tan, he looked pale around the mouth, and under the eyes. "Are you sure you're OK?" she asked, bending over, smoothing his cheek with her hand. "You look exhausted."

Cler said, "Just let me sit here, until I get up enough strength to go change my clothes."

Gwynne kissed him on the lips. They were full, and soft. "You taste like salt. Is that from sweating that landing?"

"You don't know the half of it," he said, reaching up and drawing her to him. He kissed her again, with a loud smack, "Mwah!"

That evening's paper showed a picture of the demolished jet, upside down in the brush at the end of the runway. The caption on the picture said, simply, "Air Guard Pilot Survives Crash."

GOING TO THE FAIR

The air was clear as crystal, the sun shone high in the sky, and it was too late in the year for mosquitoes. This was Fair Time, when the farmers of the Matanuska Valley, and anyone else who wanted to participate for cash prizes, brought their best livestock and produce to the fair in Palmer. The Oborn children had never been to a fair, but they were eager to go. They'd been told there'd be carnival rides, giant vegetables, all kinds of exhibits, and animals to see.

Palmer itself was started in 1916 on a branch line of the Alaska Railroad, to access the Chickaloon coal mines. In 1935, the first farmers arrived, as one of the New Deal projects of President Roosevelt. Over two hundred families from the upper Midwest were relocated at government expense, to the Matanuska Valley. They came north on a military transport ship, and then took the railroad to Palmer,

The Matanuska Project gave each farmer forty to eighty acres, by drawing lots. The first summer, families lived in a tent city, while building their cabins, assisted by paid laborers who also came from the States. The second summer, barns were built. There were several cabin plans to choose from, but every barn was the same: 32' by 32' by 32', built of logs ten feet high, with a frame upper and gambrel roof. Nails, vents, doors, windows, hinges and everything but the logs came by freight from the States.

After the initial government help, farmers were on their own to make their farms, consisting mainly of dairies and vegetable gardens, a success. The high costs of freight, far distant markets, and the short growing season combined to discourage many, and only half the families stayed. Those who stayed eventually prospered. The rich soil grew hay in abundance, and long hours of daylight produced enormous vegetables.

On this Fair Day in the fall of 1955, the local newspaper predicted temperatures in the Valley to be in the seventies. Gwynne insisted that everyone bring a jacket, because you never knew: the sun might go behind a cloud and the temperature could drop twenty degrees. She packed a lunch and blankets to sit on. Cler had cash in his pocket for tickets and cotton candy.

"What's cotton candy?" Charles wanted to know.

"You'll see," his father said, giving him a wink. "It could be the best thing you've ever tasted!"

The Glenn Highway was paved, but it was winding and narrow. It followed the Knick Arm, where broad stretches of mud flats reached inland from Cook Inlet. In the spring, acres and acres of wild Iris bloomed on the mud flats, like a great carpet of purple, as far as the eye could see. Now, the Iris blooms had faded, but the spiked leaves carpeted the flats in green.

Cler was making good time, enjoying the challenge of taking the curves at speeds just shy of making his tires squeal. Some of the children in the back seat were feeling the effects.

"Daddy, can we stop? We're getting carsick!" Corrie moaned.

"Roll the window down," Cler said. "Get some air."

"Cler, we'd better find a place to pull over," Gwynne told him.

"OK, OK!" He saw a wide place a few hundred feet ahead, and slowed down. When he stopped the car, other vehicles whizzed past on the road. *Everyone seems like they're in a hurry these days,* he thought, then smiled at himself, because he knew how fast he'd been going.

To the kids, he said, "Those who are actually car sick can get out on the right side of the car. Just walk around a little over there by those bushes. The rest of you, sit still."

Gwynne had Butchy on her lap, "I think I'll get out with Butch, too. Maybe we'll make it the rest of the way without having to stop again."

"Good idea," Cler told her.

455

She climbed out, taking Butchy by the hand, "Any of you kids need to go pee, go off in those bushes. Don't any of you go very far, and don't get near the road!"

The kids scattered into the bushes.

Refreshed and with some of their wiggles out, the children all scrambled back into the car, the girls in the back seat, the boys in the "way back."

Cler checked his rear view mirror, and watched for a break in the line of cars. He pulled into the traffic, and was forced to go slower the rest of the way. Darn! He thought. *I was ahead of the pack before I had to stop.*

After following the Knick Arm, the road crossed the long Knick River Bridge, which spanned not only the river, but a wide expanse of gray mud. Here, the flats were littered with the white trunks of dead trees, which had grown there before the river changed course and formed a new bed. They drove onto the bridge, their tires bumping over the wooden base. In awe, the children grew quiet, as they felt the bridge sway, and saw the swirling, rushing river below.

There were six spans, with open trusses overhead. After the trussed section, the bridge continued as a paved road, elevated on cement pilings, with just guard rails along the sides.

A few miles from the bridge, the Matanuska Valley came into view. It was a curiously level valley, enclosed by mountain peaks of naked blue rock topped with snow, rising straight up from the valley floor. In the fields, rows of cut hay lay drying in the sun. Stands of brush and trees separated green meadows, where small herds of black and white cows grazed. Often in a clearing, there was a log barn painted red or white, with a matching log house.

The Palmer Fair Grounds consisted of a few dusty acres on the outskirts of town. The parking lot was a grassy field where parked cars lined up side by side, in long, uneven, rows. People were streaming toward the midway, where calliope music mixed with the shrieks and screams of riders. The Oborn children ran

456

ahead, toward the exciting sounds and colorful sights ahead of them.

When they reached the gate, they waited for their parents. Cler said, "I'll buy you each one ride ticket." Lestie chose the carrousel, with its exotically painted horses and gay music. Gwynne put Butchy on a red and gold horse, standing alongside, in case he should slip off. Cler and the other kids rode the Ferris Wheel, shouting and waving to Gwynne and the kids down below.

There were flowers of every color in one tent, and fancy handwork and quilts in another. The highlight of the agricultural show were the giant vegetables. With the fertile soil in the valley, and nineteen hours of summer daylight, the farmers grew mammoth cabbages, zucchini squash, radishes, and turnips.

"Will you look at that!" Paxton exclaimed. The blue ribbon cabbage weighed seventy-five pounds. Its leaves spread out as big as a small car. There were zucchinis like logs, and radishes like footballs.

The family found a shady spot on the far side of the Fair Grounds to spread out a blanket and eat their lunch of "made to order" peanut butter sandwiches, carrot sticks and cold water from a thermos. Gwynne and Butchy rested on the blanket, while Cler took the other children for the promised cotton candy. For Lestie, it wasn't the sweet taste that intrigued her, but rather the way a handful of pink fuzz disappeared like magic in her mouth.

Too soon, it was time to go home. The children were dusty, sticky from the cotton candy, and tired out, but they'd had a wonderful day. They loaded into the car and rolled down the windows to let out the heat that had built up. Cler pulled forward and turned into the dusty aisle between rows of cars. He glanced into his rear view mirror and spotted a grubby little boy tearing after the car. Charles! Cler braked to a stop, and let the little guy catch up.

Celestia opened the back door for him. With tears making rivulets down his dusty cheeks, he cried, "You left me!"

Cler said, "But you were with us when we got to the car, or was I imagining things?"

Charles crawled over the back seat into the cargo area, where he liked to ride. "Everybody was crowding in the same door, so I went around, and you drove away!"

Gwynne said, "We're sorry! We should be better at counting heads."

As they were approaching the Knick River Bridge, the traffic slowed to a standstill. After a few minutes, Cler shifted into park, and climbed out to see what was going on.

He walked up the road. When he returned, he slid into the driver's seat, and turned off the engine. "The bridge is out. A section of road collapsed near the abutment. The men I talked to said they were doing a temporary fix. It'll take a few hours for the road crew to dump in enough rock. We might as well all take a nap!"

They rolled down the windows, and tried to get comfortable. Curled up together, the children fell asleep. When they woke up a couple of hours later, the car was still stopped in the long line of traffic. Cler was not in the driver's seat. He was standing on the side of the road, talking to a group of men.

"Can we get out?" Paxton asked. "I need to go!"

"Me, too!" Charles said.

Gwynne said, "You can all get out for a minute, but there's a lot of people around here, so pick a good bush, and don't go wandering off!"

By the time the kids returned to the car, and settled into their favorite spots, their father was sitting behind the wheel. He called to them, "OK, speak up if you're not here!"

Silence.

Corrie said, "You're funny, Daddy. If we're not here, how can we speak up?"

"Just keeping you on your toes," he chuckled. "I'm told we'll be going in a few minutes."

"I'm starving!" Charles complained.

Gwynne said. "I have a couple of pieces of bread left that you can all share.

458

"I'm alright, Mother," Corrie said, gallantly, "Give my piece to Butchy."

It was dark by the time the bridge was fixed. Everyone was so hungry that Cler stopped at Eagle River at a small café, and ordered them all dinner. Veal cutlets were the special so they all got one with mashed potatoes and gravy.

When the plates were brought, and they all dug into their dinners, Lestie said, "I always wondered what veal cutlets were." She remembered the calf that ate the window out of the barn.

The other children were too busy eating to comment.

MISSING KENNY LAKE

It was the first day of the new school year. Wearing new school clothes, Paxton and Charles, Celestia and Joyce all walked to school together. The boys and Celestia wore new flannel shirts, jeans and tennis shoes. Joyce wore a new dress and sweater. All of them proudly carried bags containing their lunches, plus new pencils, tablets and crayons. They shared a hope that their teachers would all turn out to be nice.

When they walked into the fourth grade classroom, Celestia and Joyce saw the teacher standing in front of the black board. She was tall, boney, and stern-faced. Her gray hair was cut short as a boy's, and her dress was the same color as her hair. No one made a sound as the teacher wrote her name on the board: Mrs. Campbell.

Around the classroom, one could almost hear the collective groan. *Oh, no! Not Old Lady Campbell!* She had a reputation for having made the lives of successive classes of students miserable.

The teacher turned around, "Welcome to fourth grade. I'm Mrs. Campbell and you may call me Mrs. Campbell, regardless of any other names by which you've heard me called. If you obey all the rules, and work hard, we will have a satisfactory year."

The morning was spent doing reading, spelling and arithmetic tests, which would be used to put kids in high, average, or low groups. Celestia reluctantly filled in the blanks and dragged herself through the arithmetic problems, which hurt her brain. She wasn't worried about reading and spelling, but for arithmetic, if they had anything lower than low, she figured she'd be put in that group.

After lunch, things got better. Mrs. Campbell instructed the class to draw and color pictures, using their new crayons. They could choose to draw whatever they wanted.

Celestia happily set to work. The new crayons had a wonderful, waxy smell, and the tips were all perfect. She decided to draw the scene she loved best: Kenny Lake, on a hot day in summer. As the vision took shape in her mind, she began by drawing a large oval for the lake, and then a line between the lake and the sky. She colored the sky a perfect light blue, leaving white spaces for little puffy clouds, and a round spot for the sun. Then she turned the paper up-side-down, and copied the sky onto the lake, like a reflection in a mirror. She used regular blue for the lake, because the water was always darker than the sky. She turned the paper right side up and colored dark green trees on the far side of the lake, and their reflections on the water. All around the lake, and on the bottom of her picture, she made strokes of yellow, brown and orange for the reeds. With black, she drew tiny ducks swimming in the lake.

Mrs. Campbell didn't say anything about Celestia's picture the first time she passed by her desk, but she stopped to study it. When she came back a few minutes later, Celestia was coloring the sun in the sky, using bright yellow.

Mrs. Campbell said, rather brusquely, "Celestia, your picture looked good before you colored that sun. A real artist never draws a sun in the sky."

Lestie was crushed. This unexpected criticism made it clear that she wasn't a real artist. It didn't matter that Lestie had been regularly praised for her artistic abilities. No. An authority figure had spoken. It took two years before she regained her enthusiasm for Art.

HERO AND CULPRIT ON THE SAME DAY

It was later than usual when Lestie left for school, so she made up the time by running, until she got a stitch in her side.

She cut through an alley, and flew past the doors of some apartments. She stopped abruptly, when she saw a door open, and smoke coming out. A little girl with matted hair and a boy who looked just like her, were standing in the doorway, crying. They were wearing only their nightshirts.

"What's the matter?" Lestie asked.

The girl sobbed, "My brother lit the bed on fire!"

"Who else is in there?"

"Nobody," the little girl said.

"No parents? Babysitter?"

The girl shook her head.

"Wait here!" Lestie ran to knock on a neighboring door, but no one answered. She tore across the alley and pounded on another apartment door. A woman in a bathrobe, with her hair in curlers opened it.

"There's a fire! And some little kids over there, alone!"

The woman leaned out her door and caught sight of the smoke and the kids. "OK, I'll call the fire department. Guess you better bring them kids over here," she said, shutting the door.

Lestie ran and lifted the little boy, lugging him on her hip, with his sister following, barefoot, across the muddy alley. She set the boy down, and the woman stayed on the step with the children, listening for the fire truck.

Having done what she could, Lestie took off, knowing she'd be scolded by her teacher for being late. She practiced her excuse, "Sorry I'm late, but I was rescuing two little kids from a burning building..."

By the time she kicked off her muddy boots at the door, and slipped into her shoes, class had started. Mrs. Campbell stopped writing on the board, and everyone watched Celestia make her way to her desk.

Mrs. Campbell threw her a dark look, "There's no excuse for being tardy, young lady."

Celestia had the best excuse in the world, but Old Lady Campbell wouldn't give her a chance to use it! As she took out her arithmetic book, she thought of her Potato Philosophy, one tenet of which was that sometimes a potato looks bad on the outside and turns out to be bad all the way to the center. Celestia decided Mrs. Campbell was just such a potato, and the day had only begun.

The fourth grade classes were combined to listen to a policeman talk about bicycle safety. It was a little late in the year to be thinking about bicycles, but that's what he was going to talk about.

Extra desks were brought in, which filled the room to capacity. Celestia was seated in a desk almost directly behind the policeman. She was growing bored with the safety lecture, mostly because she didn't even have a bicycle, but she was very interested in the gun and holster the policeman was wearing on his hip. The gun had a shiny, wooden handle with a carved black insignia. Without touching the gun, she reached out her index finger and traced the interesting pattern in the air.

She looked up to see Mrs. Campbell motioning to her, "Come here!" Celestia got up and zigzagged her way among the crowded desks. Her teacher led her down the hallway.

"Mrs. Mellon saw you touching that policeman's gun!" Mrs. Campbell scolded. "You are in big trouble, young lady!"

Celestia was stunned; tears filled her eyes at being unjustly accused. Her teacher never listened to excuses. What was worse, Celestia was terrified of meeting "Harvey," the white rabbit painted on a large paddle, that the principal kept in his office. North Star School believed in corporal punishment.

Instead of sending her to the office, Mrs. Campbell made her stand against the wall in the hall, until school was out. Since it was the last hour of the day, she didn't have to stand there long, but when the bell rang, she left the school seething. "I hate Old Lady Campbell! I hate her!"

When Cler came home from work, he sat down on the couch and Lestie sat beside him.

"I hate my teacher," she said, trying to hold back the tears.

"Now why would you say that? Teachers deserve our respect." He put his arm around her and jiggled her shoulder, "Look how they put up with all you rowdy kids all day long!" He was trying to make her laugh, but she was too angry.

"She scolded me for nothing! I almost got a spanking, but she sent me out in the hall...I'll never go back to that school again, ever!"

Her dad interrupted her, "Lestie. Everyone makes mistakes, but everybody has *some* good in them. I want you to go back to school tomorrow and try to find at least *one good thing* about your teacher."

Celestia sighed, "OK, but it's going to be very, very hard."

T-6 Trainer

34

WHAT IS HEAVEN?

October 22, 1955

It was only a day after she'd vowed never to go back to school again, that Celestia was walking home, as usual, with her friend, Joyce. She'd been too busy slogging through worksheets that day, to notice anything good about her teacher, even though she'd promised to try. The girls balanced on the top of the crusty snow berm at the side of the road, in order to keep from walking in the road.

The air was cold and damp. Celestia looked up at the October sky, with its swirls of gray clouds, and said, "Something has happened to my Daddy."

At that moment, a white pickup pulled over ahead of them, and stopped. Celestia recognized Larry and Laura Straley. Charles and Paxton were sitting between them in the cab. Laura rolled down the side window and leaned out, "Hop in the back and we'll give you a ride home," she said.

At home, the driveway was filled with cars, and Larry parked the pickup along the road, where several other cars were already parked. The girls jumped down from the back of the truck.

Joyce said, "Tell me when you find out what happened to your dad. Maybe he broke his leg." She ran off toward her own house, as Laura put her arm around Celestia.

"Something has happened to your daddy," she said, and led her into the house.

The principal at Central Jr. High School stepped inside the open door of Corrie's eighth grade English classroom. He beckoned to the teacher, who stopped in midsentence, "So... excuse me, please." She met the principal out in the hall. A moment later, she called Corrie Lynne out.

"You need to go to your locker, and get your things, dear. A friend of your family is here to take you home."

Corrie was surprised to see Captain Otto, Cler's wing commander, standing by the Principal's door. She knew him, because she had babysat for him and his wife, Pat, and they lived next door. Captain Otto was a slender man of medium height, with pink cheeks and dark hair shaved to a crew cut. He was in uniform, carrying his hat.

"Your mother asked me to bring you home," he said. His face was grave, and Corrie felt a chill. As she walked with him out the double doors, he replaced his hat, carefully adjusting it on his head, with the golden eagle exactly front and center. He put his hand behind Corrie, as if to steady her, and they began to descend the wide, concrete steps together.

Captain Otto said, "Corrie, your father has been in an accident."

"Is he in the hospital?" she asked.

"No. He's dead."

He caught her arm as she stumbled.

When they reached the house, Corrie was still trying to wrap her mind around the news of her father's death. She clung to Dick's arm as he escorted her inside.

The house was full of people. Some she recognized, and some she didn't. She sought out her mother, who was sitting on the sofa beside Pat Otto. When Pat caught sight of Corrie, she stood up and Corrie took her place, burying her head on her mother's shoulder. "Oh, Mama! It's so awful…"

Gwynne didn't say anything, but she patted Corrie's back.

Corrie sat up, and saw her mother's face was pale and drawn; she looked exhausted.

"Are you all right, Mama?"

"I'm OK. I…"

"Captain Otto told me," Corrie said.

"That's good," Gwynne murmured. Corrie took up her mother's soft hand, with its lovely, long fingers and perfect, oval nails. It was icy cold, and felt insubstantial, like a handful of rose petals. Her mother seemed to be looking off across the room, her eyes not fully focused. Corrie waited for her to say something.

After a moment, Gwynne said, "Your dad and I were married in the temple… That means, we'll be together forever, so we don't have to be sad."

Corrie felt tears well up, but blinked them back. "We don't have to be sad," seemed the same as, "We must not cry," and so she didn't. But her heart was broken; she felt a pain inside so sharp she thought it would kill her.

With an ache around her heart, and gnawing pain in her stomach, Corrie left her mother and slipped into her room. She crawled into her unmade bed, and pulled the covers over her head.

Paxton and Charles filed into the house ahead of Laura, who had her arm around Lestie. Larry followed them in. When he spotted Scotty, he shook his hand, and the two friends moved to a corner, where they could talk. Paxton heard Larry say, "I was told his fuel line froze up."

There were people everywhere, with shocked, pale faces. Their eyes were brimming with tears; their noses red, from crying. Paxton was beginning to think something bad had happened.

Laura stopped Paxton, as he was headed into the dining room. "Just wait here a minute," she said. "Charles, you and Celestia stay here, too. I'll be right back."

Though Laura was petite, she had a take-charge attitude, and the children did as they were told. She came back with her arm around Gwynne. "Your mother needs to talk to you in her bedroom," she said, patting Gwynne on the shoulder. She left her with her children.

They followed their mother into her room, where the curtains were closed, leaving the room in semi-darkness. The children crawled to the middle of the soft bed, while Gwynne sat down heavily on the edge.

"Your Daddy's plane crashed this morning," she said.

"Did he get hurt?" Paxton asked.

"Yes."

Gwynne was staring at the quilt on her bed; at the patterns she could just make out in the dim light. She smoothed her hand over a piece called "Texas star." Without looking up, she said, "He died, but he's up in Heaven, with Heavenly Father." She said it all in the emotionless way she'd say, "I'm going to the store. I'll be back in a few minutes."

Paxton just stared at her.

Charles asked, "What is Heaven?" But got no answer. He noticed his little brother, Butchy, asleep in the crib. "Did you tell Butchy?" he asked.

Gwynne shook her head, "He wouldn't understand."

Charles was puzzled. He didn't understand, either.

Lestie felt her whole body going numb. She didn't ask any questions, because she didn't want any answers.

Gwynne eased herself off the bed and shuffled out of her bedroom, as if she were sleepwalking. When she reached the table, she sat down on one of the chairs. Someone had left today's paper on the table. Idly she turned it over, and her eyes rested on the bottom of the front page.

"PILOT, FATHER OF FOUR, SOLDIER OBSERVER DIE NEAR EAGLE RIVER." It seemed like someone else reading those headlines. "Gwynne" was curled up in the corner of her mind, watching things happen, while some other woman was going through the motions, passively doing what other people told her to do.

She folded the newspaper and pushed it to the middle of the table. She'd read it some other day. This morning Bob Kafader had told her about the accident: Cler was talking on the radio one moment and the next moment witnesses heard his engine quit and saw his plane drop from the sky and crash into the trees. Bob said he was sure the T-6's fuel line had frozen up. He took her to see Cler's body, and it didn't look anything like him. There was no way she was going to allow an open casket. No, she didn't need to read the article in the paper; she already knew more than she wanted to.

The phone rang, and Laura answered it. After she hung up, she told Gwynne, "They're coming in an hour to pick up your foster son, Howard. They want you to have some clothes ready, to take with him."

"All right."

Laura touched Gwynne's shoulder, "She said to tell you how sorry they are, and then she mentioned the rule that foster homes have to have two parents."

When Gwynne didn't respond, Laura said, "It's probably for the best. You have enough to cope with, Honey. Where can I find Butchy's clothes? By his crib?"

Gwynne nodded, "In the trunk."

In the bedroom, Laura flicked on the light, and saw the three Oborn children still sitting on their parents' bed. "Oh! Excuse me, I just have to get some things," she said. Butchy was asleep in the crib. Trying to be quiet, she rummaged in the trunk, gathering a sack full of little shirts, pants, pajamas and underclothes. She left the room, flipping off the light again.

Gwynne remained at the table, staring at the folded newspaper. Pat Otto brought her a small plate with fruit, a half sandwich and a cookie on it. "You need to eat something, Gwynne."

"I can't."

Pat set the plate on the table. "Let me make you a nice cup of tea, then."

When a steaming cup of tea appeared in front of her, Gwynne stirred it and sipped a little from the spoon. Her throat felt as if a rope were tied around her neck, and she could barely swallow. Even so, she was thirsty. Slowly, she sipped the tea until the cup was empty.

From the table, she could see most of the front room, and the anguished faces of her friends, who had all had a shock, as she had. In the room were three other pilots in Cler's squadron: Dick Otto, Blinn Webster, and Bob Kafader.

Bob was in the corner talking to Scotty and Larry. Pat Otto was sitting on the sofa with her head on Dick's shoulder; they both had tears streaming down their faces. Beside them, Blinn sat with his head in his hands; his wife Roberta was lightly making circles on his back with her fingers, trying to comfort him. It could have been any one of these men who had crashed that day, and they all knew it.

In the bedroom, the three children waited in the semi-darkness for something; they didn't know what.

Finally, Lestie asked, "Where's Corrie?"

"I don't know," Paxton said.

Butchy stirred and saw Celestia. He stood up in his crib and called to her, "Out, Nonny!"

She slid off the bed and lifted him out of the crib. "You need to go potty," she said, taking him by the hand.

"Potty," Butchy repeated, as she led him to the bathroom.

Passing through the house, she felt sadness like heavy smoke filling every room. She washed Butchy's hands and settled him at the table, securing him to the chair with a dishtowel tied around his waist. She gave him the plate of food left sitting there, untouched. Gwynne was in the front room now, talking to Laura.

After Corrie woke up, she avoided talking to anybody, and fled into the kitchen, where she was surprised to see an abundance of food in the refrigerator, and sitting on the cupboard. Her stomach hurt, and she didn't really want to eat anything, but knew she should. A few weeks ago, Dr. Johnson had said she had an ulcer. He also said she was too thin, and had to eat more. The remedy for her ulcer was a cup of warm water and a half teaspoon of baking soda, but she hated the taste of it. She fixed herself a cup, and stirred it until the soda dissolved.

At the table, she dropped onto a chair and noticed the newspaper. "PILOT, FATHER OF FOUR..." For a moment, she wasn't sure it was about her father. But it was. These were details she hadn't been told, and she wanted to know. She sipped her soda water as she read.

"An Alaska Air National Guard pilot and his soldier flight observer were killed this morning when their small, two place plane crashed into a wooded area near Eagle River. The pilot is identified as 1st Lt. Clermont A Oborn, 33, of Fireweed Lane, Spenard, married and the father of four. The name of the staff sergeant accompanying him was withheld by authorities at Fort Richardson, where he was stationed.

"The men's bodies were found in the demolished T-6 plane of the 144th Fighter Interceptor Squadron shortly after 7 a.m. by Army Capt. Charles J. Lewis of Fort Richardson, who was also flying the support mission in an H13 helicopter.

"Capt Lewis picked up the soldier's body and flew to Elmendorf Air Force Base where he picked up a paramedic and returned to the crash scene to extricate the body of Oborn. However, a ground party headed by ANC (Alaska Air National Guard) Lt. Maurice J. Dewulf, liaison officer between the Guard and the Army, had reached the crash scene by foot by the time the helicopter returned.

"Guard authorities said the pair was apparently killed instantly. The cause of the crash could not be immediately

470

determined. No witnesses to the mishap could be located, authorities said.

"Captain Lewis saw the wreckage while flying over the area about two miles from Eagle River in the Watchtower Hill area.

"The ANG plane was taking part as a spotter aircraft in a support mission during maneuvers carried out by the 53rd Infantry Regiment at Fort Richardson. The T-6 is a two cockpit plane used extensively as an observer craft during World War II.

"Lt. Oborn, a full-time ANG flier, homesteaded here in 1947. Fellow officers went to his home to notify his wife, Gwen [sic], two hours after the crash.

"Today's crash is the first fatal mishap of the guard squadron since Lt. Albert Kulis lost his life last November in the Anchorage area. The ANG field was named in memory of Kulis."

By the time Corrie finished reading, Paxton had come to sit beside her, at the table.

"What'cha reading?"

"It's about Daddy," she said. "You can read it, but I wouldn't recommend it. Also, they spelled Mama's name wrong."

She said it as if a spelling error meant the rest of the article couldn't be accurate. But she knew the worst part, at least, was true. She closed her eyes and remembered her father saying, "Awful things happen. All we can do is try to focus on something good."As it turned out, the newspaper was missing two important facts: there were witnesses who saw the plane go down, and the cause was, indeed, a frozen fuel line.

Butchy was still tied to the kitchen chair beside her. He had reduced his food to crumbs and was eating one crumb at a time. She leaned over and kissed him. "Hey sweetie, would you like another cookie?"

"Cookie," he said, his little blue eyes lighting up. Butchy was definitely "something good." While he was breaking up the cookie, Corrie recited a verse to him, "Little Jack Horner sat in a corner eating his Christmas pie. He stuck in his thumb and pulled out a plum and said, "What a good boy am I!"

471

Paxton was almost twelve years old, and like his sister, was an avid reader. He was just as curious as Corrie, so he sat there and read the article in the paper. "An Alaska Air National Guard pilot…"

After reading the article, Paxton left the paper on the table, and walked outside. He looked up at the overcast October sky. It was cold out there, and getting dark, and he didn't have a coat on, but he didn't care. He thought maybe freezing to death would be a good and painless way to die. You just got sleepy and then you never woke up.

He stood in the snow, in his tennis shoes, letting the snow melt and seep through his socks. After a while, Paxton said to himself, "I am my father's right hand man. I have to be the man of the family now." He returned to the house and took off his soaking wet shoes and socks. As he put on dry socks, he tried to decide what he should do, as the man of the family, but he didn't know where to start. Maybe once all these people were gone, he'd come up with a plan.

A few minutes later, two women from the Welfare Agency knocked on the door. Paxton opened it.

"We've come to pick up Howard," one of them said, and Paxton stepped aside, wondering where they were taking him, and for how long.

Laura went to find Gwynne, who was lying down. "Two ladies are here from the Welfare," she said.

Gwynne hastily got up off the bed, and Laura handed her the bag of Butchy's clothing. Gwynne added a little truck, and the alarm clock he liked, and brought out the bag, handing it to one of the Welfare women.

Corrie stood in the dining room, holding Butchy's hand.

The Welfare lady leaned over the small, blue-eyed child, with his badly scared face. "Will you come and go with me?" she asked. Butchy pulled back, and tried to hide behind Corrie. He wouldn't let go of her hand, and with the other little fist he grabbed hold of her skirt and clung to it.

The woman said, firmly, "Howard, come along!"

472

Corrie unlatched his thin, vice-like fingers, and gave him to the woman, who took hold of his wrist and led him toward the door. The other woman picked up the bag of clothing.

"Where's he going, Corrie?" Charles asked.

"I'm not sure," she said, "I think they're just trying to help Mama, by keeping him for a while."

Lestie took it as an insult. "We can take care of him just fine!"

Charles and Lestie followed them outside, and the Welfare lady shut Butchy in the car. He rolled the window down, just as Corrie came running out with a box of miniature donuts. With his thin little arms waving out the window, he cried, "Out!"

Corrie handed him a donut. "It's OK, Butchy," she told him, trying to summon some enthusiasm, "You're going for a ride!"

One of the women reached behind the seat and rolled up the window.

"Goodbye, goodbye!" the children called to their little brother. They didn't know the authorities were going to send him to an institution in Oregon, called Sunnyside, and it would be seven years before his family was able to reconnect with him.

Gwynne's friends decided she'd be able to cope better if she didn't have to worry about her children, at least for one night. Larry and Laura took Paxton and Charles home with them, and Celestia went to stay with Uncle John and Aunt Ethel. Corrie stayed home with her mother.

When everyone had gone, Gwynne was sitting listlessly at the table and Corrie bent over her. "Mama, do you want something to eat? There's a lot of food in there."

"I'm not hungry, but can you put the tea kettle on? Maybe I can drink a cup of tea."

"Sure," Corrie said, rising.

It was late when Gwynne slipped into her nightgown, trying to summon the courage to go to bed; she needed to get some sleep. Tomorrow, she had to meet with the Personnel office out at Kulis. There were so many things she had to take care of, but she couldn't think straight. When she talked to Mother

Oborn, to tell her about Cler's accident, it was like talking to a stranger. Cler's mother insisted that her son be buried in Utah, "Where he belonged." Gwynne had agreed, and left it in the hands of Cler's parents and siblings to make arrangements down in Ogden, with the mortuary that had handled Oborn business for who knows how long. Gwynne sank down onto the side of her bed, feeling as if all the blood had been drained out of her body. Her limbs were heavy; her brain felt numb.

She could see a light on in Corrie Lynne's room, and knew she was still up. "Corrie Lynne? Can you come here?"

When she heard her mother call, Corrie closed the book, "Little Women," and laid it on the bedside table. She'd been engrossed in the budding romance between Laurie and Jo, the heroine of the book. For a few minutes, it had taken her mind off today's awful events. She sighed as she threw back the quilt and rolled out of bed.

Her mother was sitting on the side of the bed, in her blue cotton gown. Her feet were bare on the wood floor; they looked red from cold.

"You should get under the covers, Mama. You must be cold. Do you need anything?" Corrie asked.

"Will you sleep with me tonight?" her mother asked.

"Yes, if you want me to."

Gwynne swung her feet onto the bed, and Corrie covered her up, fluffing the pillow under her head. Her mother let out a long sigh, and cleared her throat, settling into the pillow.

"Can you get those pills in there on the kitchen cabinet? Dr. Johnson prescribed them for me, in case I have trouble sleeping."

Corrie brought the pills, and Gwynne took one, handing her back the bottle, and the half-empty water glass. Corrie set them on the dresser, side-stepped the narrow space between the wall and bed, and crawled under the covers. Her mother reached over and patted her hand.

"My sweet Corrie Lynne," she said.

At Uncle John's house, Lestie was also up late. She and her cousin, Mike, were in the kitchen, enjoying little cups of half orange and half vanilla ice cream. He was thirteen, but he didn't treat her like she was just some little girl he was stuck with entertaining; he seemed to genuinely enjoy her company.

"This is good! I've never had this before," Lestie said, licking the tiny wooden spoon.

"You can have all you want," Mike grinned, "We have a whole bag of them in the freezer."

She finished one and then another. It was like eating ice cream in doll dishes and it made her smile.

Uncle John strode into the kitchen. "How are you kids getting along?" he asked.

"Great!" Mike said.

Lestie looked up, craning her neck to see her uncle. "I love this orange ice cream!"

"Ice cream is good for little girls," Uncle John said. "Maybe I'll have some myself!" He opened the freezer and took out another cup.

While they were eating, Lestie glanced at the back of her hand, and remembered the day Uncle John had come to the cabin in Kenny Lake. She asked, "Do you remember when you bought my warts?"

John looked blank for a moment, so she showed him her hand and then her elbow. "You gave me a quarter for this one, and a quarter for this one. They both disappeared, right after you bought them! That was a pretty slick trick!"

Her uncle grinned, "Well, how about that?" He patted her head. Just like Daddy often did. Suddenly, she felt weak with sadness, but she didn't let herself cry.

That night, she had a dream. Her father was coming through the door, wearing his blue uniform. She ran and hugged him, and he smelled fresh and cool, like the outdoors. "Oh, Daddy!" she cried, "They told me you were dead, but you aren't dead!" She woke up with the feeling of his arms still around her, and the smell of his uniform in her nostrils.

The next afternoon, Uncle John took her home, where her mother and Corrie were. The boys came home later that afternoon. By this time, the question of Cler's funeral was settled. "We'll be flying to Utah," Gwynne told her children. "Next Saturday, not this week, but next, your dad's funeral is going to be held there."

Celestia knew next to nothing about funerals, but she remembered the funeral for Jerusha, the duck. A song, nice words about the one who died. Maybe she could say something about her father.

Over the next few days, friends tried to help Gwynne, but she needed more guidance than she got. For instance, Scotty and Larry said they'd take care of the airplane (the Luscombe 8 that they owned with Cler) and get it fixed. They later deeded their shares over to Gwynne. The plane was a valuable asset, but she saw it as a burden and painful reminder of Cler, and ended up selling it for much less than it was worth.

There were other things, like the assets at Kenny Lake, that required Gwynne to make decisions she didn't want to make on her own. She had depended on Cler for so long that without him she felt like a rudderless boat in a storm. She called Hal Waugh and asked him to take care of the gas station and to sell the assets like the sawmill, tractor, and dump truck. She just couldn't deal with it all.

On Saturday Gwynne took her four children to Montgomery Ward, the department store. The manager wanted to outfit the children with new clothes for the funeral, at no charge. Corrie and Celestia tried on and selected wool coats, shoes, dresses and sweaters. They also chose underwear, socks, slips and pajamas. Meanwhile, the boys were outfitted with Sunday shirts and pants, coats, and shoes, as well as socks and underwear. For the children, it was better than Christmas.

Monday arrived and the family packed their bags and headed to Elmendorf. The plane they were taking was a military transport. Inside the hanger, the family gathered, with Uncle John and Larry and Laura seeing them off. The children all wore their

476

new coats, and the girls wore dresses. Their hair was brushed and shiny, and they looked like they were headed for Sunday School. Gwynne gave Celestia a little hug and straightened her coat collar.

An Air Force officer led Gwynne and her four children across the tarmac, toward the military aircraft parked on the runway. The plane seemed massive, with four engines and a rounded body. Single file, the little family climbed the portable stairway and stepped through the open door of the cargo plane.

"Hello, Gwynne," an Air Force officer greeted her. "I'm Lieutenant Hobbs. I'll be the guy flying this box car down to Utah. If you need anything, my Sergeant over there will be more than happy to help you. The engine noise will be loud, I'm sorry to tell you; this plane isn't pressurized, but it'll get us there."

Inside, the plane was like a cavernous cylinder of cold metal, with its bare ribs apparent, and wide straps of webbing covering the walls and ceiling. The floor was a raised metal walkway; they followed it to seats set singly by small windows and each member of the family chose a seat. Boxes of freight filled part of the space, held in place with more nylon webbing. Behind a curtain, there was more freight. The children didn't know that one of those large boxes contained the casket with their father's body.

Celestia sat down on a seat by a window and the soldier strapped her in. She looked out and saw a woman hurry out of the terminal building and stop on the tarmac, staring at the plane. The engines started with a roar and the propellers blew the woman's yellow scarf off her head, but it stayed tied around her neck. Her short gray hair ruffled in the wind. It was Mrs. Campbell!

The teacher spotted Celestia's face at the window and their eyes met. The woman waved cheerfully, and Celestia waved back. As the plane taxied away, her teacher stood there in the wind, still waving. Mrs. Campbell had come to say goodbye. For a moment, tears filled Lestie's eyes; she was touched by this small kindness. She remembered she was supposed to find one good thing about her teacher. Now she'd found something. In potato philosophy, Celestia would say Mrs. Campbell was like a potato with a few black spots, but after you peeled them off, she still had some good potato left.

First Lieutenant Clermont Oborn

LOVE NEVER ENDS

They arrived in Utah and spent the week with cousins and grandparents. On Saturday, October 31st, the funeral of Clermont Arave Oborn was held in an old stone church, where Cler had gone to Sunday School as a boy. The family was seated in the front section of the chapel. There was a congregational hymn, "I Stand All Amazed," which Lestie had heard in church. "I stand all amazed at the love Jesus offers me..." She didn't sing, because she didn't feel like it, but she listened. Then Uncle Frank said a prayer, and there was another song. Lestie sat up straight on the bench, listening as she recognized the opening chords of one of Daddy's favorites. In a mellow voice, a dark-haired man sang, "I come to the garden alone, when the dew is still on the roses, and the voice I hear, falling on my ear, the son of God discloses. And he walks with me and he talks with me, and he tells me I am His own. And the joy we share as we tarry there, none other has ever known." (In the Garden, by C. Austin Miles) It was a beautiful song; one Cler's children remembered him singing in the cabin at Kenny Lake.

Sitting on the front row between her mother and Grandmother, Lestie's attention wandered as several people spoke. She focused, instead, on the long box in front of her and the flag that covered it. She followed the stripes with her eyes. They were sewn together with a double row of red thread. At one end, there was a rectangle of blue, with perfectly shaped white stars sewn onto it. She couldn't see them all, but she knew there were forty-eight stars. It did not occur to her that there was anything inside the flag-draped box.

Uncle Bill caught her attention when he started telling stories about his brother. Bill said Cler was smart and funny, and everyone's friend. "He was fearless. When Cler was twelve years old, he rode his bicycle across the water pipe that spans Ogden canyon. He nearly gave our mother a heart attack when she found out!" There were chuckles and a few gasps in response to the story.

Bill said, "My brother was a man of many talents. He had a beautiful baritone voice, and we loved to harmonize when we were growing up. He had a mind like a steel trap, and he remembered everything he ever read. If he didn't know how to do something, he read up on it."

When Uncle Bill finished, Lestie tuned out the rest of the program. Everyone was talking about her father as if he were gone. It began to dawn on her that maybe he was, and he wasn't coming back. She didn't want to be here. She didn't want to listen to these people. She fidgeted and yawned. Her mother handed her a lace-edged handkerchief, whispering, "Cover your mouth when you yawn."

Finally, the Bishop announced, "Cler will be buried with full military honors in the Ogden Cemetery. He will be laid to rest in the family plot, where his and Gwynne's ancestors are buried."

The organ began to play. Uniformed soldiers lifted the casket, three on a side, and carried it down the aisle, and out the door. First Gwynne and her children followed after it, and row by row emptied behind them, as other family joined in filing out the door, into the late autumn sunshine.

When the sunlight struck her face, Lestie looked up into the blue sky, into its vast emptiness. She closed her eyes for a moment, and let the sunlight warm her, but she was caught in a stream of mourners, and there could be no stopping. She followed her mother to a long, black car, big enough for the whole family, plus Grandma and Grandpa Oborn.

Lestie and Charles huddled together, watching out a side window, as they drove past giant trees nearly bare of leaves. The trees had great, gnarled trunks and thick branches reaching their fingers in all directions, even hanging over the streets. The children didn't realize they were in a parade of cars . They turned into the cemetery, and followed a narrow road through the lawns scattered with grave stones.

When all the cars had parked along the edge of the grass, the passengers spilled out and spread across the lawn, toward the place where a row of airmen in dress blues stood at attention and the flag-draped casket waited.

When the people were seated, Ernest Oborn, with trembling voice, dedicated his son's grave, with a blessing that Cler would "rise on the morning of the first Resurrection."

To Lestie, it seemed to be a good word, "rise," as if her daddy would wake up. "Rise and shine!" he used to call out in the morning, to wake his children. Or he played reveille on the piano, singing, "You can't get 'em up, you can't get 'em up, you can't get 'em up in the moooorn-ing!" *Rise and shine. Morning of the Resurrection.* Words to remember.

480

The airmen formed into a straight, perfect line of blue and white uniforms, and pink, solemn, faces. One called the orders, as seven airmen shouldered their rifles and aimed high over the cemetery. All at the same time, the shots rang out, followed by a long beat of silence, then again they fired. Another beat. They fired again.

Paxton leaned over to Lestie, while the echo was still dying away. "That was a twenty-one gun salute."

Afterwards, two soldiers reverently lifted the flag that lay on Cler's casket and folded it carefully into a long strip and then into a neat triangle. They stepped reverently over to Gwynne, who was seated on a chair, and stood at attention. They saluted her smartly, and handed her the folded flag.

A soldier lifted his bugle and played a tune Cler used to sing, while he played each solemn note on the piano. It had echoed through the cabin, as it now echoed through the cemetery, rebounding off the nearby mountainside. "Day is done. Gone the sun. From the hills, from the lake, from the sky. All is well, safely rest, God is nigh."

After the funeral, Aunt Ella pulled Lestie into a warm, soft hug. "People who love you are never lost. They will always love you," she said.

Later, after dinner at Ella's house, Lestie was playing quietly in a back hall, with a wonderful doll house that belonged to her cousin, Susan. The grown-ups were talking nearby, in the kitchen. "It's Halloween," Ella said, "and the children want to go trick- or-treating."

Grandma Oborn exclaimed, "Oh, Ella. That's just not right! It's the day of Cler's funeral!"

Aunt Ella said, "What do you want them to do? Sit around and mourn? I think it would be good for them to get out of the house."

Susan and her brother, David, donned costumes. Susan was a fairy, in a blue satin dress and shiny silver mask. David was a pirate, dressed in boots and a cape. The Oborn kids had only been trick-or-treating once in their life. They remembered wading through deep snow to reach a few houses and trailers. That time, no one wore costumes and they didn't get many treats.

It seemed now that Aunt Ella had won the discussion with Grandma. She cut masks for Paxton, Celestia and Charles, from green and white checked cloth, and attached a strip of elastic to go around their heads. They put on their coats and masks, and Susan and David also donned coats over their costumes. It was chilly, but not too cold outside. Each carrying a small sack, they filed out the door into the twilight. Porch lights glowed everywhere they went, and on the broad porches there were corn stalks and pumpkins carved into glowing jack-o-lanterns. There were ghosts made of sheets hanging from some porches, and some houses had paper cut-outs of black cats in the windows. This was like Halloween in a story book. It was something the Oborn children had never imagined.

The treats were even better than the decorations. At one house, there were plates stacked with homemade donuts, warm and oily, covered in crystals of sugar. The children ate the donuts and licked the sugar off their fingers. One woman even gave them apple cider in glasses and they drank it as they stood on her lighted porch.

While they giggled and ran through the darkness in their masks, the children were caught up in the magic of a Halloween that they never forgot, at the end of a day full of sadness and ritual that they had not been able to fully comprehend.

A few weeks passed. Gwynne and her three youngest children stayed with Cler's parents, and were enrolled in school. They had only to walk a few blocks to Roosevelt Elementary, the tall stone building Celestia and Paxton had briefly attended three years earlier.

Corrie Lynne was living with Gwynne's parents, Henrietta and Charles Paxton. She was in eighth grade, and Cheryl was in ninth, though they didn't go to the same school. When they crawled into their twin beds, in the gable room, they talked about events happening at school, or what classes they were taking.

When Corrie admitted feeling sad, Cheryl said, "It doesn't help to talk about sad things; it only makes you sadder." But Cheryl, in spite of all her bravado, shared Corrie's grief. She had loved Cler, too. Still, they were teenage girls, and as time passed, they discovered a host of interesting activities, including school dances and boys.

The other children accepted living with their grandparents. The boys slept in the basement, on cots set up in one corner. They hung their clothes on a galvanized pipe that ran along one wall. Celestia slept with her mother in the guest room off the living room. It wasn't home, but Grandma cooked nice meals and Grandpa often played the piano after he got home from his work at Utah Power and Light. He was a classic pianist, and he played Chopin, Beethoven and Liszt. He was also a professional at the organ, and on Sundays, he was paid to play the organ for the big Congregational Church.

The children loved to hear their grandfather play, especially waltzes like the Blue Danube, and sometimes Celestia and Charles grabbed hold of hands and danced around the small living room, trying to avoid tripping over the footstool.

Gwynne still felt like she was walking around in a fog. She let other people tell her what to do, whether it was going to lunch with her mother, attending church with Mother Oborn, or any of a number of other activities that filled her days.

One day in December Gwynne was visiting her parents. Her mother was in the kitchen fixing dinner, while Gwynne and her father sat in the living room, in adjacent chairs, talking.

"I know you want to get your family back together as soon as possible, Kitten," her dad said, patting her hand on the arm of the chair. "I think I can help you buy a little house on Adams. The man who owns it took a job in California, and his renters are moving out. The Realtor says he'd be willing to sell it for a bargain price. What do you think?"

Gwynne said, "I guess I can put my place on Fireweed Lane up for sale, and get a job here. Mother and Dad Oborn want me to stay here, too, but I'm just not sure what to do."

Her father sat forward in his chair, resting his elbows on his knees, clasping his hands. He stared at the floor. "I haven't been the best father to you, Gwynne; you and I both know that, but I've always loved you. Seems like life would be easier for you if you stayed here, and had a little help raising the kids, but it's your call. You should do what's best for you and the kids."

Gwynne kissed her father's cheek, rough with gray stubble. "Thank you, Daddy. I guess the first thing to do is look at the house on Adams. When can we go see it?"

The next week the lady Realtor took Gwynne to see the house. It was a neat, Craftsman-style house made of brown brick with white trim. It had a roomy porch with square pillars. When she followed the Realtor into the front room, she saw worn oak floors, and an archway into the dining room. The kitchen was sunny, with a window over the sink. She always liked a window over the sink. In the house on Fireweed Lane, she had been glad just to have a sink! I'm getting spoiled, she thought wryly. In this house there were three bedrooms, a screened back porch, and a plum tree in the back yard.

"I like it," Gwynne said. "This a nice house." She told the Realtor that she needed to talk to her dad, before she put a deposit down.

As the Realtor drove her back to her in-laws, Gwynne thought, with a touch of rebelliousness, *I'm back in Civilization. Why can't I just stay here?*

Later, she was sitting alone on the Oborn's back porch swing, bundled in her winter coat, hat and gloves, watching small, brown birds flitting in and out of the bare branches of an old apple tree. The winter sun warmed her face, but inside her there was a deep sadness and emptiness that a bit of sunlight couldn't heal. She thought that if she got settled here, she'd feel better, but she was uneasy about making any kind of permanent decision. If only Cler could tell her what to do. "Oh, darling, I miss you!" she whispered. "What shall I do? Shall I stay here?" All she heard was the chirping of the little birds, and a car passing on the street in front of the house.

She thought about buying the house over Thanksgiving, and into December, but she couldn't bring herself to do it. She talked to her parents and in-laws and of course, everyone thought she should stay in Ogden. Their arguments seemed sound. She had family here, who cared about her. She could depend on them for help if she needed it. To Gwynne, Ogden represented Civilization, with all its conveniences and niceties. She began to feel more at home. It occurred to her that she had come full circle: from Utah to Alaska and back. This little town with its tree-lined streets and neat houses was the place where she and Cler were born and raised, and this is where she fell in love with him. They had three babies here. They'd gone to Alaska, but now she was back.

In an attempt to finally make a decision, Gwynne put earnest money down on the brown brick house, but there was still a way out. The agreement rested on her obtaining financing. She gathered her children and took them to see the house. They walked from room to room, exploring, and they liked it. "Do we get to live in this house?" Charles asked.

"Sure we do!" Paxton said, and Gwynne thought to herself, *yes*, but she really wasn't as sold on it as Paxton.

Christmas came and of course, the grandparents spoiled the children with presents and treats. After New Year, Gwynne and her father arranged for her to move into the brick house, and rent it until the house in Alaska sold.

Corrie spent Christmas vacation with her family at Grandma Oborn's house, and slept with her mother in the guest room just off the living room. This meant Lestie had to sleep on a cot in the basement, but Lestie was glad to see her sister.

Corrie had missed her siblings and her mother, and felt happy to think that soon they'd all be together again in their own house. Her mother still seemed to be having a hard time, though. More than once she had expressed the same desire, "I just wish I could talk to your dad," she'd say.

The night after Christmas, Corrie was reading in bed, while her mother was sitting at the dressing table nearby, undoing her braids.

As Gwynne sat in front of the oval mirror, she took each section in turn and brushed it , then picked up the next section. The only sound in the room was the soft sigh of bristles moving through thick strands of hair, and the occasional turn of a page in Corrie's book.

As Gwynne was sitting there, she heard a voice. It wasn't loud, but it was clear, and it sounded like Cler. "Take the children back to Alaska and raise them there."

For a moment, Gwynne froze with the hairbrush in her hand. The sound of Cler's voice echoed in her mind. "Take the children back to Alaska." She laid down the brush and closed her eyes. Tears filled behind her eyelids, and trickled down her cheeks. When she opened her eyes again, it was as if the sun had broken through the clouds. Suddenly it was clear exactly what she should do.

"Corrie Lynne!" Gwynne stood and crossed the room, smiling. Corrie looked up from her book and saw her mother's face glowing as if lit from within. "I know what I have to do," she said, sitting on the edge of the bed.

"What?" Corrie asked, wondering what her mother meant. What did she have to do?

Gwynne looked relieved and happy, as if a load had been taken off. "We have to go back to Alaska."

Corrie was still puzzled. "I like Alaska, Mama, but how do you know we're supposed to go back? What about the brick house? You put money on it. Why can't we stay here?"

"I'm not sure why, but I'm more sure about this than I've been about anything since your dad died, Corrie. I heard him! Just a few minutes ago. I heard Cler's voice. He told me to take you children back to Alaska and raise you there." Her voice broke. "I had every intention of staying here, but now..."

Corrie closed her book and reached for her mother's hand. "Oh, Mama..."

486

Gwynne said, "Don't worry, I know I have to make some arrangements. You're right about the house. I hope I can get back my earnest money, but at least I know what I'm doing now."

A feeling of peace warmed Corrie's heart as she realized her father really wasn't so far away. She hadn't heard his voice, but she felt certain he was near, and that he cared about her life. She had felt all along that she belonged in Alaska, and now she was certain. Her dad knew what was best, and she would happily go back.

Gwynne and Corrie knelt by the bed and each said her own silent prayer.

As she was curled in bed, with the pillow fluffed under her head, Gwynne felt her heart burn as she thought about her decision to return to Alaska. It was the children's future that mattered most. She had no idea what lay ahead for her, but at least she would be where she was supposed to be.

All the struggle and sacrifice, the dream of building a life together in Alaska; the plans that she and Cler made together, could not end this way. Her children were not destined to become city kids, spoiled by well-meaning relatives. They were Alaskans, and they deserved to grow up in Alaska! It was the least she could do for them, and it was what she and Cler had intended all along.

THE END

EPILOGUE

Gwynne left her children with their grandparents for the remainder of the school year, not wanting to disrupt their schooling again. She also felt she needed time to adjust to her changed circumstances. With the earnest money in hand, she returned to Anchorage, and the house on Fireweed Lane. Being January, Alaska was in the throes of winter and the pipes and water pump under the house had frozen. She was somewhat dismayed, but she dealt with it. She knew she'd come back where she belonged. Friends helped her replace the pump, and get the house ready to live in again.

Tecane had been staying with a family in the branch. When Gwynne was home again, she picked up the dog, and he kept her company through the rest of that winter, until the children came home. While Gwynne was alone, the big collie-husky made it his job to take care of her. One evening a man she didn't know well came to the house after having had a few drinks. When he got a little too friendly with Gwynne, Tecane jumped between them on the couch and growled. The man quickly said his goodbyes. After that, Gwynne always felt safe, knowing Tecane was there as her personal guardian.

Within a few days after Gwynne was back in Alaska, she was hired to work as a secretary in the Personnel office on Kulis Air National Guard Base, and she soon rose to Personnel Manager.

Over the winter, she was able to process the loss of Cler, as she was drawn lovingly into the small circle of pilots and their wives, and others who were part of the Guard at Kulis. She and the other widows of pilots became a sort of sisterhood, supporting and aiding each other.**(see end note) She also found brothers and sisters in her church, and solace in her faith.

The Oborn children returned home in the spring and found their mother well and seemingly happy. Gwynne coped with her role as both mother and father by slipping some of the responsibility of mother onto Corrie Lynne, who rose to the

488

occasion, because she was used to it. It was Corrie who cooked dinner, bandaged cuts, supervised homework and sometimes even let her siblings put their frost-bitten feet or hands on her bare stomach to thaw them out.

After working at the Air Guard, Gwynne became an insurance adjuster, took public speaking, and blossomed in many ways, but "blue days" and headaches always troubled her. Seven years after Cler's death, she married a good man twenty years her senior. She was thirty-eight and he was fifty-nine. His name was Eugene Johnson, and he was the father of the family's long-time doctor, Cal Johnson. Gene was active in the LDS Alaska Stake, and he drew Gwynne into full activity, and deeply influenced the spiritual lives of the Oborn children. His insight and compassion helped Gwynne manage her health challenges.

Corrie, Paxton, Celestia and Charles all grew to love Gene. He was the stability they needed in their lives. He was instrumental in helping Paxton go on an LDS mission to England, when he was nineteen. Gene paid for Corrie to attend Stanford University, and later helped Celestia's husband, Van, go to Law School. He mentored Charles in business. Gene bought a sign company, which became a family business that involved Gwynne as bookkeeper as well as Charles and Paxton, who learned the skills necessary to make it into a thriving operation.

Shortly after Gwynne and Gene were married, they made a trip to Oregon, to find Butchy, who was by then, fifteen. They located him in the same institution where he'd been put when Cler died. He was only a little larger version of the boy Gwynne had known, with the same engaging smile and mischievous, blue eyes. He had the same unsteady gait, and more scars on his face from falling, his caretakers said. They called him "Howard."

Gwynne and Gene took the boy for a walk on the grounds, each holding onto one of his hands. Gwynne said, "So, Butchy, do you like it here?"

Maybe it was because she used a name he hadn't heard for a long time, but it triggered a memory. He stopped and looked up at her with those blue eyes. "Home?" he asked. "Home?"

489

Her heart melted. She hugged him, and he hugged her back. "I'm your Mama, Butchy."

"Mama," he said. "Mama!"

Gwynne and Gene made arrangements to have Butchy moved back to Alaska, where there was a new facility in Valdez, built to care for handicapped individuals with Alaskan Native heritage. It was located on a beautiful spot, overlooking the water. Gwynne adopted him, and he was part of the Oborn family until he died, at age sixty-six. He was buried in Ogden, Utah, beside Gwynne and Cler.

Corrie Lynne went to Weber College and then on to Stanford, where she got a Master's degree in English. She met her husband, Gary Player there, and they later returned to make their home in Anchorage. They adopted two sisters who were half Eskimo, and then went on to have six other children. Later, they adopted a third. Gary, a geologist, worked for an oil company and participated in the construction of the Alaska Pipeline. One year, his base camp was only eight miles away from Kenny Lake, and for that year he moved his family onto the Homestead. With six young children in a trailer, Corrie Lynne got a taste of what her mother had experienced having small children in such an isolated and challenging environment as Kenny Lake. Corrie Lynne Player is a writer with a long history of publication in magazines and newspapers, and has published several books on parenting. Over the years, she and Gary fostered forty at-risk foster children. They now live in Cedar City, Utah.

Paxton served in the Air National Guard, and then married Sherry Hanke, a local Anchorage girl he met at church. He worked in the sign business and within a few years he and Charles owned the largest sign company in Alaska. He became a pilot, bought his own plane, and while taking hunters out, crash-landed on a sandbar in a remote river. He and those with him were rescued the next day, but he hung part of the wreckage of the plane in his sign business warehouse, he said "to remind him not to buy another plane." He and Sherry had seven girls, all born in Alaska, and adopted three boys. They have a host of grandchildren and live near some of their children in Palmer, Alaska, in the Matanuska Valley.

Celestia met her future husband, Van, when he came to Alaska with a busload of Boy Scouts from Idaho. She went to Weber College, married Van Whitehead, and graduated from BYU. She became a professional artist and writer. She and Van had twelve children, many of them born in Alaska, where the family lived for eight years. Van was a physicist and a lawyer. He was killed in a tractor accident in 1997. Celestia has now been widowed twice, and lives in Draper, Utah. At last count, she had 52 grandchildren and five great grandchildren. Her daughter, Polly, and her family live in Fairbanks, Alaska.

Charles joined the Army National Guard, and then worked and owned the sign company with Paxton. He married Arlene, whose Alaskan heritage included her mother, an Alaska Native and father, a Russian fisherman. Charles worked on his father-in-law's fishing boat whenever he could get a season away from the sign business. He and Arlene moved to the Seattle area, where Charles invented a unique system of water purification, which he made into a thriving business. He has six children and four grandchildren.

Gwynne divided the Homestead and gave each of her four children forty acres. For her children and grandchildren, Alaska and the Homestead at Kenny Lake remain a cherished part of the heritage Gwynne and Clermont left for their posterity. When Gwynne died at the age of 85, she had 109 grandchildren and 38 great grandchildren.

Corrie Lynne put her forty acres of the original Homestead into a family trust, in perpetuity. Any descendant of Cler and Gwynne Oborn is welcome to visit and camp there, to feast on the natural wonders that surround that incredibly beautiful place.

**(Six months after Clermont Oborn's accident, his friend, Capt. Blinn Webster died following a mid-air collision with an Air Force trainer. In February 1957, Capt. Richard Otto, Cler's wing commander and friend, was killed in a crash, while participating in an Army National Guard training exercise north of Anchorage. His accident was eerily similar to Cler's.

In November of that same year, the Guard lost four men. Two veteran pilots-- Captain Robert Kafader (another friend of Cler and Gwynne's), and First Lieutenant Dennis Stamey, along with two staff sergeants, died when their transport plane crashed near Gustavus, in Southeast Alaska.

The tragic loss of five pilots within two years was not an anomaly in Alaska, which has always had disproportionately higher rates of crashes than elsewhere. Vast swaths of mountainous terrain, fiercely bad weather, and immense distances combine to down planes. As sophisticated forms of GPS and other technologies become available, allowing pilots to "see" hidden mountain peaks, other aircraft, and treacherous weather systems, flying in Alaska will hopefully become safer.)

ABOUT THE AUTHOR

Celestia Whitehead grew up in Alaska, first on a homestead at Kenny Lake, in the Copper River area, then in Anchorage. She has a degree in Art and English from Brigham Young University, in Provo, Utah. She taught Art and English in public schools for twelve years and has published poetry and humorous articles in newspapers, and articles in the Ensign magazine.

 Celestia is the author of the popular series, <u>The Art of Being Charlee</u>, novels that combine humor, mystery and clean romance.

Her memoir, <u>Lead Kindly Light</u>, tells the story of her marriage to Van Whitehead and their family's journey to reach their own Promised Land in Alaska, even as Celestia's parents had tried to find peace and happiness in the Last Frontier, thirty years earlier.

Celestia is the widow of Van Whitehead and currently lives in Draper, Utah. She is the mother of twelve children. The grandchildren, she says, are multiplying exponentially, but she loves them all.

She is happy to hear from her readers at celestiawhitehead@gmail.com

Other books by Celestia Whitehead:
<u>When Winter Comes</u>, The Art of Being Charlee Book 1
<u>If Spring Endures</u>, The Art of Being Charlee Book 2
<u>If Summer Ends</u>, The Art of Being Charlee Book 3
<u>Lead Kindly Light</u>, Volume 1, a memoir
<u>Keep Thou My Feet,</u> Volume 2 of <u>Lead, Kindly Light</u>